# WORKER
# PARTICIPATION

# WORKER PARTICIPATION
## Success and Problems

## Hem C. Jain

with the collaboration of
## Geneviève Laloux Jain

PRAEGER

PRAEGER SPECIAL STUDIES • PRAEGER SCIENTIFIC

Library of Congress Cataloging in Publication Data

Main entry under title:

Worker participation.

    Includes bibliographical references and index.
    1. Employees' representation in management--
Case studies. I. Jain, Hem Chand, 1928-
HD5650.W64         658.3'152        80-57
ISBN 0-03-052451-2

Published in 1980 by Praeger Publishers
CBS Educational and Professional Publishing
A Division of CBS, Inc.
521 Fifth Avenue, New York, New York 10017 U.S.A.

© 1980 by Praeger Publishers

0123456789  145  987654321

Printed in the United States of America

# FOREWORD
## R. Blanpain

Worker participation: An employer's paradise? Is it an answer to the fundamental challenges with which the enterprises are confronted? Does industrial democracy answer the workers' basic needs for human development and involvement? An unequivocal answer is impossible. The reason is simple: worker participation and/or industrial democracy constitute different things to different people, not only ideologically but also in fact. This has obviously to do with the characteristics of each society, the way of doing things, the overall societal relationships, and the philosophical outlook of employees and of the unions—whether they basically accept or reject the socioeconomic system in which they live and whether they believe in conflict or in the pursuit of harmony. Participation or democracy has also to do with the power situation in the trade union movement: whether the movement is centralized or decentralized and whether the power rests with shop stewards or with works council members. Consequently, few, if any, overall generalizations are possible.

There is however no doubt that worker participation or industrial democracy—in one way or another—is needed. To use the words of Finn Gunderlach, former European commissioner of the European Economic Community (EEC) responsible for industry:

> In societies like those of the Community, with their high
> standards of education and expectation, the managers of
> enterprises cannot expect to implement strategic economic
> decisions without adequately involving those who will be
> most substantially affected, namely, the employees of the
> enterprise. The alternative is clear: social confrontation
> to an unacceptable degree, which may even threaten the
> democratic foundations of our societies. Such confronta-
> tions will arise in one of two ways: either as an immediate
> response to changes, which those concerned do not under-
> stand; or as a consequence of the collapse of enterprises
> which could not be changed to meet the challenges of the
> time, since no adequate machinery existed for imple-
> menting changes which those concerned could understand
> and accept. [1]

What Gunderlach is saying applies to all forms of participation, direct as well as indirect.

The question remains, however, what to do, how to do it, and how to benefit from the experiences, the successes, and the failures of others. Here, there is an obvious need not only for comparative conceptual analysis but also and especially for case studies telling us what is going on. Again, caution is indicated, since comparability between industrial relations systems and participation schemes in different countries is full of traps, for reasons explained above, and transferability is often a fallacy.

Nevertheless, comparative studies, such as this book, are more than needed, not only for academic purposes but also for very practical reasons. For example, comparative studies are indeed necessary for multinationals (wanting to know what is going on in the countries in which their subsidiaries are located and vice versa) and for regional organizations, such as the EEC (aspiring to create common rules—which can only be drawn up on the basis of comparative experience). Comparative information would finally allow those who are responsible for industrial relations to read on the walls of other countries what is going to happen to them.

We are particularly happy to see that Hem Jain, who has spent almost two years in Europe, in part as a visiting professor at our institute, has been willing to help those looking for information and answers with this book and has built bridges of understanding between different continents and countries, especially between North America and Europe. He was anxious not only to spend a sufficient amount of time in Europe but also to secure the necessary collaboration of "locals," which makes his book the result of desirable intercontinental teamwork.

May I finally express my appreciation for the privilege of breaking the bottle of champagne over Jain's book, to launch the ship, and to wish "bon voyage." May this foreword also be an expression of our gratitude for his teaching at our university and testify to our lasting friendship for him and for his wife Geneviève.


NOTE

1. Finn Gunderlach, "Industrial Democracy within the European Economic Community," Excerpts from a speech given at a meeting of the European Metal Workers' Federation, Brussels, June 9, 1976.

# PREFACE

In recent years, there has been a great deal of discussion about worker participation in management. Most of the published material describes the legal and voluntary schemes in various industrialized countries. There have been a number of general surveys, such as "Workers' Participation in Management in Britain," by R. O. Clarke and D. J. Fatchett and individual country studies under the auspices of the International Labour Organisation (ILO). Particularly worthy of notice are the reports of national commissions appointed by a number of European governments to inquire into problems of worker participation, such as the Biedenkopf report (Germany), the Bullock report (Great Britain), and the Sudreau report (France). However, there is a vacuum in the published literature, namely, case studies on the actual operation of legal and voluntary participative schemes in individual companies.

This book is an attempt to fill this vacuum. The starting point was a pilot study of several Belgian enterprises conducted by the author and his Belgian associates. This and other case studies on the effectiveness of participative schemes in Belgium and other countries were presented at a seminar sponsored by the European Institute for Advanced Studies in Management (Brussels, May 1978) and chaired by this writer. Other recognized scholars and practitioners were also asked to contribute studies on the actual operation of participative schemes at the level of the enterprise.

In order to put the case studies in perspective, the various concepts and schemes associated with worker participation are examined in a series of essays. This combination of theory and practice will hopefully enable managers, personnel directors, union officials, policy makers, and students in North America to know how the various participative schemes or concepts in European countries have actually worked in practice, that is, to learn some of the benefits and problems associated with such schemes.

The main objectives of this book are to identify the range and main characteristics of legal and voluntary participative schemes existing in a number of advanced market economy countries and to assess emerging issues and trends relevant to worker participation in management; to review the practical experience with various schemes of worker participation in individual enterprises in various countries by means of case studies (these case studies will illustrate the main issues and identify factors that facilitate or hinder effective participation; and to draw useful lessons from the Western

European experience and indicate its relevance for practitioners, policy makers, and students in North America.

The first chapter of this volume presents a conceptual framework of worker participation in management. An attempt is made to define the concepts and to explain the rationale behind "worker participation" within the framework of industrial relations systems.

The main body of the book is divided into two parts. Each part has two sections. Section A describes and evaluates various forms of participation in the form of an essay. Section B consists of a series of empirical case studies. Part I deals with indirect forms of participation, that is, employee representation on boards, works councils, and collective bargaining. Part II examines current practices of direct participation by workers at the job or shop floor level with the objective of improving the working environment or the quality of work. There are two concluding chapters. Chapter 6, "Information, Training, and Effective Participation," emphasizes the importance of communication, disclosure of information, and training and education for all those involved in participative schemes. The last chapter discusses the implications and relevance of the Western European experience for North America. Special emphasis is placed on the adaptation of some of the more successful Western European experiments in worker participation to fit the North American environment.

The discussion in the introductory chapters (essays) and in the case studies in this book is limited to various participative schemes in the more advanced market economy countries, such as Western Europe, North America, and Japan. Most workers perceive profit sharing and coownership schemes as important because they have a stake in the survival and growth of the firm that employs them. However, such schemes do not necessarily in themselves afford the workers an opportunity for active participation in decision making. Therefore, these schemes are not included in this book.

In certain Western European countries, organized labor and employer associations participate in the formulation of socioeconomic policy at the national level. They consider political action as an important vehicle for influencing public policy, which has implications for industrial democracy far beyond the level of the enterprise. Since the focus of this book is on the effectiveness of direct and indirect schemes of participation at the enterprise level, the question of public policy formulation and political action is discussed only to the extent that these factors influence worker participation in management at the level of the enterprise.

# ACKNOWLEDGMENTS

I am indebted to so many individuals and organizations for assisting me in this project that it is difficult to acknowledge all of them. I am grateful to the University of New Brunswick and the Fondation Industrie-Universite (Belgium) for providing me research grants during my study leave (1976-78). I am thankful to the several institutions that offered me the use of their research facilities. In the fall of 1976, I served as an external collaborator with the International Labour Organisation (ILO) in Geneva on a research project on worker participation. During my stay in Belgium, I was a visiting professor at the Catholic University of Leuven, the European Institute for Advanced Studies in Management, and Boston University in Brussels.

In these and other educational institutions, such as Antwerpen University (Belgium) and the University of Groningen (the Netherlands), I conducted seminars and courses on worker participation. My colleagues and students, many of them practicing industrial relations professionals, helped me to gain a better understanding of European industrial relations. My research activities at the European Institute for Advanced Studies in Management enabled me to travel and meet many distinguished European scholars, labor and management leaders, and government officials. Discussions with them on current industrial relations topics helped me in clarifying my own thinking. Throughout my stay in Belgium, Professor Roger Blanpain, the director of the Labor Relations Institute of the Catholic University of Leuven, and the members of his staff were most gracious in giving me their time and professional advice. This book would not have been possible without the assistance and cooperation of all these people.

I am most grateful to the following scholars who contributed empirical case studies on the actual operation of participative schemes: from the ILO, Geneva—Dr. A. Gladstone and B. Essenberg (IILS) from Canada—Professors D. Ondrack and M. Evans (University of Toronto), A. Whitehorn (Royal Military College), and M. Gurdon (University of New Brunswick), Bert Painter (British Columbia Research Institute), and J. Mansel (Ontario Department of Labour); from France—Professors H. Douard and J. D. Raynaud (Conservatoire National des Arts et Métiers); from Japan—Professor S. I. Takezawa (Rikkyo University); from the Netherlands, Professors B. Hovels and P. Nas (Katholieke Universiteit Nijmegen); from Sweden —Professor S. Rubenowitz (Göteborg University); from the United Kingdom—Dr. E. Chell (University of Nottingham); and from the United States, Professor S. Doyle (Iona College).

I am particularly grateful to the following professors and colleagues who read individual chapters and gave me their constructive criticism. Although they had very little time to review the material I sent them, their comments and suggestions proved to be most helpful: Professors G. Dion, editor, <u>Relations Industrielles/Industrial Relations</u>, Université Laval, Quebec; C. W. Summers, University of Pennsylvania; D. Ondrack, University of Toronto; G. Hunnius, York University, Canada; Alan Whitehorn, Royal Military College, Canada; Michael A. Gurdon, University of New Brunswick, Canada; M. Derber and A. Strumthal, University of Illinois; and R. O. Clarke, principal administrator, Industrial Relations division, Organization for Economic Cooperation and Development (OECD), Paris.

My special thanks are due to Professor Roger Blanpain, director of the Labor Relations Institute, for writing the foreword, and to my wife, Dr. Geneviève Jain, who collaborated with me from the very beginning and who gave continuous encouragement and professional guidance in the completion of this project. Finally, I am appreciative of the editorial assistance provided by Hazel Kerr. Ronald Brennan, editor with Praeger Publishers, has been helpful to me in the final stages of the publication of this manuscript.

# CONTENTS

PART II:

DIRECT FORMS OF PARTICIPATION

Section A

Section B:  Case Studies

# INTRODUCTION

# *Chapter One*

## WORKER PARTICIPATION AND INDUSTRIAL RELATIONS—A CONCEPTUAL FRAMEWORK

Worker participation in management decision making has always been a controversial subject. One of the problems central to this controversy is management's prerogatives. Business leaders are feeling increasing pressures for participation from workers and their organizations in areas that were once exclusively reserved for management. The pressure for worker participation in management is a natural outgrowth of economic and social change. The new generation of workers is better educated, more affluent, and more mobile than previous ones. With advanced technology, longer years of schooling, and rising affluence, workers are becoming independent and are asserting their individuality. They are less tolerant of boredom, lack of proper health and safety provisions, and of discomfort in their working environment. As a result, they have begun to challenge established authority.

Recognizing the changing social and economic situation in Western Europe, the European Economic Community (EEC) Green Paper on Employee Participation and Company Structure states:

> The current economic situation, with its reduced possibilities of growth has emphasized the need for mechanisms, which will adequately ensure the pursuit of goals other than economic growth, such as improvement in the quality of life and working conditions. . . . The pursuit of such goals can probably be secured only by the existence of decision making processes in enterprises which have a broader, more democratic base than such processes often have at present. [1]

This chapter sets out the concept of worker participation in management within the broad framework of the industrial relations system. Such a framework could serve as a base from which the success of, as well as the problems associated with, the implementation of participative schemes at the level of the enterprise in advanced market economy countries can be evaluated. A brief review of the literature is presented in order to shed some light on the basic issues in worker participation in management. Finally, this chapter lists some of the essential conditions for the effective operation of a participatory enterprise.

## PARTICIPATION DEFINED

Participation is one of the most misunderstood concepts in industrial relations because it is one to which people assign different meanings. Much of the confusion arises from the absence of a precise definition of the term participation. It is important to make a distinction between the concepts of "worker participation" and "industrial democracy." Industrial democracy has broad social objectives. It seeks to eliminate or restrict the rights of the dominant industrial hierarchy and calls for the expansion of employee rights. It also aims at exerting "political pressures on governments, making them more responsive to employee and union views for redesigning the total economy toward more socially oriented goals."[2]

By contrast, the concept of worker participation has a narrow focus in the sense that it deals primarily with the participation of workers in the management of the enterprise. To be more specific, participation is a process by which employees can influence management decision making at various hierarchical levels in an enterprise. In an enterprise, decision making usually takes place at three broad levels: the corporate level, the plant and department level, and the shop floor level. The participative processes whereby employees are involved in decision making through their representatives or delegates are known as indirect forms of participation. These are collective bargaining, works councils, and worker-directors on corporate boards. Some of these participative schemes may involve more than one level of organizational hierarchy. The participative processes whereby employees are involved in decisions relating to their immediate tasks or environment are known as direct forms of participation.

Participative processes or schemes may range from the mere disclosure of information to the work force about decisions already made elsewhere to self-management, that is, full worker control of the total management process, such as in Yugoslavia. In most advanced market economy countries, worker participation in decision making at the various levels of an enterprise has been established either through voluntary agreement between worker representatives and management or through legislation. These participative schemes can be grouped under four main headings:

TABLE 1

Participation and Organizational Decision Making

| Organizational Hierarchy | Nature of Decisions Undertaken | Participative Processes |
|---|---|---|
| Corporate level (long-range) | Strategic policy decisions<br>Setting goals and objectives; choice of products and geographic locations; pricing and marketing policies; major capital expenditures; diversification; mergers, acquisitions, raising of capital; disposition of profits. | Indirect<br>Employee-directors on corporate boards. |
| Plant and department level (short-term)<br>Plant: one or two years<br>Departmental: weeks to months | Administrative decisions<br>Organizing and controlling of resources at plant level with the objective of accomplishing goals set at corporate level; capital expenditures within budgets; plantwide work arrangements; production layouts; product lines; hiring, firing, and promotion of employees. At department level, cost and quality control; resource allocations; achievement of targets and quotas; planning and coordination of activities. | Indirect<br>Works councils, joint labor-management consultative committees at department and plant level. |
| Shop floor (day-to-day) | Operating decisions<br>Scheduling of work; safety regulations, work methods; workplace layout; quantity of output; quality control; training of new employees, and so forth. | Direct<br>Job enrichment; job rotation, job enlargement, job redesign or restructuring of work semiautonomous work groups, and so forth. |

Source: Compiled by the author.

1. Participation in management and supervisory boards: The workers may, by law or by voluntary agreement, elect representatives to the top level of management (board of directors); the worker representatives on a board of directors may participate in strategic policy-making decisions, as well as in the administration and government of the enterprise in varying degrees.

2. Joint consultation: The term is used to cover many different types of management-worker relationships; usually, the employees elect delegates to represent them on joint labor-management committees. These councils provide workers with a forum for discussion and exchange of ideas with management, as well as an opportunity to give management advice on a wide variety of production, safety, and welfare matters. These bodies are known by different names in different countries, such as works or worker councils, labor councils, joint-production committees, and so forth. These bodies are integrated into the managerial decision-making process at the plant, department, and shop floor levels.

3. Collective bargaining: This process involves participation by workers through representatives who are part of the formal union structure; decisions concerning wages, working conditions, and so forth are arrived at by a process of negotiations between management and representatives of the workers.

5. Participation at the shop floor level: Workers, along with members of management and technical specialists at the shop floor level, participate in the analysis of production problems and make suggestions for improvements in the methods of work or of working conditions and for the development of new job designs. Semiautonomous work groups or special joint committees are set up for this purpose at various levels of the organization.

The nature of decisions undertaken at each level of the organizational hierarchy and the participative processes associated with these levels are illustrated in Table 1.1.

WORKER PARTICIPATION AND
INDUSTRIAL RELATIONS

Worker participation in each country must be seen within the context of its industrial relations system. The actors in an industrial relations system, namely, the workers and their organizations (formal and informal), management, and government operate in a given environment. The goals, values, and power of these actors are conditioned by the environmental forces (political, socioeconomic, legal, and so forth) in each country.

TABLE 2

Industrial Relations System and Participative Processes: A Conceptual Framework

| Actors | I.R. System | | Functioning of Participative Processes |
| --- | --- | --- | --- |
| | Goals, Values, and Power | Environmental Influences | |
| 1. Workers and their organizations (informal and formal) | Goals: Objectives of the actors | External Economic; political; social and legal | Dependent upon: 1. Goals, values, and power of the actors in the I.R. system and perception of their role within the framework of organizational networks and vis-à-vis each other. |
| | Values: Norms and standards that an actor observes in accomplishing his objectives | Internal Structural: Organizational structure; size of the enterprise; technology. Forms and content of participation. | 2. Their understanding of the environmental influences. |
| 2. Management | Power: Ability of an actor to satisfy his needs or goals despite the resistence of others | Behavioral: Actor's perception of the work situation; organizational climate; managers and supervisors autonomy; leadership styles and expectations; interpersonal and inter-group interactions. | 3. Relationship among various forms of participation and their integration at all levels of the enterprise. |
| 3. Government | | | |

Source: Compiled by the author.

7

The functioning of participative processes in an enterprise is dependent upon (1) the goals, values, and power of the actors and the perception of their roles within the framework of organizational networks and vis-à-vis each other; (2) the actors' understanding of environmental forces—these forces may inhibit or encourage the actors to develop appropriate goals, attitudes, and perceptions of roles necessary for the successful functioning of the participative processes; and (3) the relationship among the various forms of participation and how well they are integrated at all levels of the enterprise.

Each actor in the industrial relations system has his or her own particular set of goals and values. The roles these actors play in a given environment are usually consistent with their respective ideology, that is, goals and values. The ideology of each actor has a profound influence on his or her social behavior and, in consequence, on the actual operation of the participative schemes in an enterprise. These will be discussed here. (See Table 2.)

Goals and Values (Ideology)
of the Actors (Workers)

In the context of participation, the question is often raised whether workers want to participate in managerial decision making. According to an Organization for Economic Cooperation and Development (OECD) report on worker participation:

> Workers evaluate participation schemes basically in terms
> of a perceived personal pay off. . . . "What do I get out of
> it?" Numerous participation schemes have failed in the
> past, precisely because the workers did not perceive any
> personal pay off resulting from them. If workers do not
> see this personal pay off in a participative scheme, the
> likely result will be that the scheme is perceived as a
> management instrument—or even a trade-union instru-
> ment geared to union organizational ends—which really
> does not serve the workers' need.[3]

Various studies and surveys on worker attitudes and motivation toward participation suggest that generally speaking, most workers wish to participate in decisions that are likely to affect their interests, especially their own work and conditions of employment. Institutions (labor or management) that ignore such findings are likely to breed worker apathy and discontent, which, in turn, may manifest themselves in a higher rate of absenteeism, wildcat strikes, artificial restrictions of output, higher rate of accidents, and so forth.

Whether workers who wish to participate will try to do so depends on how much power to influence decisions they believe they possess. "The critical factor in this respect is the workers' perception of their relative power rather than the actual balance of power, since workers will try to participate when they think they have sufficient power, even though events may prove them wrong."[4] The workers' perception of their relative power may be based on their informal organizational network within the enterprise or on the strength of their unions.

Furthermore, worker goals are multidimensional in character, such as income security, job security, higher wages, good working conditions, pleasant social relations, and interesting and satisfying work. Some of these goals cannot be advanced through direct worker participation at the shop floor level. It is only through a system of indirect or representative participation, such as collective bargaining, worker-directors, and so forth, that worker interests, such as job security, income security, and high wages, can be protected.

While a relatively small proportion of workers express interest in personally taking part in participative bodies concerned with higher-level decision making, it does not automatically imply lack of worker support for these participative bodies. The OECD final report on worker participation concludes that

> workers are not so much interested in the processes of indirect participation [trade unions, collective bargaining, board representation] as in the outcomes of these processes: the general protection of their individual jobs and income. . . . From the perspective of the individual worker, the different forms of participation serve his different needs and interests. Effective management will only be possible if these different needs and interests are explicitly recognized in organizational policies and practices.[5]

## Union Ideology

It is difficult to generalize about the attitudes of the trade union movement toward worker participation in management. Differences in the organizational structure, ideological orientation, and the climate of the industrial relations in various countries influence the unions' outlook toward participative schemes.

Union leaders in West Germany believe that they can best protect the interests of their members by participating in decision-making bodies at the highest level of the enterprise, such as company boards. In France and Italy, those union leaders who have socialist leanings believe that it is not possible to accomplish meaningful results by changing the structure of the firm within the present framework of capitalist society. They are critical of the system of "codetermination" in West Germany, holding that "the workers' leaders are in this way incorporated into a structure which remains no less hostile than ever to the interests of the work force as a whole."[6]

Unions in North America, and to a degree in the United Kingdom, perceive their role as being that of a countervailing power to management, whose main function is to bargain with management as equal partners. They do not wish to become managers or to assume any responsibility for the administration of the enterprise. They believe that through the bargaining process, they will be able to establish a fair balance between the demands of their members and the overall interests of the enterprise.

Union Structure and Industrial Democracy

Unions differ from business firms in goals and in organizational structure. The union structure is democratic in the sense that union officials are elected by the rank and file. Power and authority in unions flow upward rather than downward, as is the case of business organizations. However, unions, like companies, have become big bureaucracies. They have staff specialists, a hierarchy of offices, and a set of impersonal rules and regulations.

A union is not monolithic. It is a coalition of diverse groups of people, such as international and national officers; local officers, such as shop stewards and local union presidents; workers—white collar, blue collar, skilled, and unskilled; workers with long years of service and relatively young workers; male and female workers; and shift workers and regular workers. For example, shift workers may have other interests than regular workers. They have little time to attend union or joint labor-management committee meetings. When across-the-board pay increases lead to narrowing the wage differentials between skilled and unskilled workers or between blue collar and white collar workers, union leaders in many countries deem it wise to switch to percentage increases. Young workers prefer cash, while older employees prefer higher pensions and other fringe benefits. Bargaining demands must balance the interests of these groups in order to hold them together.

A union is also a political organization. Union leaders perceive their role as directing various political alliances and settling jurisdictional disputes (crafts versus industrial). They must cope with national and international policies. It is safe to assume that a high degree of union organization and participation in power centers of the society provides unions with a degree of institutional security that is generally conducive to their responsible behavior in the operation of a participative scheme.

In countries where workers are organized on the basis of industry, such as in West Germany, industrial unions can serve as an agency of organized workers to have an effective voice in participative schemes; however, even in Germany, the existence of a separate and fairly small white-collar union poses problems. The problem of developing a genuine representative form of industrial democracy is compounded in a country like the United Kingdom, where a large number of unions claim to speak for different groups of workers in the same plant. In some other countries, where two or more unions with different ideological orientations and confederal affiliations claim to represent the same groups of workers, it would be even more difficult to develop a system of participative process acceptable to all unions.

Management Ideology

Management ideology in market economy countries seeks to legitimize the goals defined by business leaders and the various stakeholders—that is, the customers, employees, shareholders, government, and local community—which the enterprise is designed to serve. Business leaders are concerned with the financial and organizational well-being of the enterprise. They emphasize that business is primarily an organization of people whose activities must be coordinated for a common purpose, that is, the production of goods or services at a profit. This calls for teamwork and loyalty on the part of managers and workers in increasing the efficiency and productivity of the enterprise.

Though managers have many goals in common with the owners of the enterprise, their respective ideologies are not always necessarily identical. The increase in professionalization of management in the last decade has changed the role of managers and has led to a greater degree of ideological independence on the part of managers. Managers perceive their role as negotiators of acceptable working arrangements between various stakeholders. Managers attach great importance to the growth of the enterprise, which brings them increased power, status, and financial rewards.

In part, management's objection to sharing authority with employees or their representatives is based on the fear that their lack of technical knowledge and expertise, as well as their limited perspective, will jeopardize the viability of the enterprise. Some managers believe that labor participation in management will ultimately result in the breakdown of the institution of private property and is, therefore, inconsistent with the free enterprise system. They argue that management is responsible to the owners of the enterprise and cannot legitimately share its authority without abdicating its responsibility.

Legally speaking, under British law, the board of directors is elected as representative of the shareholders and is deemed to be accountable solely to them. There is, legally speaking, no responsibility on the part of the board of directors to its employees collectively or individually to negotiate or consult with union representatives. Furthermore, management insists that worker participation in management is legitimate only to the extent that it is provided for in legislation or in a collective agreement.

North American corporate law is based on the assumption of private ownership, with the control of the corporation residing with the owners in their capacity as shareholders. The law grants shareholders the collective right to participate in the voting to elect directors. Almost invariably, directors delegate the management of the company to appointed officials. In practice, important organizational decisions are made by these appointed officers, usually known as "management." In most collective agreements in the United States and Canada, the "management rights" clauses spell out in some detail and in positive terms the functions that are exclusively managerial and outside the scope of mutual determination. Management argues that rights not restricted by contract or prohibited by law belong to it.

In European countries, employers in general have been in favor of voluntary schemes of joint consultation, such as joint labor-management committees at the shop floor level and plant councils. Where legislation requires the existence of works councils, employers have viewed such bodies as a mechanism for providing necessary information and consultation with employees and have showed a willingness to cooperate as long as these bodies did not develop into joint decision-making bodies. Albeda, at a seminar in 1975, discussed employer attitudes toward various participative schemes in OECD member countries.[7] His view can be summarized as follows. Employers, in general, (1) favor the schemes that are voluntary rather than legally imposed, as well as the schemes that do not discriminate between union and nonunion members; (2) prefer to deal with their own personnel rather than with unions representing their personnel; (3) give preference to direct floor shop democracy over representative schemes of industrial democracy; (4) accept representation of worker representatives on the company boards in a minority position (if at all); and (5) believe strongly in schemes that integrate the workers in the firm and give the workers more responsibility for their work, as long as such schemes do not lead to a change in power relationships within the firm.

## Governmental Objectives

In the context of worker participation, the government's objectives in most market economy countries seem to be the promotion of cooperation between labor and management and the minimization of industrial conflict. The multiplicity of legal and quasi-legal participation schemes, such as works councils and worker-directors, in several European countries has been stimulated by a belief that the adversary model of labor-management relations, symbolized by collective bargaining, is not an adequate method of "participation." In West Germany, the adoption of codetermination, as well as the resulting legislation, has been greatly influenced by the political circumstances and the existence of close ties between the ruling political party and the major trade union federations in that country. This close alliance in several European countries accounts for the unions' influence on governmental policy in industrial relations. Efforts to combat wage push inflation forced the ruling Labour party in the United Kingdom to develop a "social contract" with unions. The social contract represented a wide-ranging set of promises, including union representation on boards of private companies, given by the Labour party in return for the acceptance of voluntary wage controls by the unions.

The role of governmental agencies may vary considerably from one country to another and is closely linked with the legal framework. Legislation in North America requires both labor and management to bargain in good faith. The governments' objective there is to assist parties to reach an agreement without work interruption. In recent years, direct governmental involvement in industrial relations has resulted in many countries in freezing wages and setting up wage guidelines and controls. Government through legislation has regulated unfair labor practices, standard hours, minimum wages, health and safety provisions, and so forth.

## BASIC ISSUES IN WORKER PARTICIPATION

In most market economy countries, unions, management, and government are separate identifiable entities. Each of them have a multiplicity of goals. An attempt to pursue such wide-ranging and diverse goals will bring some of them into conflict with the others.

For example, management perceives worker participation as a means of stabilizing labor-management relations at the workplace— of promoting cooperation between workers and managers, leading to employee commitment and, thereby, greater productivity and efficiency. On the other hand, unions view worker participation more as a means of establishing a new balance of power between employer and unions than as improving the organizational performance of the enterprise.

It does not necessarily follow that unions are not concerned about the organizational performance and efficiency of the enterprise, but it does emphasize the fact that unions and management have partially conflicting goals and priorities. Hence, the question is how the enterprise operating in a democratic framework ought to be controlled and directed. To be more specific, the concept of worker participation addresses itself to two basic issues, namely, power sharing and promotion of cooperative and harmonious relationships between labor and management. Each of these issues may require a solution in its own right or may be considered as a means to an end, such as (1) increased efficiency and productivity through effective utilization of human resources, (2) minimization of industrial conflict and increased stabilization of labor-management relations at the level of the enterprise, or (3) increased job satisfaction and alleviation of feelings of powerlessness felt by many employees at the workplace.

Power Sharing

Many of the problems arising from the implementation of participative schemes at the level of the enterprise arise from the fact that worker participation involves a change in power relationships. The participatory organizational model accepts the existence of a variety of interest groups within an enterprise, all of whom are stakeholders in it and have different goals, interests, and values. The participatory model also assumes that individuals make decisions to a certain extent on the basis of self-interest.

> It is therefore likely to happen that the greater the distance of an organizational member from the place where a decision is made the less his own interests are likely to be compatible with that decision. The different forms of workers' participation are all attempts to assure that workers, as much as possible, shall be able to influence these decisions which are of concern to them.[8]

The concept of participatory enterprise is in sharp contrast with the traditional hierarchical organizational model. The traditional model assumes that management alone is responsible for planning, organizing, and controlling work and that worker responsibilities are restricted to the performance of specified tasks. Management sees the enterprise as an organization in which all parties work together as a team for the common good of the enterprise. This unitary view of the enterprise as an organization ignores the existence of conflicts of interest among members of the enterprise and the fact that workers and their representatives have needs and objectives of their own, which may not be compatible with those of management. Therefore, this unitary view is not consistent with the participatory organizational model. According to Walker,

> An enterprise is not a unitary but a pluralist-system containing many related but separate interests and objectives which must be maintained in some kind of equilibrium. . . . An important feature of the concept of participatory enterprise is that it accommodates the possibility of conflictual as well as co-operative participation.[9]

One of the conflictual aspects of the participatory processes is the scope of issues subject to collective bargaining. Should collective bargaining be extended to issues that traditionally have been regarded as management prerogatives? Generally speaking, unions feel that in order to protect the interests of their members, collective bargaining must be extended to a wide range of managerial decisions that might have consequences for workers. Such areas might include mergers, investment in new plants, changes in work methods and technology, closing down of a plant, and so forth. Unions would also like to see collective bargaining extended to groups not previously covered, such as middle management, professional staff, and so forth.

The British Trade Union Congress (TUC) has taken the position that

> enterprises can no longer be run on the basis of the unchallenged prerogatives of employers and unilateral actions by management. Many industrial difficulties arise from decisions taken without prior agreement with the working people directly affected. Widening the range of issues on which negotiations take place, and making the procedures more speedy and equitable, will go a considerable way toward improving industrial relations.[10]

Historically speaking, unions in North America have pursued a strategy aiming at the equilization of power in the bargaining relationship, not only by opposing what management does or proposes but also by creating new positive issues, that is, extending the scope of issues to be bargained.

In many European countries, the unions' desire for sharing power over decisions affecting workers extends far beyond the conventional North American bargaining view. Unions in these countries have taken the position that they can protect the interests of their members only if they are fully informed about the economic conditions of the enterprise, its problems, activities, and future plans. Such information can only be obtained by employee representation on company boards, and it is here that worker-directors can influence management policy. Unions are also advocating increased bargaining rights for works councils.

Furthermore, unions in most European countries contend that such institutions cannot be effective if they are established voluntarily or by agreement. They argue that it is only legislation that can put teeth into the various provisions by authorizing worker representatives to take the matter to the courts or to take industrial action in the event of such provisions not being implemented.

Some managers seriously question worker capacity to make a meaningful contribution to decisions at the level of the enterprise. They argue that in a free market economy, performance and productivity still remain the major goals of most companies in the private sector. Performance will be judged not on the effectiveness of worker participation schemes but on the criteria of economic viability and productivity. "The proof of success, then, continues to lie within the competitive labour market rather than in the participative structure of the organization."[11]

As far as worker capacity to participate effectively is concerned experiments on shop floor democracy in Scandinavian countries show that rank-and-file workers at the shop floor level can make a significant contribution to the practical aspects of work. They can make useful suggestions about improving technical aspects, design of equipment, plant layout, and so forth. Worker delegates on works councils at the plant level in many European countries have participated effectively in decision making in personnel matters, such as terms of employment, plant rules, discipline, welfare programs, and so forth. However, in order to participate effectively in decision making in highly technical and financial matters at the enterprise level, worker representatives need specialized and general training. Their capacity to communicate clearly and persuasively and to operate effectively in participative bodies can also be developed considerably by training and experience.

Managers are afraid that worker participation will restrict the managerial freedom necessary for the efficient conduct of the enterprise. They also believe that various participative schemes tend to increase worker and union influence and power in managerial decision making at the level of enterprise. However, some observers believe that

> despite the restrictions put on management during the
> last century, performance does not seem to have been
> seriously hampered. . . . That management's capacity
> to adapt itself to new conditions is generally underesti-
> mated by managers themselves, and that further restric-
> tions on the managerial prerogative and the execution of
> some management functions by the workers would be
> more likely to improve than to endanger organizational
> performance. [12]

Batstone's analysis of research findings in countries with legal participative schemes leads him to conclude that "schemes which apparently develop industrial democracy have often been less an extension of worker influence than a recognition of its existence and an attempt to channel it."[13]

In his research on the power distance theory and its implications, Mulder argues that participative systems may reduce rather than increase the power of workers and staff delegates. For example, at the works council level, managers and top specialists have more expertise and information about problems pertaining to the organization than ordinary workers simply because they spend more time on such items as financial resources, the relationship between technology and production, and relationships between the organization and outside influences. These are crucial to the survival of the system. Managers and specialists have more experience in communication and human relations than workers and/or their representatives. [14]

While legal and quasi-legal schemes do not appear to enhance worker and worker representative control, it does seem that such schemes do increase total control, that is, both of workers and of management.

According to Tannenbaum,

> The participative system differs from the nonparticipative
> system in the way control is exercised and distributed.
> . . . participation is often thought to imply taking power
> from the managers and giving it to subordinates but in
> fact managers need not exercise less control where there
> is participation. A reduction in managerial power may
> occur but it need not and there is evidence to suggest that
> participation may be the means through which managers
> actually increase their own control along with that of
> workers. . . . In fact many participative schemes are
> really designed implicitly, if not explicitly, to legitimize
> if not to enhance the control exercised by managers. [15]

Promotion of Labor-Management Cooperation

The lesson one can learn from the West German experience is that representative integrative participation through works councils and employee representation on boards has had no effect on the immediate work environment and personal fulfillment of individual workers at the shop floor level. Whether institutions such as works councils or worker-directors foster greater cooperation and harmonious labor-management relations depends upon how well the various forms of participation are interrelated and jointly regulated at all levels of the enterprise, as well as on the total labor relations climate in the enterprise. From the studies on the effectiveness of works councils in several European countries, it would seem that there has been general dissatisfaction with the efficacy of works councils at the enterprise level in the promotion of cooperative relationships between workers and management or as a means of representing employee interests.

Moreover, works councils cannot be a substitute for unions as a means of representing worker interests at the plant, industry, or national level. There is a greater likelihood of cooperation between management and workers in the areas where a worker can share directly in the managerial functions relevant to his or her job and his or her work situation. This implies organization or reorganization of work so as to give employees greater freedom in deciding how it is to be done and, then, in carrying it out. Greater potential for labor-management cooperation lies in joint labor-management committees, plant production committees, quality of working life projects, and so forth.[16]

Labor-management relations in North America are based on the adversary system. Except in a few well-publicized cases, unions remain suspicious of cooperating with management in experiments with work reorganization at the shop floor level. Involvement of unions and management in cooperative endeavors therefore requires a change of attitudes and value systems on the part of unions and management.


CONCLUSION

The establishment of contractual or legal schemes of participation in themselves or the mere presence of employees and/or their representatives on joint committees or management boards does not guarantee that participative schemes will be fully effective. If a participatory enterprise is to operate effectively in the interest of all parties, it must fulfill certain conditions. Some of these conditions include the following:

1. Various stakeholders in the enterprise must recognize the problems inherent in the operation of participative schemes and set realistic goals. The goals cannot be handed down from on high. Its members must be encouraged to contribute to such objectives.

2. Participation must be perceived as instrumental to the attainment of goals valued by each party. For management, it should lead to increased productivity and efficiency; for unions, participation should not threaten or impinge upon their established rights, such as collective bargaining; unions should also be made to feel that they have a meaningful role to play. For workers, participation should provide practical and psychological gains, such as a safe and secure job environment, a sense of dignity and responsibility, and a share in the economic benefits.

3. A firm belief in, and commitment to, the participative processes on the part of key management officials at all levels of the enterprise is crucial. The role of top management in setting an organizational climate conducive to participatory democracy is very important. Autocratic management at the top level is likely to beget similar management at the middle and lower levels, because managers know that their performance is likely to be judged by their superiors not only on the basis of what they accomplish but also on the basis of their style.

4. Availability of accurate, opportune, systematic, and relevant information about the enterprise to all those involved in participative schemes and meaningful communications to the work force at all levels about the operations of participative schemes are important elements.

5. Acquisition of systematic knowledge and experience in managerial, economic, and technical fields on the part of all those involved in participative schemes will go a long way in ensuring their effective implementation.

6. Finally, to be real, participation should take place at the appropriate levels in an enterprise in a spirit of mutual trust, and various forms of participation (for example, collective bargaining, shop floor democracy, labor-management committees, and board representation) must be integrated into the total system. [17]

NOTES

1. Employee Participation and Company Structures in the European Community, Bulletin of the European Economic Community, supp. 8/75 (Brussels, 1975), p. 11.

2. Solomon Barkin, "Labour Participation: A Way to Industrial Democracy," Relations Industrielles/Industrial Relations 33 (Canada, 1978): 395 and 402.

3. "Workers' Participation" (Final summary, Organization for Economic Cooperation and Development, Paris, March 1975), p. 44.

4. K. F. Walker, "Worker Participation in Management Problems, Practice and Prospects," International Institute for Labour Studies Bulletin no. 12 (Geneva, 1974), p. 14.

5. "Workers' Participation," p. 413.

6. K. Coates, ed., Can the Workers Run Industry? (London: Sphere Books, 1968), p. 232.

7. W. Albeda, "Workers' Participation" (Organization for Economic Cooperation and Development, Paris background paper for the International Management Seminar, March 1975), mimeographed, pp. 28-29.

8. "Workers' Participation," p. 39.

9. K. F. Walker, "Toward the Participatory Enterprise: A European Trend," Annals of the American Academy of Political Science 431 (May 1977): 4-8.

10. G. Lloyd and M. Gregory, "Workers' Participation in Decisions within Undertakings in the United Kingdom" (Paper delivered at the International Labour Organisation Symposium, Oslo, August 1974), p. 1.

11. E. Rose, "Work Control in Industrial Society," Industrial Relations Journal 7 (1976): 30.

12. "Workers' Participation," pp. 41-42.

13. E. Batstone, Industrial Democracy and Worker Representation at Board Level: A Review of European Experience (London: HMSO, 1977), p. 35.

14. Mauk Mulder, "Power Equalization through Participation," Administrative Science Quarterly 16 (March 1971): 31-38.

15. A. Tannenbaum, "System of Formal Participation," in O. B.: Research and Issues, IIR Association Series (Wisconsin, 1974), pp. 78-79.

16. Ibid., p. 97.

17. Hem C. Jain, "Information, Training and Effective Participation," Industrial Relations Journal, vol. 9 (Spring 1978); see also "Leadership—A Management Perspective," Journal of European Training 5 (1976): 46-61.

# Part I

## INDIRECT FORMS OF PARTICIPATION

### Section A

# Chapter Two

## WORKER PARTICIPATION ON
## SUPERVISORY AND MANAGEMENT BOARDS

Worker participation may take place at various levels in an undertaking—the shop floor, the plant, or the board level—with varying outcomes in terms of power relationships and actual opportunity to influence decision making. However, employee representation on a board of directors has an added symbolic significance. It enhances the status and prestige of the workers. The presence of employee representatives on the board serves as a constant reminder to management that worker interests are to be taken into account along with those of shareholders. It also emphasizes the fact that the personnel aspects of management are as important as the technical, marketing, and financial aspects. From a utilitarian point of view, worker participation on the boards offers labor an opportunity to influence fundamental policy decisions.[1]

Employee representation on baords gives rise to problems that are of great concern to unions, management, and shareholder representatives on these boards. The following issues are the most controversial:

1. Should employees be represented on boards of private, as well as of public, enterprises?

2. Should labor have equal representation with shareholders on the boards, or should labor have only minority representation?

3. How should such employee-directors be chosen—should they be employees of the company or outsiders nominated by unions, or should employee-directors be chosen from both groups? and

4. Should worker-directors be responsible to the general shareholders meeting or to the unions, and should their rights and responsibilities be the same as those of other directors or should they be different?

The purpose of this chapter is to examine the role of worker-directors through a case study of worker participation on supervisory and management boards in West Germany. The influence of the German model on other countries will be examined briefly. In the context of these experiences, an attempt will be made to shed light on the issues listed above.

## CODETERMINATION—THE GERMAN MODEL

For varying lengths of time in a number of industrialized and developing countries, workers have had representatives on the boards of public sector enterprises.[2]

As far as the private sector is concerned, very few non-Socialist countries have come close to matching West Germany's system of codetermination. It is one of the oldest and best developed examples of worker participation at the board level and deserves special consideration. The intent of the codetermination legislation is to establish a new equilibrium in the power relations between employers and employees in the industries affected by the law. Before discussing the main features of this legislation and its impact upon the actual operation of worker participation at the level of the enterprise, it is necessary to understand the functioning of the industrial relations system in West Germany. The reader must also have a clear idea of the structure and functions of corporate boards.

### Industrial Relations System in West Germany

Unions in West Germany are organized at the industry level and represent all employees in an industrial branch. However, they do not represent employees within individual plants. The main issues arising at the plant level are dealt with by negotiations between management and the members of the works council. The works councils represent all the employees in a plant except for the executives. Therefore, at the plant level, the unions do not influence personnel management issues directly.

At the national level, the unions concentrate on influencing large-scale social and economic policies. They are represented on many administrative councils and standing committees. At present, in the West German Parliament, more than half of all deputies are union members. Unions have acquired considerable power and are able to influence policy decisions affecting the conditions of life and work of the labor force. They have pushed certain demands through parliament that in their opinion they could not have hoped to obtain through collective bargaining.[3]

The right to bargain collectively is for all intents and purposes vested in the 16 industrial unions federated in the German Trade Union

Federation (DGB), and the Federation of Salaried Employees (DAG), which plays a relatively minor role. On the management side, it is the Confederation of German Employers Associations with its sectoral subdivisions that negotiates with the unions. Such negotiations usually take place at the industry level and result in master agreements on wages and other working conditions. Lately, some attempts have been made to negotiate agreements at the plant level in order to close the gap between the minimum wage rates set at the industry level and the actual earnings in a plant. The purpose of plant negotiations is "to establish a system of 'wage leadership,' instead of orienting wage policy toward wage levels in the least effective marginal companies. Thus far the German employers' organizations have strictly resisted these attempts to weaken their solidarity."[4]

Functions of Management and Supervisory Boards

As opposed to a single board, as in the Anglo-American system, German companies have two boards, the supervisory board and the management board. The supervisory board consists of at least 11 members. It meets four or five times a year and oversees the activities of the company. Its main legal function is to appoint and control the management board. The members of the management board are appointed by the supervisory board and must be approved by a two-thirds majority. There are usually three members in the management board—a financial, a technical, and a labor director. Their main responsibility is the day-to-day operations of the enterprise. The supervisory board has the right to ask management questions concerning the company's finances and to scrutinize its books, accounts, and correspondence. While the management board usually makes the major policy decisions on such things as mergers, takeovers, closure of plants, increases of capital, and overall manpower planning, the supervisory board must formally approve such decisions. It also has an important advisory function in terms of policy coordination.

Structure and Functioning
of the Codetermination System

Early in the modern industrial era, Germany experimented with various forms of worker participation. However, the system did not become institutionalized until the 1920s. In 1920 and 1922, the Weimar Republic passed legislation strengthening works councils and granting the workers the right to elect one-third of the members of the

supervisory board in certain firms. However, these participative
bodies exerted little influence on management decision making.[5] During the Nazi period, there was a form of worker participation, but it
was, of course, completely controlled by the government. Immediately
after the fall of the Nazi regime, many segments of German society
supported the concept of codetermination rights for the workers. Both
the employers and the labor movement were deeply committed to the
industrial reconstruction of Germany and believed that the allied oc-
cupation powers would not let it proceed unless a system of worker
participation in management was instituted.

As a matter of fact, as early as 1947, the British occupying
authorities had set up in their zone a system of works councils and
employee representation on company boards in the iron and steel industry. West Germany adopted this system by passing the Codetermination Act in 1951 and the Works Constitution Act in 1952. In later
years, a series of legislative measures consolidated and extended the
codetermination system.

The system operates at both the plant and board level. At the
plant level, the Works Constitution Act decrees that works councils
must be established in firms employing more than five employees;
this law was amended in 1972 and 1974, so that it now applies to all
industrial and commercial firms and to public sector employees.

Worker representation on the management and supervisory
boards in the coal and steel industry is regulated by the Codetermination Act of 1951. This act establishes parity of representation on the
supervisory board for employees and shareholders. The chairman
must be a "neutral man" co-opted jointly by both sides. He is supposed to represent the public interest and has a deciding vote in the
event of a deadlock between worker and shareholder representatives. In the case of an 11-member supervisory board, five labor
representatives have to be chosen—two of them are proposed by the
works councils and two of them are appointed by the unions in the
firm in consultation with the works councils. At least two members
from the labor side must be company employees. There must be at
least one blue collar and one white collar worker. The fifth member
is nominated by the DGB.

It is important to note that although in theory the worker
representatives on the supervisory board are elected by the shareholders' general meeting, in practice, the shareholders do not exercise any influence in the choice of candidates. They have to accept
the list of candidates submitted to them jointly by the works councils
and the unions. As far as the shareholder representation on the
supervisory board in the coal and steel industries is concerned, four
shareholder representatives can be appointed by the general meeting without restriction. The fifth member on the shareholder side

is an independent one. He or she must not belong to shareholder
or employer groups or to their respective organizations. In theory,
the fifth member on the shareholder, as well as on the labor, side is
supposed to represent the public interest.

All the members of the supervisory board elect the members of
the management board by a two-thirds majority. In the coal and steel
industry, the labor director cannot be appointed or dismissed without
the consent of the majority of the worker representatives on the supervisory board. He or she is therefore a person who must enjoy the
trust and confidence of both the unions and employees. Although the
labor director shares in all management responsibilities along with
the two other members of the management board, he or she usually
concentrates on personnel, social policy, and administrative matters
within the undertaking.

The new Codetermination Act of 1976 does not bring any change
to the participation system in the coal and steel industry, but it extends a somewhat watered down version of the principle of worker
parity representation on the supervisory board in limited companies
outside the coal and steel industry employing more than 2,000 people.
Under this law, the supervisory board in such firms must be made up
of an equal number of representatives from worker and shareholder
sides in the following proportions:

| Number of People Employed by Firm | Number of Worker Representatives | Number of Shareholder Representatives |
|---|---|---|
| Up to 10,000 | 6 | 6 |
| Between 10,000 and 20,000 | 8 | 8 |
| More than 20,000 | 10 | 10 |

In a company where there are ten worker representatives,
seven are chosen from the shop floor and from the staff of the company and three must be union officials from outside. All of them are
elected by the work force. The labor representatives on the supervisory boards must represent all employees regardless of whether
or not they belong to unions. One of the worker representatives
must be a senior official of the company.

Both sides of the supervisory board elect jointly a chairperson
and a deputy chairperson, one from each side, from the entire membership of the supervisory board by a two-thirds majority vote. If
the parties do not succeed in electing the chairperson and deputy by
this procedure, then the shareholder representatives on the board
can appoint their candidate as chairperson, and the workers can ap-

point their nominees as the deputy. This has a considerable effect on the decision-making power of the parties on the supervisory board because, in the event of a deadlock, it is the chairperson who will have the deciding vote. The unions claim that although the act gives them equal representation on the supervisory board, it is not parity in the true sense of the word because in the case of a deadlock, the shareholder representatives on the board will have the final say.[6] Under the 1976 legislation, the concept of the chairperson being a neutral person was not retained. While the firms affected by the law are still required to have a labor director on the management board, the employee representatives no longer have veto power over his or her appointment or dismissal.

In all joint stock and private limited liability companies outside the coal and steel industry employing between 500 and 2,000 people, the Works Constitution Act of 1952 gives workers one-third of the seats on the supervisory board. These members are elected by direct and secret ballot of all the employees of the company.

OPERATION OF THE SYSTEM

Worker Reactions

Summarizing the results of various studies conducted in the 1950s on worker attitudes toward codetermination, Fürstenberg points out that

> about three-quarters of the workers knew that co-determination had been introduced within their firms. . . .
> Not more than one worker in ten had some knowledge of the actual composition of the supervisory board. Obviously among workers the level of their perception was much centred around the individual work place and the situation within their own factory.[7]

These findings are not surprising if one considers the fact that workers do not play any direct role in management decision making. A worker participates in electing the members of the works council, who, in turn, appoint some members to the supervisory board. It is the supervisory board that, in turn, appoints the management board, which is directly responsible for running the company's day-to-day operations. In such a hierarchical system, the workers feel that the locus of decision making is quite remote from their day-to-day concerns.

The main question is whether the system of codetermination, howsoever remote it may be, is of any real interest to the employees.

Fritz Voight, head of the Industrial Research Institute in Bonn, says that it definitely is: "If you ask the workers what they think of co-determination, then they will tell you they don't care much. But if you ask them about taking it away, they say they would strike if anybody tried."[8] Fürstenberg also noted that

> though most of the interviewed workers seemed to evaluate the idea of co-determination rather favorably, there were quite a few skeptical comments concerning its achievements in practice. . . . It was found that there was a positive evaluation of co-determination practices among workers with a high degree of job satisfaction. The comments of those employees who were active trade union members were also more favorable than the average."[9]

## Employee Reactions

Generally speaking, the Confederation of German Employers Associations accepts the Works Constitution Act of 1952, which grants workers one-third representation on supervisory boards. On the other hand, they are opposed to the concept of parity representation of the supervisory boards in the steel and coal industry under the Codetermination Act of 1951. The criticism leveled by the employers against parity representation on supervisory boards can be summarized as follows:

1. Studies conducted in the coal and steel industry indicate that parity representation has not substantially increased the influence of the workers and employees on the affairs of their companies; it does not guarantee employment for the workers or bring them any other substantial advantages.
2. Delays and postponement of decisions have been very frequent and have harmed the effective functioning of the enterprise.
3. Codetermination is harmful to the economy: "It isolates us from the E.E.C." and "restricts us in markets abroad."
4. It "upsets the social equilibrium and undermines property."
5. Demands made by unions for the extension of codetermination are motivated less by economic than by political considerations.[10]

In 1966 the Confederation of German Employers Associations sponsored a study of employee reactions toward codetermination. This study compared worker attitudes in the steel and coal industry with parity representation on supervisory boards with those in other industries that had only one-third representation on these boards. The findings of this study showed that workers were not as satisfied with parity representation as had been anticipated. In particular, only one-fifth of them reported that codetermination had been to their personal advantage. However, most scholars, as well as the DGB, the largest trade union federation in West Germany, were critical of the methodology and standards of scientific research used in this study. [11] According to Jenkins, "Most of the opposition to co-determination appears to be poorly documented and highly emotional, such as the Employers Confederation's simultaneous assurances that the system means nothing and that it means so much that it is damaging the economy. "[12]

However, not all the employers subscribe to the Confederation of German Employers Associations' views. Executives at Hoesch A. G. stress that

> codetermination in our company has been successful. The employees are aware that the system means power but also means responsibility. . . . The frequently voiced complaint that workers were incompetent to serve on boards was unfounded. . . . There might have been some difficulties in the beginning, but now they have the capacity to participate in decision-making.

Another executive at Krupp Works states: "Co-determination is not a menace either to labour or management as long as it works. . . . The idea that a worker is too stupid to become a manager is just silly. "[13] This wide discrepancy of opinion regarding the codetermination system reflects the difficulties in its operation.


Problems of Codetermination

The functioning of codetermination gave rise to certain problems at the supervisory board level and at the management board level. In the latter case, these problems concerned the role of the labor director. The labor director is required to perform two important functions. He must participate fully along with the two other members of the management board in the shaping of general company policy in the best interest of the undertaking. At the same time, he must effectively represent the worker interests. Observers of codetermination recognize that this dual allegiance can be a source of problems. However, Fürstenberg maintains that such problems are not uncommon in modern life. He points out that the amount of time and effort devoted by the labor directors in their managerial role has not prevented them from giving greater consideration to the social needs of employees when major changes in technology and plant layout

were being planned. The effectiveness of the labor director in performing both functions, that is, effective management and effective
representation of workers, depends upon his functional integration
and social recognition. The degree to which the labor director becomes integrated and recognized depends in turn upon his competence.
According to Blume, labor directors listed the following qualities as
being indispensable for the fulfillment of their proper tasks: "ability
to achieve social contact so as to find the right way of getting along
with employees, fairness, reliability, good fellowship, ability to
maintain close contact with the trade unions, diligence and a dynamic
personality. "[14]

The second major problem concerns parity representation on
supervisory boards. The unions are very sensitive to the fact that
employers are hostile to the idea of equal labor representation on the
supervisory board. They argue that the employers try to circumvent
labor equality on the supervisory board by the formation of subcommittees (on investment policy, for example) on which labor is under-
represented or not represented at all. "These committees then made
recommendations to the full board which accepted them without proper scrutiny, because it did not have the time to go through all the
data with which the sub-committee had worked. "[15]

Other critics claim that parity codetermination leads to a situation that gives rise to two factions (labor and capital) with opposing
interests. It is alleged that usually each side's representatives on
the supervisory board meet before the sessions and agree on the position they will take at the full board meeting. The result is confrontation and a series of delays and adjournment in the decision-
making process. The neutral member of the supervisory board is
constantly faced with the necessity of balancing the interests of the
shareholders with those of labor. In some cases, he or she encourages the groups to reach an amicable settlement, but in others, where
agreement cannot be reached, he or she votes alternatively for one
or the other side. In practice, many of the decisions are made by the
so-called horse trading principles. In short, the neutral person on
the board is in constant danger of becoming a tool of the opposing
factions rather than remaining an independent and equal partner.


The Biedenkopf Commission

In response to union pressure for the extension of parity representation on supervisory boards to all large firms, the German government appointed in 1967 a commission under the chairpersonship
of Kurt Hans Biedenkopf to study the history and results of codetermination in the steel and coal industry. In January 1970, the Biedenkopf Commission issued a unanimous report in which it concluded:

> Even though conflicts of interest remain . . . the repre-
> sentatives of shareholders and workers, after some initial
> difficulties, have cooperated in the supervisory boards in
> the steel and coal industries as well as in the industries
> where the Works' Constitution Act applies. The integra-
> tion which was intended when worker representatives were
> given places on the boards has, in fact, taken place. [16]

Furthermore, the commission did not find any evidence in support of
allegations that "unions were manipulating companies by 'remote-
control,' nor that workers were exercising an unhealthy influence on
the companies investment policies." [17] Other interesting findings of
the commission included the following:

1. that the present practice of co-determination is influenced more by the leadership style and decision-
   making conceptions of top managers in the management hierarchy than by the legal provisions of the Act.
2. that the profit orientation as the guideline of entrepre-
   neurial decision-making is not disputed by labour representatives, though they demand that decision-making
   should have an additional parameter, the interests of
   employees. The commission is of the opinion that this
   is accounted for by the two main goals of unions today,
   namely, the increase in standard of living and security
   of employment.
3. that co-determination never prevented projects initiated
   by management from being carried out.
4. that the areas where the labour representatives initiated
   action were most frequently social, personnel planning
   and policy; investment restructuring, mergers and dividend payments, etc., were usually left to management's
   initiative.
5. that co-determination did not slow down the process of
   concentration of enterprises but on the contrary promoted it, because labour representatives are susceptible to the argument that international competition demands large enterprises and because they do not think
   that there is any danger of misuse of economic power.
6. that the presence of labour representatives on supervisory boards did not bring about revolutionary changes
   in company policies; that these boards have operated
   rather smoothly and that unanimous votes are reported
   to be the rule rather than the exception. [18]

These findings of the Biedenkopf Commission contradicted the often-made predictions of management that the codetermination system would be detrimental to the good running of the enterprise. Other findings contradicted the claims of unions that worker influence on participative bodies was consistently undermined by management. For example, the commission reported that shareholder representatives had not been able to restrict and determine the flow of information in such a way as to undermine the capacity of the workers to participate; that discussion format and agenda for meetings of the supervisory board were not unilaterally determined by the chairperson, a shareholder representative in most cases, but by an executive committee on which the workers had representation; and that workers in the coal and steel industries were adequately represented on the subcommittees, where important issues are worked out in advance. [19]

While the commission strongly endorsed the principle of codetermination, it opposed the extension of parity representation on supervisory boards to other industries. It recommended that the Works Constitution Act of 1952 be modified to give labor a small amount of additional influence. The outcome of the Biedenkopf Commission's recommendations was the Works Constitution Act of 1972, which established a network of works councils throughout German industry, and the new Codetermination Act of 1976, which extended parity representation for supervisory boards to limited liability companies outside coal and steel with more than 2,000 employees.

Both unions and employers dislike the new legislation. Management is unhappy because the commission recommended an extension of labor influence, no matter how small. The unions are equally unhappy because their demand for the extension of parity representation to all industries was rejected. However, they are hopeful that one day there will be sufficient parliamentary support for the extension of all the provisions of the coal and steel model to all other undertakings.

Impact of Codetermination

One should not be surprised to find that management and unions disagree on the impact of codetermination. Management's prime concern is with how the system affects the productivity of the enterprise. On this point, Thusing, head of the Department of Economics and Social Structure, Confederation of German Employers Associations, had this to say: "Due to experience in the Federal Republic of Germany, I must establish the fact that participation of workers is at best irrelevant to productivity; that the special form of equitable co-determination has a negative effect on productivity. "[20]

On the other hand, the unions are primarily interested in the effect of the system on the well being of the workers. DGB, the largest trade union federation in Germany, claims that the codetermination system can be credited for the following achievements. It has improved communication within the enterprise, broken down the often oppressive anonymity of the administration process, and made it apparent that the interests of the employees are taken into consideration by elected representatives in all decisions taken by management of the plant.

It is particularly difficult to evaluate the impact of codetermination because it cannot always be separated from the results of the prevailing economic and social situation. For example, in a generally booming economy, the cost of "social plans," in case of rationalization and/or automation, is easily absorbed by the enterprise, and there is no way to tell what has been the effect of codetermination on decisions concerning automation, plant closures, and mergers. The question is often asked whether the system has contributed to industrial peace. The evidence is inconclusive. According to available data, the man-days lost declined from 1.59 million in 1954 to 37,723 in 1960. Undoubtedly, the reduction in industrial unrest was due to the economic prosperity, which benefited the workers a great deal, but part of the improvement in the industrial climate could be attributed to the interest evinced by labor in the welfare of the enterprise through its participation on boards. [21] However, codetermination did not prevent the wildcat strike in the metal industry in 1969 nor the strike of 1971.

One of the major contributions of codetermination is its usefulness in times of crisis. For example, the coal industry has suffered for many years from a structural crisis, which led to the shutting down of quite a few mines, company mergers, and the putting out of work of a large portion of the work force. Management was required to discuss every move with the labor representatives on the supervisory and management boards. Faced with these problems, labor representatives have shown remarkable understanding of the economic necessities. All this was accomplished without any major upheaval. The labor representatives helped in introducing technological changes, in improving vocational training, and in maintaining a relatively strike-free record. [22] Codetermination also facilitated the restructuring of the steel industry. Observers agree that

> due to co-determination, management has become more rational, more professional and more efficient. . . . In some cases, co-determination does seem to have slowed down managerial decision-making. However, once reached, the quality of decisions has been better than might have been

expected in other circumstances, due to a supervisory and
management board which can balance and reconcile a variety of points of view, resulting in worker commitment to
the ultimate decision. [23]

There is no evidence to show that firms experienced difficulty in at-
tracting sufficient capital or that potential foreign investors and current German investors have been induced to go elsewhere on account
of the codetermination system. Neither has it crippled the competitive drive necessary for survival in a free enterprise system.

The question of wages, personnel practices, and conditions of
work affect the workers more directly. It has been argued that codetermination has contributed in some enterprises to an upward adjustment of wages from the minimum agreed on an industrywide basis,
the so-called wage drift. However, the matter of wage adjustment is
usually dealt with at the works council level and not at the board level.
Labor directors do have some influence on the actual wage level and
have supported "high and just wages." It is a fact that wages in the
coal and steel industry, where codetermination is most successful,
are not substantially higher than elsewhere. While the tight labor
market probably contributed to the small spread of remuneration, it
can also be partly attributed to what has been called the "demonstration effect"—which is to say that employers in other branches of the
industry have attempted to keep up with coal and steel in order to alleviate political pressure for the expansion of parity codetermination.

The demonstration effect is also evident in the area of administrative and personnel practices. In industries affected by the Codetermination acts, the action of labor directors, combined with
union and works council pressure, has succeeded in bringing about
more rational, objective, and equitable systems of administration.
This change is also slowly occurring in firms where codetermination
is not in operation. However, it must be acknowledged that codetermination has been least effective in affecting working conditions at
the shop floor level. Herding notes that "exhausting physical effort,
excessive heat, hazardous safety and health conditions have been far
less points of attention (and redress) than in the American industry."[24]

Summary

The underlying objective of worker participation legislation
in Germany was to avoid conflict between employers and labor. The
unions believe that there is an inherent conflict between the aims and
interests of employers and workers, both at the level of the individual
undertaking and at the level of the economy as a whole. They argue

that worker rights can only be protected when labor is granted equal rights in management through legislation—in other words, the basis for worker participation is legal provisions and not mutual agreement reached through negotiations. Furthermore, the unions consider that worker participation in management should be indirect, that is, through the union representatives. The fact that unions concentrate on industrywide or nationwide issues leads to a certain apathy on the part of most workers, who are primarily interested in their immediate work situation. "The basic idea of giving the individual worker real opportunities for self-expression and influence in those matters of actual concern to him is overshadowed by strategic and political considerations of both the employers and the trade unions."[25] While the new legislation strengthens the position of unions and works councils, it does not provide individual workers with opportunities to play a more active role in shaping their workplace relations.

In retrospect, employee representation on the boards in West Germany seems to have worked remarkably well. The majority of the workers have a favorable attitude toward the institutional changes. They feel that their interests have not been ignored. The German experience has shown that labor representatives can participate in decision making at the highest level within an enterprise in a competent and responsible manner. Unions and employers accept the principle of codetermination, though not its detailed mechanism. In a larger economic and social context, both labor and management have cooperated in helping the steel industry to expand and in easing the suffering of the coal industry as it went through a process of painful restructuring. This was done without any strike or major upheaval. In short, board members have shown interest not only in the technical and economic aspects of the business but also have shown a great deal of sensitivity toward the personnel problems and social planning of companies.

## BOARD REPRESENTATION
## IN OTHER COUNTRIES

It is intriguing that while the debate on codetermination continues in West Germany, the system of worker participation in other European countries is being influenced by the German model.

Worker participation at the board level is widely prevalent in the public sector. For example, when the British Steel Corporation was renationalized on May 1, 1968, three employee directors were appointed to serve on each of the corporations' four divisional boards for a period of three years. They were paid the same salary as other part-time directors. They continued their existing jobs but had to attend board meetings and fulfill all other duties and responsibilities assigned to them as part-time directors. These employee-directors served in a personal capacity, not as a representative of a trade union, even though the Trade Union Congress and the unions in the industry were consulted prior to their appointment. During the first five years that the scheme was in operation, they were required, where appropriate, to relinquish their union offices for the period of their directorship. In 1970 their number was increased from three to four on each divisional board. All persons selected as employee-directors had considerable experience as part-time union officials.[26] They were given an extensive five-week training course (jointly organized by the steel corporation and the TUC) on the problems and policies of the steel corporation. They were also taught managerial techniques and procedures. It is generally recognized that the employee-directors reflected the feelings and attitudes of the employees and that they made useful contributions to the discussions in the individual boards and brought a different and fresh point of view to the problems under discussion.

In France, legislation provides for worker minority representation on the management boards of nationalized enterprises. The labor representatives on the boards are generally nominated by the most representative union organizations (coal, mining, gas, electricity, and railways), but in some cases, they are appointed by the works committee (Renault) or elected by the staff (Air France).

While worker minority representation on boards is fairly common in nationalized industries or in undertakings in the public sector, it is not so frequent in the private sector. However, in recent years, legislation has been introduced in many countries providing for labor representation on the board in private sector companies. The influence of the German model on the Netherlands, Denmark, Sweden, and Norway is obvious in their introduction of two-tier boards and employee-directors. On the other hand, other countries, such as the United Kingdom, seem to be steering away from the German system of codetermination. Because of the many similarities between the industrial relations system and company structure in Britain and in North America, recent developments in the United Kingdom are analyzed here in greater detail than those in other countries.

Recent Developments in the United Kingdom

The British TUC has strongly advocated the adoption of a worker participation system similar to the codetermination model in West Germany, asking that 50 percent of the directors be appointed by the unions. The employer group is opposed to the introduction in the United Kingdom of two-tier boards and union-appointed worker-directors. It prefers to maintain the present British company structure of a unified board of directors, but would be willing to see a wider appointment of outside directors. In 1976 the British government appointed Lord Bullock to head an official commission of inquiry on industrial democracy. The terms of reference of the Bullock Committee read:

> Accepting the need of a radical extension of industrial
> democracy in the control of companies by means of repre-
> sentation on the board of directors, and accepting the es-
> sential role of trade union organizations in this process,
> to consider how such an extension can best be achieved,
> taking into account in particular the proposals of the
> Trades Union Congress report on industrial democracy
> as well as experience in Britain, the E.E.C. and other
> countries. [27]

It can be seen that the terms of reference were heavily slanted in favor of the unions' position. The committee's final report, published in 1977, consisted of two parts: the official majority report and a minority report giving the views of the three commission members who represented the employers. The main recommendations of the Bullock Committee (majority) were the following:

1. Equal representation of shareholders and employees on the board of directors; in addition, a third group of directors should be co-opted with the agreement of a majority of each of the other two groups, that is, the employee and shareholder representatives;
2. Unions are given the responsibility of devising a satisfactory method of selecting employee representatives on the board (unfortunately, the report does not state in practical terms how this should be done, especially in cases where competing unions are operating in a company); and
3. A unitary board of directors instead of a two-tier board; the report recommends that the present company law be amended so that the right to take a final decision in certain areas would rest with the board of directors and the board could no longer delegate authority for such decisions to senior management (such areas include the winding up of a company, changes in the capital structure of a company and disposal of a substantial part of the undertaking, recommendation to shareholders on the payment of dividends, and so forth).

These recommendations have met with strong opposition from the employer federation, the Confederation of British Industries

(CBI). Basically, the CBI accepts the need for greater employee participation provided it is achieved by consensus. They particularly object to the imposition of a rigid formula for apportioning the number of board level representatives to stockholders, union nominees, and additional outside directors. This formula, known as $2(X) + Y$, means that shareholders and employees have X directors each and the Y element would be the co-opted directors. The committee is of the opinion that the size of the boards should be left for the parties to agree, but in case of deadlock, minimum figures are proposed. For example, in a company employing between 2,000 and 10,000 workers, the board would have 11 members, namely, 4 employee and 4 shareholder representatives and 3 co-opted directors. The formula is based on the principle that the number of co-opted directors must always be uneven and must always form less than one-third of the total board. The employers are of the opinion that the formula is, at best, a recipe for deadlock and, at worst, for deepening conflict.[28]

The British employers also oppose any moves that would weaken their managerial prerogatives. They argue that parity representation would put managers under considerable strain. It would result in the slowing down of the process of decision making when speed is an essential element in the making of effective decisions in a highly competitive economic environment.

Unions in the United Kingdom are divided on the issue of worker representation on the board. At the 1974 TUC convention, a number of union delegates voiced strong reservations about the appointment of worker-directors. A resolution was passed, "recognizing that the best way to strengthen industrial democracy is to strengthen and extend the area of collective bargaining giving union representatives increasing control over elements of management." The resolution rejected the mandatory imposition of a supervisory board with worker-directors and called for a flexible approach, giving statutory backing to the right to negotiate on these major issues but relating control more directly to collective bargaining machinery.

Many left-wing unionists believe that worker representatives on the board are exposed to potential conflict of interest. They believe that the trade union movement is in danger "of falling for theories that will tie the movement lock, stock and barrel, with the interests of capital and to the detriment of our movement."[29]

Because of the strong opposition of employers and some unions, the British government rejected some of the more controversial elements of the Bullock report, including parity representation on the board for workers and management. In its latest (May 1978) White Paper on Industrial Democracy, the government proposed:

1.  Companies employing more than 500 people should be under a legal obligation to discuss major policy deci-

sions (such as mergers, investment, redundancies and takeovers) before they are taken, with a joint representation committee (JRC) representing all the trade unions in the company.

2. After a JRC has been operating for three or four years, workers in companies employing over 2,000 people will have the legal right to board-level representation. If this cannot be agreed voluntarily, then workers (Which workers? It is left vague) will be able to appoint one-third of the directors either to the top policy board in a new two-tier structure, or (if the company prefers) to the existing unitary board.

3. The establishment of an industrial democracy commission to provide advice and conciliation and to give rulings on disputes and to monitor and evaluate the operations of the planned legislation. [30]

Commentators have pointed out that the whole thrust of the white paper is to encourage voluntary participation agreements. The only universal obligation on companies would be to consult employee representatives on a range of major issues before decisions are taken. This represents a major extension of participation into central and strategic policy decision making. Legislation is to intervene only if companies fail to work out satisfactory arrangements by themselves.

New legislation on the basis of the above proposals is unlikely before the next general elections, which must be held before the fall of 1979. Nevertheless, the general principle of extension of industrial democracy and board representation is a certainty. All political parties in the United Kingdom are committed to it.

Worker-Directors in Other European Countries

In France, worker representatives attend board of director meetings. However, they participate in an advisory capacity only. They are nominated to the board by the works council. A new law that became effective in 1972 extended the nonshareholder membership on the board from two to four, one of whom represents the foremen and the other graduate engineers and other supervisory staff. The Sudreau Commission, which was appointed by the government in 1975 to make recommendations on the reform of the enterprise, proposed a one-third worker representation on the board of directors. The idea was not to institute comanagement but, rather, a form of joint supervision. This would allow employee representatives to be informed about decisions without being necessarily involved in making them.[31] In Austria and Luxembourg, recent legislation allows one-third labor representation on the supervisory board in companies of a certain size.

A new act relating to board representation for employees came into effect in Sweden in 1976. Its stated purpose is "to afford to the employees insight and influence in respect to the enterprises' activities." The act states that companies that have 25 employees can have two employee-members on the board. The most interesting feature of the act is the fact that it comes into operation only if the union or unions recognized by the employer and representing more than half the company's employees so request. The representatives on the board are nominated by the unions, usually from among company employees.[32] The labor representatives on the board have the same responsibilities as other corporate board members in formulating company policies. The worker board members are not permitted to participate in board decisions affecting collective bargaining agreements and matters involving labor-management disputes, such as strikes and lockouts. In Norway, a new law, which became effective in 1973, requires companies in mining and manufacturing industries that employ 200 or more people to set up a new type of assembly, a "board of representatives," with one-third members to be elected by the personnel. This board is empowered to appoint the company's management board and has the final authority concerning important investment decisions and any rationalization or reorganization plans that would affect the labor force to an appreciable degree. A similar system was introduced by the government in the construction industry after both parties reached an agreement. Firms not yet covered by the legislation are expected to be covered by other laws or decrees. Thus, the commercial and agricultural undertakings, cooperatives, the hotel and catering industry, banks and insurance companies, and so forth will also have labor representation on boards.

In Denmark, the government introduced in 1973 a plan for economic democracy under which employees in limited liability companies employing 50 or more persons would have to contribute each year a certain percentage of the total amount paid in salaries to a central investment fund. Under this scheme, employees would acquire a collective stake in the central investment fund. This fund would be used for purchasing shares in Danish companies. One implication of this proposal is that workers, as owners of corporate shares, would have the right to elect a number of representatives of their own choosing on the board. The number of representatives on each board would correspond to the employees' share of the capital in the undertaking, up to a maximum of 50 percent. The main difference between the profit-sharing schemes that have been in operation in other countries, such as France (1967) and the Netherlands (1972), and the Danish scheme is that in Denmark, the employees will have the right to own shares of Danish companies and the central investment fund will be governed by a majority of the worker representatives.

The Netherlands have devised a unique plan, which became legally effective in 1973. This plan gives workers an indirect voice along with shareholders and management in the selection of members of corporate boards. The principles of the system are the following:

1. Every supervisory board member must retire every four years, but he or she may be reappointed.

2. Supervisory board members are no longer appointed or re-appointed by the shareholders' meeting but by the supervisory board itself.

3. The shareholders' meeting, the works council, and also the management may make recommendations for appointments, but the supervisory board is not bound by these recommendations.

4. The supervisory board cannot co-opt a person as a member of the supervisory board if either the shareholders' meeting or the works council objects.

5. If the supervisory board does not agree to the objection, it can appeal to the "Social Economic Council."

6. There is no appeal against the decision of the Social Economic Council, which is composed of representatives of the unions and employee associations, as well as of appointees of the Crown.[33]

The idea behind the new Dutch system appears to be that the supervisory board should be a harmonious body, in which individual members are not tied to the vested interests of either labor or the stockholders. Its purpose is to ensure that all supervisory board members have the full confidence of both shareholders and employees and, therefore, will be guided by the interests of the company as a whole.[34]

Perhaps the most important influence exercised by the Dutch and German models has been on the EEC Commission. In 1970 the commission proposed the European Company Statute, which would provide for the establishment of supervisory boards. The workers would be represented on the supervisory board unless two-thirds of the total number of employees in a company voted against such representation. The worker representatives would constitute one-third and the shareholder representatives two-thirds of the board membership. In seeking to promote the development of a common social policy in respect to the structure of corporate enterprise and the rights of employees, the heads of government of the enlarged EEC issued in October 1972 a draft directive for the harmonization of national company laws in member countries. It is interesting to note that the commission offered two alternative patterns from which the employees could choose one. In the first model, the appointment of the members of the supervisory board for the company in a member country is made partly by the general assembly of shareholders and partly by the employees. Labor representatives on the board should account for at least one-third of the total supervisory board membership (German model). In the second model, appointees to the supervisory board may be co-opted. Shareholders and employees may object to the appointment of a particular candidate to the position of a corporate director on the grounds that he or she is not suitable for the task or for other reasons. The final decision over the soundness of objections must be made by an independent institution (Dutch model).

Because of internal dissensions within the committee on the issue of worker participation, a Green Paper, Employee Participation in the European Community, was issued in 1975. The new revised European Company Statute recommended that the membership of the supervisory board consist of one-third labor, one-third shareholders, and one-third appointed jointly by labor and shareholders. The last category in some respects represents the public interest. In this paper, the commission had to acknowledge the fact that for an indefinite transitional period, no standard patterns could be generally agreed upon, and in some cases, workers and their unions might not even want to be represented on boards at all. This acknowledgment is not surprising, since unions in many European countries are still not favorably disposed toward employee representation on the boards. For example, the Belgian General Federation of Labor (ABV/FGTB) prefers to remain outside the management structure. The Italian trade union movement is also opposed to becoming involved in management decisions.

AN OVERALL VIEW

In the beginning of this chapter, we listed a number of controversial issues concerning employee representation on boards. These were the following:

1. Should employees be represented on boards of private as well as of public enterprises?

2. Should labor have equal representation with shareholders on the boards, or should labor have only minority representation?

3. How should such employee-directors be chosen—should they be employees of the company or outsiders nominated by unions, or should employee-directors be chosen from both groups? and

4. Should worker-directors be responsible to the general shareholders meeting or to the unions, and should their rights and respon-

sibilities be the same as those of other directors or should they be different?

Even though employee participation at the board level in the private sector is no longer a new and untried concept in Europe, it still meets with opposition from some quarters on ideological grounds. At one end of the spectrum, unions with Marxist leanings claim that industrial democracy is meaningless unless the structure of society is changed radically. At the other extreme is the argument advanced by many academics and employers that the political notion of democracy cannot be applied to the enterprise because management is primarily a productive and not a political function. However, as Batstone remarked, the European experience indicates that

> the introduction of worker-directors, as indeed other forms of "industrial democracy," has typically reflected a compromise between contrasting philosophies in the face of industrial crises. Schemes which apparently develop "industrial democracy" have been less an extension of worker influence than a recognition of its existence and an attempt to channel it. [35]

Is the institution of worker-directors an effective mechanism to protect and enhance worker influence and interests? In most European countries, the prevalent form of worker participation at the board level is that of minority representation, regardless of whether the company has a unitary or two-tier board structure. The only exception is labor representation on a parity basis, as practiced in the coal and steel industry in West Germany.

The effectiveness of labor representatives on the board is limited by a series of factors. In West Germany, for example, the legal function of the supervisory board is primarily to elect the members of the management board and to control its overall activities. In practice, in times of economic prosperity, the actual activities of the supervisory boards do not amount to more than coordination, advice, and formal ratification of the decisions already made by the management boards. Supervisory boards in West Germany usually meet three or four times a year. Thus, the activities of supervisory boards are rather remote from the day-to-day management activities within the enterprise. This is equally true of other countries in Western Europe.

In the case of labor minority representation on the supervisory boards, labor representatives do not have real power to make decisions against the will of the shareholder representatives, who are in the majority. In terms of actual power relationships, minority representation on the supervisory boards must be viewed by labor as a means of gaining firsthand knowledge and information on important aspects of business. Though labor representatives in Germany do not have any veto rights, in practice, their approval is usually sought and considered valuable by the shareholder representatives. For example, the shareholder representatives on the supervisory board of a large German automobile company decided in favor of declaring a sizable dividend. The labor representatives first objected to their decision, but later on gave their consent, when the shareholder representatives agreed to grant a big bonus payment for all employees of the firm at the same time.

Labor representatives on the board also have influence over the decisions that are likely to affect employment conditions, such as changes in the ownership of the firm, plant closures, and the introduction of new products and production methods. Early information on these matters can help the members of the works councils at the plant level to take appropriate measures. In summary, the legal provisions for labor representation on supervisory boards in countries with market economies do not amount to real codetermination in all management decisions. The very structure of the supervisory boards and the legal framework within which they operate provides labor representatives with only indirect opportunities for influencing the decisions of the management board. It is the management board that decisively shapes the technical, economic, and financial policies of the enterprise. Labor's influence is usually felt at a time when the enterprise is faced with a serious labor relations crisis—and here again, it mostly is with social and personnel matters. Past experience indicates that labor representatives on boards seem to conform to the established norms of conduct set by shareholder representatives.

If minority employee representation on boards does not amount to real codetermination, is parity representation the answer? Most European unions think it is. The arguments they advance in favor of parity representation on boards can be summarized as follows. They maintain that parity representation

1. Would put an end to the autocratic regime of management and would introduce an element of democracy in the control and management of industrial and commercial undertakings, which is necessary to supplement political democracy;

2. Would also safeguard the interests of workers, such as job security;

3. Is necessary to avoid concentration of power in the hands of management—it is argued that the repercussions of management decisions are felt not only by the owners but also by labor and the general public; and

4. Would provide a better balance within the undertaking between the interests of shareholders and those of labor—particularly in view of the growing tendency toward concentration in large production units.[36]

Many employers in Western European countries look favorably upon labor minority representation schemes because it gives them an opportunity to provide the worker representatives with firsthand information on the economic situation of the enterprise, thus encouraging their cooperation with management. However, employers groups are opposed to labor parity representation on the boards of directors. At an OECD seminar, employer representatives raised serious doubts and objections about parity representation schemes. Their arguments can be summarized as follows:

1. The demand for parity representation does not come from the workers but from the unions, who have difficulties in explaining the rationale for parity representation to their own members.
2. The appointment of management boards by the supervisory board on which labor has parity created unstable conditions, which will deter able managers from seeking high-level positions.
3. Parity representation means the end of the free market system and of the concept of private property. It would slow down the process of decision making, when speed is an essential element in the making of effective decisions.
4. Parity representation means a redistribution of power, which might result in the unions having a dominant influence in the national life, in the economy, and in collective bargaining.
5. Parity representation could affect the process of collective bargaining adversely, that is, it could lead to the extension of collective bargaining into board rooms and to the development of decision making by horse-trading and other undesirable deals.[37]

Evidence from the West German experience indicates that while worker-directors have contributed to the improvement of personnel practices within the company, they have tended to adopt a perspective of "company egoism." For example, "they have supported managerial proposals for rationalization of economic power, viewing these as a means of promoting security of employment."[38] Even though past experience does not seem to justify management's skepticism and suspicions, nonetheless, management's opposition to parity representation at the board level remains as strong as ever. It is based partly on the fear of potential deadlocks and confrontations. An array of procedures for solving these deadlocks provided by legislation in a number of countries indicates that the governments seem to share these fears to a degree.

Among the above list of objections of management to parity representation, two deal with its potentially negative impact on collective bargaining and on the danger of upsetting the balance of power between union and management. The problem of the degree to which unions should exercise control over worker–directors is a complex one. In the case where the employees of a firm are represented by a multiplicity of unions, such as in the United Kingdom, the question arises which union or unions should represent labor on various management organs. There is also the additional problem of providing adequate representation on boards for middle and senior management. They would like to be treated as a group distinct from blue and white collar workers, that is, to be represented by a "cadre" union and have separate representation on boards.

Several participants at the ILO seminar in 1974 expressed the fear that worker participation on boards would weaken collective bargaining. Such fears are widespread among the union leaders in the United States and Canada. Even the leaders of some sections of the trade union movement in the United Kingdom, France, and Italy believe that employee representation on the board would undermine the bargaining power of the unions. They argue that labor representation on the board does not solve the problem of dual allegiance or divided loyalty. Some participants from West Germany and Sweden at the ILO seminar contended that in their countries, where collective bargaining is conducted mainly at levels higher than the undertaking, minority representation of workers on supervisory boards was not incompatible with collective bargaining.[39] They pointed out that participation on company boards was a particularly effective safeguard of certain interests of the workers, such as job security, and that it could promote information and, thus, collective bargaining.

In conclusion, then, consideration of the European experience at the board level suggests that in most cases management has resigned itself to accepting the concept of worker representation on company boards. Unions perceive employee representation on the board as complementary to collective bargaining and other forms of industrial democracy, such as works councils. Furthermore, in the long term, worker representation on company boards is seen as a potentially important development in Western Europe's continuing movement toward greater industrial democracy.

NOTES

1. International Labour Organisation, Management and Productivity, ILO Bulletin 38 (Geneva, 1973), p. 7.

2. International Labour Organisation, Symposium on Workers' Participation, Background paper (Oslo: ILO, 1974), pp. 4-5.

3. Rudolf J. Vollmer, "Industrial Democracy in Germany" (Paper delivered at the International Conference on Industrial Relations, McGill University, Montreal, June 1976), p. 25.

4. Friedrich Fürstenberg, "Worker Participation in German Industry," in Industrial Democracy, ed. C. P. Thakur and K. C. Sethi (New Dehli: Shri Ram Centre for Industrial Relations, 1973), p. 311.

5. For an analysis of the weakness of early worker participation systems in Germany, see Roy J. Adams and C. H. Rummel, "Workers' Participation in Management in West Germany: Impact on the Worker, the Enterprise, and the Trade Union," Industrial Relations Journal 8 (Spring 1977): 5-6.

6. Vollmer, "Industrial Democracy in Germany," pp. 21-23.

7. Friedrich Fürstenberg, Workers' Participation in Management in the Federal Republic of Germany, International Institute for Labour Studies, Bulletin no. 6 (Geneva, 1968), p. 37.

8. David Jenkins, Job Power: Blue and White Collar Democracy (London: Heinemann, 1974), p. 125.

9. Fürstenberg, Workers' Participation in Management, p. 38.

10. Jenkins, Job Power, p. 127.

11. Friedrich Fürstenberg, Workers' Participation in Management in the Federal Republic of Germany, International Institute for Labour Studies, Research Series, no. 32 (Geneva, 1978), p. 27.

12. Jenkins, Job Power, p. 130.

13. Ibid., p. 129.

14. Fürstenberg, Workers' Participation in Management, p. 31.

15. N. Das, Experiments in Industrial Democracy (New York: Asia Publishing, 1964), p. 76.

16. Jenkins, Job Power, p. 123.

17. Ibid., p. 124.

18. H. Daheim, "The Practice of Co-Determination on the Management Level of German Enterprises," in Industrial Democracy in the West European Countries, ed. W. Albeda (Rotterdam: Rotterdam University Press, 1973), pp. 23-30.

19. "Biedenkopf Commission Report," as quoted in Adams and Rummel, "Workers' Participation in Management in West Germany," p. 10.

20. Rolf Thusing, "Productivity under Co-Determination," in Industrial Democracy, ed. Albeda, p. 339.

21. Das, Experiments in Industrial Democracy, p. 75.

22. Jenkins, Job Power, p. 121.

23. For a detailed analysis, see Adams and Rummel, "Workers' Participation in Management in West Germany," pp. 15-21.

24. R. Herding, Job Control and Union Structure (Rotterdam: Rotterdam University Press, 1972), p. 329, as quoted in ibid., p. 15.

25. Fürstenberg, Workers' Participation in Management, p. 54.

26. R. O. Clarke, D. J. Fatchett, and B. C. Roberts, Workers' Participation in Management in Britain (London: Heinemann, 1972).

27. Industrial Democracy, Report of the Committee of Inquiry on Industrial Democracy (Bullock Report) (London: HMSO, 1977).

28. Ibid., p. 103.

29. Benjamin C. Roberts, "Employee Participation: Trends and Issues," in Employee Participation and Company Reform, ed. F. Basagni and F. Souzey, The Atlantic Papers, 4/1975 (Paris, 1976), p. 13.

30. Economist (London, May 27, 1978), pp. 77-79.

31. Yves Delamotte, "The 'Reform of the Enterprize' in France," Annals of the American Academy of Political and Social Sciences 431 (May 1977): 60.

32. P. L. Davies, "European Experience with Worker Representation on the Board," in Industrial Democracy, European Experience, Prepared for the Industrial Democracy Committee (Bullock Committee) (London: HMSO, 1976), p. 75. For further details, see J. Kalvenback, Worker Participation in Europe (Kluwers, Deventer, Netherlands, 1977), pp. 45-47.

33. Kalvenback, Worker Participation in Europe, p. 62.

34. Ibid., p. 63.

35. Eric Batstone, "Industrial Democracy and Worker Representation at Board Level: A Review of European Experience," in Industrial Democracy, European Experience, p. 39.

36. Ernst-Gehrard Erdmann, The Myth of Co-Determination (Kaln: Confederation of German Employers Associations, 1972), pp. 17-30.

37. Organization for Economic Cooperation and Development, "Workers' Participation" (Final summary, Paris, 1975), p. 51.

38. Batstone, "Industrial Democracy and Worker Representation," p. 40.

39. International Labour Organisation, Symposium on Workers' Participation, Summary of discussions (Oslo: ILO, 1974), pp. 11-15.

# Chapter Three

## WORKS COUNCILS

With the possible exception of collective bargaining, the works councils or works committees appear to be the most prevalent form of worker participation in management. Essentially, works councils are joint labor-management bodies that operate mostly at the plant or enterprise level. Their objectives are to promote cooperation in the undertaking, to encourage greater productivity, and to give employees a say in matters that concern them. The size, composition, and competence of works councils vary among different countries. Generally speaking, works councils have limited powers of decision making.

Great diversity is evident in the attributions of the works councils or works committees, which generally deal with clearly specified matters. Their field of competence ranges from mere receipt of information (in particular on the general economic and financial situation of the undertaking and its prospects), often followed by consultation on a variety of subjects, to the right of co-decision, mainly concerning personnel matters and working conditions. In addition, they are often entrusted with the management of welfare services. In the majority of cases, their attributions have been clearly defined to distinguish them from matters which are subject to collective bargaining between employers and trade unions.[1]

The works councils have been established by one of the following three ways: (1) through national collective agreements between central trade unions and employer confederations, such as in the Scandinavian countries; (2) through voluntary local agreements between employers and workers, such as in the United Kingdom, the United States, Canada, Australia, and so forth; and (3) through legislation, such as in Belgium, the Netherlands, West Germany, and so forth.

The purpose of this chapter is to study the functioning of the works councils (works committees) system and to evaluate its strengths and weaknesses. Recent developments are examined in an attempt to discern the direction works councils will take in the years ahead. With the object of illustrating the influence of various factors that account for the success or failure of the system, a case study of works councils in France will be presented here. The French experience with works councils is also interesting because nowadays "the question of participation is a more burning question in France than elsewhere; the difficult problem of translating desires into action appears, due to the prevailing social, political, ideological and psychological background, to be harder to resolve than in several other industrial countries."[2]

THE FRENCH CASE

France has long been in the forefront of the trend to make the actual producer responsible for the management of production. Yet it is generally acknowledged that in spite of having passed progressive pieces of legislation in the past (France was the first European country to grant the right to strike to workers—in the 1860s), nowadays, the climate of social and industrial relations in France is unfavorable to the functioning of schemes of worker participation in management.

The Creation of Works Councils after World War II

The profound national, social, and economic crisis brought by World War II provided an occasion to introduce elements of worker participation in France. The Communist party had been very deeply involved in the activities of the underground resistance movement. The need to strengthen and reaffirm the national unity and to give priority to reconstruction in the economic field led to a regrouping of all political forces under the leadership of General Charles de Gaulle. This common front lasted until 1947. During that time, the Communist party held important portfolios in the government, including the ministries of Labor and Industrial Production.

In the final days of the war, groups of workers had set up "management committees" to run enterprises whose owners, some of whom had collaborated with the enemy, had fled. Rather than allowing the situation to deteriorate into anarchy, the government thought it wise to give legitimate sanction to this spontaneous movement. Thus, because of the play of special circumstances, the 1945 and 1946 legislation introducing works councils in France had a dual objective, namely, to introduce a reform that could be seen by the workers as a step on the way to more far-reaching achievements while, at the same time, preserving to a large extent the traditional authority of the employers.

Works Councils Legislation until 1968

The Ordinance of February 23, 1945, and the Act of May 16, 1946, define the rights and functions of works councils in France. While later amendments and new legislation enlarged to an extent the scope of their powers, the basic provisions of the early legislation remained unchanged between 1946 and 1968. The 1946 act extended the obligation to set up works councils to all firms, whether commercial and industrial, which had 50 or more employees. The only exceptions were the public services and the nationalized companies, to which a system of works councils and other forms of worker participation were extended by collective agreements or by governmental decrees.

The works council is chaired by the company's chief executive officer. Its members number from 3 to 11, according to the number of employees in the firm. Elections are held every two years. Each group of employees (rank-and-file workers, salaried people, technicians, and supervisory personnel) elect representatives from lists proposed by the principal unions in the firm. Should half the electors abstain from voting, a second ballot is held for which any one may be a candidate. For each firm, collective agreements regulate the proportion of council members attributed to the separate voting "colleges." The June 18, 1966, amendment apecified that a third such college, representing engineers and higher supervisory staff (cadres), could also elect members to the works council and that the total membership could be extended subject to collective agreement. The law protects the members of the works council from arbitrary dismissal by management.

Where undertakings have several separate plants, "establishment committees," with more limited powers, take the place of the works council. The establishment committee, however, elects representatives to the central works committee of the undertaking. The rules of procedure for the works committee are also prescribed by legislation. They include provisions for monthly meetings, advance circulation of the agenda, and, most important, the obligation of the chairperson to reply at each meeting to proposals put forward by staff representatives at previous meetings.

Before defining the scope of activities of the works councils, the law states clearly that the councils are "not designed to press demands" nor to present individual or collective grievances. Those aspects of collective labor relations are specifically reserved for collective bargaining and for "employee delegates" (shop stewards), respectively. However, employee delegates may communicate to the works council the comments of the employees on all matters within the jurisdiction of the council. The intent of the legislation was that the works councils' sphere of activity cover economic and financial problems. The ordinance of 1945 stated that the members of the works council had the right to be informed and to have access to the annual report on operations and prospects and to quarterly communications on the progress of production and employment. In limited liability companies, they could also look at the balance sheets. The 1946 legislation went further: the right to information became the right to be consulted on these matters. The loosely worded legislation was made more specific, and therefore more effective, by the 1966 amendment, which stated that the council must now be consulted, among other things

> on any measure affecting the size or structure of the staff. Thus, while it is always the head of the undertaking who in the last resort decides on any collective dismissals, the committee has a chance to express its views and desiderata, which are communicated to the labour inspectorate, together with a reply by the management justifying its proposal. The same holds good for a certain number of organizational problems (including the drafting of work rules), questions of vocational training or the possible allocation of profits. [3]

It must be noted also that works councils elect two representatives to sit in an advisory capacity (without voting rights) on the company's board of directors. Thus, the opportunities for the works council to participate in the running of the enterprise are of a very limited type. On the other hand, the works council has practically free rein insofar as the welfare activities are concerned.

> On their own responsibility, they actually administer those activities within the undertaking which do not have separate legal personality—canteens, children, homes, libraries, etc. They also share through their duly appointed representatives, in the administration of certain independent institutions for staff welfare—cooperatives, mutual benefit societies, building or housing societies, etc.
> The committees also contribute to the working of the medical, health and safety services of the undertaking and

must approve the appointment or dismissal of the medical officer and the chief women employment officer. [4]

In addition, works councils are empowered to negotiate and sign profit-sharing agreements provided for by an ordinance of 1959, which set up a voluntary scheme for worker participation in the benefits accruing from the expansion of the undertaking. The Vallon Amendment of 1967, which made the scheme compulsory for all enterprises employing more than 100 persons, greatly expanded this aspect of the works council activities.

> By March 1974, 8971 collective agreements had been concluded implementing the ordinance. They benefited four million employees and covered a total of 10,051 enterprizes. Of this total, 15% of the enterprizes had less than one hundred employees and therefore submitted voluntarily to a law which was not obligatory for them. More than 80% of the agreements were concluded by enterprize committees. [5]

Problems of Works Councils—
The Industrial Relations Climate

It is a generally recognized fact that worker participation in works councils has been effective with regard to the social and welfare aspects of the councils' activities. On the other hand, except in a few cases, the works councils have had little impact on the economic aspects of the running of the enterprise. There is little doubt that the attitudes of management, the unions, and the workers account for these disappointing results.

A number of historical factors account for this situation. The French Revolution of 1789 had social as well as political objectives. While the latter were eventually implemented in the course of the nineteenth century, the social equalitarian ideal did not become a reality, and the class system in France remained rigid. As a result, the working classes, whose numbers were swollen by the Industrial Revolution, inherited a legacy of bitterness. These feelings erupted occasionally—sometimes in bloody struggles, such as the Commune Uprising in 1871, which aggravated a social malaise that has lasted to this day. Another factor, also originating in the French Revolution and its Napoleonic aftermath, is the belief in centralization and the reliance on bureaucracy to maintain order and stability and, at the same time, to be an instrument of economic progress. Jenkins's analysis shows how this factor influences the labor relations climate:

The key to the situation is the position of the government, which intervenes at numerous points in the relations between the two, in establishing certain aspects of working conditions and social security measures, as well as in direct participation in negotiations and in its own considerable role as an employer. This arrangement has certain advantages—notably, it skirts "the emotional difficulty which direct contact would constitute"—but its cumbersomeness also carries obvious disadvantages. Though both parties have the theoretical possibility of influencing the other through pressuring for state action of some sort, this is not very efficient. As a consequence, both sides get increasingly locked into their rigid positions. The unions remain weak because whatever influence they are able or willing to apply on management is all but invisible to the potential dues-paying member. Management remains aristocratically backward because the resentment of the state's interference in company affairs "reinforces a complex of reactionary attitudes and an anachronistic attachment to prerogatives which, in fact, are largely outmoded."[6]

Insofar as the employers are concerned, a strong belief in the authority of the head of the enterprise, coupled with an ingrained desire for discretion, is at the root of the majority of employer hostility to the idea of participation. Since absolute authority is thought to be essential for maximum efficiency, any sharing of this authority is inevitably suspect. As Jenkins puts it:

A generally accepted attitude is that the president of the company is alone capable of making decisions, that pressures from workers and/or unions are to be resisted under all circumstances, and that maximum efficiency can be attained by exerting maximum severity of authority. The money-instrumental idea of workers and work is accepted without question: No worker would do anything at all if he were not forced to by threats, bribes, or fear of starvation, and workers are incapable of taking any real interest in their work or of accepting responsibility. [7]

Indeed the general attitude of the National Council of French Employers (CNPF), the largest and most influential employers group, has been traditionally one of opposition to participation.

One reason for the overall failure of the system is that it depends too heavily on the goodwill of management. The ability of the works council to fulfill its advisory function is largely contingent on the quality of information received and on the actions taken by management on the council's suggestions. Past experience has shown that employers have tried to weaken the influence of the works councils or to bypass them by holding informal management meetings when key issues came up for consideration. Nor have all employers complied with the legislation concerning works councils. In 1964 only 10,000 of the 15,000 enterprises affected by the law had established works councils. Similarly, the attitude of the unions has hampered the development of employee participation through works councils. The majority of the French unions, faithful to their revolutionary traditions, which rejects the established order, have generally been unwilling to accept any employer-employee relationship that implies cooperation. Greyfie de Bellecombe describes the objectives of the General Confederation of Labor (CGT) at the time of its organization in 1895 as follows:

> A new order in which the producer would eventually assume responsibility for his work and at the same time be free to dispose of the product of his employment; this went hand-in-hand with the greatest reluctance to be involved in the play of forces of the established economic or political institutions even with a view to transforming them from within. Even in connection with the improvements in the lot of the workers resulting from legislation or from employers' initiatives, the attitudes of the trade union leaders were unclear: in most cases it was one of suspicion. Still less were they prepared to show any interest in the working of the mechanism of production which some of them in any case dreamed of destroying. [8]

The general attitude of the unions, as summed up by the CGT, is that "works committees constitute a weapon in the class struggle and should not be considered as an instrument for cooperation between employers and workers."[9] Indeed, despite provisions for secrecy, information from works councils has been used to back up worker demands in other areas. This attitude, coupled with the general disinterest of the worker representatives, has encouraged the employers to retain their traditional ways.

Yet it would be a mistake to believe that the attitudes of all managers and trade unionists are entirely rigid. Some employers and managers welcome the idea of worker participation. They are mostly found in independent employers associations, such as the Association of Industrial Managers, the Christian Employers Federation, and the Organization of Young Managers. Similarly, some unions show a willingness to consider participation as an acceptable alternative to

class struggle. This is the case of the French Democratic Confederation of Labor (CFTD). This evolution is a result of a shift in the
thinking of those who criticize the defects and inadequacies of the
present social system.

> Of the two accusations made against capitalism by the fol-
> lowers of Marx—which may be summed up as exploitation
> and alienation—the former was the one on which attention
> was almost entirely centred until a recent date. Alienation
> was little more than a subject of speculation for a few spe-
> cialists; to attempt to put an end to it without first destroy-
> ing the basis of exploitation—the private ownership of the
> means of production—was generally held to be futile. Now-
> adays there is a growing and deepening interest in the prob-
> lem of alienation to which many would wish to find a solution
> by way of participation in economic decision making—without
> waiting for the perhaps distant day when the question of ex-
> ploitation may be solved along the lines of traditional social-
> ist thought.[10]

Whether the rank-and-file workers feel exploited and/or alienated is related to their apparent lack of interest in participation in the
works councils. This attitude is often thought to be the result of the
lack of opportunity to move upward socially and of the low degree of
social integration of the working class. According to Greyfie de Bellecombe:

> These factors, even more than low wages, lead the worker
> to consider his environment, and especially that of the un-
> dertaking in which he works, as a hostile or at least for-
> eign world, towards which the only conceivable attitude
> must be one of negation and demands. This has for long
> been the spontaneous reaction of the French worker towards
> his employer, and it would still seem to be the attitude of a
> far from negligible fraction of the working population, who
> look on profits as a reflection of exploitation rather than of
> efficiency. One is tempted here to quote a distorted ver-
> sion of the famous dictum of Charles Wilson, President of
> General Motors, and say that "what is good for the under-
> taking is bad for the workers"—bad or at least suspect.[11]

The above general comments need to be qualified in several
important respects. Rank-and-file workers have shown a great willingness to participate in the works council's running of social and welfare activities. Opinion is divided as to the reasons for this. It has

been contended that the workers can better identify with, and are therefore more interested in, the social aspects of the work of the council. It is felt that this contributes greatly to the greater success of the social, rather than the economic, tasks of the council. Other observers think that the decision-making powers of the workers in this area are responsible for the workers' active movement and for the successful functioning of the works councils in the social welfare field.

There is also some evidence that the psychological obstacles described above are waning. This is due to the improvement in the workers' living standards, the progress of education, and their growing tendency to identify with the middle classes. This is particularly true among the higher grades of staff, who show a fairly active interest in participation. The recent changes in the attitudes of the working class have led some observers to believe

> that the evolution which is at present taking place and which, especially in sectors in which the most advanced techniques are used, gives an increasing number of wage earners a mastery over complex production processes, will lead to the emergence of a "new working class," conscious of its importance and its strength and anxious to see its responsibilities for the running of the undertaking brought on a par with those for the operation of these processes. [12]

In May and June 1968, some 20 years after works councils were introduced in France, student-originated disturbances led to riots and a long general strike. The incidence of the demand for participation in this crisis and the society's response to it will be examined next.


The 1968 Crisis

According to Jenkins, who has studied the impact of the 1968 events on the evolution of worker participation in France, the union-management equilibrium worked quite well during "the balmy Gaullist 1960's":

> The inflexibilities on both sides tended to maintain a kind of dynamic stagnation—there could be a great deal of movement and development within each position, but the positions themselves remained in place and helped immensely in maintaining stability and therefore in promoting economic growth. But pressures for changes were building up in a situation that could not change and that could not adapt to the needs of a modern society and a modern economy. [13]

None of the warnings that "a very profound upheaval" was coming had any effect whatsoever. Yet, when the revolt occurred, it became manifest that it was wholly spontaneous—that the students and the workers were not manipulated in any way. Furthermore, an examination of the type of workers involved and of their demands and behavior convinced Jenkins that the conflict was "an extremely instructive manifestation of the new working class":

> Though almost all workers were striking, the most important initiatives were those provided not by the traditional low-skilled workers with doctrinaire socialist or antimanagement views, but by a new generation of highly skilled workers, technicians, and high-level white-collar workers. . . . It was no accident that the first shut-down occurred at an advanced technology company, Sub-Aviation. Moreover, some of the most significant strike actions were conducted in electronics, atomic power, and other such sophisticated industries.
>
> The aims of the strikers were also sharply different from the traditional ones. . . . The major demand was no longer for a "redistribution of wealth," but for "self-management." . . .
>
> They were seeking principally to fulfill their needs for "achievement, dignity in work and freedom (freedom of expression, freedom to control the norms and results of their work)." A recurrent strain in the testimony given by workers was criticism of management. Demands for "participation," "democratization of the enterprize," "cogestion" (co-management), and "autogestion" (self-management), were common. . . . Perhaps the most innovative feature of the revolt was the behaviour of the strikers. Far from trying to wreck the hated capitalist physical equipment, the workers took great pains to maintain the machinery, in order to show that "we cared as much about it as the boss and we could run it by ourselves." Many hoped to get back into production "without waiting for management." In a few cases the workers did in fact resume production, under their own management, especially to fill urgent orders, while they continued to strike "part-time." . . . The point of all this was to show that workers had sufficient interest, sense of responsibility, and intelligence to be trusted with some of the decision-making power hitherto monopolized by management. This was no far-away thought, since many workers and other observers were convinced that the day of workers' manage-

ment was not on the horizon, but just around the corner.
The show of responsible behaviour had its comic aspects
—as when strike committees solemnly informed the boss
that they were taking over the plant but that he had been
selected to continue in his job—but it did demonstrate that
both the unions and management had been wrong in their
long-held assumption that workers did not want to share
in management decisions. [14]

After consultations with management and unions, a monetary
settlement was offered to the workers. The government, still headed
by de Gaulle, also promised that demands for participation would be
met. In spite of a general belief "that the workers had somehow
gained an important victory and that a permanent transformation had
taken place that would leave a heavy mark on the country's industrial
structure," the expected changes did not take place. The vice-president
of the employers' association declared that worker participation
should remain limited to three forms: "information, consultation and
participation in results." The unions' position did not change either.
According to CGT spokesmen: "We believe the workers can only
genuinely participate in management through nationalization of the
means of production. . . . What would we co-manage with them?
The exploitation of the workers?"[15]


Works Councils Legislation since 1968

After de Gaulle's resignation in 1969, the government seemed
to lose all interest in the issue of reforming the structure of French
industry. Yet, some small and unspectacular developments showed
that the revolt had left its mark. New legislation was enacted to enlarge the scope of activities of works councils and to encourage the
building up of more positive attitudes toward participation. A national collective agreement on job security was signed in 1969 providing that the works councils must be consulted when collective dismissals were envisaged. These provisions were further extended in
1975. Works councils are also directly involved with vocational training since the act of 1971. Finally, their control of working conditions
was extended in 1973, when another act provided for a special committee of the works councils to be set up in enterprises with 300 or
more employees.

Finally, shortly after the 1974 presidential elections, the French
government appointed the Sudreau Commission to examine how firms
could be restructured to allow more influence for employees. In its
report, made public in 1975, the commission acknowledged the need

to strengthen the consultation which occurs within the enterprize committee for it expresses a true though imperfect

recognition of the community of employees as a constituent part of the enterprize. The representative character
of the committee has to be improved and its competences
reinforced by way of full consultation, but not by way of
co-decision which the social partners do not want. It is
necessary to provide also for a personnel representation
within groups of companies, since, within such extensive
structures, local enterprize committees could form the
impression that they were not talking with the real holder
of management power. Therefore, foreign multinational
groups should be obliged to appoint a representative for
each of their French subsidiaries to be answerable for the
group's overall policy. [16]

For the Sudreau Commission, the top priority was the reform
of the enterprise and the improvement of working conditions. The
final report recommended strongly "that the extension of the rights
of the employees should neither undermine the authority and role of
managers, nor be a substitute for the trade unions and collective bargaining." While the commission did not recommend any changes in
the role and powers of the works councils, it did suggest that enterprises provide "the maximum degree of consultation and supply of information between managers and employees in the period when the
decision is being prepared. "[17] According to Delamotte, the political
conditions at present are not as favorable as they were in 1975 for
taking new steps in the area of worker participation. Furthermore,
the government has adopted a pragmatic attitude: "Instead of immediately preparing new laws, it is encouraging industry to experiment.
Once the results are in, laws might then be prepared. "[18]

Assessment of the French Experience

The recommendations of the Sudreau report have not received
much support from management circles nor from the CGT, which
calls the whole exercise a "political maneuver." Yet, there is evidence that the idea of worker participation and the reform of the structure of the enterprise is slowly gaining ground in France. According
to a briefing paper issued by the European Association of National
Productivity Centres, "More employers now express quite progressive views on social matters." The national employers' association
held a congress on the nature of work and structures of companies in
1973. In 1974 the Centre des Jeunes Dirigeants (grouping 3,000 managers from smaller companies) published a program aiming at changing the fundamental nature of the company. The unions' outlook is

also changing. They now accept the idea of negotiating with employers—the CGT, for example, has set up a negotiating department.[19]
While the CGT still opposes participation, other unions have been
more flexible.

The CGT-FO (Workers' Strength), while skeptical of being overly

> involved with the enemy (management), has nevertheless
> expressed cautious willingness to "consult before deci-
> sions are taken" and "to be associated in checking on the
> execution as well as the results of the decisions." The
> CFTC affirmed at its 1969 congress that "the right of
> workers to participate effectively in the formulation of
> decisions constitutes an indispensable element of eco-
> nomic life."
>
> The boldest initiative of any union was taken by the
> CFDT, which, at its 1970 congress, reshaped its entire
> program around the idea of "democratization of the enter-
> prize" and placed "self-management" as its primary ideo-
> logical goal. . . . Though the CFDT program insists that
> socialism must accompany worker control, it nevertheless
> recognizes that the key to efficient functioning of companies
> is not political action but sound organizational principles,
> and that it is useless to talk about worker control without
> also reworking organization structures.[20]

Some positive results have come from the functioning of works
councils during a period of 30 years. The overall success of the
works councils' activities in the social field has resulted in both a
decline in paternalism on the part of the employers and in the development of the workers' own sense of responsibility and interest in
work-related matters. It has also given the workers a greater opportunity to follow the progress of the undertaking and to play a more informed role in the discussions concerning its administration. This,
in turn, has given them a greater insight into the economic and financial aspects of industrial management. Finally, the existence of
works councils and of worker representatives has greatly stimulated
the efforts of unions to train members to fill these posts successfully.
However, it has been suggested that all these factors can more accurately be described as preparation for participation than participation itself.

In spite of signs pointing to a degree of acceptance of the idea
and practice of worker participation, the truth remains that the results of the works councils' experiment in France are disappointing:

> Despite the law, many French companies do not have works
> councils and where they exist both employers and employees

often do not fulfill their mission. Employers do not
always provide the information and works councils
members seldom use their right to give their opinion on
financial matters nor do they provide the cooperation
that they were intended to promote.[21]

Many observers believe that mere structural reform of the works
councils and of the enterprise would not be effective: "It would probably not change the fundamental conditions or put an end to the dia-
logue of the deaf. It therefore seems probable that the blockage in
communication will continue unless a political settlement of one sort
or another is reached."[22]

## WORKS COUNCILS IN OTHER EUROPEAN COUNTRIES

Given the variety of industrial relations systems in the world
and the diverse cultural values and socioeconomic climates, worker
participation has been given very different expression in the institutions developed in various European countries. Yet, there are certain similarities. In particular, many countries have developed plant-
level institutions of labor-management relations, which, though they
go by different names (such as works councils, works committees,
and so forth), are essentially "joint labour-management bodies of a
purely advisory character in which problems of mutual interest to the
two parties may be discussed."[23]

As pointed out earlier, works councils are generally established
by national agreements between central unions and employer organizations (covering the majority of workers in those countries), by local
agreements at the enterprise level, and by law.

### National Agreements

Industrial relations in Denmark have long been characterized
by a spirit of cooperation between labor and management, the keystone
of which has been the cooperation committee.[24] The system was first
established in 1947 by a national agreement between the Danish Federation of Trade Unions and the Danish Employers Confederation. It
was based on the fundamental principle that labor and management
should together attempt to create a better work environment and ensure satisfactory economic results.[25] Several revisions have been
made in the original agreement—the last in 1970. The system as it
exists today is characterized by the establishment of labor-management

TABLE 3

Examples of Works Councils Based on National Agreements

| Country/Name of the Works Council Year of the First Agreement | Formal Powers | | Size of Undertakings Covered Categories Represented | Election of Worker Representatives— Terms of Office | Other Features |
|---|---|---|---|---|---|
| | General Principles | Particular Items | | | |
| Denmark Samarbejdsudvalg, 1947  Last revised in 1971 | Codetermination assumes an obligation on both parties to strive for agreement. Should either party in the council refuse to strive for agreement this shall be regarded as a breach of the agreement. Coinfluence means that the management shall afford the council good opportunities for the exchange of | Codetermination in formulating principles governing the organization of local work, safety and welfare conditions and in formulating principles governing the staff policy of the enterprise. Coinfluence on the general policies of day-to-day production and work planning and on the implementation of major alterations in the enterprise. Information from the management relating to the enterprise's economic situation and future prospects. Notice: Given agreement, and provided agreement proce- | In any firm where at least 50 workers are employed. Workers and employers. | Representatives are elected by all workers in the undertaking, whether organized or not. However, shop stewards are ex-officio members of the works council. Two years. | Shall not deal with questions affecting the conclusion, extension, termination interpretation or adjustment of national or local wage agreements which are normally settled by negotiation or statutory means. |

(Continued)

ideas and suggestions for subsequent incorporation in the management's decision.

dures enable this to be done, the council may discuss basic structure, functioning and applicability of productivity—linked wage systems, and possibilities of establishing funds with educational and social aims.

| | | | | |
|---|---|---|---|---|
| Norway<br>Bedriftsutvalg,<br>1945<br><br>Last revised in<br>1969 | The works council is an advisory and informative body. When the council has expressed its opinion on a question, the management shall deal with it as soon as possible and inform the council at the first meeting after it has reached a decision. | Major changes in production plans.<br>Questions of quality.<br>Developments of products and plans for expansion and restrictions of reorganization that are of major importance to the workers and their working conditions.<br>Shall work for sound and correct rationalization.<br>Improve safety and health.<br>Social measures, vocational training.<br>Information from the management on the financial status of the undertaking, such information shall be given to the same extent as to the stockholders. | In any firm where at least 100 workers are employed. Workers and employers.<br><br>Representatives are elected by all workers in the undertaking, whether organized or not. However the chairman of the shop steward committee is ex-officio member of the works council.<br>Two years. | Shall not deal with questions of wages and working hours or disputes on the interpretation of collective agreements or work agreements. However, working hours and standard wage and piece-work systems may be discussed in general but no agreements may be entered into by the council. |

Table 3 (Continued)

| Country/Name of the Works Council Year of the First Agreement | Formal Powers | | Size of Undertakings Covered—Categories Represented | Election of Worker Representatives—Terms of Office | Other Features |
|---|---|---|---|---|---|
| | General Principles | Particular Items | | | |
| Sweden Foretagsnämnd, 1946 Last revised in 1966 | Questions having an essential bearing on the firm and its personnel will be made the subject of information and consultation within the works council. | Production matters such as techniques, organization, planning. Personnel matters such as principles and methods of recruitment, selection and promotion, overall planning of recruitment and training, the preparation of introduction programs. In economic matters information should be given. Should there arise any question of a shutdown, suspension or major cutback in the operation, there must be consultation in the works council. | In any firm where at least 50 workers are employed. Workers and employers. | Elected by the local trade union organization in the manner it prescribes. The chairman of the works club, or a person holding a corresponding position should normally be a member of the works council. At least two years and at the most four years. | Has no right to deal with disputes concerning any collective wage agreement and the regulation of employment terms which are normally to be handled by a trade union organization. |

Source: C. D. Asplund, Some Aspects of Workers' Participation (Brussels: International Confederation of Free Trade Unions, 1972), pp. 17, 18.

councils in every company with more than 50 employees. The councils are intended to promote the widest possible cooperation in the day-to-day management of the companies. Specifically, they have "codetermination rights" with regard to general personnel matters (such as safety, health, and work organization). They also have the right to influence decision making insofar as production plans, new capital investment, and the day-to-day running of the company are concerned (see Table 3).

Originally established in 1946 and slightly strengthened in 1966, the Swedish works councils are seen as a medium for information and joint consultation between management and employees who should— through continuous collaboration—"fulfill the function of working for greater productivity and greater occupational satisfaction."[26] Until the late 1960s, the councils—which are required in every undertaking with more than 50 employees—"were regarded as vapid discussion groups."[27] However, since the early 1970s, management's recognition of the fact that councils could be used to promote communication and to partly satisfy labor's demands for greater influence has resulted in the revitalization of the system.[28] This is demonstrated by the fact that in the 1968-72 period the number of works councils with working committees and subcommittees increased greatly, involving workers more closely in the running of the enterprise and increasing their impact on it.[29] More recently, an agreement signed in 1975 between the Swedish Employers Confederation and the labor organizations created financial subcommittees with the right to examine virtually all company books and to hire outside consultants for assistance when needed.

In Norway, also, the works council system was first established in the 1940s, through a national agreement between the Norwegian Federation of Trade Unions and the Norwegian Employers Confederation. Revised several times, this agreement was replaced in 1969 by a new one, which established the main function of the councils as "the promotion of the most efficient production possible and the well-being of workers through labour management cooperation."[30] Like the Swedish and Danish councils, the Norwegian bodies—which are required in firms with at least 100 workers—are workers/employer bodies. Their functions include the right to be consulted on some economic matters, such as productivity, expansion, relocation, organizational structure, and so forth; the right to be informed on general business trends; and the right to be informed and consulted with regard to such personnel matters as working hours, wage systems, and safety and health. Altogether, the powers of the Norwegian works councils appear to be less developed than those of its immediate neighbors. It can therefore be said that they are "inadequate to give workers real power in company decision-making,"[31] a factor that has undoubtedly contributed to the early interest in experiments in shop floor participation in that country.


Local Agreements

The piecemeal nature of these agreements makes this kind of participation difficult to describe. Under the terms of these enterprise-level agreements, the formal works council machinery that is set up is purely voluntary in character. Among the developed countries, such agreements are found in Canada and the United Kingdom. In Canada, the idea of union-management cooperation through works councils (joint consultation committees) was pioneered by the Canadian National Railways as early as the 1920s. However, despite the support provided by a special governmental agency, which acts in an advisory and consultative capacity for both parties, the system's development has been limited. Essentially, the council is a forum for the discussion of day-to-day problems and "can deal with any subject, with the prior mutual consent of both parties, as long as the council is not considered as a substitute for the collective bargaining agency."[32]

In the United Kingdom, collective bargaining is also seen as the main channel for worker participation, and the establishment of works councils is purely voluntary. In this country, works councils (joint production committees) originated during World War II because of the need to maximize efficiency and production for the war effort. Although the immediate postwar years saw some continued support for the idea of consultative participation, the development of the councils has been rather limited, and support for them has been waning. In 1973 a proposal for works councils (of a purely consultative character) by the Confederation of British Industry met with opposition from both the employers and the TUC.[33] As they exist in the United Kingdom, works councils are mixed labor-management bodies, the duties of which vary, depending on the terms of the local agreements.


Law

By far the most common way of instituting this form of worker participation would appear to be through the promulgation of legislation (see Table 4). Some critics of the French system have argued that "a strict law is a priori less likely to establish a system of cooperation than are voluntary agreements, which can be more readily adapted to concrete circumstances."[34] However, the experience of some countries, notably West Germany and the Netherlands—where the attitude toward works councils is generally favorable—contradicts this view.

While a long tradition, dating back to the 1840s, lies behind the West German experience with works councils, the first series of laws establishing the present system of works councils was passed between 1952 and 1956, providing for worker participation in private and public enterprises through works councils and supervisory boards. The original act was amended in 1972, considerably expanding the councils' powers and giving them "a very strong position in the company and constant contact with and influence over day-to-day happenings in virtually every area that could affect individual employees."[35]

Like the 1952 act, the new Works Constitution Act of 1972 stresses that employer and works council have to work together in a spirit of mutual trust. Under the terms of the current legislation, works councils that "consist solely of chosen representatives of the employees" must be established in all undertakings with more than five permanent employees with voting rights. They can range in size from 1 to 31 members, according to the size of the enterprise, and provisions have to be made for the representation of white and blue collar workers, young workers, and women workers.[36] As Table 4 indicates, the works council system is highly developed in Germany and functions quite successfully. A study conducted in 1961/62 showed that 95 percent of interviewed workers had a basic knowledge of the functions of the works council.[37] It has been said of the German experience that it has "served as a source of inspiration for increased activity and advancement among the workers and their representatives."[38] However, observers have pointed out that even though "the legal rights of works council members in West Germany by far surpass the rights of equivalent bodies in other countries, nevertheless, the system of works councils creates certain problem areas which limit that effectiveness of participation."[39] Fürstenberg points out some of these problem areas:

1. Certain groups of workers are under-represented, for example female employees, shift workers, foreign workers and to a certain extent lower skilled employees.

2. Some works council members who are elected repeatedly have a tendency to become professionalized. This creates a distance between the new workers elite and the rank and file.

3. Attendance at plant meetings in which works councils reports are presented and discussed is low and such meetings are held infrequently.

TABLE 4

Examples of Works Councils Based on Laws

| Country/Name of the Works Council Year of the First Agreement | Formal Powers | | Size of Undertakings Covered—Categories Represented | Election of Worker Representatives—Terms of Office | Other Features |
|---|---|---|---|---|---|
| | General Principles | Particular Items | | | |
| Austria Betriebsrat, 1947 Amended in 1971 | Information and consultation. The 1971 law requires management to provide information about everything touching the interests of the workers in social, economic, cultural, and hygienic matters. | Job pricing and average rates of wages applicable in the undertaking, where not regulated by collective agreements. According to the 1971 law, all forms of incentive rates have been included. Codetermination in the establishment of work rules. Limited veto right in the case of dismissals. Information (1971) in any question of a shutdown, suspension, or cutback in the operation of the firm. | In any firm where at least 20 workers are permanently employed. Only workers. | Elected by all workers in the undertaking, whether organized or not. Three years. | Has to watch over the application of the provisions of collective agreements. Disagreements with the employer are settled by special arbitration boards. It elects two members of the supervisory boards of joint stock companies. |
| West Germany Betriebsrat, 1952 | There are rights for codetermination, consul- | Codetermination: regulation of daily working hours and breaks, the time and place | In any firm where at least five workers are | Representatives are elected by all workers in the | No codetermination right as to individual measures. The |

| | | | permanently employed. Only workers. | undertaking, whether organized or not. Two years. | works council has no right to call a strike. If differences arise that cannot be settled jointly, a mediation body is to be set up. It elects two representatives on boards of enterprises covered by the co-determination system. |
|---|---|---|---|---|---|
| Amended in 1971 | tative rights and rights of information. The employer and the works council cooperate on the basis of the collective agreements in force, in conjunction with the unions and employers' associations. | for payment of remuneration, the preparation of the leave schedule, the carrying out of vocational training, the administration of welfare services, disciplinary matters, fixing of job and piece rates, principles of remuneration, introduction of new methods for remuneration, major alterations contemplated involving substantial disadvantages for the staff. After the 1971 reform, the works council can offer more effective opposition to unjustified transfers, regroupings, and dismissals. | | | |
| Belgium Conseil d'Entreprise, 1948 Supplemented by collective agreement, 1970 | Information, consultation, and some rights of codetermination. | Examination of general principles in respect to hiring and decisions on general principles for the dismissal of workers. Establishment of work rules, administration of social services, establishment of the leave schedule. The employer has to communicate to the council any information concerning the productivity and the economic situation. | In any firm where at least 150 workers are employed. Workers and employers. | Representatives are elected by all workers in the undertaking, whether organized or not. Four years. | The employer serves as chairman of the council. Grievances and union matters are not dealt with by the works council. |

(Continued)

Table 4 (Continued)

| Country/Name of the Works Council Year of the First Agreement | Formal Powers | | Size of Under-takings Covered— Categories Represented | Election of Worker Representatives— Terms of Office | Other Features |
|---|---|---|---|---|---|
| | General Principles | Particular Items | | | |
| The Netherlands Ondernemingsrand, 1950<br><br>Amended in 1971 | Information and consultation. | Working conditions that affect a greater number of workers. Matters that concern moving of the enterprise to another place or abandoning the enterprise. Fundamental changes in the organization of the enterprise. Important increase or decrease of production pensions, holidays, working hours, and so forth. Advice on measures that may contribute to technical and economic improvements. The law also obliges the employer to provide all information needed. | In any firm where at least 100 workers are employed. Workers and employers. | Representatives are elected by all workers in the undertaking, whether organized or not. Two years. | The employer serves as chairman of the council. The law does not impose penalties on employers who fail to establish a works council or to operate one that is in existence. |

Source: C. Asplund, Some Aspects of Workers' Participation (Brussels: International Confederation of Free Trade Unions [ICFTU] 1972), pp. 23, 24.

⅋ councils are often used as an executive ✓
↲agement, especially the personnel de-

5.  The relationship between works councils and unions ✓
    poses the problem of solidarity.[40]

The last two points will be examined in greater detail in a later section of this chapter.

Like West Germany, the Netherlands is characterized by a relatively well-developed system of participation through works councils and supervisory boards. Under the terms of the Joint Consultative Committees Act of 1950, the works council was established merely as an instrument of consultation between employers and worker representatives and was intended "to contribute its utmost to the best possible functioning of the enterprize."[41] The 1971 amendment to the act has considerably extended the powers of the works council, which must be established as a mixed worker/employer body in all undertakings with more than 100 workers. The new works council is more than a consultative body, having the additional task of representing and defending workers' rights. Meetings of the works council may deal with any matter concerning the undertaking that the employer or employees may wish to bring up. The council has the right to be consulted on various economic matters, such as mergers, transfers, or closure of the firm; on productivity issues; and on layoffs and wage systems. It must also be informed about general business trends and has decision rights in social matters, such as training, pensions, hours of work, vacations, safety and health, and so forth. In general, in the Netherlands, workers favor the works councils and consider them to be useful, though this does not mean that they are satisfied with the system's actual achievements.

RECENT DEVELOPMENTS

In his book on industrial democracy, Crispo assesses the recent developments of works councils in the following terms: "Currently, works councils in Western Europe are either disappearing or losing influence or undergoing a kind of rebirth or resurgence."[42] These trends are still too tentative to enable observers to state conclusively what the future of European works councils is going to be. It is possible, however, to analyze the factors that contribute to these recent developments.

Revitalization of Works Councils

One valid criticism that has often been leveled at works councils and other consultative bodies is that the worker members of these councils do not have the expert knowledge required for a meaningful discussion of organizational problems. This lack of expertise means that the workers cannot meet management on an equal footing and are dependent on the latter for the requisite information. Management is, therefore, in a more powerful position, and as has sometimes been noted, managers take advantage of their position. One of the solutions to this problem is to provide paid educational leave for worker representatives, because "without special training, the different legal structures, even with wide-ranging powers, will be meaningless institutions."[43]

Works councils have often been faulted for being "marginal institutions," which, at best, give only limited opportunities for participation to employees.[44] However, new legislation and agreements extend the rights of works councils in the sphere of information, consultation, and codetermination. In a number of countries, management is now required to communicate to the works council comprehensive general data on the social and economic situation, as well as on the future prospects of the enterprise. (For a detailed treatment of this topic, see the last part of this book.) This includes advance information on prospective organizational and technological changes, possible acquisitions, mergers, and shutdowns—in essence, virtually every change that could have an impact on the employment or working conditions of the labor force.

In many countries, both law and practice now force employers to consult and seek the advice of works councils in matters that were previously within the exclusive domain of management rights. Each and every activity or policy that can affect the employees' vital interests are now subject to some degree of discussion within the council. One of the major developments in recent years has been a shift toward granting works councils codetermination or even veto power over certain managerial actions. For example, in West Germany, works councils now have such power over recruitment and layoff policies, as well as on a host of personnel and social issues. In the Netherlands, works councils have an equal voice with management in health and safety matters, work regulations, pension plans, and so forth.

Another factor in the revitalization of the works councils has been the efforts made by the EEC to promote unified legislation relating to industrial and commercial companies. One aspect of the proposed European Company Statute concerns employee participation and was put forward in a green paper released in 1975.[45] According to this proposal, European-wide works councils would enjoy wide information privileges, general consultative rights, and extensive co-decision-making powers. Not only would the council have access to all data and documents provided to shareholders but management would be required to provide written information on any matter that in the opinion of the council affected the fundamental interests of the company or its employer. Management would also have to consult the council on matters pertaining to job evaluation, the payment system, and devices designed to control or regulate the pace of work. Management would not be allowed to proceed with any changes that affected the employment or income level of employees without prior consultation and approval of the council. The council would have co-determination power over most personnel and social matters, ranging from recruitment, promotion, and dismissals to work-scheduling criteria and practices.

Given the range and scope of the proposed European works councils' powers and rights in the spheres of information, consultation, and codetermination, it is hardly surprising that both unions and employers view such a council with a great deal of skepticism. Unions are worried about the tremendous potential overlap between the functions of the works councils and the traditional activities of the unions, particularly in the area of collective bargaining. Unions also have strong reservations about submitting to an arbitrator disputes arising from the effects of technological or organizational changes on the workers. The European works council proposal provides for such a procedure in case the parties are unable to resolve their differences.

Unions and Works Councils

The problem of the relationship between the unions and the works councils deserves critical examination. The question is often asked whether works councils and unions are rival organizations or whether one is subservient to the other.

Historically speaking, in many Western European countries, works councils were created to fill the void left by the absence of effective union organization at the plant or enterprise level. The intent of the legislation in most European countries is that the works councils are to serve quite different and distinctive representative functions from those of unions, and as such, they are not considered rival organizations. To be more specific, works councils represent all the workers in an enterprise. There is often a form of proportional representation, which is designed to ensure that shop floor, salaried, and young employees are adequately represented. In some countries, there is separate representation for professional workers, as well as for supervisory and lower-level managerial employees. Works council members are selected by all workers of the enterprise and hold office for a specified period of time. The members of the works councils are not necessarily union members.

Furthermore, in most countries, the role and powers of the works council are clearly demarcated from the activities reserved for unions. The primary role of the works council is to promote cooperation between employers and employees at the plant level with a view to improve the well-being of the enterprise and the welfare of its workers. Unions in most European countries concentrate their efforts on collective bargaining at the national and sectoral level and direct their energy at influencing public policy on social and economic issues. Works councils cannot call a strike. In case of breach of contractual or legal provisions, they may refer the matter to labor courts or to arbitration tribunals. Only the unions can have recourse to strike in the event that they are unable to conclude a collective agreement.

Even though unions and works councils have distinct rules and spheres of activity, there is a certain amount of overlapping in both areas. In some countries, such as West Germany and Austria, union influence on works councils is not negligible, leading some observers to think that unions are intent on taking them over. Except in Belgium, where unions have the exclusive right of nomination, union influence in the election of works council members is usually limited to the nomination of slates of candidates. In practice, however, union candidates usually do well in these elections. For example, in West Germany, 70 percent of works council members are union members. This is despite the fact that only about 40 percent of the paid labor force is organized. The case of Germany is particularly significant because it is the country where the works councils are the most effective. Fürstenberg notes that the unions are the only organizations that can strengthen the power of the works councils in their dealings with management.[46] In that country, it is the unions that provide training for works council members and give legal aid and other support in case of conflict with management. When nonunion employees are elected to the works councils, they soon join the union.

Even so, it does not necessarily follow that works councils are subservient to unions. Although works councils in West Germany often work closely with unions, they do not see eye to eye with them on all important issues at the plant level. This is partly due to the fact that industrywide or national unions are much more interested in the progress of the whole industry than in the problems of a single factory. It must also be recognized that in order to function successfully at the factory level, the works council members must take into consideration both the workers' interest and managerial goals. Employee representatives have a tendency to develop a "company orientation" while working together with management representatives over a period of time. In order to counter this relative independence of the works councils, unions in some countries are trying to play a more active role at the plant level.

The question of whether or not works councils are subservient to unions takes on added significance in view of the fact that works councils are acquiring greater powers. Will this lead to their greater involvement in the collective bargaining process? It has been suggested that having the right to bargain over certain matters would probably stimulate worker interest in the works councils. However, the inclusion of a bargaining function in these bodies would undoubtedly be suspect to many unions and might have unfortunate consequences for the system as a whole. [47] Certainly, any shift in the orientation of works councils from consensus and collaboration to bargaining and confrontation would be opposed by the employers.

One possible trend that is being advocated by some unions, notably in the Netherlands, is the possibility of having workers' councils instead of works councils. A case could also be made for the wider recognition of the idea of the conflicting interests of labor and management and the inclusion of an interest-promoting function in the operation of the works council. Data from the Dutch works council system suggests that the most lively councils are those that recognize and allow for this disparity. [48] The experience of the Works Council Plan of the Glacier Metal Company in the United Kingdom and of the Danish cooperative committees suggest that it is possible to reconcile and integrate worker participation in management with independent interest group representation, leaving intact both the managers and unions as separate entities. [49]

## GENERAL ASSESSMENT
## OF THE WORKS COUNCILS

Taken as a whole, the performance of works councils in their present form has generally been disappointing, and there is some justification for the view that "the works council as a concept is not perhaps an ideal solution to the enterprize level employee-employer relations." [50] Even with regard to the often-quoted objectives, that is, worker motivation, increased productivity, and the promotion of industrial democracy, works councils have fallen short of their goals. As job motivation is more directly influenced by the immediate work situation and as the functioning of works councils is usually very remote from the job itself, it cannot be said that either motivation or productivity are directly improved by the presence of works councils in the plant. Indeed, works councils have been criticized as being instrumental in creating elites among workers and for increasing the isolation of the rank-and-file worker. The perceived need for, and development of, shop floor participation in countries where works councils have operated for over 20 years clearly illustrates the fact that the individual employee does not feel affected by the functioning of the council.

It has also been claimed by both labor and management that works councils promote industrial democracy. Indeed, a glance at the statutes setting up the various types of councils shows that this has been one of the primary goals of these bodies. However, insofar as most works councils have little or no decision-making power, it cannot be said that works councils have—up to the present—contributed greatly to industrial democracy. A 1972 International Confederation of Free Trade Unions (CFTU) study estimated that the works council system was "inferior to fully-developed collective bargaining, largely because it does not involve the worker to the same degree in decision-making."[51]

Among the criticisms that have been leveled at the functioning of the works council is the unions' fear that these bodies, by giving the worker an illusion of power, would inhibit rather than promote industrial democracy. Unions in many countries, such as France, the United Kingdom, the United States, and Canada, feel that participation in works councils causes workers "to lose their combativeness and become docile instruments in the hands of the power wielders and become absorbed and 'encapsulated' in the existing structures."[52] Conversely, management's suspicion of works councils arises from the diametrically opposite viewpoint, which is that the councils threaten the status quo, by encroaching on the prerogatives and responsibilities of the managers. This, they feel, endangers efficient business operations. Managers are also suspicious of the role of unions in this context. Given the present weakness of the average works council, neither argument can be sustained. On the one hand, the severely limited powers of the council do not encourage a shift in the balance of power and, on the other hand, while the majority of workers are not involved in, and are generally apathetic to, the functioning of the councils, it cannot be claimed that they have a tranquilizing effect on all workers.

The above conclusions are of necessity tentative ones. Since the various countries of Europe have different traditions of industrial relations, the degree of power and influence of works councils has been uneven among them. However, Fürstenberg's assessment of works councils in West Germany, where they function efficiently, may be a valid estimate of the potential value of the system itself:

The establishment of works councils has helped to neu-
tralize quite a few conflict situations which would otherwise provoke wild-cat strikes. Modern methods of personnel management are being promoted and the communications structure within individual firms has improved
to an extent where every employee has the opportunity to
submit his complaints, suggestions and demands to the
competent committee.[53]

## NOTES

1. International Labour Organisation (ILO), Workers Participation in Decisions within Undertakings (Oslo Symposium, 1974),
Labour Management Relations Series, no. 48 (Geneva, 1976), p. 10.
2. L. Greyfie de Bellecombe, Workers' Participation in Management in France: The Basic Problem, Reprinted from the International Institute for Labour Studies Bulletin no. 6 (Geneva, 1970), pp.
54-55.
3. Ibid., p. 86.
4. Ibid., pp. 86-87.
5. European Economic Community, Commission of the European Communities, Employee Participation and Company Structures in the European Community, Bulletin of the EEC, supp. 8/75
(Brussels, 1975), p. 71.
6. David Jenkins, Job Power: Blue and White Collar Democracy (London: Heinemann, 1974), p. 138.
7. Ibid., p. 139.
8. Greyfie de Bellecombe, Workers' Participation in Management in France, p. 64.
9. Ibid., p. 90.
10. Ibid., pp. 67-68.
11. Ibid., p. 73.
12. Ibid., p. 75.
13. Jenkins, Job Power, pp. 141-42. Most of the analysis in
this section is taken from Jenkins's excellent chapter, entitled
"France: The Elusive 'Participation.'"
14. Ibid., pp. 145-47.
15. Ibid., pp. 147-48.
16. European Economic Community, Commission of the European Communities, Employee Participation and Company Structures, p. 69.
17. Benjamin C. Roberts, "Employee Participation: Trends
and Issues," in Employee Participation and Company Reform, ed. F.
Basagni and F. Souzey, The Atlantic Papers, 4/1975 (Paris, 1976),
p. 15.

18. Yves Delamotte, "The 'Reform of the Enterprize' in France, Annals of the American Academy of Political and Social Sciences 431 (May 1977): 62.

19. European Association of National Productivity Centres, "Industrial Democracy, France," mimeographed working document (Brussels: European Association of National Productivity Centres, 1976), p. 4.

20. Jenkins, Job Power, p. 150.

21. European Association of National Productivity Centres, "Industrial Democracy, France," p. 9.

22. See Greyfie de Bellecombe, Workers' Participation in Management in France, p. 92; and Jenkins, Job Power, p. 154.

23. Chester Asplund, Some Aspects of Workers' Participation (Brussels: International Confederation of Free Trade Unions, 1972), p. 12.

24. David Jenkins, Industrial Democracy in Europe: The Challenge and Management Responses (Geneva: Business International, 1974), p. 59.

25. Asplund, Aspects of Workers' Participation, p. 15.

26. Ibid., p. 16.

27. Jenkins, Industrial Democracy, p. 53.

28. Jenkins, Job Power, p. 262.

29. Jenkins, Industrial Democracy, p. 53.

30. Asplund, Aspects of Workers' Participation, p. 16.

31. Jenkins, Job Power, p. 247.

32. Asplund, Aspects of Workers' Participation, p. 20.

33. Jenkins, Industrial Democracy, p. 91.

34. Greyfie de Bellecombe, Workers' Participation in Management in France, p. 91.

35. Jenkins, Industrial Democracy, p. 39.

36. Roger Blanpain, "Influence of Management on Decision Making by Labour: A Survey of Belgium, Denmark, Germany, the Netherlands, the Societas Europaea and Sweden," unpublished (March 1974), p. 27.

37. Asplund, Aspects of Workers' Participation, p. 26.

38. Ibid., p. 22.

39. Friedrich Fürstenberg, "West German Experience with Industrial Democracy," Annals of the American Academy of Political and Social Sciences 431 (May 1977): 47.

40. Ibid., pp. 47-49.

41. Asplund, Aspects of Workers' Participation, p. 22.

42. John Crispo, Industrial Democracy in Western Europe: A North American Perspective (Toronto: McGraw-Hill-Ryerson, 1978), p. 115.

43. Blanpain, "Influence of Management," p. 38.

44. Freidrich Fürstenberg, Workers' Participation in Management in the Federal Republic of Germany, International Institute for Labour Studies, Research Series, no. 32 (Geneva, 1978), pp. 15, 17.

45. European Economic Community, Commission of the European Economic Community, Employee Participation and Company Structures.

46. Fürstenberg, "West German Experience," p. 16.

47. International Labour Organisation, Workers Participation, p. 8.

48. Organization for Economic Cooperation and Development, Final Report on the International Seminar on Workers' Participation, Held at Versailles, March 1975 (Paris: OECD, 1975), p. 51.

49. Jacques Elliot, The Changing Culture of a Factory (New York: Dryden, 1952); see also Wilfred Brown, Exploration on Management (London: Heinemann, 1960), p. 6.

50. International Labour Organisation, Workers Participation, p. 8.

51. Jenkins, Industrial Democracy, p. 8.

52. J. A. P. van Hoof, "The Works Council," Paper prepared for an OECD Seminar on Workers' Participation, Versailles, March 1975, mimeographed (Paris: OECD, 1975), p. 44.

53. Fürstenberg, Workers' Participation, p. 18.

# *Chapter Four*

## COLLECTIVE BARGAINING AND PARTICIPATION

Collective bargaining is related to worker participation in management in two ways. It can be an instrument for introducing worker participation schemes or institutions. This is best exemplified by the practice followed in the Scandinavian countries, which have a long tradition of collective bargaining. In these countries, works councils or production committees were first introduced by collective agreements between employer associations and unions. Second, the actual process of negotiating the collective agreement at the plant or enterprise level, as well as the extension of bargaining to issues that in the past were considered as managerial prerogatives, is itself the process by which participative management is implemented.[1]

In North America, the concept of worker participation in management is almost exclusively viewed within the context of the institution of collective bargaining. With a view to illustrating the strengths and weaknesses of collective bargaining as a form of worker participation, the U.S. experience with the bargaining system is presented in this chapter. Furthermore, an attempt is made to analyze recent trends toward the enlargement of the range of negotiable issues in North America, as well as in certain Western European countries, such as Sweden and Italy; and the extension of collective bargaining downward to the level of the enterprise in certain European countries where collective agreements are concluded at the national and regional level.[2]

### COLLECTIVE BARGAINING AND PARTICIPATION: THE AMERICAN MODEL

"The belief that collective bargaining is the main road toward industrial democracy, and that the collective agreement in its widest sense is its principal expression, is almost unchallenged by contemporary thought in the U.S.A."[3] While this quotation sums up the present position in regard to worker participation in management in the United States, it does not necessarily mean that attempts to introduce certain employee representation plans were not made in the past.

In the 1920s and early 1930s, a number of companies introduced employee management councils. These councils were formed of elected representatives of workers that sat together with management to consider problems of mutual concern. These councils, known as company unions, were dominated by management and were primarily designed to counter the growth of unions. These schemes could not survive the Great Depression of the 1930s and were finally outlawed by the Wagner Act of 1935.

The Wagner Act and successive labor legislation both in the United States and in Canada affirmed the workers' right to form or belong to a labor organization of their own choice without the employer's interference. Once a particular union has been lawfully established as the bargaining agent for a given group, it has the exclusive right of representation for the purpose of collective bargaining. Employers are obliged to bargain in good faith with the union, lawfully established as bargaining agent, over wages, hours, and other terms and conditions of employment. Both parties may conclude collective agreements, which are legally enforceable. If the parties cannot reach an agreement after bargaining in good faith and complying with statutory conciliation requirements, they may legally engage in a strike or lockout. Employee grievances and complaints over the interpretation or administration of the labor contract are subject to due process through a formal grievance procedure specified in the contract. If there is a stalemate in the settlement of a grievance, it is usually referred to binding arbitration.

It should be noted that employers have the same rights to form their own representative associations without outside interference.

A number of questions arise if collective bargaining is to be accepted as a form of industrial democracy so conceived. Some of these questions are the following: "To what extent can union participation in industrial government be regarded as workers' participation? Which areas of managerial decision making are subject, directly or indirectly, to the impact of the union? How great is that impact?"[4]

Union Structure and Internal
Democracy within the Unions

Before we can answer the above questions, it is essential to understand the union structure in North America, which is quite different from that of European countries. Another important question is, Do the local unions enable union members to participate effectively in plant management? The answer to this last question depends upon the degree to which the union itself practices internal democracy and is participative in nature.

In North America, the local union that represents the workers in a plant is the dominant force. The size of local unions may vary from less than 100 to several thousand members. The local unions are primarily responsible for negotiating collective agreements at the plant level or for assisting the national representatives in negotiations, for the appointment of shop stewards and grievance committee members, and for the conduct of strikes within the framework of the union constitution.

The union in North America is basically a job conscious, not class conscious, organization in the sense that it expresses the views and interests of particular groups of workers rather than those of the working class as a whole. The union members look up to shop stewards and other local union officials for help and guidance in matters that affect them in their immediate work environment. The leaders of national labor federations, such as the American Federation of Labor-Congress of Industrial Organizations (AFL-CIO) in the United States and the Canadian Labour Congress (CLC) in Canada, remain "prestigious but distant figures" and have neither any power over their affiliates nor any influence in matters pertaining to the plant or enterprise.[5]

Generally speaking, local unions are responsive to the members' wishes. For example, the demands they make at the bargaining session are usually decided at a meeting that is open to all rank-and-file members. The constitution of many unions requires that collective agreements must be ultimately ratified by all workers. However, in certain situations, labor leaders have ignored the wishes and interests of rank-and-file members because of ignorance, prejudice, or their desire to stay in power. Some labor leaders have also indulged in corrupt practices, such as collusion with corporate bosses. Apathy of rank-and-file members is partly responsible for this phenomenon. Except at certain times, when crucial decisions—such as whether or not to call or settle a strike—are taken, the proportion of rank-and-file members who attend union meetings has been relatively low. In short, the democratic principles that underlie union philosophy have not always been followed in practice. Experience has nevertheless indicated that when rank-and-file members are sufficiently aroused on a specific issue, they do not hesitate to express their views openly, sometimes even in opposition to the local leadership. Refusal by rank-and-file members to ratify collective agreements is not unknown.

Another factor that affects how much the rank-and-file worker may be directly involved in the participative process is the structure of collective bargaining, that is, whether bargaining is conducted at the industry level, company (multiplant) level, or primarily at the plant level. In the United States, "the dominant trend in the structure of the bargaining system appears to have been in the direction of larger bargaining units and increased concentration of power within units."[6] Larger and more centralized bargaining units usually mean that decision making is further removed from the rank-and-file members and that their power is reduced to the approval or rejection of the outcome of negotiations. Yet,

> in spite of the centralizing tendencies in bargaining, there are still in the U.S.A. some 150,000 agreements in existence, so that the average agreement relates to some 100 organized workers (plus a sizable number of unorganized workers covered by the agreement under the majority rule). . . . The decentralized bargaining is still very strongly entrenched. . . . Collective bargaining in the U.S.A. has retained a high degree of adaptability to a great diversity of conditions. This is a distinctive feature of American collective bargaining which brings the union close to the plant and the individual worker, and thus retains for collective bargaining—in spite of the giant proportions of the U.S. economy—some of the features of living industrial democracy.[7]

Scope of Collective Bargaining

If collective bargaining is regarded as the main form of worker participation in management in North America, the question arises, What are the subjects or issues covered explicitly by collective agreements or by informal union management understandings? Unions in North America perceive their role as that of a countervailing power to management, whose main function is to bargain with management as equal partners. Unions do not challenge management's prerogatives that lie outside of bargaining, but they do insist that any of these prerogatives may be brought within the scope of collective bargaining whenever the welfare of workers makes it necessary.

As far as the large range of managerial decision making which does not have anything to do with wages and working conditions are concerned, union leaders have maintained that they are management's responsibility. The unions do not wish to assume any responsibility for the administration of the enterprise. They prefer to be critics rather than partners in management. In 1948 a noted observer of the labor scene in the United States elaborated on this point as follows:

The union is not concerned with the strictly business procedures; such as budgeting, raising the necessary capital,
capital structure, dividends, reserves, types of machinery
and equipment, advertising or credit policies, etc. It
should be noted however, that should any policies of the
company adversely affect the wages and working conditions
of its membership, the unions would have to challenge management's unilateral authority over the problem. [8]

Even today, the union's position has not changed. Thomas R. Donahue
executive assistant to the president of the AFL-CIO, recently expressed similar views in even stronger terms:

We do not seek to be a partner in management. . . . We
do not want to blur in any way the distinctions between the
respective roles of management and labour in the plant.
We guard our independence fiercely—independent of government, independent of any political party and independent of management. [9]

Since almost any managerial decision directly or indirectly
may, in a given set of circumstances, have an impact on the wages
and working conditions of union members, it can be argued that in
principle there are no areas of managerial decision making that are
completely beyond the scope of collective bargaining. Furthermore,
if the union has a strong bargaining position, it could compel management to discuss and negotiate on any issue of concern to its members,
be it plant closure or the future plans of the corporation. However,
management has strongly opposed any union attempts to extend the
scope of collective bargaining beyond the traditional sphere of wages
and working conditions. Management has usually insisted that a general "management rights" clause be included in the collective agreement. The impact of the management residual rights clause is significant because it takes a number of issues, which affect employees
closely, outside the range of worker influence through collective
bargaining for the duration of the collective agreement, except insofar as express provision is made in the agreement itself.
Recent trends indicate that the scope of collective bargaining
in the United States has been broadening. An ILO study lists the following main topics of managerial decision making, which may provide
a general picture of how far the impact of collective bargaining has
gone:

1.  Corporation finance: no direct union intervention,
    but profits play a part in collective bargaining by

way of "ability to pay"; profit sharing, though not
widely applied, has some relevance; the form of investment of pension funds may be the subject of negotiations.

2. Personnel matters: this is of course the area of
deepest union penetration and of the most detailed
regulation by joint union-management decisions.
Under this heading come such matters as—

Size of the work force (guaranteed annual wage
establishes the minimum size of the work force for
a period).

Who is to be hired and in what sequence (anti-dis-
crimination clauses, seniority systems).

Transfer to new jobs.

Transfer to other shifts.

Promotions.

Lay-offs (the order in which workers are to be
temporarily laid off and in which they are to be re-
hired).

Dismissal and severance pay.

Discipline.

Seniority systems and their application.

Job classification.

Job evaluation.

Wages.

Fringe benefits such as pensions, life insurance,
health insurance.

3. Production policies that may be influenced by con-
tractually regulated personnel policies. Under this
heading may come "featherbedding" (that is, the employment of more people than a job may require),
reabsorption of displaced workers, retraining, severance pay.

4. Procurement—hiring of outside contractors ("con-
tracting out")—has become a frequent issue in labour-management negotiations.

5. Technological change; changes in job content, rates
of operation, regularisation of operations over time.[10]

## Innovations in Collective Bargaining

The evolution of collective bargaining in the United States over
a period of more than four decades has shown over and over again
that the institution of collective bargaining has been an extremely

versatile and adaptable instrument of joint action between unions and management.  Unions and management in certain cases have extended the scope of union-management interaction beyond its conventional boundaries and established joint labor-management committees. These committees are serious endeavors, freely and cooperatively undertaken, to enhance company profits and to improve jobs and the workplace.  The U.S. experience with some well-known union man- agement collaborative endeavors will be reviewed here.

Soon after World War II, several major collective agreements (enterprise and industry level) revived interest in developing new pro- cedures for dealing with problems of technological changes, the pro- tection of employee job rights, and other special economic and social problems.  The following are the most noteworthy examples. [11]

### The Armour Automation Committee

Armour & Company, the second largest meat-packing company in the United States, closed several meat-packing plants between 1956 and 1958.  The plants employed 25 percent of its production workers. Loss of jobs created frustration among union members and brought about intentional slowdowns and wildcat strikes.   Unions demanded in the negotiations a short work week, limitations on subcontracting, guaranteed employment, advance notice of plant shutdowns, and the right to reopen the entire contract in the event of another plant closing.

However, guaranteed employment was the main issue in bar- gaining.  The company was afraid that a costly strike would ensue if something was not done to assist the displaced workers.  It agreed to the establishment of a committee having equal representatives from union and management, chaired by a neutral executive director, to study the problems and make recommendations.  The six main rec- ommendations of the committee, which were accepted by unions and management, can be summarized as follows:

1.  The company must give 90 days' notice before closing plants.

2.  Transfer seniority rights were established.  Included herein was a clause relating to "replacement plants," which was to loom very large in the future of the committee.  Employees transferred to a replacement plant were to be "credited with all continuous service and seniority rights held at the closed plant."

3.  The fund was to pay relocation costs.

4.  Technological adjustment pay was established, which was to provide funds for displaced workers awaiting transfer.

5.  Severance pay was improved.

6. Provision was made for early retirement at age 55 at one and one-half times full retirement pay.

Pacific Maritime Association Plan

Another example of the establishment of a fund to cushion the effect of technological changes is found in the agreement reached in 1960 between the Pacific Maritime Association and the International Longshoremen's and Warehousemen's Union. The management of the shipping industry was greatly concerned with rising costs and was interested in mechanizing cargo handling and loading methods. The union, as a matter of policy, viewed mechanization and modernization of operations as a threat to their jobs and would not readily agree to such changes. However, in 1957, the union realized that though it had succeeded so far in protecting jobs by the so-called system of work rules, management went ahead anyway with the technological changes. The union felt that these changes would affect the job security in the long run and decided on a change in tactics. The union demanded "a share of the machine in return for the employers' demand for full freedom to modernize." In other words, the union would agree to permit the introduction of labor-saving devices and methods on the docks if workers were allowed to share in the benefits from mechanization. Finally, in 1961, both parties signed an agreement under which

> the shipowners and stevedoring contractors are freed of restrictions on the introduction of labor-saving devices, relieved of the use of unnecessary men and assured of the elimination of work practices which impede the free flow of cargo or ship turn around. These guarantees to industry are in exchange for a series of benefits for the workers to protect them against the impact of the machine of their daily work and of their job security.

Under this agreement, a fund called the Mechanization and Modernization Fund was created to provide security for the workers. The fund, which will amount to $5 million, is to be financed on an annual basis from the contribution of the members of the Pacific Maritime Association.

As a result of this agreement, the labor relations of the industry on the West Coast became highly centralized. The Joint Coast Labor Relations Committee, which was originally set up to settle grievances at the top, became a forum for exchange of ideas and mutual problems on a continuing basis. The greater centralization of authority on both sides has resulted in greater uniformity in contract administration.

The Pacific Maritime Association agreement is different from the Armour Automation Committee in that the Pacific Maritime agreement was reached without the participation of neutrals. Both parties were committed from the beginning to work out the solutions of their problems among themselves. They had faith in each other, which helped reach an eventual agreement.

. Kaiser Plan

Another unique plan, called the Kaiser Plan, has been widely discussed and publicized all across the continent. The plan was developed in 1959 when the Kaiser Steel Company broke away from the other companies during a 116-day industrywide steel strike and established a tripartite committee, consisting of union and management representatives and third-party neutrals. Kaiser, who took the initiative in forming this committee, hoped that it would develop a plan for equitable sharing between the stockholders, the employees, and the public of the fruits of the company's economic progress.

The committee agreed upon a plan that divided savings resulting from cost reductions through increased efficiency. The plan also provided job security. In substance, it protected jobs and income against technological changes. It guaranteed wages and benefits equal to, or better than, the rest of the steel industry. It provided for lump sum payments to such employees who were willing to withdraw from the incentive systems.

From management's point of view, the replacement of the existing incentive system for those workers who chose the plan was the most desirable feature of the plan. Management is becoming increasingly aware of the fact that wage incentive systems instituted earlier for the purpose of increasing productivity have become outmoded and that it is the machines, not the men, that increase production. Many other large companies are seriously considering doing away with the wage incentive systems.

Under this plan, management is assured of uninterrupted production, free from the threat of strikes at least for four years. As far as the success of the plan is concerned, in the first few months of its operation in 1963, the monthly bonus for the employees averaged $100, and it dropped to $14 in April 1964. As the bonus dropped sharply in 1964, it gave rise to some concern. The committee discovered that reduction in bonus payments could be attributed to several reasons: inexperienced employees, problems in accounting and administration, and so forth. The committee recommended several changes in the plan to fit it to the changing circumstances. One such change was that new employees were to be barred from sharing in cost-savings until they had been on the job for six months.

The Kaiser Plan has proved to be successful and beneficial to both parties so far because union and management have demonstrated their willingness to change the cost-sharing plan or even replace it with something else if the present plan does not meet the specific objective of both parties. George Taylor, chairman of the Long-Range Committee, in assessing the success of the Kaiser Plan had this to say:

> If this plan works, it will be because the people on both
> sides want it to work. If there is anything transferable
> about it, it is not the specific arithmetic but the basic
> principles of progress plus security on which it is built.
> It grows out of the determination of both sides to get
> away from crises bargaining and work out realistic
> programmes of dealing with the human problems of
> technological change.

The Human Relations Committee

In January 1960, the Human Relations Committee in the Basic Steel Industry was established to plan studies and recommend solutions for mutual problems. To be more specific, the committee was asked to study problems in the following areas: (1) guides for the determination of equitable wage and benefit adjustments; (2) the job classification system; (3) wage incentives, including development of appropriate guides for determining fair incentive compensation; (4) seniority, including maximum practicable protection for long-service employees against layoffs; (5) medical care; and (6) such other oral problems as the parties by mutual agreement may from time to time refer to such committee. The composition of the committee as provided in the agreement was as follows: (1) the Human Relations Research Committee shall be composed of an equal number of representatives designated by the parties to such memorandum agreement (the number of which by agreement of the parties may be changed from time to time), and shall be under the cochairpersonship of two persons of outstanding qualifications and objectivity, one to be designated by the company parties to such memorandum agreement and the other to be designated by the union; (2) the Human Relations Research Committee shall be empowered to retain, by mutual agreement of the cochairpersons thereof, qualified experts and services in the various fields of study for the purpose of consultation and advice; and (3) the expense of the Human Relations Research Committee's work shall be shared equally by the parties.

In the initial stages, the Human Relations Committee worked very well. However, later on, due to the internal crises in the union, the committee had to be abolished.

In all of the above-mentioned plans and experiments, there is one common characteristic: they provide for a joint continuing study of the problems and issues of mutual interest to both parties. These experiments indicate that the institution of collective bargaining was adapting itself to a new climate. In many instances, the remedies adapted were tailor-made for specific situations. All these programs and many others like them had a limited life, but they made important contributions during their lifetime.

## Recent Cooperative Efforts

In the 1970s the efforts to extend union-management cooperative relations beyond traditional collective bargaining have accelerated. Two major concerns have played a large part in stimulating this acceleration. They were the slackening in productivity and a widespread feeling among behavioral scientists and influential members of the media, industry, and government that worker alienation and dissatisfaction was excessively high. [12] The outcome has been the setting up of what is now known as Employment Security and Plant Productivity committees in the steel industry, as well as the creation in 1974 of the National Commission on Productivity and Work Quality.

## The Steel Industry Committees

Anxiety over lagging productivity in the steel industry in the 1960s and the potential loss of jobs because of foreign imports gave impetus to the establishment of joint labor-management committees in 1971 in ten basic steel companies. These committees were set up under the terms of the 1971 basic steel contract. An essential guideline of the committee was that it was in no way to interfere with the existing rights of the parties under the provision of the collective agreement. The goal of these committees was fivefold: (1) to advise management on ways of improving productivity; (2) to promote orderly relations in the plant in order to ensure uninterrupted production; (3) to promote the use of domestic steel; (4) to encourage company progress and, thus, worker prosperity; and (5) to review issues of special concern to the parties.

The committees have reviewed such issues as the improvement of quality control, the more efficient handling of scrap, energy conservation, more efficient phasing out of old equipment, the reduction of breakdown and delays, more efficient use of time and facilities, reduction of overtime, the improvement of worker safety, and so forth.

It is estimated that some 230 committees were in operation by 1973, with widely varying results. I. W. Able, president of the Steel

Workers of America, conceded that some committees had showed indifference and a lack of cooperation. It appeared that workers in some plants continued to suspect that productivity gains would be made at their expense by means of speedup and loss of jobs. On the other hand, examples of successful committees were cited to illustrate that by reducing costs and improving quality, job security was enhanced and worker morale was strengthened. The union leadership claimed that the existence of these committees had contributed to substantial improvements in productivity and to mature collective bargaining relationships throughout the industry. They also attributed the inclusion in the contract of provisions barring strikes over wages and other terms of the contract to the groundwork laid by the Basic Steel Joint Employment Security and Plant Productivity Committee.

Jamestown Area Labor Management Committee

Another project that has received wide publicity is the communitywide effort to improve the labor relations climate in Jamestown, New York. Jamestown, a factory town of 40,000 people in the western part of the state of New York, was a deteriorating industrial community. In the early 1970s, unemployment was reaching 10 percent, and the number of manufacturing jobs had been in a steady decline for a long time. Faced with loss of plants and jobs because of a bad labor relations climate, the mayor, on the advice of the Federal Mediation and Conciliation Service, took the initiative in bringing together a substantial number of local management and union leaders to discuss ways of halting the community decline. After several meetings, the Jamestown Area Labor Management Committee was formed in 1972. It included representatives of international and local companies, as well as of the machinists, auto workers, steel workers, and furniture workers unions.

The Jamestown area committee received financial assistance from the National Commission on Productivity and Work Quality and from the Department of Commerce to intensify its program at the plant level. The committee hired a full-time coordinator to get plant union-management committees started and to carry out a program of demonstration projects and educational activities. The parties in each plant determined their own structure, procedure, and problem priorities. The objective of each plant committee was to maintain close communications among all participants and to initiate joint productivity improvements projects, including experiments in redesign of work.

As the plant committees took over the function of initiating joint projects, the communitywide labor management committee assumed the role of a clearinghouse, serving as a facilitator and sponsor of joint conferences and other educational activities.

In the three years (1972-75) of the Jamestown Labor Management Committee's existence, despite a nationwide economic recession, it can be credited with notable progress in increasing productivity and reducing strikes and grievances in its 36 member enterprises. New employment opportunities were created through expansion and arrival of new employers. Despite a refusal by some employers in Jamestown to participate in the project, the leaders of the program feel that the Jamestown Labor Management Committee was enough of a success to set an example for other communities with similar problems that wished to develop such collaborative programs themselves.

The Rushton Coal Mining
Autonomous Work Group Program

As far as the improvement of the quality of work life programs are concerned, the most widely publicized project involving unions and management is the autonomous work group program in the Rushton Coal Mine in Pennsylvania. In 1974 the Rushton Mining Company, in agreement with the United Mine Workers of America, undertook an action-research project in one section of the underground mine. The project was initiated by the private National Quality of Work Center and sponsored by the National Commission on Productivity and Work Quality.

Initially, the 27 work group members in the experimental section were given training to enable them to perform a variety of jobs. Each crew member was trained how to do every job in the section. The section decided where each crew would work each day. The foremen had no direct authority over the crew, but were responsible only for their safety. Pay and classification differences were eliminated. All workers in the experimental section received the highest possible rate. Grievances were to be settled, if possible, by a joint committee of elected representatives from the crew, the local union, and management. Both sides were entitled to settle any unresolved grievances through the regular grievance procedure. The company and the miners were to share any increased profits that resulted from the new work arrangement.

As a result of this new program, the average rate of absenteeism was reduced to 1.5 percent, as against 5.8 percent for the whole mine. Crew members were enthusiastic about their work, accidents declined, and the company experienced the highest rate of productivity in the experimental section it had ever achieved. However, the attempt to extend the new work arrangment to the whole mine encountered difficulties. After considering the workers' objections and ideas, the experiment was modified and extended to the entire mine.

Other examples of labor-management cooperation and consultation are found in individual plants, at the company level as well as at the industry level, in the United States and in Canada. [13]

## COLLECTIVE BARGAINING IN WESTERN EUROPE

While in North America collective bargaining is central to worker participation in management, in most of the Western European countries it is usually treated as distinct from other forms of industrial democracy, such as works councils and worker representation on company boards. The differences in the collective bargaining system between North America and continental Europe, as well as differing attitudes and philosophies of unions and management toward the bargaining system, help explain the contrasting American and European approach to industrial democracy. These differences will be discussed here.

### Structure and Philosophy

While plant- and enterprise-level bargaining is the dominant pattern in North America, industrywide bargaining at the national and regional level has been a common practice in most Western European countries for some time. Typically, collective agreements concluded at the national or regional level establish minimum standards of pay, hours of work, holidays, and so forth. In many instances, such agreements also set up procedures for negotiating further agreements at lower levels. Although some enterprise-level bargaining does take place, such as Volkswagen in West Germany and Renault in France, it is the exception rather than the rule. The reasons for the neglect of plant and enterprise bargaining on the European continent, as opposed to North America, are historical as well as institutional. Unions in many Western European countries are divided along the same ideological and religious lines as the political parties they support. They attach great importance to class-oriented industrial unionism and are much more politically inclined than their counterparts in North America. [14] Most of the European unions assign priorities to socioeconomic matters at the industry or national level. "In return for a more influential voice at the macro level in national socio-economic policy formulation, these unions have apparently been prepared to moderate and restrain their demands at the micro level in collective bargaining." [15]

While the unions have been concentrating on larger socioeconomic issues and neglecting the individual enterprise, the employers
have been equally keen to set firm boundaries to the bargaining relationship at the industry or multifirm level. In this way, they hope to
safeguard their managerial prerogatives against union encroachment.
One result of the contrast between the emphasis upon industry-level
collective bargaining in Europe and the more dominant enterprise-
and plant-level bargaining in North America is the relatively lower
level of collective employer organizations on the American continent.
European employers, on the other hand, have established closely knit,
highly structured, well-financed associations that conduct national bargaining with unions, coordinate regional and enterprise bargaining,
and play a major role in shaping and maintaining national norms for
employment standards.

Current Trends

In considering collective bargaining as a form of worker participation, two developments in Western Europe seem to stand out: a
trend toward enterprise-level bargaining and a trend toward increasing the scope of collective bargaining.

The changing orientation of works councils and similar bodies
of employee representation is likely to extend the bargaining structure
downward, that is, to the enterprise and plant level. According to
Windmuller:

> Formal schemes of worker participation generally tend to
> promote the integration of works councils in the bargaining
> structure. They do so most frequently by allocating to the
> works councils explicit bargaining rights in certain subject
> areas or by entrusting them with responsibility for super-
> vising the implementation at plant level of macro-type col-
> lective bargaining concluded between unions and employers
> associations. They may of course do both.[16]

In recent years, there has been a shift toward granting works
councils codetermination rights and even veto power over certain
managerial decisions. As pointed out in a previous chapter, works
councils in the Netherlands have equal rights with management in
health and safety matters, work regulations, and pension plans. Furthermore, according to newly proposed amendments, their role is to
become first and foremost "a watchdog over management and an agency
for plant level bargaining over issues supplemental to industry-wide
bargaining."[17] In West Germany, works councils have codetermination

powers over recruitment and layoff policies, as well as over a host of personnel and social matters. Though under the law the works councils in West Germany do not have the right to bargain collectively with management on wages and working conditions, in practice such bargaining often takes place.

In Italy, the pattern of bargaining has shifted in recent years. Industrywide bargaining, which was once the dominant pattern, still is prevalent in some industries. However, plant bargaining has now become the most significant form of collective bargaining in many Italian industries. The shift to plant bargaining has paralleled two other developments, namely, the rejection by rank-and-file workers of the old works councils, which they believed were dominated by management, and the spontaneous emergence of worker delegates at the plant level. Since the late 1960s, collective agreements negotiated at the plant and enterprise level have begun to place emphasis on the improvement of the quality of working life. In the 1970s collective bargaining took on a new dimension. Agreements were concluded that dealt with investment and development policies to be followed by certain major companies. For example, unions at company-level bargaining sessions in the metal, chemical, food, and textile industries insisted that firms place more of their new investment in the chronic unemployment areas of the South to create new jobs. [18]

In Sweden, the 1976 Act on Codetermination at Work enables workers and their representatives to exert greater influence over the organization of work and management of company affairs. However, the provisions of this act can be implemented only through appropriate collective agreements. Unions are entitled to negotiate on such issues as changes in working environment (restructuring of work organization, allocation of work, switching to new lines of business, and selling the firm), industrial health services, personnel policy, personnel transfer, the organization of work hours, and choice between alternative remunerative systems. [19] In case of disagreement, the unions were granted the right to impose their own interpretation concerning employee obligations to work and the meaning of the provisions of the act. The union's interpretation was to be binding until the labor courts made a decision.

## COLLECTIVE BARGAINING: AN EVALUATION

Collective bargaining, as it is usually known and practiced in North America, has a number of drawbacks. It is not continuous in character. Bargaining takes place at the end of a certain period, which may range from one to three years, which makes immediate and direct response to day-to-day problems impossible. For example, in a recent survey of collective agreements covering bargaining units of 200 or more employees in Canada,

> 75 percent of the agreements did not contain clauses which provided advance notice or consultation prior to the introduction of new equipment and production methods. Only about half of the agreements provided for joint labour management committees. There were hardly any provisions which dealt with industrial safety problems of old or handicapped workers.[20]

Apart from the limited coverage of such important issues, the success of collective bargaining depends to a large extent on the power relationship between the parties, as well as on the leadership qualities of union and management. Experience has shown that there is an inherent variability in the results of the bargaining process because circumstances can arise that could have a tremendous effect on the parties' bargaining power. These circumstances could include wage and price guidelines, product obsolescence, and so forth. New technological advances could make a whole range of traditional skills unwanted. The collective bargaining process seems to be quite inadequate in coping with these circumstances.

It is generally recognized in North America, as well as in Western Europe, that the key to effective collective bargaining is the presence of a strong, well-informed union. In most European countries, both law and practice now force employers to provide extensive information on the existing socioeconomic situation and on future prospects of the enterprise, as well as on all matters that could affect the employees' vital interests. Employers in North America are not obliged to provide detailed information to unions about their future plans. The legislation in North America requires both parties to bargain in good faith, which essentially means that employers are obliged to furnish information necessary and relevant to the performance of the union's collective bargaining responsibilities. In many instances, the unions have to negotiate agreements without adequate data or pertinent information, which could conceivably result in plant shutdown or in the reduction of staff. It has been argued that "collective bargaining is unlikely to remain central to North America's approach to industrial democracy as it is today, unless unions are provided with more information heretofore generally held back from them and the scope of negotiations in widened."[21]

In North America, the system of collective bargaining is overburdened with distributive decision-making issues that are primarily economic in nature. Many of the issues on which rank-and-file worker should be informed and consulted are not the sort of issues that can always be reduced to a demand in a bargaining session, let alone included as a condition of employment in the collective agreement. Consequently, the rank-and-file workers feel alienated, and it is this alienation that undermines the effectiveness of unions. Furthermore, a large number of unorganized employees cannot rely upon the collective bargaining system for protection.

Despite these limitations and imperfections, many respected observers of the U.S. industrial relations scene contend that collective bargaining will continue to retain its dominant role in U.S. society. According to Derber:

> The strength of collective bargaining has been its pragmatic quality in response to changing conditions and needs. It has never been constant or static. . . . Most of the recent innovations in job redesign, employee-supervisor relations and flexible work schedules are compatible with collective bargaining. [22]

Other observers argue that the history of U.S. industrial democracy, the legacy of individualism, and distrust for governmental control leave little room for any dramatic change in the workplace during the foreseeable period ahead.

More important, it has been argued that in the last decade, the scope of bargainable issues in North America has considerably increased. It now includes matters of work organization, such as employee dislocations or disruptions brought about by technological changes, health and safety matters, and even productivity matters, as is exemplified by the negotiations in the steel industry. Many union leaders and intellectuals in the United States believe that the degree of control exercised by unions and workers over managerial decision making in the United States is greater than in most countries in Western Europe. According to Tannenbaum:

> While the American union is not formally defined as playing a management role, it does so in fact. The result, ironically, is that the American worker, who does not seek control as an end in itself, exercises more control over matters in the plant that are important to him than does his counterpart in many European countries, who is ideologically committed to the concept of workers' control. [23]

NOTES

1. Adolf Sturmthal, "Unions and Industrial Democracy," An-nals of the American Academy of Political and Social Sciences 431 (May 1977): 14.

2. Most of the material in the following section is based on International Institute for Labour Studies, Workers' Participation in Management: A Review of United States Experience, IILS Bulletin no. 6 (Geneva, 1970).

3. Ibid., p. 160.

4. Ibid., p. 166.

5. Ibid., p. 167.

6. Ibid., p. 170.

7. Ibid., pp. 171-72.

8. Neil Chamberlin, The Union Challenge to Management Control (New York: Harper, 1948), p. 93, as quoted in International Institute for Labour Studies, Workers' Participation in Management, p. 174.

9. T. R. Donahue, "Why Unions Reject Co-Determination?," Labour Gazette (Ottawa) 76 (September 1976): 474.

10. International Institute for Labour Studies, Workers' Participation in Management, pp. 177-78.

11. The material in this section is taken from an article written by the author, Hem C. Jain, "Continuous Bargaining—Recent Developments in the U.S.A. and Canada," Indian Journal of Industrial Relations 6 (October 1970): 135-39.

12. See Harry M. Douty, "Labour-Management Productivity Committees in American Industry," mimeographed (Washington, D.C.: National Commission on Productivity and Work Quality, May 1975). See also Edgar Weinberg, "Labour-Management Cooperation: A Report on Recent Initiatives," Monthly Labour Review, April 1976; William L. Batt, Jr., and Edgar Weinberg, "Labour Management Cooperation Today," Harvard Business Review, January-February 1978; and Charlotte Gold, Employer-Employee Committees and Worker Participation, Cornell University, Industrial and Labor Relations, Series 20 (Ithaca, N.Y.).

13. Ontario Ministry of Labour, An Inventory of Innovative Work Arrangements in Ontario (Toronto, 1978); see also Jain, "Continuous Bargaining."

14. See International Labour Office, Collective Bargaining in Industrialized Market Economics (Geneva: ILO, 1973); see also European Economic Community, Commission of the European Communities, Employee Participation and Company Structures in the European Community, Bulletin of the EEC, supp. 8/75 (Brussels, 1975).

15. John Crispo, Industrial Democracy in Western Europe: A North American Perspective (Toronto: McGraw-Hill-Ryerson, 1978), p. 36.

16. John P. Windmuller, "Industrial Democracy and Industrial Relations," Annals of the American Academy of Political and Social Sciences 431 (May 1977): 26.

17. Ibid.

18. See European Economic Community, Commission of the European Communities, Employee Participation and Company Structures, pp. 21-22; see also Crispo, Industrial Democracy, pp. 48-49.

19. See Hem C. Jain, "Information, Training and Effective Participation," Industrial Relations Journal 9 (Spring 1978): 53.

20. Paul Malles, "Co-Determination in Canada," Labour Gazette (Ottawa), August 1976, p. 419.

21. Crispo, Industrial Democracy, p. 151.

22. Milton Derber, "Collective Bargaining: The Approach to Industrial Democracy," Annals of the American Academy of Political and Social Sciences 431 (May 1977): 94.

23. A. Tannenbaum, "System of Formal Participation," in O. B.: Research and Issues, Industrial Relations Research Association, Association Series (Wisconsin, 1974), pp. 90-91.

# *Part I*

## Section B: Case Studies

# *Case 1*

## SUCCESS AND PROBLEMS WITH PARTICIPATIVE SCHEMES— THE CASE OF BELGIUM

### H. Jain, O. Vanachter, and P. Gevers

This pilot study examines the benefits and problems associated with the actual operation of participative schemes
in four Belgian enterprises.

In recent years, there has been a great deal of debate and discussion on worker participation in management. Most of the published
material has described the legal and voluntary schemes in various industrialized countries. There have been a number of general surveys
and individual country studies, but there is a noticeable gap in the
published literature, namely, case studies on the actual operations
of legal and voluntary participative schemes in individual companies.
The present pilot study is an attempt to fill this gap and to obtain insights into the practical operations of participative bodies in four enterprises.

The purpose of this study is (1) to identify the range and main
characteristics of schemes of worker participation in management in
Belgium, and (2) to review the practical experience with various participative schemes in four individual enterprises in Belgium by means
of case studies and to explore the benefits and problems associated
with the actual operation of the schemes.

The focus of this pilot study is on disclosure of information, as
well as on the comprehension and use of information by all parties involved in participative schemes. Because both major unions in Belgium are pushing for a worker council (as opposed to the existing
works council), which will exclude management, and will give them
veto power over such matter as work rules, methods, layoffs, and
closures, this pilot study takes an added significance.

This study was conducted by H. Jain in collaboration with O.
Vanachter, University of Leuven, and P. Gevers, University of Antwerp.

THE BELGIAN LABOR RELATIONS SYSTEM

There are three major blue collar unions in Belgium. Each is affiliated to a political party. These include the Confederation of Christian Unions (ACV/CSC), which has 1.08 million members and is affiliated with the Christian Democratic party; the Belgian General Federation of Labor (ABV/FGTB), which has 970,000 members and is affiliated with the Socialist party; and the General Center of Belgian Liberal Unions (ACLVB/CGSLB), which has 149,000 members and is affiliated with the Liberal party. The Belgian trade union movement derives its strength from a high rate of union membership and from its actual participation in national economic and social policy-making bodies. Belgium has one of the highest rates of union membership (71 percent of the labor force) in the industrialized world. Unions have close links with major political parties. Many union members are members of the Parliament and even ministers of the government. The political power of the unions explains the extensive protective labor legislation, the absence of legislation regulating unions, and the almost absolute freedom to strike. The principal organization on the employer's side is the Belgian Federation of Enterprises. This association is active in all labor-management affairs and represents employers in national negotiation with the three major unions. According to Blanpain, "Collective labour relations in Belgium rely almost entirely on practices and de facto agreements between the social partners. There is no significant legislation on strikes, settlement of industrial disputes and the like."[1] One illustration of this fact is found in the functions of the labor courts, which are restricted to dealing with individual worker grievances and have no power to intervene in strikes.

Since the end of World War II, labor-management relations in Belgium have been influenced by a "Pact of Solidarity" between the Belgium Employers' Association and the major unions. This pact established the main directions along which a modern labor relations system should be developed. This working relationship led in 1960 to national agreements called Social Programming, which established a joint program for social advancement in industry. Three fundamental principles were laid down: (1) a concerted policy of economic expansion must enable workers to share in a regularly improving standard of living; (2) this must be realized through collective agreements at the interindustry level; and (3) social programming is possible only if industrial peace is observed during the life of the agreement.[2]

Both social partners also participate at the national level in the shaping of economic and social policies through the Central Economic Council, the National Labor Council, and the National Committee

TABLE 5

Collective Bargaining—Belgium and North America
(a comparison)

| Belgium | North America |
| --- | --- |
| 2 or 3 unions with different ideological orientation represent the same group of workers in a plant. | A single union is the exclusive bargaining agent of the production and maintenance workers. |
| Trade unions do not have legal status. | Collective agreements are binding on both parties. |
| National collective agreements become law by Royal Decree and have to be followed by individual companies. Local conditions are not taken into account. Result is a lack of flexibility. | Collective agreements are mostly concluded at the plant level. |
| Scope of agreement (plant level) is limited mostly to wage and income issues and special problems that can have financial repercussions. | The scope is broader. |
| Unions feel that they can discuss, bargain and strike if necessary, for all items not expressly covered by specific clauses in the agreement. | Items not expressly covered by collective agreements are considered managerial prerogative. Management claims residual rights. |
| Fringe benefits include syndicate benefits (fixed amount each trade union receives for its members); benefits for laid-off workers (over and above unemployment benefits); unique separation allowance (for the uninterrupted employment after 2 years); fidelity bonus (seniority); additional pay (13 month). | Most of these benefits are unheard of in North America. |
| In one Belgian company the combined effect of holidays, vacations, and shift-break days has been to hire 5 men to man one position. | Such vacations and holidays would be considered excessive by North American standards. |
| Management freedom: Very little restriction is placed on management on reasonable subcontracting, specially job transfers within maintenance categories; lot of flexibility in craft handling in maintenance group, provided the labor relations climate is good and wages and job security is not adversely affected. | Craft jurisdiction is very rigid and union rivalry does not allow flexibility in craft handling, and so forth. |
| Union delegates are provided with more free time and better facilities for the performance of their duties. | |
| Rules and regulations against layoff are more strict (minimum notice for layoff of an hourly worker is 4 weeks). | |

Source: Compiled by the author.

for Economic Expansion. The National Labor Council is made up of an equal number of union and employer representatives and concludes nationwide agreements, involving such diverse matters as minimum wages, guaranteed monthly incomes in the event of disability, maximum number of hours worked each week, vocational training, and so forth. Some of the most noteworthy agreements resulted in the works councils being given the right to extensive information and the automatic indexation of all wages and salaries to the cost of living. As a result of these agreements between employers and unions, there have been relatively few conflicts and strikes in Belgium.

Most collective bargaining in Belgium is handled at a national, industry-, or sectorwide level. The organizations responsible for the negotiations of collective agreements are the Labor-Management Joint committees (commissions paritaires), which have an equal number of management and union representatives, with an independent chairperson and vice-chairperson appointed by the crown. Besides conducting negotiations, the joint committees also have a conciliation role during disputes, and they give advice on social legislation from their sector to the government.

Belgian unions have no legal personality, and therefore, they cannot be sued in court for breach of collective agreement. However, one of the fundamental principles of social programming is the maintenance of industrial peace during the time of the agreement. Consequently, most agreements signed at the industrial or sectoral level contain a "no strike clause," through which unions guarantee social peace during the life of the agreement. The peace obligation is generally accompanied by a clause in the agreement that guarantees that each union will receive a fixed amount in proportion to the number of its members (and for the faithful observance of the collective agreement). (See Table 5.)


PARTICIPATIVE BODIES AT THE
LEVEL OF THE ENTERPRISE

Present Laws and Practices

Representative institutions at the level of the enterprise include the works council, the union delegation, and the safety and health committees. Although formally separate, these bodies have overlapping functions and personnel. Health and safety committees have been required by law in plants with 50 employees or more. These committees are elected by all workers in proportion to their numerical strength. They are purely consultative and work to enforce safety regulations and improve working conditions.

Union delegations (delegations syndicales) operate at the shop floor level, but employers are not compelled by law to recognize them. However, once they have been granted recognition by the employer, they can negotiate collective agreements, which supplement national agreements. The union delegation in Belgium has some similarities with the North American shop steward and grievance committee system. Generally, the union delegation in Belgium plays an important role, particularly in the settlement of individual grievances and problems at the plant level. The union delegation in Belgium, like their counterpart shop stewards and grievance committee in North America, is the principal medium for union activity in the plant. Union delegates have a considerable influence over the enforcement of terms and conditions laid down in legislation and national agreements.

In contrast to union delegations, which are established by collective agreements, works councils (comités d'entreprise) are required by law. Every enterprise employing more than 150 people is required to have a works council. All employees in an enterprise, except supervisory personnel, are entitled to vote in works councils elections, but only the three recognized unions can nominate candidates. Manual and white collar employees are elected in proportion to their numerical strength. The councils meet under the chairpersonship of the chief executive, who may nominate a number of management representatives. The size of the council varies from 4 to 22 and is determined by the number of employees. The number of management representatives may not exceed that of employee representatives. The purpose of the works council is to promote cooperation between the employer and employees. The works council is entitled to receive detailed information on investment plans, sources of financing, and on the competitive position of the firm. Furthermore, the works council has the right to be consulted when the enterprise contemplates measures that might alter working conditions, the structure of the organization, or the rate of output. An element of codetermination has been introduced in that the council is empowered to examine the general criteria for recruitment, and it determines the criteria to be followed for layoffs. Finally, the council has power of codecision with regard to work rules, social welfare schemes, vocational training programs, and so forth. Employee representatives can call an expert for advice, though management may object to a particular individual appearing as an expert. In case of disagreement or complaints, the matter may be referred for conciliation to the Minister of Economic Affairs or to the joint committees. The royal decree makes it clear that the purpose of providing detailed information about production costs and about plans for future investments is to help the members of the works council to assess the relationship between the prevailing economic and financial conditions in the enterprise and their effect on the organization, employment, and personnel.

## Unions and Management Attitudes toward Works Councils

Management is generally favorably inclined to the works councils because the system gives them a good opportunity to explain their point of view. Works council meetings are neutral grounds, where management is not exposed to union demands. Although both major unions favor the continued existence of works councils, they differ sharply on the question of the value of the system to the workers and on its future direction. The Christian unions (CSC) consider that the works councils are useful because they provide an opportunity for monthly encounters between management and employees. They demand that more information and greater power be given to the works councils and would like to see them transformed into worker councils representing the employees exclusively. A recent CSC document stated that the "present holders of economic power (high finance, management, large capitalists, both Belgian and foreign managers) should accept the right of workers' participation not only in administration but in the totality of the common task." The document argued for the need for worker control and, calling it "a step toward self-management of the enterprize and the economy by workers," made a favorable reference to the Yugoslav system. [3]

In general, the Socialist unions (FGTB) consider that any failure of the works councils is bound up with an unrealistic belief that conflict-free worker representation is a real possibility. They are opposed to any form of worker integration. Like the CSC, the FGTB is asking for worker control, but its approach is different. The CSC puts the emphasis on the "common task," that is, the fact that unions and management have a common stake in the welfare of the enterprise, while the FGTB emphasizes the right to strike and to give workers the power to control the enterprise without the responsibility for decisions. Within the existing social and legal framework, however, the FGTB is in favor of the continuation of the works council system, not only because of the company information they receive through this channel but also because they believe the system can be educational for the workers. Both major unions are in favor of workers' councils that will exclude management and will give them veto power over such matters as work rules, methods, layoffs, closures, and so forth.

## OPERATION OF PARTICIPATIVE SCHEMES
## IN FOUR BELGIAN ENTERPRISES

Methodology

The research team included psychologists, sociologists, and labor law professors from four well-known universities in Belgium. Two members of the team had previous experience with studies on works councils and were fully familiar with the Belgian scene. The team agreed upon two criteria for selecting firms: (1) to select those firms where works councils and other participative bodies were formally established and functioning reasonably well and (2) to select those firms where union and management were fulfilling the minimum legal requirements but were not interested in joint consultation or cooperation.

The interview guide used in the collection of data was fairly comprehensive (24 typed pages) and covered the following items: (1) personal background of the interviewees; (2) general data about the enterprise; (3) general data about the unions in the enterprise; (4) general data concerning participative bodies—works councils, health and safety committees, and union delegations; (5) guideline for the disclosure of information—philosophy of disclosure of information, list of information items received by members of the works councils, consultation and negotiation machinery, preparation and presentation of information, practical problems, and overall evaluation; and (6) guideline for training of management and labor delegates in participative bodies in the enterprise. We tried to gather all the necessary data about individual companies and the unions in the enterprise prior to conducting interviews. We had serious problems of entry with several Belgian, as well as multinational, firms where we wanted to conduct this study. In one case, the head office in the United States allowed us to do our research, but the Belgian enterprise refused to cooperate. (See Table 6.)

Three interviewers spent a minimum of one full day interviewing the chairperson of the works council and other management representatives. We interviewed members of the union delegation, the works councils, and the health and safety committee in their own language. In some instances, the same people belonged to more than one representative body. Except in one case, where unions objected, all interviews were taped. It is important to underline again the exploratory nature of this study and the fact that the proposed conclusions are mainly impressions based on discussions with a limited number of people. At times, it was difficult to distinguish between the personal views of the individuals and the official view of the body to which they belonged.

TABLE 6

General Data about the Companies

| | A | B | C | D |
|---|---|---|---|---|
| 1. Corporate structure | | | | |
| Nature of activities | Car assembly | Manufacturing food pro-cessing machinery | Production of synthetic fibers and filter tips | Oil refinery |
| Nationality | (Belgian) subsidiary of a French multinational company | Subsidiary of an American multinational company | Subsidiary of an American multinational company | Subsidiary of an American multinational company |
| Head office location | Paris | European head office Saint-Niklaas | European head office Brussels | Belgian head office Antwerpen |
| Plant location | Vilvoorde | Saint-Niklaas | Lanaken | Antwerpen |
| 2. Number of employees | 4,404 | 564 | $\pm$300 | 1,333 |
| Blue collars | 3,993 | 354 | (mass layoff in 1974) | 516 |
| White collars | 339 | 140 | — | 503 |
| Cadres–executives | 72 | 70 | — | 314 |
| 3. Union representation (in percent) | | | | |
| CSC/ACV (Christian) | $\pm$50 (majority of white collars) | $\pm$64 (majority of blue collars) | $\pm$80 | 50 (majority of white collars) |
| FGTB/ABVV (Socialist) | $\pm$46 | $\pm$27 | $\pm$20 | 50 (majority of blue collars) |
| CGSLP/ACLVB (Liberal) | $\pm$4 | $\pm$9 | — | — |

4. Personnel practices

| | | | | |
|---|---|---|---|---|
| Hiring | The firm's policy is to hire an equal number of CSC and FGTB members (blue collars); mostly Flemish (99 percent); no foreigners; male workers; country workers | Inside and outside the firm; union delegates informed about vacancies | Mostly from neighboring areas; country workers; mostly Flemish | Inside and outside the firm; white collar workers mostly from outside; mostly Flemish; blue collars; mostly male country workers |
| Job evaluation and performance appraisal | Annual performance appraisal of blue, white collars and cadres; points system | Annual performance appraisal | Job evaluation and performance appraisal for white and blue collars | Performance appraisal for white collars; job classification for blue and white collars |
| Promotion | When position available within plant; based on merit and seniority | Based on merit | — | Based on merit and seniority; a new plan for promotion under discussion |
| Training and education | Few opportunities, but have recently started a training program for foremen | Conducted by the unions | First two sessions of W. C. devoted to training and explanation of balance sheet and other financial information | Organization development for executives and supervisors |
| 5. Labor relations climate | Accommodative; collective conflicts are avoided; importance attached to resolving individual grievances at shop floor level | Very good; no strikes | Very good according to management | Distrust between management and blue collars; friction between blue and white collars; Company involved in sectorial strike; no strike at company level |
| Turnover (percent) | 15.3 | Below 5 | Very low except for shift workers ($\pm$25) less than 2 | Less than 4 |
| Absenteeism (percent) | 11.65 (1976) | Less than 1 | Less than 2 | — |

Source: Compiled by the author.

113

Data on Firms Visited

Company A

Company A is a car assembly plant employing 4,404 people. It is a subsidiary of a French international company and is located near Brussels. Virtually all blue-collar and white-collar workers are organized by the two dominant unions, Christian and Socialist. The work force is homogeneous (predominantly male and Flemish). The Works Council has 7 management representatives and 14 employee representatives. All employee representatives belong to the unions: 9 out of 14 of them have dual membership (in the Works Council and Union Delegation). No formal meetings are held between the members of the unions delegation and management. The Works Council is chaired by the general manager. The secretary, an employee representative, draws the agenda in consultation with other employee and management members. The Health and Safety Committee consists of 2 members of management and 14 employees, all union members. The chairperson of the Health and Safety Committee is the Personnel and Human Relations director, a member of the top management executive committee. The firm is affiliated to Fabrimetal, the national employers association for the metal industry, and is a party to national collective agreement.

The labor relations climate in Company A can be characterized as accommodative. Real efforts are made to avoid collective conflicts and to resolve individual grievances at the shop floor level.

Company B

Company B is a food-processing machinery manufacturing company. It is a subsidiary of a U.S. multinational company and employs about 564 people. The plant, as well as the company's European head office, is located in Sint Niklaas, half way between Antwerp and Brussels; 98 percent of blue collar and 75 percent of white collar employees are unionized. The dominant union in the plant is the Christian union. The Works Council has eight representatives each from management and employees.

All employee representatives to the Works Council belong to unions. Four out of eight employee representatives hold two positions at the same time, that is, as members of the Works Council as well as of the Union Delegation. The secretary of the Works Council makes the agenda in consultation with the general manager, who is the chairperson of the Works Council. The Health and Safety Committee has been organized in a similar way. The firm is affiliated with the Fabrimetal group and is a party to the collective agreements that are concluded at the national level. The labor relations climate in Company B can be termed as very good.

## Company C

Company C is a subsidiary of a U.S. multinational company and manufactures synthetic fibers and filter tips. In 1976 the company experienced serious financial difficulties and had to lay off almost half of its labor force. At present, the number of its work force is approximately 300. It is located in Lanaken, on the border of the Netherlands. Virtually all blue- and white-collar workers are unionized. The Christian union is the largest union, with 80 percent of the members. The personnel manager is the chairman of the Works Council. It consists of an equal number of representatives from management and employees. The Health and Safety Committee has a similar structure and is chaired by the production manager.

The Union Delegation holds formal weekly meetings with management. The company, which is a member of Febeltex, the national employers' association for the textile industry, pays its membership dues and receives all useful information, but it is not a party to the national sectoral bargaining.

Collective bargaining takes place at the plant level. Cases of plant bargaining in Belgium are exceptions and require permission from the government and the employers and unions federation. Full-time union officials outside the plant represent the employees at the bargaining table. The scope of bargaining is limited to wages and other matters related to the income of hourly employees. According to management, the labor relations climate is very good.

## Company D

Company D is an oil refinery and is a subsidiary of a U.S. multinational company. The plant employs 1,333 people and is located in Antwerp. Except for cadres (executives), all blue- and white-collar workers are organized by the two dominant unions. The labor relations climate is marked by suspicion and mutual distrust.

The Works Council consists of eight employee representatives and the same number of management representatives. All the eight employee representatives to the Works Council are also members of the Union Delegation. The secretary of the Works Council has kept the same position for the last 20 years. The agenda for the Works Council is prepared in a special meeting of the council. The Health and Safety Committee has the same structure. The company is a party to the national and regional sectoral-level collective agreement.

## Findings

Because of the limitations of space, we shall present only the highlights of our pilot study.

## Works Councils

Management's attitude toward works councils in two of the plants (B and C) we studied seemed to be highly positive. This can be inferred from such statements as: "We believe in the spirit of the law. Some mechanism is needed for communications and consultations. Problem solving should not be limited to formal participative bodies." In one of these plants, the director of personnel, who is a member of the executive committee of senior management, was the chairperson of the Works Council (C), and in the other, the present general manager started his career as personnel manager (B).

Both these plants are relatively small, and the Christian union is the dominant union. Employee representatives to the Works Councils in these two plants were not as enthusiastic as management, but felt that the Works Councils were functioning reasonably well and that there was a climate of mutual trust. In the other two plants (A and D), which were the largest ones, management strictly conformed to the letter of the law. In the car assembly plant (A), management admitted that they attached less importance to the Works Council than to the other two participative bodies. Employee representatives shared this view. In the fourth plant (D), management described its major objectives in a company document as follows: "Faced with the union's and the political parties' leftist strategy . . . we want to maintain the traditional right to manage and to avoid importation of foreign union schemes in our culture." Management strategy in this plant was to maintain direct channels of communication with all personnel and to bypass the unions. Union strategy at the Works Council in this plant was to mix bargaining with consultation. The labor relations climate was marked with distrust and mutual suspicion.

## Disclosure of Information

In a paper on "Information, Training and Effective Participation,"[4] H. Jain stated that there seemed to be a general agreement that the disclosure of company information was desirable. However, he pointed out that those who argue for disclosure often do so for different reasons. For example, proponents of disclosure from the employers' side tend to believe that it will lead to rational and objective bargaining. They claim that it will influence the behavior of trade unionists and is likely to result in moderating some of their demands and attitudes. On the other hand, unions may support disclosure in the belief that it will redress power imbalance and will enable them to bargain as "equal" partners. They also think it will assist them in mapping out their strategy, for example, giving an indication as to when management can least afford a strike, and will force management to justify their decisions. "Some observers believe that dis-

closure will promote acceptance of redundancy and the need for cooperation and change to avoid it; others view it in terms of advance
warning and the need to prepare for factory occupations and other
forms of resistance. "[5]

Disclosure of information goes much farther in Belgium than in
North America. In the United States, there are no direct legal requirements for the disclosure of corporate information to the unions.
However, various labor laws impose on both labor and management
the obligation to "bargain in bood faith. "

As a result, if the employer claims "inability to pay," he is required to provide proof, and the unions have the right to appeal to the
National Labor Relations Board for a ruling. A number of cases,
some of them having gone as high as the U.S. Supreme Court, have
set minimum standards of disclosure. However, North American
unions, especially in Canada, think that corporations should be required to disclose more information. At its 1978 congress, the CLC
demanded that full disclosure be made in the following areas: firm's
status, its competitiveness in the market, its production and productivity, firm's financial structure, budget and cost accounting, staff costs,
firm's programmed outlook for the future, scientific research, all
forms of public support received, and firm's organizational chart.
These are precisely the ten areas in which the Belgian law requires
companies to make full disclosure to the works councils (see Appendix).

In our study, we found that management and employee representation in all the four plants did indeed favor disclosure of information,
but for different reasons. In two out of the four plants (B and C), the
chairperson of the Works Council said that "provision of adequate information to employee representatives and helping them to understand
it was absolutely necessary to maintain social peace. " To a large extent, this philosophy contributed to the unions' acceptance of the need
for layoffs in both plants. For example, in 1974, one of those companies (C) laid off 300 employees, more than half of the total labor
force, and in the other (B), 100 employees, in both cases with the
agreement of unions. Management in one company (C) claimed that the
provision of adequate information had resulted in moderating union demands, for example, there had been no wage increase in this plant for
the last three years. The importance management attached to the disclosure of information, consultation, and verbal communications can be
seen from the fact that in Company B, a small plant with 564 employees,
employee representatives spent approximately 70 hours of production
time every month in the meetings of various participative bodies. Also,
employee representatives on the Works Council met on their own once a
week. They could discuss any problem that arose with management representatives on company time outside the regular Works Council meetings. The general manager had an open door policy. He and other management representatives met frequently in the evenings with a group of

12 to 15 workers and union representatives (from one section) to discuss operational problems and answer questions. Union delegations in both these plants received automatically the information given to Works Council members. According to management, all matters subject to codecision were made by consensus ("We never had to vote"). Occasionally, Company C invited union specialists and experts in finance and auditing to attend Works Council meetings to give additional explanation to workers on economic and financial matters.

Employee representatives at both Plants B and C acknowledged that management provided adequate information on such issues as job security, overtime, work load, and vacation regulations, as well as on future investments in new equipment and machinery and the impact of these investments on employment. These were the issues in which workers were primarily interested.

Other economic and financial information provided by management was in accordance with the legal requirements. Though management was willing to give information on such matters and discuss it with employee representatives, it still made all the final decisions.

The attitudes of the Christian union, which was the dominant union in both these plants, were highly pragmatic. It accepted the view that the subsidiaries of multinational companies in Belgium were under greater pressure to make a profit than the national companies, because of the possibility of the parent company closing down an uneconomic unit and relocating it in another country. Union representatives believed that management was sincere in its attempt to resolve personnel problems in consultation with employee and union delegates.

In the two larger plants (A and D), management interpreted the legal requirements for the disclosure of information in a highly restricted sense. For example, the management of Plant A did not provide any information on the production costs of the car, nor did it divulge the profit and loss statement issued by the head office. Their attitude was: "We are not obliged to give information about the head office. We do not have time or money to prepare graphs or charts to explain economic and financial information." In the other large plant (D), unions claimed that "management tells what it wants to tell. Employee representatives complained that only partial answers were provided by management to the questions asked, with the result that the agenda of the Works Council ended up each time with the same topics. Management's explanation was that the existing structure of the Works Council did not lend itself to the disclosure of all the information that employee representatives wanted because certain items were confidential. While management considered the Works Council as a strictly advisory body, many employee representatives considered it more as a bargaining agency. Many members of the Works Council from both sides did not have a clear understanding of its objectives and operations. As a result, Works Council meetings ended up in frustration for both sides, which in turn created social tension and morale problems.

## Comprehension of Information

In all the four plants, management argued that it was the union's responsibility to provide adequate training in economic and financial matters to help worker representatives understand the economic and social information made available to them. According to both unions and management, understanding the information was indeed a problem for employee representatives in the four plants investigated. In certain cases, it was also true of management representatives. However, there was one exception.

One employee representative in Plant A, whom management claimed was a radical Socialist, understood all the information provided by management and asked questions at each meeting of the Works Council. He wanted to know the breakdown of costs, the budget of each department, and the profit and loss statement of the head office. Management admitted that he was hard working, intelligent, and capable of understanding all the information, but it believed that the Socialist union was using him as a tool to further its ideological aims. We were surprised that one senior management official talked about the same delegate for almost one-half of the time during our interview. Our impression is that management finds it difficult to handle him because he is a constant challenge and a nuisance. Of course, management did not want to provide all the information. Their attitude was, "We are under no obligation to do so."

The Belgian royal decree on disclosure of information became operative in 1974. Since then, the Belgian unions and employers have conducted independent studies of the actual operations of the royal decree over a period of three years. The CSC surveyed the situation experienced by its members in 319 undertakings in Flanders and the Brussels metropolis. About one-half of these firms provided the necessary information. Two-thirds of the remainder were deficient on technical grounds: "inadequate documentation, late information, no special meetings." The rest ignored the royal decree altogether.

The employers' federation in a survey of 200 of their member firms found that in the French-speaking Wallonia region, the implementation of the decree was much slower than in Flanders, because the "employers in Wallonia seem more prepared to defend their traditional managerial prerogative."[6] The findings of these surveys indicate the following obstacles to the free flow of information as outlined in the royal decree:

1. There was little or no information on price calculation, on the details of management budgets, or on the salaries of higher management.

2. In the union survey, it was claimed that many firms treated even basic information as confidential; they did not allow the members of the works council, who already had access to the information, to release it to all employees.

3. There was ambivalence of unions concerning their role vis-à-vis the works council; the FGTB was primarily interested in extending worker control through bargaining rather than in the effectiveness of the works councils.

4. The CSC estimated that 5 percent of its members were true activists, who played a leading part in both the works council and the union delegation. These were the ones who really benefited from disclosure of information and served as catalysts to make the royal decree operational.

5. The use of outside experts caused major problems. The employers resented the manner in which the expert tended to become the leader or chief spokesman for the employees. They feared that the presence of an outside expert in the works council detracted from its consultative cooperative role and increased the possibility of employer representatives in the works council engaging in bargaining. [7]

## Shop Floor Consultation

It appears that most meaningful exchanges at the shop floor level in all the four enterprises between employers and workers involved the union delegation rather than the works council. The most outstanding example is Plant A, where management attached a great deal of importance to establishing interpersonal relationships with workers and to maintaining informal contacts with union delegates at the shop floor level. To this effect, this company had devised, to the best of our knowledge, a unique human relations-information program through the introduction of "social assistants." For approximately every 500 workers, the company appointed one social assistant, who kept daily contacts with the workers on the assembly line and helped them with their social and psychological problems. He or she knew each worker by name in his or her section and worked hand in hand with technical assistants. The Health and Safety Committee enjoyed a privileged position in this plant. Unlike the three other plants, where usually the safety engineer or production manager chaired this committee, in Plant A, it was chaired by the Personnel and Human Relations director, who was a member of the top management executive committee. It should be noted that while the official meeting of the Health and Safety Committee was held once a month, an informal meeting was held prior to this one, which lasted three hours or more. While all the 14 employee representatives attended the informal meeting, the management side was represented by the safety engineer and his assistant only; according to management, the purpose of this informal meeting was to allow employee delegates to talk about their day-to-day problems, such as speed at the assembly line, working environment, comfort, and hygiene and technical problems, at their own pace and at their own educational level. They were assured that management would listen sympathetically to their problems. In addition to the informal meeting, the Health and Safety Committee appointed two employee delegates on a permanent standby basis to examine problems on the assembly line as soon as they arose. They had access to all management officials. These delegates also represented the employees and met with Labor Ministry inspectors when they visited the plant. Management believed that such meetings and daily contacts with employees and union delegates provided an outlet for their frustration and had an impact on productivity. Without such contacts work flow can be disturbed; lack of contact may lead to the spreading of rumors, affect the quality of output and increase discontentment.

As far as the grievance machinery for individual workers at the shop floor is concerned, a worker could approach his or her foreman, union delegate, or the social assistant in his or her area. But a union delegate could not approach the foreman directly; he or she had to go through the area social assistant. The social assistant would investigate the problem and would get in touch with all concerned in an attempt to find an equitable solution. Management argued that if the grievance was handled by the social assistant, there was greater likelihood that the solution to the problem would be objective and fair to all concerned, since the social assistant was not directly involved in the dispute. At the same time, the foreman would be able to maintain his integrity and authority because he could not be accused of favoritism or prejudice against the employee who filed the grievance.

Union delegates are never brought together for a formal meeting with management. However, management keeps in touch with them on an individual basis almost daily and keeps them informed of problems.

CONCLUSION

Much more empirical research is needed before one can evaluate properly the benefits and problems associated with the functioning of participative schemes over a period of time. Further studies could examine such variables as size of the firm, technology, location,

degree and type of unionization, philosophy of national versus multinational companies, and so forth, and the influence of these variables
on the effectiveness of participative bodies. As far as this pilot study
is concerned, the benefits and problems associated with the functioning of participative bodies in four Belgian enterprises can be summarized as follows.

The main advantage of participative bodies is that they function
as a forum, where management can inform, consult, and explain its
viewpoint and decisions to employee representatives. However, the
works councils have the right of codetermination on social issues,
that is, on work rules relating to hours of work on holidays and welfare matters. In this sense, they do limit management rights. There
seems to be a general agreement, however, that works councils can
be a useful instrument in promoting two-way communications, in un-
covering problems, and in reducing social conflicts within the enterprise.

The problems relating to the functioning and effectiveness of
participative bodies arise from the differences in attitudes and interests of management, unions, and employee representatives toward
such bodies. For example, in two out of the four plants studied,
which were also the largest in size, management interpreted the requirements for the disclosure of information in a restrictive way,
which antagonized employee representatives. The role of the works
council in such cases tends to become factional, that is, interest promoting rather than collaborative.

The very nature of participative bodies reduces their effectiveness. These bodies are mostly consultative. The decision-making
power of works councils is limited to certain social and personnel
matters designated by law. Both major Belgian unions would like to
see this power extended. They would like the works council to exercise a right of veto on all major financial decisions that have an impact on employment. The quality of the people elected to representativ
bodies is equally important. Lack of experience and adequate training
in economic and financial matters greatly reduces the contribution of
employee representatives on such bodies.

In spite of these problems, most members of works councils
who were interviewed favored the retention of the works council system. Because of the overlapping of functions and personnel between
works council and union delegations, the difference between the two
bodies is narrowing. The unresolved issues at the works council
level in many cases are referred to the union delegation for negotiations and settlement.

The situation in the four enterprises we studied cannot be taken
as representing the Belgian industry in general. However, our findings do indicate that when the attitudes, goals, and priorities of the

parties are different, the efficacy of participative institutions in furthering cooperation between labor and management is greatly reduced. When this occurs, participative bodies can become an instrument in the hands of each party to pursue its own interest. Furthermore, the employer may attempt to circumvent the legal institutions of works councils.

Our pilot study described one such case. In Plant A, cooperation was not possible because of the antagonistic attitude of the Socialist union and the indifference of management. The employer appears to have set up an elaborate system of shop floor consultation to bypass the Works Council and the union delegation and to increase its control over day-to-day operations at the same time. It is worth noting that the institution of social assistants at the shop floor in this company was highly effective and may be of particular interest to nonunionized companies in North America.


APPENDIX

The Rights of Belgian Works Councils
to Economic and Financial Information

A. The purpose of the information that must be communicated by the managing director or his delegate to the works council is to give the employees a clear and correct view of the situation of the company. The operation of the decree is policed by officers appointed by the Ministry of Economic Affairs. Their most important function is to authorize the chief executive not to disclose information that could be detrimental to the company. This can be authorized on the following points: distribution margins, the absolute value of turnover and its division into the subgroups, the level and evolution of costs and selling prices, the allocation of costs by product or department, new selling points in the distribution sector, information on scientific research, and the profit and loss of subgroups. The officer is empowered to do this after examining the minutes of the works council when the request for exemption was made and any documents produced in justification by the employer and after consulting a special ministerially appointed committee.
B. Experts can be invited to attend by either side, and the other side has the right to refuse that same expert twice. If the disagree-

This appendix is a general summary of the royal decree of November 27, 1973.

ment remains or if there is disagreement between the works council and the chief executive on which information is to be disclosed to the council that the company wishes to treat as confidential, the disagreement is resolved by the same government official (articles 1-3, 27-39). The actual information provisions, which apply separately both to whole companies and to subunits, can be summarized as follows (articles 4-26):

1.  Basic information: This information is to be communicated to council members within two months of election or reelection and discussed within a period of 15 days to two months. It consists of ten categories, in the first three of which a report must be given in writing.

    a.  Company statutes, including the directors and officers; medium and long-term financing, including relations with other legal entities; and agreements having basic consequences on the company

    b.  Financial structure, including an explanation of the accounting methods that is sufficiently detailed for a full understanding of the annual accounts, and a detailed comparison of accounts for the last five years

    c.  Organization chart, explaining the distribution of powers and responsibilities, including a plan of the enterprise and the financial group

    d.  Competitive position, including the main national and international competitors; competitive possibilities; fundamental sales or purchasing agreements; government contracts; general information on the sales patterns, distribution channels, and profit margins of the company's products; turnover; costs and selling prices by unit of production; and the general market position

    e.  Productivity, including production by number, volume, and weight, as well as value per man-hour and per head

    f.  Budget and calculation of costs, including sufficient information on the elements or structure of costs to make informed criticism of the evolution of costs, set out under cost headings by products or groups of products or department

    g.  Personnel costs, including remuneration split between hourly, salary, and managerial pay; social charges; and accident and retirement insurance

    h.  Program and general prospects on all aspects, including financial, social, and research aspects, and the financing of forecast investment

    i.   Scientific research, including the people and institutions in charge and the direction of the research

    j.   The nature and volume of public aid

2.  Annual information: Within three months of the end of the financial year and before the general shareholder assembly, a written report must be given updating all of the basic information, and copies and explanations must be given of:

    a.   The balance sheet, comparing it to the two previous balance sheets and analyzing changes in capital; changes in, and destination of, the reserves; depreciation and the amortization taken; change in debt; changes in fixed and current assets; and the solvency and profitability of the company

    b.   The profit and loss account, comparing it to the two previous years and analyzing the evolution of the level of the different profits and expenses; profit distribution; means foreseen for dealing with possible losses; remuneration of directors, managers, and supervisors; and changes in rentability

The annual information will also include copies of any enclosures given to shareholders and any reports by management, auditors, or commissionaires.

3.  Periodical information: This information is to be supplied at least every three months so that it is possible to undertake a proper comparison to the basic information and make a judgment on the attainment of objectives. This should cover in particular the foreseeable evolution of sales, orders, the market, production, costs and cost prices, stocks, productivity, and the numbers employed.

4.  Occasional information: Any event or internal decision with important effects on the company. Communication of this information should not await the periodical information, and decisions should, wherever possible, be communicated before their execution.

NOTES

1. Roger Blanpain, "Labour Relations in Belgium," in <u>Western European Labour and the American Corporation</u>, ed. A. Kamin (Washington, D. C.: Bureau of National Affairs, 1970), p. 221.

2. Commission on Industrial Relations, (CIR), Worker Participation and Collective Bargaining in Europe, CIR Study, no. 4 (London: HMSO, 1974), p. 81. Much of the material for this introduction to the pilot study is derived from this CIR study and from the green paper issued by the European Economic Community, Commission of the European Economic Communities, Employee Participation and Company Structures in the European Community, Bulletin of the EEC, supp. 8/75 (Brussels, 1975).

3. As quoted in Marc-Henry Janne and Guy Spitaels, "Belgium: Collective Bargaining and Concertation Mold a New System," in Worker Militancy and Its Consequences, 1965-1975, ed. Solomon Barkin (New York: Praeger, 1975), p. 180.

4. Hem C. Jain, "Information, Training and Effective Participation," Industrial Relations Journal 9 (Spring 1978).

5. Ibid.

6. Robin Smith, "Company Information to Trade Unions: Can Britain Learn from Belgium?" unpublished (1977).

7. Ibid.

# *Case 2*

## LABOR-MANAGEMENT COMMITTEES: THE CANADIAN EXPERIENCE

### Jacquie Mansell

This case study examines the functioning of labor-
management committees in two Canadian organizations:
Ontario Hydro and Supreme Aluminum. It highlights
some of the benefits and problems associated with this
particular form of worker participation in Canada.

The purpose of this case study is to examine two functioning
labor-management committees in order to explore the nature and effects of one particular form of worker participation. The cases cover
two quite different organizations—a medium-sized nonunion organization in the private sector and a large unionized organization in the
public sector. The participative mechanisms in both cases are voluntary and indirect. In both organizations, the workers do not participate directly at the point of their immediate work situation; rather,
they choose representatives to participate on their behalf in certain
decisions at higher levels of the organization.

Hopefully, a joint examination of two related but different cases
will help to provide some insights into the more general characteristics of labor-management committees, as well as into certain conditions that either facilitate, or even are necessary for, the effective
operation of worker participation.

The following case study was written by Jacquie Mansell, while
she was employed at the Research Branch of the Ontario Ministry of
Labour. Although much of the information in the cases is based on
work done under the auspices of the Research Branch and published
by them in an Inventory of Innovative Work Arrangements in Ontario,
the major work on Supreme Aluminum was done by the author as a
graduate student.

## RESEARCH METHODOLOGY

The information on Supreme Aluminum was collected through a variety of methods, including a questionnaire survey in 1976 of all employees; examination of the minutes of the meetings of the labor-management committee from its inception in 1972 to May 1976; attendance at all meetings of the committee from January 1975 to May 1976; and numerous interviews with several levels of management, with committee representatives, and with a small sample of nonsupervisory workers. The Ontario Hydro case is based on more limited sources of information—several interviews with the union president and with the manager of Industrial Labor Relations for Hydro, examination of internal documents relating to the establishment and functioning of the labor-management committee, and a short case report done in 1976 by Labour Canada.

## ORGANIZATIONAL BACKGROUND

### Supreme Aluminum Industries Limited

Supreme Aluminum is a private, primarily family-owned and managed nonunion organization. It was founded in 1920 by the father of the two men who are presently the chairman and president of the company. Supreme currently employs about 460 people in Ontario, spread over five manufacturing plants of about 50 to 60 workers each, two warehouses, a small division that handles wholesale distribution of imported specialty items, and a head office located within metropolitan Toronto. Approximately 325 workers and 65 managers are covered by the labor-management committee; a small unionized subsidiary is excluded.

Supreme Aluminum is a prosperous company. Its major products are cookware, pressure cookers, and aluminum ladders. Rates of pay are equivalent to average rates in the cookware industry and in the local area. Everyone in the company participates equally in a profit-sharing plan, which has been in operation since 1948. In 1972 the company began a share-ownership plan, by which both management and nonmanagement employees may purchase company stock. About 50 percent of the employees own some shares in Supreme. Most employees work a four-day, 36-hour week.

From all evidence, it appears that the founder of the company was well liked by his employees, whom he managed in a kindly, but paternal, manner. Labor-management relations have historically been good at Supreme; the company has not lost a day of work through a labor dispute since 1938. There have been a few close, but eventually unsuccessful, attempts to unionize the company.

Ontario Hydro

Ontario Hydro is a large, unionized public sector organization with its head office in Toronto. Spread across the whole province of Ontario, Hydro employs approximately 24,000 people in the production and transmission of electric power. It is a complex organization, made up of many different types of operations. The bargaining unit, which includes about 15,000 people in more than 100 locations, is the largest local of the largest union in Canada. The collective agreement includes such diverse classifications as stenographers, janitors, librarians, helicopter pilots, over 100 categories of tradespeople, artists, and electrical, thermal, and nuclear operators.

The workers at Ontario Hydro have been unionized in some form since 1935 and became a local of the Canadian Union of Public Employees (CUPE, local 1000) in 1963. Hydro and the union have traditionally had a poor relationship, characterized by a history of difficult negotiations, strikes, and bitter feelings. The three rounds of negotiations from 1968-72 reflected a progressively deteriorating relationship, marked by numerous work-to-rule slowdowns and several work stoppages, including a bitter and sometimes violent strike in 1972.

PARTICIPATIVE MECHANISMS

In both organizations, the participative mechanisms first originated in response to a particular problem and were conceived and designed primarily by management. However, in both cases, the nature and purpose of the committees were developed considerably over time by labor and management working together.

Supreme Aluminum

Prior to 1972, worker participation at Supreme was limited to an employee Plant Council, which had virtually no power over decisions of any importance. By 1972 many of the workers had become quite dissatisfied with the Plant Council, until finally the council members went to management for help. Management suggested creating an internal labor-management council and let the employees decide, by secret vote, whether they preferred a union of their choice or such a council. The vote was over 80 percent in favor of the latter, and the first council was elected and began operations in April 1972.

Although several workers were involved somewhat in the design of the council, it was conceived and designed primarily by the current chairman of the company. The chairman was also responsible for designing the original composition of the council.

All management and nonmanagement employees at Supreme belong to an employee association called the Supreme Association for Effective Results (SAFER). The labor-management committee (or council), called the Governing Body, is the controlling body for the employee association and is, therefore, the major structure for worker participation. It is composed of 18 elected representatives— two from senior management, two from middle management, three from the foremen and supervisors, two from the office staff, eight from the nonsupervisory nonoffice workers, and one from all levels of employees of a subsidiary company (thus far, this has usually been a supervisory person).

The term for an elected member is two years, and no person may serve more than two consecutive terms. Each year, the 18 elected members choose a chairperson, who does not have to be a member of the Governing Body. There is no limit to the number of terms a chairperson may serve. The Personnel and Employee Relations managers are also permanent nonvoting members of the Governing Body. The personnel manager keeps the minutes of the meetings. The Governing Body must meet, by constitution, at least quarterly; however, in practice, meetings are held approximately eight to ten times per year.

The issues subject to worker participation and the formal structures and procedures through which workers may participate are outlined in the Constitution, By-laws, and Agreement of the employee association. Theoretically, the powers of the SAFER Governing Body are quite extensive. According to the agreement, the issues subject to some form of joint decision making include all issues generally contained in a standard union-management contract, plus assignment and transfer of employees, operating speeds and methods of production, changes in the size of the work force, and changes in working conditions. The social activities of the company are also handled by the Governing Body.

The issues reserved for exclusive management consideration include the following: establishment of remuneration for all levels of management, including sales representatives;* all hirings and dismissals (subject to grievance); establishment of costing standards, sales targets, and profit objectives; new product development; and all financial requirements and planning for growth.

---

*As of February 1979, the Governing Body was seriously considering amending the agreement to give itself the right to set supervisor's salaries.

The Governing Body participates in decisions by two means— the Governing Body itself may make the final decision or management may make the final decision, but in consultation with the whole Governing Body, the Governing Body chairperson, or the representative(s) of the workers who will be affected by the decision. Decisions on issues covered directly by the agreement (that is, those issues generally covered by a union contract) are made by the Governing Body. Decisions are made by vote, often by secret ballot, and require a two-thirds majority.* However, the company has not formally agreed that these decisions are binding on them; it has retained the formal right to accept or reject any terms of the agreement recommended to it by the Governing Body. The Governing Body has only formally been given final decision-making powers with respect to grievances, that is, with respect to the interpretation of the agreement.

For issues not covered directly by the agreement, but which according to it are open to joint decision making (for example, methods of production and changes in working conditions), the method of worker participation is unclear. The wording of the agreement is vague and does not provide clear guidelines as to either the mechanisms of participation or the distribution of decision-making authority. In most cases, these questions are left to the discretion of management.

In addition to the operations of the Governing Body, monthly divisional meetings are held between every plant and office manager and his or her workers. The meetings are primarily to enable the manager, and sometimes the Governing Body representative(s), to report current information to the workers.


Ontario Hydro

Since the labor-management committee at Ontario Hydro is not the major mechanism for worker participation, it is more limited in purpose and scope than is the Governing Body at Supreme. At Hydro, the collective bargaining process already provides a mechanism for most of the decision-making activities that in practice occupy most of the time of the labor-management committee at Supreme. The joint committee at Hydro was developed to complement the traditional means of worker participation and to make it function more effectively.

By 1973 both senior Hydro and union officials felt that something had to be done to improve their relationship. In September 1973,

---

*Interestingly, the two-thirds majority requirement does provide the seven management representatives with effective veto power should they wish it.

the chairman of Hydro wrote to the president of the union to suggest
the establishment of a union-management study team. The purpose
of the study was for the two parties to work together to find a "better
way" to conduct their relationship. They were to study such areas
as "relationships, alternatives to a strike, co-operation versus confrontation, size of bargaining agendas, communications to employees,
etc." The union executive agreed to the proposal and further proposed
that all activity in connection with strike discipline be abandoned.
Management agreed, and the Joint Committee on Relationships (JCR)
was established in February 1974.

The JCR is a senior-level committee composed of the union
president and two vice-presidents, the director of Labor Relations,
the manager of Industrial Labor Relations, and two line managers.
Two outside "group leaders" were involved in the early stages to help
establish more open and effective communications. Union and management soon found they were able to handle the process on their own
and discontinued the use of outsiders.

The first meetings of the JCR focused on exploring the reasons
for past conflicts and on discussing problems of issues and relationships involved in the 1972 strike. Once areas of misunderstanding
and misconception were resolved, the committee was able to shift its
attention to current issues and relationships. The goals of the JCR
became to "remove unnecessary conflict, reduce the level of conflict
where it could not be removed, and develop a more workable ongoing
relationship." The first task of the JCR was to consider the general
area of contract administration, with particular emphasis on the
grievance procedure and communications.

The JCR recognized that it was necessary to improve communications at all levels of the organization, especially at the intermediate level, where many of the more important decisions are actually
made. They, therefore, recommended that union-management meetings be held at least twice yearly at the divisional level. These meetings include the union divisional chairperson and chief stewards and
appropriate management representatives, including the director, regional manager, or plant manager. It was agreed that staff of the
Labor Relations division and union staff officials would not attend the
meetings. The JCR encouraged the discussion of a wide range of
topics, including the responsibility and authority of line management,
the role of the union steward, communication with employees by supervisors and stewards, administration of personnel policies, union
policies and procedures, and joint study of some corporate policy
areas of mutual interest. In some plants, local-level meetings are
also held between plant management and the elected union officers,
but this is not an organizationwide policy or practice.

In May 1974, the JCR established a Grievance Review Board,
composed of the three-man executive committee of the union and three

senior Hydro representatives. The board was designed to consider unusual grievances whose resolution could not be justified financially by an expensive arbitration procedure; it is not seen as an alternative to regular arbitration. Each side can veto whether a grievance will be handled by the board. Veto powers were given in order to encourage those handling grievances at lower levels to resolve most disputes themselves.

The current operation of the JCR is fairly unstructured and informal; it administers itself and meets only when necessary. There is no chairperson for the meetings, no set agenda, and no minutes. The JCR meets to review the bargaining process and to design the process for the next round of negotiations. It determines the use of subcommittees and develops a bargaining timetable to provide a framework for more prompt negotiations. Generally, the JCR looks at problems in the bargaining process; it is not a vehicle for continuous bargaining.

BENEFITS AND PROBLEMS

Supreme Aluminum

Although there is no doubt that there are some serious limits with respect to the effective participation of workers at Supreme and that much of the traditional control of management remains in full force, it still cannot be denied that workers do have some real control over issues of importance to them. Relations between labor and management at Supreme are very good. Employee satisfaction is high: 72 percent of the people feel that Supreme is a better place than most to work. Most employees feel that workers and managers are working together toward common goals.

Since 1972 the general management style throughout the company has become more participatory, and the workers have come to believe that it is their right to participate in decisions that affect them. The Governing Body has made several changes to ensure that workers will be treated more fairly, especially with respect to pay and promotions. Many of the worker representatives have become quite effective in helping individual workers to deal with floor-level problems. In addition, several worker and management representatives on the Governing Body have worked hard, with management, to establish and maintain a safer working environment.

In many ways, the actual operation of the Governing Body goes beyond what is formerly specified. The terms of the agreement are usually determined jointly by the labor and management representatives in a smooth manner and to the general satisfaction of both parties. The company has rarely exercised its power to reject the terms

recommended by the Governing Body. Since senior executives of the
company have often publicly stated that decisions of the Governing
Body will be final, it could cause serious problems were they to go
back on their word. In the most major case where they did do so (the
company rejected the Governing Body's 1976 wage decision and re-
opened negotiations so that, in effect, the final decision was made
through negotiations between senior management and the Governing
Body chairperson), it caused considerable outrage among key workers
in the company.

The actual extent of participation on issues not directly covered
by the agreement varies with the nature of the issue and the nature of
the relation between the workers and managers involved. Although
workers can theoretically share in decisions on job assignments and
transfers, changes in the size of the work force, and methods of production, in practice, such decisions are usually made exclusively by
management. It is more common, however, for workers to participate in decisions on such things as operating speeds or immediate
working conditions.

Worker participation, through the Governing Body as a whole
or through individual labor representatives, is greatly affected by the
strength of the affected worker representative(s) and the dominant
management style of the affected manager(s). Some worker representatives have been unwilling or unable to participate effectively, so
that participation in areas covered by them has been low. In contrast,
a few worker representatives have been able to increase the scope and
effectiveness of participation in their areas considerably.

The effect of some individual managers has also been significant. Some people have had great difficulty in changing from an authoritarian to a more participatory management style. The authoritarian style of certain managers has caused problems in the past,
not only for individual representatives but also for the Governing
Body as a whole. Around issues where senior management and the
Governing Body have felt participation to be essential (for example,
individual grievances and changes in immediate working conditions),
considerable pressure has been put on these people to change their
approach. Over the past few years, there have been some very striking changes at Supreme in the styles of several key managers.

In several plants, the plant manager and Governing Body representatives have established regular bimonthly meetings to deal with
plant-level problems. The Governing Body is encouraging this practice, as it would like to see more discussions of problems at the
floor level rather than at the level of the Governing Body.

Giving workers access to joint decision-making procedures,
however, does not automatically mean they will participate effectively
in determining the outcome of the procedures. The workers must

also be willing and able to participate. However, a significant number of both workers and managers at Supreme believe that it is not totally safe to disagree with one's superiors. They fear the repercussions that may come from "getting in your boss's bad books." They also believe the Governing Body cannot ultimately protect people—that management retains enough control to win in the end. Thus, many workers will not run for the Governing Body, and even some of the elected representatives are hesitant to speak their minds freely.

However, even if workers were not afraid to challenge management, most management representatives would still have a decided edge over their nonmanagement counterparts with respect to actual power to influence decisions. Management's power is derived largely from the advantages they have with respect to training and experience. Almost all information is collected, interpreted, and presented by management. Most worker representatives have no access to, or experience with, management-level information. Whereas management representatives have access to, and know how to use, management's full-time trained experts, the workers have no nonmanagement sources of information and expertise. In addition, most workers have little experience with either the semiformal debate procedure common in meetings of the Governing Body or the informal processes of group decision making generally. As a result, many of the discussions of the Governing Body leave some of the worker representatives feeling confused and inadequate, a situation that they often handle by simply deferring to "management expertise."

The above criticisms should not be taken to mean that the Governing Body is totally controlled by management—it is not. Especially in less complex issues that affect them directly (for example, shift bonuses and vacations), many worker representatives are willing and able to participate quite effectively and have had considerable influence over decisions. Several worker representatives have also become highly skilled at handling the decision-making processes of the Governing Body. However, since there is no way at Supreme for an interested and able worker to progress to a more challenging and responsible position and remain a "worker" (for example, through a union), several of their best representatives at Supreme have been "lost" to the workers via promotions into the ranks of management.


Ontario Hydro

The situation between Hydro and the union has improved dramatically since the inception of the JCR. Both parties have overcome original feelings of mistrust and skepticism to develop a more mutually trusting and credible relationship. They have come to respect each other more and to communicate more openly and effectively. These improvements have led to important changes in labor-management relations at Hydro.

In September 1974, the JCR developed two midterm agreements that resolved the contentious issues of employment security and mutual protection, which had been left over from the 1972 strike. In 1975 the number of items on the bargaining agenda was reduced to 90 from a previous high of 270, and negotiations were shortened to three months, compared with the 13-month average of the past three rounds. For the first time, a new agreement was reached before the existing one had expired and without a strike. This pattern of reaching agreements quickly and without work disruptions has continued since 1975.

Union and management firmly believe that both sides still bargain just as hard in negotiations and that the above kinds of changes have been achieved through making the bargaining process more effective. Prior to negotiations, a prebargaining seminar is held, where both parties are provided with a range of information on the bargaining agenda items. In addition, certain issues of a more local nature are no longer taken to the bargaining table, but are handled at the divisional level. This escape from bargaining over issues that are not understood by everyone, plus a great reduction in feelings of personal antagonism, has meant that negotiations have become much less emotionally charged. The parties are now able to find solutions to problems where a common resolve is possible and to channel their energies more efficiently to areas of real conflict.

Both union and management agree that the greatest accomplishment of the JCR has been to work itself out of a job. There is now much less reason for the JCR to meet, and therefore, it does so only infrequently. The relationship between senior union and management people has so improved that they are able to work out most problems on a day-to-day basis. For example, a large layoff in 1979 was handled without any serious difficulties. In addition, many problems that in the past would have gone to the JCR (for example, a change in one plant to 12-hour shifts) are now being handled at the local level. However, both union and management want to preserve the JCR as a permanent structure so that it will be there if and when it is needed. The problem now is to find a way to maintain the mechanism over a period of low use.

The divisional meetings, which are held regularly in most areas, have also been highly successful. Union and management people at the intermediate and local levels have improved their abilities to jointly resolve local issues. An anonymous questionnaire survey done by Hydro in 1978 on the functioning of the divisional meetings showed that most unionists and managers involved felt that the meetings contained important material, were interesting and generally effective, enhanced union-management relations, and should be continued. It is interesting to note that, overall, the views of the union people were more positive than were the views of management. It was also found that relations are significantly related to the frequency of meetings: the greater the number of meetings, the better the reported relations.

Within meetings at all levels at Hydro, the labor representatives are able to participate very effectively. As one outside observer of the JCR commented, "Union and management are both well served by their respective representatives. They all know their business and they aren't afraid to speak their mind."[1] The comment also holds true for the divisional level. Senior union people carefully explained the intended purpose and nature of the divisional meetings to the chief stewards, and almost all union representatives at that level are quite experienced with meetings per se and with discussing issues with management. In addition, whenever necessary, they have access to the research facilities and trained experts of not only their own union but also the labor movement as a whole. Overall, the balance of power in union-management meetings at Hydro is quite even; in fact, in the few cases where one person has tended to dominate at divisional meetings, it is as likely for this person to be a steward as a manager.

One part of the Ontario Hydro system that does not seem to have been very effective is the Grievance Review Board. It has handled only three grievances in its history and has not been used since 1977. There has been no real change in the number of grievances, at all stages, including arbitration, since 1972. The union, however, does not feel this is a problem, since the number of grievances (approximately 70 to 100 per year) does not seem excessive given the size and complexity of the bargaining unit.


CONCLUSION

The above two cases, although different in many ways, do share some important characteristics, benefits, and problems. It is interesting to note that three key aspects of both the Supreme and Hydro cases were also found to be central in a larger study of labor-management committees in Ontario—the importance of communications, the importance of the attitudes of key people, and the overall positive effect of joint committees on labor-management relations.[2]

Communications appears to have a central and two-way relation with labor-management committees. Good communications are necessary in order for committees to work; if committees do work, they generally lead to improved communications. It also appears that the chances for communicating effectively are best where the parties are

open to and respect each other, where there is an atmosphere free of
intimidation, and where appropriate structures are available. Despite tremendous differences in size, the senior-level labor-management committees at both Supreme and Hydro needed to establish additional lower-level structures in order to extend communications
throughout their organizations. In fact, communications problems
between the Governing Body itself and the rest of Supreme are still
seen as important enough that the Governing Body is currently considering hiring someone to deal largely with internal communications.

The importance of the attitudes of key people to the actual operation of participation schemes would indicate the need for some
form of education. The lack of an educational program may not have
been too serious at Hydro because of the more limited scope of the
committee and the greater need for change. At Supreme, however,
a well-planned educational program probably could have helped many
people to adapt to the new approach and may have helped to ease several managers through what was, in fact, a very difficult and often
harsh adjustment.

The committees at both Supreme and Hydro had positive effects
on several aspects of labor-management relations. There is an important difference, however, which is worth noting. At Supreme,
there is a common belief that cooperation is possible because the interests of labor and management are the same. This attitude would
be unacceptable to many people. At Hydro, however, both labor and
management accept that there will always be differences between
them. The JCR and its offshoots are based on the belief that there
exists both areas of mutual interest where cooperation is appropriate
and areas of conflict where confrontation is necessary.

Another important difference between Supreme and Hydro is the
level of effectiveness of the labor representatives on the joint committees. The labor people at Hydro, in general, appear more able
to participate effectively. One reason for the difference is that workers at Hydro have less reason to fear management—they have a strong,
independent union that is well able to protect them. The fears of
some people at Supreme, whether justified or not, underline the importance to any system of worker participation of a system to guarantee employees protection from reprisals for voicing criticism and
of an independent apparatus for the settlement of disputes.

A further reason for the differences between the labor representatives at Supreme and Hydro is the different levels of training and
experience of the two groups. Unions not only provide a wide range
of formal and informal educational opportunities for their elected representatives but also involve them in a variety of progressively more
complex labor-management situations. In a unionized setting, someone would not usually be taken straight off the shop floor with no train-

ing or experience and be put cold into important discussions with senior management. At Supreme, no real attempt has been made to provide the worker representatives with the kinds of training and experience that have been provided by the union at Hydro.

In conclusion, it is interesting to note that despite important differences in the intended extensiveness of the two participation schemes, the mechanisms at Supreme and Hydro both represent fairly limited forms of participation that do not directly involve many people. Although both central labor-management committees found that they could not achieve even fairly narrowly defined goals without some decentralization, neither committee has had any real effect on the amount of worker participation at the level of the job itself. Opportunities for workers to participate in the work situation at the point where it affects them most often and most directly have not really increased in either organization. The above comment, however, is not meant to detract from the significant improvements that have been achieved at both Supreme and Hydro. Only time will tell whether the labor and management people within these organizations will be able to use the mechanisms they have developed to extend the benefits of participation even further.

NOTES

1. D. A. Ondrack, Hydro Supervisor (Toronto), June 1974, p. 1.

2. J. Mansell, R. Wilkinson, A. Musgrave, An Inventory of Innovative Work Arrangements in Ontario (Toronto: Ministry of Labour, September 1978).

# Case 3

## RATIONALES FOR A SCHEME OF WORKER PARTICIPATION AT THE BOARD LEVEL: THE BRITISH EXPERIENCE

### E. Chell

> This case study highlights some of the issues that may
> cause potential problems for worker-directors. The
> findings are based on a sample of seven firms, six
> unionized and one nonunionized, in the private sector
> in the United Kingdom that voluntarily installed a
> scheme of worker representation on company boards.

### PROLOGUE

The focus of this particular case study is the role of the worker-director in the private sector companies of British industry. There are a number of points that first and foremost should be made concerning the developments of worker participation in the United Kingdom over the last few years. This will help put into perspective the reasons why there are so few private sector companies that have worker-directors and, second, why a study has been commissioned by the government to investigate the role, needs, and problems of worker-directors and their relationship to other participative machinery in the same firm.[1]

Worker participation is not a new concept in the United Kingdom; several initiatives have been taken in this direction since the late nineteenth century, in the form of guild socialism, nationalization, joint consultation (following the Whitley committees), and so on.[2] In the mid-1960s, initiatives were taken to examine to what extent worker-directors might be a potential form for the development of industrial democracy in British industry. Consequently, an experiment was set up in the British Steel Corporation—a public sector industry—to have worker-directors on their regional boards, a level

---

This study was conducted by E. Chell, the University of Nottingham, England.

below the main board. This experiment was monitored by a group of researchers.[3] The scheme was developed, and some rather crucial changes were made—for example, the worker-directors were allowed to retain their union membership. A further piece of research was carried out that focused specifically and almost exclusively on the worker-directors themselves, presenting their perspective of their role and problems.[4]

Following this particular development, there were several other events that ensued that tended to narrow the focus from worker participation to the possibility of worker-directors on the boards of private sector British companies of a certain size. There was, for example, some pressure from the EEC for member states to conform to a particular model[5]—the so-called German model of worker-directors sitting on the upper tier of a two-tier board.[6] This particular initiative was not resolved for some time. However, another more localized source of pressure was brought to bear on the government of the day by the TUC.[7] A Committee of Inquiry was commissioned by the government "to advise on questions relating to representation at board level in the private sector."[8] While the committee was sitting, a number of research projects were set up to examine the nature, feasibility, and function of various forms of worker participation as they revealed themselves in actuality. One such project was the Worker Director Project, as it became known.

The Worker Director Project had as its aims to investigate the role, needs, and problems of the worker-directors in those firms that have appointed them to their boards and to investigate the relationship between the worker-director and participative machinery within the same firm.

It is now the objective in the remainder of this case study to focus more narrowly upon the Worker Director Project itself: first, to give information about the firms involved; second, to outline the research methodology; and third, to concentrate on some specific issues, with an overview of some of the findings of the project to date.

## RESEARCH SAMPLE: THE FIRMS INVOLVED

At the present time, the government has not legislated on industrial democracy; therefore, those firms that have taken it upon themselves to install such a system within their particular company have done so of their own volition and for their own particular reasons. The companies concerned, which are thus few and far between (there are seven in the sample), span a wide range of industries, from the heavy engineering side to computers and printing. Moreover, in terms of size of company and organizational structure, the companies again differ. The largest company in the sample has upward of 8,000 employees, while the smaller companies are in the 200 to 500 range.

In order to describe these companies, it is most useful to think in terms of a threefold scheme of classification:

1. There are companies that are highly organized by at least one union, but that typically have multiunion structures, where the domestic union organization has brought a high degree of union penetration among the work force and of commitment to union values and principles both from within the shop steward network and the work force. The unions are thus highly involved in some way, directly or indirectly, in determining the operation and direction of participation within the company.

2. There are companies that are medium to highly unionized (50 to 100 percent membership), but where there is a distinct lack of union organization in the sense of there not being a highly developed shop steward network; neither is there a strong union commitment among the work force or lay representatives. The unions had little or nothing to do with the introduction of a scheme of participation in the companies, and the operation of the scheme, especially that of the worker-director, is not dependent on the involvement of the unions

3. There are companies that have not to date recognized a union for collective bargaining purposes.[9]

There are two companies that fall into category 1, four that fall into category 2, and one that falls into category 3.

RESEARCH METHODOLOGY

Research was carried out by the author in seven private sector companies, all of which had some form of worker-director system. It is pertinent to state here what is meant by a worker-director system. The working definition that has been adopted on the project is that "the companies in question have initiated a scheme whereby at least one subexecutive level employee shall be chosen either by election or by appointment to take up a seat on the main or a subsidiary board of the company."[10] The companies were chosen because they had such a scheme in operation and thus were not randomly selected.

Consistent with the aims of the project, it was decided that the research would be carried out and interviews with the following groups of people would take place.

1. It was decided to ascertain, by interview, from the worker-director what he thought his role, functions, and skills were as

worker-director and to identify the individuals and groups that made up his role set.

2. It was decided to interview the executive and nonexecutive members of the board in each company to ascertain the rationale for setting up a worker-director scheme, to assess their perceptions of the role and functions of directors, and, additionally and most important, to assess their perceptions of the role, function, and necessary skills required of the worker-director.

3. Interviews would also be conducted with members of the role set (there might include branch secretaries of the unions concerned, full-time officials, key members of other participative arrangements within the firm, and any other people who might form the network of persons the worker-director contacted in the course of performing his functions as worker-director).

4. In some companies, where possible and appropriate, an attitude survey of a 10 percent sample of the work force would be carried out with a view to discovering the extent of shop floor knowledge about the worker-director scheme and their attitude toward it.

It is beyond the scope of this case study to present in a coherent fashion all the findings of the project to date; it is therefore thought to be most appropriate to concentrate on certain issues that are most pertinent. These will be (1) the motivation and rationales of companies in installing a worker-director scheme and the implications of this for the worker-director; (2) the relationship of the worker-director to other forms of participation within the company; (3) the extent to which information is disclosed to worker-directors and how structural factors, such as the degree of centralization of the company, the structure of the board, and the location of the worker-directors within the company structure may delimit their ability to be influential as regards policy matters; and (4) the training of worker-directors.

FINDINGS

Insofar as the findings will be examined, I propose to adhere to the threefold classification of the firms and examine each in turn under the four headings listed above.

The Motivations and Rationales of Companies
Installing a Worker-Director Scheme

First of all, it is necessary to explain what is meant by a rationale for a scheme of worker-directors. It was possible to identify three such rationales, which have been labeled the <u>distributive</u>, the

incorporative, and the cosmetic. [11] A distributive orientation to a
worker-director scheme suggests an open attitude toward the scheme
—that is, that employees have a right to influence decision making in
the firm and that the worker-director is merely a mechanism by which
they can get their views heard at senior policy-making levels in the
firm. Moreover, the worker-director himself is a channel of communication from the board room to inform employees in this, a two-
way process of distribution, information, and influence. The incorporative orientation, on the other hand, because those who espouse
this view believe there is only one interest to pursue, that is, the
prosperity of the company, emphasizes a unidirectional flow of information, which is information about employee attitudes and likely
reactions to board policies for the use of the board in making its decisions. Employees may indirectly have an "influence," but it is not
seen as theirs of right, but merely as an adjunct to managerial decision making. The third rationale, the cosmetic, has as its basic
tenet the notion that a scheme of participation has been introduced to
the firm as a public relations exercise; it is thus shallow and without
substance (for any real benefit to accrue to employees).

What is the evidence that the companies in the sample of worker
director firms were differently motivated in initiating the worker-
director scheme, and how might this difference in rationale impinge
upon the role the worker-directors have subsequently to perform?

There are three sources of evidence that may be used to examine
the question of the rationale of the company in installing a worker-
director system. These are (1) Who or which party was responsible
for initiating the scheme?; (2) From the interview data, what was the
attitude of the top executives of the firm to the scheme—and how did
it appear to work out in practice?; and (3) How, if at all, did the level
and activity of the union(s) within the firm affect the operation of the
scheme?

## Highly Organized Firms with Some Union
## Involvement in the Worker-Director Scheme

There are two companies, A and B, that fall into this category.
Both are in heavy male-dominated industries, and both firms were
100 percent unionized. In both cases, the initiative for the scheme
was taken by senior management, although the unions were drawn into
the discussions at an early stage.

In Company A, it was decided that the convenor of shop stewards
should in addition take on the role of worker-director. * Being a man

---

*Convenors are lay officers of the engineering section of the
Amalgamated Union of Engineering Workers (AUEW) and are appointed from among their own number by the shop stewards or shop

who was influential in his union at a national level, as well as within his own firm, there was evidence to suggest that he was both trusted by the Joint Shop Steward Committee (JSSC) and by senior management. * It was clear also from the interview data that the worker-director/convenor reported back regularly to the JSSC and that he was not interested in the confidentiality argument as a reason for withholding information from the work force. There thus appeared to be quite considerable distribution of influence throughout the plant, operating via a single channel of union organization within it.

In Company B, on the other hand, the setup was rather different. Again, the initiation of the scheme came from senior management levels, but very quickly, the unions (it was a large multiunion company) were brought in to discuss the fine details. There had for some time been a full-time official of the union sitting on the board of this particular company, and so what was being offered to the unions was another seat, which could be taken by one of the internal trade unionists, a senior shop steward rather than a shop floor employee. Apart from the obvious problem of which unions should be represented on the board, the JSSC decided against the idea until they were offered 51 percent of the board seats. The scheme, however, went ahead. The first worker-director emerged from within the ranks of the union hierarchy in the firm. He was virtually ostracized from the start, being thrown off various union committees. The second worker-director had a slightly smoother ride, while the unions made it clear that they saw the major thrust of participation in that firm in terms of the three-tier consultation structures that had been developed. At the very top level, the Central Consultative Committee, six senior shop stewards meet six executives of the board to discuss policy-level

---

committee. Their role is formally defined as being synonymous with that of shop stewards and shop committees, generally. In practice, their experience and senior status tend to give them a special role in grievance procedure and in negotiations, especially in federated engineering establishments. The expression convenor is sometimes used to describe a lay officer of another union performing similar functions, but outside the AUEW, the term senior shop steward or some variation of this is usually preferred. (See Marsh and Evans, The Dictionary of Industrial Relations [London: Hutchinson, 1973].)

*JSSCs are committees of shop stewards belonging to different unions within an establishment in the engineering industry. Similar committees of shop stewards exist in other industries, usually by tacit agreement among unions and sometimes with management also. (See Marsh and Evans, The Dictionary of Industrial Relations [London: Hutchinson, 1973].)

issues; here was the source of information disclosure and the point
from which a distribution of information percolated downward to the
shop floor and back through the shop stewards. The middle layer—
the Joint Consultative Committee—consisted of shop stewards representing each union within the company and a handful of managers, including the managing director. The committee tended to be somewhat
unwieldy, as there could be as many as 50 members. The participation thus tended to be dominated by the managing director and convenor. [12] The discussion centered on day-to-day issues that concerned the work force generally, but which were not of a policy nature. At the lowest level, each department would have its own consultative committee, on which members of the department would sit
and discuss local issues of working conditions, day-to-day problems,
and so forth. Interviews with the managing director and the senior
shop steward and convenor separately underlined each other's point
that as far as that particular firm was concerned, the three-tier consultative committees were of prime importance and, in terms of influence, the worker-director scheme was of little consequence.

Highly Unionized Firms with Little or No
Union Involvement in the Worker-Director Scheme

While the rationales of the worker-director scheme of the two
companies in category 1 appear to fall into our definition of a distributive orientation, in category 2 we find the schemes operate rather
differently.

As regards initiation of the schemes, we find that all were initiated by top management. At Company C, for example, the "edict"
came from group level, * and the personnel department set up the system of elections whereby nominees could be elected to sit on the subsidiary boards of the company. The company was a multiplant operation, with small units (less than 100 employees) located in different
sites. The worker-directors were to be elected on a basis of one to
every 50 employees in the plant, and initially, there were 15 nominees. This fell to 12 worker-directors due to three worker-directors
leaving the company or resigning their office. The worker-directors
sat on the local plant boards, which were effectively management
committees, policy being made at group level. The unions in the

---

*This group of companies was organized on the centralization-
of-policy principle. Thus, policy was made by the directors on the
board of the holding company (group level, as it is known) and was
transmitted downward and taken up by the managing directors of each
company within the group.

company were not highly organized and active. Most of the worker-directors had had no experience of holding union office of any sort, and there was no obvious channel for them either to glean information or to distribute information from the board meetings they attended. Moreover, boards met very irregularly, and the impression that some of these worker-directors gave was of a seeming impatience by other board members whenever some of the worker-directors attempted to put forward their or the shop floor point of view. * In terms of the lack of any provision of seats for worker-directors at the group level, where policy-level decisions are made in this company, in terms of the inability of the worker-directors to be influential at the level at which they do operate, it appears that this scheme is largely cosmetic. Whether in its original conception in the minds of the top executives of this firm this outcome was intended is of little consequence to the future of the scheme. What is clear is that in order for the worker-directors to operate effectively and influentially, there needs to be some rather major changes introduced into the scheme.

In Company D—a medium-sized multiplant engineering concern—there was one worker-director. Here, senior management not only initiated the scheme, they also nominated and finally chose which shop floor employee should become the company's worker-director. Interviews with members of the board revealed that the worker-director was expected to keep in confidence most of the sensitive issues that were discussed on the upper tier of the two-tier board that the company had instigated coincident with the worker-director scheme. The role of the worker-director in this company was thus to bring a shop floor point of view to the board room in order to help management in policy formation. There appeared to be no way in which it could be seen as a distribution of influence of the shop floor. Moreover, the worker-director himself was in a sense isolated; the unions were not interested in the scheme and, therefore, to all intents and purposes, ignored its existence, while the worker-director himself was not an active member of the union. Thus, if the worker-director had wanted to report back (if he had seen himself as having a responsibility to a constituency of shop floor employees), there was no vehicle through which he could operate. On the other hand, as he was not elected by the employees or the unions, then it was quite consis-

---

*For example, one worker-director graphically described an occasion when toward the end of a board meeting, at the point of "any other business, " he started to put forward the items he had been saving for the duration of that meeting when one board member started to put on his coat.

tent with this scheme that he should have a narrow view of his role, which did not include a reporting back function. In terms of the degree of influence the worker–director appeared to have, and of its narrow focus, the objective would appear to be cosmetic; however, it could, and probably would, be claimed by its initiators to have an incorporative rationale.

The next two companies included in this category were different from the previous two, as they were companies where the worker–director scheme was of much longer standing and certainly predated the recent debate concerning worker–directors described in the prologue. Both schemes were initiated by the senior executive and managing director of the company as an act of paternal benevolence.

In Company E, over 40 years ago, the then-managing director set up a trust on behalf of the employees of the company; along with this was organized the Company E Society. This was a social and welfare society whose aim was to look after the interests, welfare, and well-being of all members of the company. The Company E Society has a president, secretary, treasurer, and a constitution. It was felt appropriate that the president of this society should sit on the board. At the time when the scheme was initiated, the company was not unionized. However, in the last decade, with the advent of two unions, there have been some interesting developments. The unions saw the society as a body encroaching on their prerogatives: the right to negotiate wages and conditions on behalf of their members. There ensued an interparty dispute between the society and the unions, with the unions gaining ground steadily. While the level of unionization in this company is about 60 percent, the unions argue that the society is no longer representative of all employee interests and that it (the union) is better equipped to carry out that task. Despite this restriction of the society's functions, the president continues to attend board meetings. His function is seen by him and by the board as that of a communicator of the employees' point of view to the board to enable it to make better decisions; insofar as this is the case, the scheme appears to be incorporative in its rationale.

Finally in this section is Company F, a medium-sized printing firm that also has financial participation as part of the totality of its worker–director scheme. Here, the company has for some 20 years or more operated a savings scheme. From their savings, employees can buy shares in the company. Only those employees who have £100 worth of shares are eligible for the position of worker–director.

As is the case in most printing firms in the United Kingdom, the level of unionization is 100 percent. However, the relationship between the worker–director and the union is minimal. The senior union officials in the firm do not appear to agree with the principles underlying the scheme and see participation for them in the form of the traditional collective bargaining mode (and that other issues be resolved through the Works Council). The worker-director himself is not seen as having, nor could he have, a constituency under the terms of his appointment, and therefore, any information or opinion that goes to the board must necessarily be his own. At best, this scheme can be seen as being incorporative in nature; in terms of the ineffectiveness of the worker-director, it may be termed cosmetic.

## Nonunionized Companies and the Worker-Director Scheme

The last of the companies in the sample, Company G, is a medium-sized company that does not recognize a union for any purposes, negotiation or otherwise; there are thus no shop stewards. The scheme, again initiated by the chief executive of the company, has been in operation for four to five years. There were to be two worker-directors, elected from all the employees of the company in a ballot organized by the Personnel department. The term of appointment would be one year, and each worker-director would overlap the term of the other by six months. The board was to be split into a two-tier board, with a small top executive board, which had policy-making powers, and a second board, made up of managing directors and heads of departments, and upon which the worker-directors would sit. This second board would be executive in function. There appeared to be a lack of clear conception on the part of the top executives as to what the worker-director scheme was supposed to achieve, and this certainly did not help the worker-directors. They were expected to keep sensitive information in confidence, although there was no channel through which they could report back to their constituency, which was the company as a whole. From our interview data, it appeared that the worker-directors were ineffective and lacked influence, mainly because of the deficiencies in the scheme than through any fault of their own. Although the scheme may have been initially conceived as an attempt to improve managerial decision making, in practice, there was little evidence of such worker-director influence, and it thus appears rather more cosmetic in its actual function.

## Worker-Directors and Their Relationship to Other Forms of Participation in the Firm

A further way of conceiving of the rationales for worker-director schemes is to ask oneself the question, What are the limiting/determining factors weighing upon the effectiveness of the worker-director scheme? The fact that the rationale for such a scheme is conceived by management, initiated by management, and put into operation by management has had apparent effects for the functioning of such a scheme in practice. However, that conception and the ensuing event (the "becoming" of the worker-director scheme) occurs at $t_0$ (time zero). It is thus merely one factor that necessarily has an effect upon the scheme itself, but which in itself is not sufficient to determine the future operability of that scheme. In the next few sections, I am therefore going to examine briefly other factors that contribute to the ongoing effectiveness or otherwise of the schemes. The data again will be drawn from interviews carried out in the firms concerned; no attempt will be made at this stage to quantify such data, and to that extent it may be regarded as "soft." In terms of the broad brush strokes of such research, however, these kind of data are important insofar as they give a qualitative feel for the kind of interaction that is going on in such organizations—a picture that could not be sufficiently well-drawn by numbers alone.

In terms of the effectiveness of the worker-director's role, it is clear that in order for him to function effectively (that is, to perform minimal necessary functions, such as reporting back to a constituency of some sort), there should be some mechanism whereby he can do this.[13] The issue concerning the relationship of the worker-director to other forms of participation within the firm is thus crucial and one that, because of the scope of this chapter, may only be sketched.

### Highly Organized Firms with Some Union Involvement in the Worker-Director Scheme

It may be recalled from the above section that the worker-director schemes operated rather differently in the two companies included in this category. In Company A, the worker-director/convenor worked very closely with the JSSC and also negotiated in collective bargaining situations concerning pay and conditions on behalf of his union. The wearing of two hats in this particular instance did not apparently create problems for this particular individual. One can only assume that because of his standing in the union at national levels, with his own shop steward committee, and with the board that he was able to overcome any potential problems.

By way of contrast, in Company B, every attempt was made initially by the unions concerned to divorce the worker-director from the other forms of participation. Now that the unions are assured that the three-tier structure of consultation is established and works for them, they do not appear to mind that the second worker-director to be elected sits on the upper two tiers of the consultative structure. However, they regard his influence as negligible, and therefore, one is led to believe that this in effect is what makes his presence acceptable.

## Highly Unionized Firms with Little or No
## Union Involvement in the Worker-Director Scheme

In the companies that fall under this heading, the extent to which the worker-director was involved with other forms of participation in the firm was minimal. The unions concerned had, principally on ideological grounds, decided to wash their hands of the worker-director system. The two forms of participation thus functioned separately—the worker-director posing no threat to the unions, except in the case of Company E. In the latter company, the unions, being second on the scene, challenged the already existent system of participation, and interparty conflict ensued. How long the two parties can coexist is impossible to predict; certainly, however, the unions will not be too happy until the Company E Society has disappeared.

## Nonunionized Companies and the
## Worker-Director Scheme

In the only company representative of this category, there was in fact no other participative machinery for the worker-directors to lock into. The absence of a union to organize employees meant that there was no collective bargaining machinery, a joint shop steward committee, or even a works council. The worker-directors were thus without support of any organized kind from below.

In other words, in few of these companies has one criterion of effectiveness of the worker-director scheme been met. In only a couple of cases was there any supportive interaction between the worker-director and a subordinate participative structure. In the majority of cases, therefore, the worker-director was left to operate in vacuo, with his sole lifeline of communication being left to the remaining source of interaction at an individual level with his peers in a localized part of the plant. This could not bode well for his image vis-à-vis the work force at large or for his influential functioning within the decision-making hierarchy of the organization.

## Disclosure of Information

The extent to which information is disclosed to worker representatives and their freedom and ability to use that information for union purposes are two aspects of the one issue that are contentious and unresolved. Certainly, one important factor that seems to be forgotten is not, surely, the quantity of information that is disclosed but its quality—how it is presented and whether or not it is usable. [14] On the other hand, from the shop floor representative's point of view, it is also a matter of what his needs are and whether or not he is capable of using the information once he has received it.[15] Additionally, factors such as organizational structure[16] and the role and function of the board within the company[17] are other broad parameters that have a bearing on the type of information disclosed and the extent to which the worker-director might be influential at the higher echelons of the organization.

### Highly Organized Firms with Some Union Involvement in the Worker-Director Scheme

In line with previous research findings quoted above, the companies within this category could not be faulted for the extensiveness of their disclosure of information to the worker-directors concerned: it appeared to be very high. Moreover, in terms of the worker-directors' abilities to handle such information, in Company A, the worker-director was used to handling financial information by virtue of the other position he held on the National Executive Committee of his union, while in Company B, the ex-worker-director, who was involved in local government, was familiar in the handling of complex committee papers. The problem was, in Company A, the extent to which policy-level decisions were actually made at board level and, in Company B, the limited use that the worker-director could make of the information once he had acquired it. In both cases, the question of the locus of power of decision making at the highest levels and of power invested in the worker-director to use that information were crucial and yet not seen to be met.

### Highly Unionized Firms with Little or No Union Involvement in the Worker-Director Scheme

In terms of organizational structure, the setup at Companies C and E was one of a holding company board, where all top-level policy decisions were made, and subsidiary company boards, where management decisions were made or proposals formed to be pushed upward for sanctioning. Even if the locus of decision making were not at top board level, the worker-directors themselves are divested of any power to influence decision making at this level.[18] The decisions upon which they could have any impact are of a day-to-day variety for the most part; the planning horizons the worker-director is thus expected to think in terms of are of a shorter term than of the top-level directors within the company.

In Company C, by way of contrast, the role and function of the board was the operative factor, determining in part the degree of influence of the worker-director. The board of this company was split board was the operative factor, determining in part the degree of influence of the worker-director. The board of this company was split into a two-tier board, after the German model of supervisory (policy-making) and management (executive decision-taking) board structure.[19] The worker-director was thus placed on the supervisory board, but the question of locus of power then becomes one critical criterion of worker-director effectiveness.[20]

Finally, within this category, Company F was a medium-sized family business. Here, several members of the board were members of the family, three were top executives of the company, and all were major shareholders. Not all top decisions or the formulations of proposals for sanctioning by the board took place within the boundaries of the board room. A high degree of interaction took place along the corridor where most of the executive board members had their offices, from which the worker-director was duly divorced. Certainly, this appears to be one of the clearest cases of a situation whereby the locus of decision making was not principally or in practice within the board room.

### Nonunionized Companies and the Worker-Director Scheme

Company G had several overseas subsidiaries and sales offices in many parts of the United Kingdom.* In terms of the board structure, it was suggested that with the advent of worker-directors, the board should be split. The main top executive board should remain the same and have as its function policy-level decision making, while at a lower tier, a management "board" should be created on which the two worker-directors should sit. Apart from any other frustrations that these worker-directors might have felt, there was no way in which they could influence or change company policy.

### Training

The conception of the role of worker-director by various groups within the organization in question has a bearing upon the perceptions of those individuals as to how he might operate and what skills and abilities he might need in order to operate at the desired level. The arguments for or against the training of worker-directors within the same enterprise may thus be convoluted and contradictory, and it may be only when one takes into account a broader framework within which the individual or group is ordering its perceptions that any conclusions can be drawn. It is beyond the scope of this case study to go into these

---

*Company G has recently been taken over by a U.S.-based firm.

broader perspectives in detail or to put forward alternative proposals. However, the following will attempt to sketch briefly what in fact were the principal attitudes of worker-directors themselves to training and whether they had received any training for the job.

### Highly Unionized Firms with Some Union Involvement in the Worker-Director Scheme

The worker-director in Company A felt that his wealth of union experience was sufficient training—and in this particular instance, he may have been right. However, in Company B, despite the experience of the worker-directors concerned, they still felt a grounding in some of the business studies-type subjects would have been useful.

### Highly Unionized Firms with Little or No Union Involvement in the Worker-Director Scheme

In Company C, the worker-directors felt a great need to understand more about what was presented to them in board meetings. They felt the need to acquire some of the most basic skills in order that they might on some issues be able to counter some of management's arguments and put forward an alternative case. In Companies D and E, the worker-directors had received some training, and they had apparently gained some self-confidence as a result of it, but because they accepted the, at best, incorporative rationale of the scheme (as it presumably must have been perceived by them) and the unitary view of the firm, they were merely concerned to be able to follow board room business and did not see it as part of their role to challenge management.

### Nonunionized Companies and the Worker-Director Scheme

Finally, the worker-directors of Company G all felt that some training was essential; however, the extent to which these worker-directors might want to use that knowledge might well be limited by management attitudes, lack of any support from an alternative body (such as a union), and, generally, because of the heavily weighted structure of the scheme in management's favor.

## CONCLUSION

It is not possible in a case study of this length to include all the data that one would ideally wish. However, it has been the objective of this particular case study, consistent with the theme of the book as a whole, to highlight some of the issues that may cause potential problems for worker-directors and, from a sample of British private sector firms, to describe the worker-director scheme in each company and show how the factors selected appeared to operate upon the worker-director scheme as a whole.

As the government has not as yet legislated in the area of industrial democracy, few private sector companies in the United Kingdom have taken it upon themselves to initiate such schemes. The handful of firms that have are thus very different in size and structure, and they represent a range of industries. In terms of organizing the research findings into a more coherent whole, a scheme of categorization of the firms was used. It could then be seen that in fact the behavior of worker-director firms in each category differed as a result seemingly of the constraints and factors which were in operation. For example, the relative strength of unionism in the firm was a factor that appeared to influence the degree of involvement of the union in worker participation in the firm and the extent to which the worker-director could be a success or failure.

Other factors also appeared crucial. The orientation of management to, and its rationale for, the scheme of worker-directors tended to shape how the scheme was seen and how it operated in practice. Thus, where a distributive rationale was held, there was a two-way dissemination of information within the company; the incorporative rationale, on the other hand, meant that information tended to be seen as for the benefit of senior management and the company as a whole, rather than to extend the boundaries of shop floor participation. A cosmetic orientation tended to occur where the worker-director was cut off from all channels of effective communication and influence, consciously or otherwise. The idea of the worker-director then became symbolic in name only; in practice, it was ineffectual.

Other issues were cited to demonstrate how the role of the worker-director could be affected. For example, the lack of any support from some other participative body—of the inability to lock into such a body—tended to isolate the worker-director, with inefficacy being the net result. Finally, and closely linked together, were the issues of information disclosure and training. It was discovered that the issue in most of the companies was not so much the lack of information disclosure, but the organizational constraints, that is, the structure of the board, which imposed severe limitations upon the power of the worker-director and on his ability to use that information. A lack of power of worker-directors and of their expertise in handling company information were again the major factors observed.

Many other countries of Europe have already legislated for worker participation.[21] There is some evidence to show that these countries have not completely resolved the problems that surround the notion of worker participation at the board level.[22] The United Kingdom is in a position now to learn from the experience of others, both internationally[23] and from "experiments" that have been carried out within its own national boundaries.[24] It is hoped that its future legislation will be based on informed opinion as to what structures will lend themselves to effective and meaningful forms of worker participation. Eventually, however, it is up to the actors themselves and the parties concerned to make worker participation work.

NOTES

1. See Department of Employment Manpower Services Commission Research 1976-77 (London: HMSO, 1977).

2. Derek C. Jones, "Worker Participation in Management in Britain: Evaluation of Current Developments and Prospects," in Worker Self-Management in Industry: The West European Experience, ed. G. David Garson (New York: Praeger, 1977).

3. Peter Brannen, Eric Batstone, Derek Fatchett, and Philip White, The Worker Directors: A Sociology of Participation (London: Hutchinson, 1976).

4. John Bank and Ken Jones, Worker Directors Speak (London: Gower Press, 1977).

5. European Economic Community, Proposed Statute for the European Company (Brussels: 1970); and idem, Commission of the European Communities, Employee Participation and Company Structures in the European Community, Bulletin of the EEC, supp. 8/75 (Brussels, 1975).

6. See G. David Garson, "The Co-Determination Model of Workers' Participation: Where Is It Leading?," Sloan Management Review 18 (1977): 63-78; Arndt Sorge, "The Evolution of Industrial Democracy in the Countries of the European Community," British Journal of Industrial Relations 14 (1976): 274-94; Adrian Dicks, "The New Shape of Worker Participation in Germany," Financial Times, July 3, 1978; and E. Chell, "Report on Worker Participation: The State of the Art," Introduction to a bibliography of worker participation (Aberystwyth: ERIS, 1979).

7. Trade Union Congress, Industrial Democracy, Statement of policy endorsed by 1974 TUC, rev. ed. (London, 1977).

8. United Kingdom, Parliamentary Papers, "Report of the Committee of Inquiry on Industrial Democracy (Chairman Lord Bullock), Cmnd. 6706, January 1977.

9. E. Chell and D. Cox, "Worker Directors and Their Relationship with Collective Bargaining Machinery and Shop Stewards in Seven Private Sector Companies," Industrial Relations Journal, vol. 10 (Summer 1979).

10. Ibid.; see also E. Chell, D. Cox, and B. Towers, "Industrial Democracy in the UK: The Worker Director Project Described," mimeographed (Nottingham: University of Nottingham, Department of Adult Education, 1977).

11. E. Chell, "Worker Participation: Some Problems Facing the Worker Director," Industrial Society, March 1979.

12. See also E. Chell, "Organisational Factors and Participation in Committees," British Journal of Clinical & Social Psychology, in press; and idem, "Participation in Joint Consultative Committees" (Ph.D. diss., University of Nottingham, October 1977).

13. See E. Batstone, "Industrial Democracy and Worker Representation at Board Level: A Review of the European Experience," in Industrial Democracy—European Experience (London: HMSO, 1976); and United Kingdom, Parliamentary Papers.

14. Trade Union Research Unit, Trade Unions and Their Use of Company Information, Interim reports, June 1-5, 1977 (Oxford: Ruskin College, TURU, 1977).

15. Ibid.

16. Brannen, Batstone, Fatchett, and White, Worker Directors.

17. Batstone, "Industrial Democracy."

18. Brannen, Batstone, Fatchett, and White, Worker Directors.

19. G. David Garson, Worker Self Management in Industry (New York: Praeger, 1977).

20. Brannen, Batstone, Fatchett, and White, Worker Directors.

21. Batstone, "Industrial Democracy."

22. Ibid.

23. Industrial Democracy in Europe, International Research Group, "Industrial Democracy in Europe (IDE): An International Comparative Study," Social Science Information 15: 177-203.

24. See R. Oakeshott, The Case for Worker Cooperatives (London: Routledge & Kegan Paul, 1978).

# Case 4

## EFFECTIVENESS OF WORKS COUNCILS IN THE NETHERLANDS

### Ben Hovels and Peter Nas

This study examines the structure and actual functioning
of works councils in the Netherlands in an attempt to assess their effectiveness as a form of worker participation. A sample of 90 works councils at the plant level
and 19 central works councils at the enterprise level
were chosen for this study.

WORKS COUNCILS: THE LEGAL FRAMEWORK

Before examining some results of research among 100 works
councils in the Netherlands,[1] a brief outline is given of the development of the legal framework within which the country's works councils
function. The works council in the Netherlands is a legally regulated
organ of worker participation in management. A characteristic of
industrial relations at the enterprise level is that they have been established, in the main, via legal channels. The unions have played a
considerable role in the framing of laws with regard to works councils
(but they have held fast to the regulation of working conditions by
means of collective bargaining and not through works councils). It is
only in the past ten years that an effort has been made within firms
to build up a union organization (comparable, for instance, with the
déléques du personnel in France). Before the first law relating to
works councils in 1950, there already existed a modest number of
factory committees that represented the employees in joint consultation with management. These committees frequently enjoyed the support of the management as a means of promoting peaceful labor relations. Idealistic considerations, the accentuation of the business as

---

This study was conducted by Ben Hovels and Peter Nas of the
Catholic University of Nijmegen, the Netherlands.

a community, and a desire to curb the influence of the unions within the enterprise all played a role in this.

The first law relating to works councils (1950) came entirely within the scope of the prevailing collaboration between employers and employees.[2] The works council constituted an organ of the business enterprise intended to serve the interests of the firm as a whole. Elected members (members chosen from among and by the employees) had no powers of their own, as contrasted with the chairperson of the works council (a member of the management appointed by management). There was, in principle, no room for promotion of the employees' interests. The works council existed chiefly as a channel of communication.

The second law (1971) offered greater possibilities because other changes in the law relating to enterprise occurred at the same time. For instance, the appointment of a board of directors superior to the chief executive was henceforth mandatory for large enterprises. An obligatory requirement for the appointment of all members of such boards was the agreement of both the shareholders' board and of the works council. The works council remained a body whose aim was to ensure proper functioning of the business enterprise toward all its objectives. This requires not only consultation with but also representation of the work force. Thus, one is brought to a recognition of the dual character of works councils, that is, not only to enable consultation focused on the interests of the enterprise but also to ensure the possibility that the worker representatives should advance specific worker interests within this consultation. The position of elected members was strengthened: they now had the right, during working hours, to consult both together and with third parties without the presence of a management representative and to invite their own experts. The powers of the works council have been similarly reinforced. There is a right of veto with regard to a number of internal social directives; the right to advise upon policy relating to personnel and upon a number of management decisions affecting, notably, working conditions; and the right to information on the current position of the enterprise (especially in relation to matters arising from annual reports of the company and to questions of staff policy).

The present research is concerned with works councils as they operated during the 1972-75 period, that is, under the regulations of the law enacted in 1971.

Rather more light is cast upon the limited significance of these regulations by consideration of new proposals (put forward in 1976 and 1978, but not yet given legal force by the legislature). These proposals take a cautious step toward increased independence for works councils as the worker representatives. The works council would consist only of employee members. The objective, however, would continue to be consultation with the management, and works councils would only be able to exercise their powers after prescribed consultative meetings with higher management. The powers of the works councils would be expanded: management, for instance, would be obliged to justify any eventual deviation from advice put forward by the works council (which could, if necessary, appeal to a judge to decide whether the executive had carefully weighed the various interests involved). The works council would have deciding or, more accurately, veto rights with regard to policies involving personnel. There remains, however, a general hesitation whether to afford the works council more than advisory powers with regard to typical strategic management decisions. The unions are apprehensive of workers taking responsibility for management; employers fear an attack on their prerogatives. Both parties are, on different grounds, reluctant to grant more authority to councils. Employers insist on the works council being an instrument for consultation within the existing organization and power relation of the firm; the main trend among unions is to recognize this dependent position of the council and to evaluate this position as "too weak for self-management" and "not enough under union control."

OBJECTIVE

The objective of our study was to acquire systematic, empirical information concerning the actual structuring and functioning of works councils, to identify different types of works councils, and to look for relevant explanatory variables at the enterprise level. Such an empirical supplement was deemed desirable to round out various theoretical and political speculations posited by some opinion researchers and found in a number of case studies. With the aim of attaining our objective, an attempt has been made to collect data from a large variety of enterprise and works councils; 90 works councils and 19 central works councils cooperated in all its phases.* We were concerned with councils from different branches of industry: five industrial sectors (metal, food, textile, printing, and chemical), building, commerce, banking, and insurance. The nonprofit sector was not included. These works councils do not constitute a representative sample of all works councils in the Netherlands, but they do offer a

---

*Central works councils exist in enterprises with several establishments or affiliates and operate on the level of the enterprise. Their members are appointed from and by the members of the works councils of the several establishments.

picture of the important variations among the 1,343 works councils that existed in 1973 in the sectors mentioned.

The focus of this research is on works councils as a form of participatory democracy,[3] as expressed in the structure and working methods of the councils. These are reflected in the procedures of joint consultation, the degree of autonomy of worker representatives vis-à-vis the management, the degree of its acceptance by management, and, in essence, the possibilities of influencing managerial decisions. The main question with regard to participation is, To what extent do elected worker representatives as such manage to formulate their own issues and demands and ensure discussion of them? If so, it may emerge that they can enlarge top management's definition of the situation by putting forward supplementary worker viewpoints. This constitutes an essential first step in a more democratic management of the enterprise. Thus, the emphasis comes to be on the independence of elected members, as worker representatives, vis-à-vis the executive. This can lead to the identification by elected members of subjects that in their opinion should or should not be discussed in the works council, to the clarification of their viewpoints with regard to subjects discussed, and to their possible influence on conclusions reached in works council meetings.

RESEARCH METHODOLOGY

Information regarding the works councils in question was obtained in various ways. Use was made of a content analysis of the minutes of works council meetings (over a period of a year); of oral interviews (in each case with four elected members, the chairperson, the secretary—two-thirds of whom are elected members—a personnel official, and, where present, a representative of the unions at enterprise level); and of questionnaires (to be filled in for each works council by the secretary, the chairperson, and the personnel official).

Information was gathered on the following aspects of each works council.

1. The domain a works council covers: this includes subjects that (according to minutes) are discussed in its meetings, as well as those that are not; the latter appear from comparison between councils' minutes and from interview questions on failures to reach agenda status. Issues are ordered into spheres of action: financial-economic policy, internal organization, personnel management, and working conditions (including conditions of employment). In this order, issues range from strategic to peripheral importance for the firm and from less to easily accessible for workers. A works council

demonstrates less participation in management when it does not cover strategic spheres.

2. The methods used by the works council in dealing with subjects: this includes processes of drawing up the agenda of the meetings and, especially, the control by elected members of the domain they wish to cover. The management on its own will be able and willing to maintain control by preventing the discussion of annoying issues that threaten their prerogatives or that might stir labor disputes. Also included are the processes of discussion at council meetings; this subject was discussed in interviews. Four subjects from different spheres for each particular works council, identified as relatively important by prior analysis of minutes, were examined. What level of decision making does the council reach? Do elected members develop their own points of view, and do parties frankly discuss possible differences of opinion? To what effect are conclusions reached in favor of worker representative views?

3. The works council as an institution: this includes relationships among elected members and with the rank and file (Do they form a representative body instead of merely being a number of individuals?); relationships between elected members and the chairperson as representative of top management; composition; facilities; and so forth. To what extent is the works council structured in fact as a political organ for participation by labor in management?

4. Various characteristics of the firm, its management, and labor force, the history and structure of industrial relations: these condition the needs and opportunities of both parties for joint consultation.


## MAIN TYPES OF WORKS COUNCILS

A considerable diversity appears to exist among works councils. The differences are too great to allow one to sketch "the typical Dutch works council." Four main types are outlined; they are primarily identified by the nature of the relationship between the elected members and the chairperson and other institutional characteristics. Differences in working methods, especially processes of discussion in meetings, go along with these structural types.

The first type of works council, a fifth of those researched, leads a marginal existence. Such councils do not satisfy the minimum requirements for joint consultation. They meet only the minimum six times per year laid down by law. The elected members show scarcely any solidarity as a party, making little or no use of their right to prior consultation together. In the definition of worker participation in management, one of the principal questions is the nature of the relations between management and worker representatives. Within these marginal works councils, however, there is scarcely any question of a relationship between the two parties, let alone the possibility of inquiring into its nature. Elected members do not initiate any activities as a group vis-à-vis the chairperson; when they do act, they act as individuals. Elected members maintain little contact on works council affairs with the workers they are supposed to represent; in fact, the relationship with other employees is so tenuous that elected members do not even know to what extent their position in council meetings differs from opinions of their coworkers. Accordingly, top management hardly takes the works council seriously as a discussion partner. It either ignores the elected members or, from time to time, feeds them a few scraps of information during the council meetings, which are, in any case, held fairly infrequently. At best, these works councils constitute channels of communication, though even then of strictly limited scope. When a works council leads a marginal existence, neither the elected members nor the chairperson see much reason to exert themselves. As long as elected members do not combine to form a party, there is no need for the management to strive for more intensive consultation. As long as the chairperson ignores the works council, the elected members have little opportunity and/or see little reason to act purposefully as a group.

The other councils exhibit a stronger relationship between worker representatives and top management. The procedure for determining the agenda of the council appears to be a crucial indicator for this relationship and for the functioning of the works council. There is, on the one hand, the question whether elected members and top management consult together about agenda composition and, on the other hand, whether elected members as a group—that is, independently of the management—discuss the agenda of works council meetings. In the latter case, elected members themselves decide what problems ought to be or ought not to be debated in the council, and in this respect, they participate independently in the joint consultation. A discussion between management and one or more of the thus prepared elected members about the agenda before the works council meeting can have different meanings. At least, it indicates the desire of management to prepare seriously for the meeting, even if only by preventing elected members from slipping embarrassing questions into the agenda.

The second type of works council (constituting one-fifth of those researched) forms an organ of the management of the enterprise. As far as joint consultation is concerned, these councils are comparable with the first type of works councils (those leading a marginal existence). We are concerned here with councils where the agenda for the meeting is drawn up by the management. Elected members do not consult each other about matters to be placed on it. The chairperson occupies a predominant position when it comes to deciding upon the scope of the councils' business; the elected members do not protect their own sphere of operations.

Despite the fact that the chairperson quite frequently provides prior information concerning the subjects to be discussed, elected members do not make use of this opportunity to develop their own standpoint before the meetings. Consultation between elected members and contacts with their constituents are very poorly developed. Elected members evidently do not seek opportunities to acquire information of their own and to reflect critically on the information provided by the top management.

The works councils in question can be typified, on the one hand, as "downward communication" and, on the other hand, as "comment offering." When this latter is the case, that is, when members offer their own comments upon a subject—introduced by the chairperson—such opinions are often not unanimously held by the elected members. Here, too, the isolation of elected members, both from their grass roots and from each other, plays its role.

The remarkable fact is that such a large proportion of the central works councils researched belong to the type described above. Representatives from the various establishments or branches listen to what the chairperson has to say, then hurry back home, each to his or her own affairs, without any effort to advance the communal interests of workers in the different divisions of the concern. In view of all this, we seem justified in typifying these works councils as organs of management. In the absence of any coordinated action on the part of elected members, the management defines what problems are to be discussed and the terms on which this "discussion" takes place. Accordingly, there is a low degree of worker participation in management in these councils.

A third type of works council (a sixth of those researched) can be termed an organ of the employee representatives. Elected members draw up their own (draft) agenda, without any prior consultation with the management. The chairperson waits to see what items emerge on the agenda drawn up by the elected members, but he himself proposes his own agenda points during works council meetings, when legally required to do so. He frequently restricts himself to mentioning these only for information—and not for discussion. Moreover, sometimes he refuses to discuss points placed on the agenda by elected works council members. It is characteristic of these councils that the two parties—often well prepared—effectively oppose each other as parties. On the part of management, however, the strategy often is to ignore and to avoid the works council; despite the best efforts of the elected members, they are not respected as a party. One weapon available to, and indeed used by, the management is the withholding of relevant information, certainly on strategic issues. Elected members can thus achieve very little by way of result in the council meetings.

A fourth type of works council (fully 40 percent of the works councils and 60 percent of the central works councils) forms organs of consultation. In these, elected members discuss the agenda with each other, but at the same time, points for the agenda are talked over with the management in, for example, an agenda committee. It is in these categories that one must look for the works councils that most closely meet the criteria for joint consultation that we have specified.

In many of these councils, elected members adopt a position independent of that of the chairperson. This finds expression both inside and outside works council meetings. There is frequent preliminary discussion between elected members; their differences of opinion with the chairperson are expressed as such in meetings. Thus, we can really speak here of joint consultation: elected members define their own standpoints on management decisions, and the possible conflict between these and the viewpoint of the top management is openly discussed.

The attitude of elected members is a factor in persuading the chairperson to take the council seriously. He even tries to gain the cooperation of elected members by, for example, providing them with sufficient information before meetings and by giving them scope to participate in the decision-making process. The reaction of elected members to the possibilities offered them by the chairperson differs. In a number of these councils, they operate with striking caution: especially on strategic questions relating to economic policy problems, they do not always make use of the opportunities the chairperson affords them to contribute their own suggestion and advice. Helping to decide on matters relating to investment, product-market combinations, and so forth is evidently beyond them. One reason for this may be that they are unwilling to share responsibility for decisions on matters over which they feel they do not have sufficient insight and control. In matters relating to internal social policies of the enterprise, elected members feel more competent, and they then seek for a high degree of participation in decision making. Generally speaking, the group of works councils under discussion may be typified as one in which business gets done by interaction between the chairperson and the elected members. The manner in which this is achieved varies. On some occasions, a tactical compromise is reached, whereby elected members refrain from airing their differences with the chairperson on a number of points in order to be able to achieve results on others. On other occasions, results are obtained through negotiation.

The procedures followed in drawing up the agenda appear to constitute an important indication of the nature of the works council and its joint consultation. The distinctions between these types of works councils show a few lines of prime importance. Joint consultation requires a relationship between two parties: on the part of worker representatives, their formation as a group that has the courage to develop and to put forward views of their own vis-à-vis the chairperson; on the part of the management representative, the willingness to accept such an independent stand of worker representatives.

The question then is raised which party is more influential with regard to the development of the works council and its participation in decision making. The research suggests the dominance of the chairperson in this respect, as well as in the effects of the works councils' activities.

## SOME EXPLANATORY CONDITIONS

### Activities of Parties in the Works Council

A direct corollary is to be found in the activities of each party. In nonactive councils (marginally existent or organ of the management), elected members hardly ever convene before council meetings; they do not develop a common stand vis-à-vis the chairperson. The other councils display, in contrast, frequent consultations among elected members, and within specific subgroups (for example, the members of one union), they do demand adjournment at council meetings in order to adapt their common stand to new information supplied by the chairperson. In works councils that are organs of elected members or organs for joint consultation, elected members act as a group—a party vis-à-vis the chairperson. Often related to the latter position is an active relationship between worker representatives and the rank and file, their constituency.

The chairperson also can act as a representative of the management (the board, his fellow directors, and higher line and staff managers). If so, the management takes the works council as a party that is to be taken into account, either because of its possible interference with management or because of the accepted idea of joint consultation.

### Relationships between Elected Members and Rank and File

As indicated, stronger relationships exist between elected members and the workers they represent in those works councils where in their dealings with the chairperson, they function as a group and promote common value orientations. It appears also that this closer relationship with other workers increases their chance of being accepted by management as partners in joint consultation.

Trivial as it may sound, this is a remarkable datum for works councils in the Netherlands. Apart from the periodic election of members, legal regulations give no guidelines concerning relationships with the workers represented. In each firm, elected members can decide for themselves whether or not to build up a relationship within which they may justify their actions to their electorate, gather information concerning issues to be discussed and standpoints to be adopted, and mobilize active support for their approach to management. In only 40 percent of the works councils did elected members report more than occasional contact about topics concerning the council with a group of workers or with workers as spokesmen for a group. * In the remaining 60 percent, elected members had no contact on the topic of the works council with other employees, or if they had, it was merely incidental, usually with an individual colleague. The analysis suggests an interdependence of representative and worker activities. Active representatives seek the commitment of the rank and file; the latter commit themselves to elected members of active councils. The existence, however, of channels of communications plays a vital role.

For more structured contacts, the significant factors seem to be a union presence among the workers of an enterprise (this is so in 21 of the 90 councils), and/or the habit of holding shop floor meetings between departmental managers and subordinates in every department of the organization. The works council plays hardly any role in the emergence of such channels. The function of a union branch with respect to the works council is to provide a forum in which elected members—at least insofar as they are members of the same union—can discuss with others what issues merit consideration in the works council and what standpoints they ought to adopt. In addition, the union sometimes mobilizes support for the council.

Departmental joint consultation, found in 62 of the 90 cases, has a real if limited significance; because groups of workers in the department discuss their problems together, elected members are in touch with some of the wishes of their coworkers. It is noticeable that in firms of this sort, elected members are thereby encouraged

---

*These data relate only to the 90 "ordinary" works councils. Central works councils are excluded because their base consists of the works councils of constituent units of the total concern. Information concerning relations between works council members and other workers was gathered from ordinary council personnel.

to put strategic matters on the agenda of their councils, even when they say that the workers as a whole display little interest in joint consultation (in banks and insurance companies for instance).

Even these very limited opportunities for contact concerning the works council affect the activities of elected members as representatives of the employees vis-à-vis the management. None of this, however, implies any breakthrough in the tendencies to oligarchy.[4] Elected members often form a small and relatively closed group. New candidates are hard to find or, when presenting themselves, have difficulty in gaining admittance. Elected members arbitrarily reject questions from the constituents as "not relevant" and adopt standpoints during council meetings that they know are not shared by those they represent. Elected members themselves maintain this distant attitude toward other workers, with a view to preserving a confidential relationship with the chairperson so that they, as members of a political body, may conserve the possibility of exercising influence. Evidence of this is the fact that elected members (in 84 percent of the works councils) frequently refuse to reveal what was discussed in the council, even on issues at which the chairperson did not enjoin secrecy upon them. Partly for this reason, not all chairpersons need to resort too frequently to their power of swearing elected members to secrecy (as obtains in 59 percent of the councils). This isolated position of the works council not only limits its significance for the democratic participation by workers in management but also the influence of the works council as a political body. In the last resort, the management of the enterprise has the final say as to what attention is to be paid to the ideas of the elected members. These possess hardly any powers of their own apart from their strictly limited legal competencies. If they were to succeed in mobilizing the active support of large groups of workers, they would be in a better position to reinforce their standpoints, as incidentally is apparent with threatening factory closures or actions initiated from the union side.

Characteristics of Firms

Interrelated characteristics of firms contribute to the explanation of differences between works councils, activities of chairpersons, elected members, and the rank and file. Such patterns characterize various industries and size levels. In industrial firms (especially metal, printing, and foods) with over 500 employees, works councils have become a tradition since 1950. In this period, these works councils matured to well-equipped organs for joint consultation. In the building industry, commerce, and banking, the recent (1971) obligation of works councils to be installed contributes to the often marginal or management-dominated position of works councils.

Works Councils' Fields of Activity:
Nondecision as a Management Method

In principle, all aspects of management and its policy are open to discussion in works councils. In this research, concrete topics are divided into categories on the basis of the terms in which the situation involved and the measure to be taken are formulated: financial-economic policy, internal organization, personnel management, and working conditions. These categories are understood to be sequential (arranged from more to less strategic issues in the policy of the organization as an economic and administrative unit). This also implies that they are of greater or lesser consequence for future decisions.[5] It is accordingly assumed that a works council has more participation in management if it also discusses the more strategic issues in the policy of the organization. On the basis of a systematic analysis of the minutes of works council meetings over the period of a year, it was determined, for each council, what percentage of the topics discussed related to each of the above-mentioned categories.

Generally speaking, it does indeed seem that works councils that score high on other indications of worker participation also devote a relatively large part of their discussions to more strategic issues.* This is important chiefly because these more strategic issues also make great demands upon the expertise of works council members. With regard to personnel management and working conditions, the worker representatives are in a better position to acquire the necessary knowledge, information, and viewpoints. In general, therefore, they regard themselves as exercising greater influence in discussing such issues than when discussing issues relating to financial-economic policy and internal organization.

It is important now to inquire into issues that do not crop up in works councils, even when they do constitute a problem within the organization. For this comparative research, we are, to a certain extent, justified in assuming that in all organizations, these issues are equally problematic to a more or less equal degree and that it

---

*In every works council, in accordance with legal regulations, financial-economic policy must be placed on the agenda at least twice a year: in 3 percent of the councils, however, no subject relating to this was discussed. Of the works councils, 48 percent paid relatively more attention to more strategic issues (compared with the average paid to these issues throughout all works councils); 52 percent of the councils devoted, relatively speaking, a good deal of attention to less strategic issues (including 19 percent that to all intent and purpose discussed only pay and conditions of work).

depends chiefly upon the activity of the works council whether they are discussed.

Information was gathered by means of interviews concerning topics that according to elected members and/or the chairperson were considered to be material for the works council but did not come up for discussion.

Sometimes, there are issues referred to other bodies (unions, central works council, and so forth) either by the elected members or with their approval. With such topics, elected members play an active role in defining the field of activity of the works council. In addition to the more frequent referral of issues relating to personnel management, it is striking that a number of councils, in contrast to others, also refer strategic issues. The councils in question are those that discuss such strategic areas fairly frequently in their meetings, but then limit themselves to comment. This again appears to be a deliberate strategy: elected members are informed about such problems, but confine their discussion to issues (or aspects of them) of which they consider themselves to have sufficient grasp.

In contrast to referral, nondecision is a process whereby a subject is either not discussed at all in council meetings or else not discussed at the desired time or in the desired form, whereas it ought to fall within the council's field of activity.[6] Here, the nub of the matter is the definition of the field that the elected members have arrived at: such members do not succeed in discussing all those matters that they think ought to be discussed, or that they might think it desirable to discuss, if they had been made aware of the existence of this matter by management.

In our research, we have gathered information concerning three forms of nondecision.

First, in over half (55 percent) of the works councils, the chairperson confessed that he had left one or more issues out of discussion. Usually (in 43 percent of the cases), the issues involved were strategic policy issues. An important factor leading chairpersons to take this course was the likelihood of unrest among the workers should these matters be made known and discussed. The chairperson has the legal right to ban discussion of subjects if this would tend to harm the interests of management or of persons immediately involved. In actual fact, chairpersons seldom refer explicitly to this right when banning discussion on a given matter. One result of this managerial strategy is that elected members may not realize that the chairperson is censoring discussion of certain matters. In two-fifths of the works councils (41 percent), the elected members claimed to be aware of the mechanism. There is scarcely any correlation between these two variables, that is, information of the chairperson and of elected members. However, it is clear that elected members recognize this mechanism more often in works councils that have been typified as "organs of consultation" and in councils that pay relatively more attention to more strategic issues.

In three-quarters of the works councils, elected members say that they sometimes fail to have particular issues placed on the agenda and/or that they have not attempted to do so for fear of failure. This form also occurs more frequently in councils where elected members act as a party and wish to consult with the chairperson/chief executive.

There is another closely connected form of nondecision that occurs in over a quarter (28 percent) of the works councils. Elected members sometimes reject a question from other workers as "not relevant." Here, worker representatives, on their own authority, pass judgment on the purposes of other workers' wishes. In view of the close correlation with actual or anticipated failures to have some say in the agenda, this indicates a deliberate attitude on the part of elected members toward the agenda: they wish to propose only "feasible" topics. It also shows elected members as members of a political body acting in an independent fashion: they do not act simply as the spokesmen for their fellow workers.

Despite its legal base, the Dutch works council is dependent on the management for its functioning as a structure for proper joint consultation. As a strategy for the development of industrial democracy, legislation is not sufficient and could even be an impediment. What is needed is a form of worker representation that will articulate the worker viewpoint in consultations with management. Such a worker representation is able to develop its own program of issues to be tackled, especially regarding personnel management, conditions of employment, and work. On those kinds of issues, worker definitions of situations are available independent of the management. Workers (representatives) know themselves what improvements they desire and what measures would be effective. Direct linkage with problems as experienced by groups of workers ensures to the representative body the necessary support of the rank and file. Moreover, inevitably conflicting interests of various groups of workers are to be solved by worker representatives themselves. By reaching unanimity of demands on management in the case of internally divided interests, the worker representatives take over the traditional managerial role of deciding on the distribution of (dis-)advantages among various groups of workers.

On that basis, a worker representation could make joint consultation inevitable for the management. A representative body can develop a nuisance value to the management—and is able to negotiate on that basis. Objects of negotiations are the procurement by management of information on economic-financial policies, as desired by the worker representation. The mobilization of external support and guarantees for joint consultation (from unions and/or legislation) will then result in the proper character of external devices, and it will provide a safeguard against a withdrawal of joint consultation as a tool of workers.

NOTES

1. Ben W. M. Hovels and Peter Nas, "Ondernemingsraden en medezeggenschap: Een vergelijkend onderzoek naar struktuur en werkwiyze van ondernemingsraden" [Work's councils and worker participation: A comparative study of the structure and functioning of works councils] (Ph. D., diss., Alpen aan de Rijn, Nijmegen, 1976). This research was commissioned by the Steering Group of the Foundation for Social Scientific Research and carried out at the Institute for Applied Sociology, Nijmegen, under the auspices of the Commission for Increased Productivity of the Social Economic Council.

2. John P. Windmuller, Labor Relations in the Netherlands (Ithaca, N.Y.: Cornell University Press, 1969), pp. 399–433.

3. See, among others, Carole Pateman, Participation and Democratic Theory (Cambridge: At the University Press, 1970).

4. Robert Michels, Political Parties: A Sociological Study of the Oligarchical Tendencies of Modern Democracy (Magnolia, Mass.: Peter Smith, 1960).

5. A. S. McFarland, Power and Leadership in Pluralism Systems (Stanford, Calif.: Stanford University Press, 1969).

6. C. van der Eyk and W. J. P. Kok, "Non-Decisions Reconsidered," Acta Politica 10 (1975): 227–301.

# Part II

# DIRECT FORMS OF PARTICIPATION

## Section A

# *Chapter Five*

## JOB IMPROVEMENT AND
## WORK HUMANIZATION THROUGH
## DIRECT WORKER PARTICIPATION

In some countries, the idea of worker participation in decision making in an enterprise has been associated with the legal forms of employee representation, such as representation on boards, works committees or works councils, collective bargaining, and so forth. Since representative participation does not in itself guarantee democracy at the shop floor level, it must be supplemented by arrangements for direct participation by the rank-and-file worker that affect him or her and his or her immediate work environment.

In the face of extensive evidence supporting the view "that the rank and file worker is primarily concerned with his immediate work situation, rather than the broader aspects of managerial policy," various attempts are being made to introduce changes in tasks and authority structure, such as job enrichment, work restructuring, autonomous work groups, job redesign, and so forth. [1] The purpose of this chapter is to examine past and current practices in direct participation by workers at the job or shop floor level with the objective of improving the working environment. It also analyzes union and management attitudes toward joint projects on work reorganization and humanization and suggests criteria for a successful model of union-management involvement in the quality-of-working-life projects.

### BACKGROUND—THE TRADITIONAL MODEL

In many highly industrialized countries, the organization of work based on mass production techniques has been one of the major factors contributing to an extraordinary rise in productivity, with a corresponding rise in material standards of living.

In the late 1960s and early 1970s, many mass production industries in the Western world were faced with personnel problems, such as a high rate of absenteeism and turnover and an increase in worker indifference and apathy, leading to unsatisfactory standards of work, accidents, and so forth and numerous wildcat strikes. One significant example was the strike that occurred in 1972 in the Lordstown (U.S.) auto production plant. Similar actions against coercive coordination and control were reported in many parts of Western Europe as well.

For many years, behavioral scientists and others have been critical of the authoritarian management style and hierarchical organization structure that are the basis of the traditional model of work organization. They have denounced the excessive fragmentation and simplification of machine-paced tasks, pointing out the repetitive and monotonous nature of such jobs and the frustrations, the feelings of powerlessness and alienation they engender among workers. Furthermore, changes in living conditions and values, along with a rise in educational levels among workers, have brought about new expectations, such as demands for a higher quality of working life, the humanization of work, and the democratization of the workplace.

Workers are looking for more satisfying work, greater control over the organization of their work, greater freedom of movement, more opportunities for self-development and promotion, and wider scope for the exercise of their intellectual capabilities and skills. Young workers, particularly, feel frustrated with repetitive work, such as assembly line operations, and with the limited scope of many jobs in office or factory.

## RECENT CHANGES—THE PARTICIPATIVE MODEL

In recent years, various attempts have been made to adapt organizational structures and forms of work organizations to changing human requirements. According to a recent IILS research study, the purpose of the different forms of work organization is to extend the worker's scope for action along two dimensions:

1.  Firstly, in a horizontal direction, in order to open up greater opportunity for activity through job design. This can be achieved through job rotation and job enlargement.
2.  Secondly, in a vertical direction, with the objective of extending the worker's scope for decision and control, which can be achieved through modified forms of work organization, namely job enrichment, autonomous work groups, etc.[2]

According to the study Work in America, in a work group, one may find workers participating in decisions on:

—their own production methods;
—the internal distribution of tasks;
—questions of recruitment;
—questions regarding internal leadership;
—what additional tasks to take on;
—when they will work (flexible hours). [3]

Not all of the work groups make all these decisions, but the list provides the range within which the workers are able to control the aspects of work intimately affecting their lives. The most important feature of an autonomous work group is the fact that

> it entails the direct participation of rank and file workers in decision making with the minimum amount of time delay in feedback. Certainly the practice allows direct involvement of the largest number of workers, if only in small scale decisions, when compared with other forms of work organization or even some of the workers' participation schemes. [4]

It is primarily the changes in the authoritarian structures that represent the essential elements or building blocks in the modification of work content.

The participative model contains the important elements of a sociotechnical system and is now followed in several companies. For management, the participative approach involves open communications, experimentation with new forms of work organization, and the participation of rank-and-file workers in managerial functions, that is, sharing in planning, organizing, and controlling the work he or she does. The participative approach has the potential for achieving all of management's major objectives, that is, increased productivity, increased job satisfaction, and improved industrial relations.

Some of the most thoroughgoing experiments concerning the effectiveness of working groups were carried out by the Tavistock Institute of Human Relations of London. These experiments were conducted in an Indian textile mill, British coal mines, a U.S. coal company, and a number of enterprises in Norway.

## TABLE 7

### Spread of Experiments

| Country | Frequency of Instances | Percent |
|---|---|---|
| United States | 21 | 29.50 |
| Sweden | 14 | 19.74 |
| Norway | 6 | 8.46 |
| Denmark | 7 | 9.87 |
| Italy | 4 | 5.64 |
| France | 2 | 2.82 |
| Netherlands | 2 | 2.82 |
| England | 3 | 4.23 |
| Switzerland | 2 | 2.82 |
| Australia | 1 | 1.41 |
| India | 1 | 1.41 |
| West Germany | 7 | 9.87 |
| No indication | 1 | 1.11 |
| Total | 71 | 100.00 |

Source: Reinold Weil, Alternative Forms of Work Organisation: Improvements of Labour Conditions and Productivity in Western Europe, International Institute of Labour Studies, Research Series, no. 4 (Geneva, 1976), p. 12.


## TABLE 8

### Distribution of Experiments by Industry

| Industry or Branch | Frequency of Instances | Percent |
|---|---|---|
| Automobile industry | 11 | 15.5 |
| Electrical industry | 13 | 18.1 |
| Metal trades industry | 11 | 15.5 |
| Chemical industry | 11 | 15.5 |
| Services | 4 | 5.6 |
| Building industry | 3 | 4.2 |
| Others | 11 | 15.8 |
| No indication | 7 | 9.8 |
| Total | 71 | 100.0 |

Source: Reinold Weil, Alternative Forms of Work Organisation: Improvements of Labour Conditions and Productivity in Western Europe, International Institute of Labour Studies, Research Series, no. 4 (Geneva, 1976), p. 12.

TABLE 9

Breakdown by Functional Areas

| Functional Area | Percent |
| --- | --- |
| Engaged in assembly jobs | 43.0 |
| Engaged in production depending on the use of machines | 9.5 |
| Engaged in process supervision | 14.0 |
| Engaged in service operations | 9.5 |
| Engaged in other functions | 24.0 |

Source: Reinold Weil, Alternative Forms of Work Organisation: Improvements of Labour Conditions and Productivity in Western Europe, International Institute of Labour Studies, Research Series, no. 4 (Geneva, 1976), p. 12.

EXPERIMENTS IN WORK REORGANIZATION
IN VARIOUS COUNTRIES

The results of a survey of 71 cases of group work with varying degrees of autonomy in various countries are shown in Tables 7, 8, and 9.

It is estimated that there are now probably about 200 documented case studies available. For the most part, such experiments have been developed at the level of industrial firms or organizations, but in some instances, the changes in work organizations have become institutionalized at wider levels. In the United Kingdom, following the publication of a report on the quality of working life, a tripartite steering group, made up of the government, the TUC, and the Confederation of British Industry, was established to examine how jobs could be made more satisfying for workers. In West Germany, the Ministry of Labor, in cooperation with employers, unions, and other appropriate institutions, sponsored a large-scale study on job satisfaction, with its focus on problems of alternative technologies and work organizations including semiautonomous work groups.

A number of companies, in various countries and for a variety of reasons, voluntarily made innovations in work organizations that attempted to make work more meaningful and satisfying. For example, the results (human and economic) of experiments in work organization in 33 large corporations representing various sectors of the economy are found in a study entitled Work in America. All the companies surveyed reported favorable results.[5] In other cases, management and unions have joined to introduce changes in work organization. Such is the case in Scandinavian countries (Norway, Denmark, and Sweden), where national agreements between employer and worker organizations have set the stage for experiments in the reorganization of work at the plant level.

In Denmark in 1970 a committee formed by three labor market organizations in the metal industry (unions, the employers' association, and the formen's association) launched experiments on work organization in seven companies. All the parties signed a cooperation agreement to experiment with semiautonomous work groups. The committee concluded that the establishment of semiautonomous groups affects all levels of the company organization. It noted the following conditions that affect the planned work reorganization in a plant:

1. Size of the establishment: the smaller the establishment, the greater is the progress in developing and testing new forms of cooperation. Two factors are significant: the distance between the factory floor and the senior management and the relationship of the experimental department with the other departments in the plant.

2. Work methods and techniques: the work methods, techniques and system of wage payment selected by a particular company will affect the individual worker. A new production technique may make more demands on the worker (a great number of operations, adjustments, and so forth) or the worker may be subjected to a more mechanical control. In such cases, a greater variation in technical work is desirable. This in turn will help vary the planning of work and mutual human relations.

3. Composition of the labor force: the composition of the local labor force and the generally prevailing attitude have a major influence on the speed in which changes in work organization can be introduced. It is impossible to create an atmosphere of cooperation if any of the parties involved are forced to participate.

4. Experiences, information, and education: it is necessary to ensure that information is circulated to those staff and auxiliary departments with whom an experimental group has contact. Otherwise, misunderstanding will occur, and the atmosphere of cooperation can suffer. There is not the slightest doubt that if employees are to be involved in decision-making processes, they must be knowledgeable.

5. Initiative: supervisors concerned must take the initiative in bringing up specific topics or problems for open discussion and debate.

6. Selection of experimental area: it is necessary to select a specific area for experimentation, with a clearly defined boundary between it and the rest of the company, so that it is easy to see where the duties and responsibilities of the group begin and end. The size of the group may vary between 5 and 15. It is important to have the group working in one geographical area to facilitate contact and the flow of information.

7. The time factor: from the moment the decision is made to start the experiment, a considerable period of time may elapse before the appearance of changes or results.

8. Costs: the direct costs (lost wages, course expenses) may vary between 1.5 to 2 percent of the total payroll. In companies where there was little or no changes in productivity, these costs could be written off as welfare expenses. However, the companies that have recorded the greatest progress were those that experienced an increase in productivity and were able to treat such costs as investment expenditures. [6]

In Sweden during the last few years, there has been a dramatic growth in activities connected with increased participation by workers in new forms of work organization. Not only private enterprises but also departments of central and local governments have participated in such activities. The Swedish Employers' Confederation (SAF) has played an active role in stimulating the search for new work systems among its members, with a view to promoting job satisfaction and higher productivity. Though in many instances, initiative for changes has come from management, the unions, as well as the workers themselves, have been directly involved. For example, in the SAAB and Volvo automobile companies, management has worked very closely with all the unions, as well as the workers, in introducing systems of group production. These experiments have received wide publicity in North America and in European countries.

Belgium provides a very interesting example of participation of workers in decisions concerning work organization at the shop floor level. The following plan, which was voluntarily introduced by one company, will give an idea of what actually happens in a specific case. This plan should, however, be considered only as an example among many others, since methods differ somewhat from one firm to another. [7]

The first stage consists of organizing contact meetings at the level of certain production units, with the aim of providing better information and encouraging exchanges of views on the work and on relations between those in charge and the workers. The second stage consists of extending throughout the undertaking these informal contact meetings and creating, at the level of each department, a specific committee. The aim of this is to encourage collaboration through the exchange of information between those in charge of the work units of the department and the workers employed there. The third stage consists of the constitution at the level of each work unit of a group composed of the chief of the unit; a representative of the department, belonging either to the union delegation, the works council, or the safety and health committee; and a workers' delegation equivalent to 10 percent of the personnel concerned. Half of this delegation, which is appointed by all the workers concerned, is renewable each year. The aims are (1) to provide information from the higher to the lower levels of the firm; (2) to conduct exchanges of views on this information, as well as on the running of affairs at the level of the work unit; and (3) to examine all proposals apart from those relating to wages and individual disputes. The fourth stage is the creation at the level of each section (that is, each group of identical jobs) of a standing working party made up of three to six workers, two representatives of the technical supervisor, and of the engineer in charge, who becomes the chairperson of the working party. The aim of this group's mission, defined in agreement with the union delegation, is to extend effective participation by the workers in the preparation of decisions. These will subsequently be taken by the person who will assume responsibility for them.

In many other countries, a great many different types of experiments, which allow for greater participation of workers in decision making at the shop floor level, have been carried out, mainly at the initiative of management. While unions are rarely involved directly in the planning stage of the restructuring of work or redesigning of jobs, they frequently exercise an influence on these changes through the process of collective bargaining. In Italy, for example, the national agreements negotiated in 1973 between the employers' association and the Italian Metal Trades Union provide for occupational mobility of workers through training, as well as for the redesigning of jobs to facilitate interchangeability among jobs. In addition to the national agreements in Italy, several collective agreements at the level of the enterprise require management to provide advance notice to union representatives about the introduction of new methods of work and to set up mechanisms for joint study of the effects of such changes. [8]

In France, in the publicly owned Renault automobile company, management introduced a variety of new systems of work organization without consulting the unions concerned or giving prior information to them. However, in January 1973, the company signed an agreement with the unions at the plant level that contained a clause whereby the unions agreed to implement the positive results of these experiments. In West Germany, unions in the automobile industry negotiated an agreement with management that provided for improvements in job design and elimination of monotony on assembly lines. In 1973 an agreement between the Metal Workers' Union and the employers' organization representing companies in Nord Württemburg-Baden provided for a minimum length of the work cycle (one minute and a half) and increased rest periods. [9]

In the United Kingdom, changes in work organizations have taken place within the framework of productivity agreements. For example, at the nylon-spinning factory of the Imperial Chemical Industries at Gloucester, the company signed a productivity agreement with the unions. The agreement authorized the local management to work out, in cooperation with the unions at the plant level, a more flexible system of operations, which would give the workers more freedom of movement and greater autonomy in the organization of their work and production schedules. From the very beginning, shop stewards and workers were closely associated in the planning and execution of such changes. [10]

In the Soviet Union, governmental policy is deliberately oriented toward encouraging new initiatives for organizational change in enterprises. The economic plan provides for the gradual elimination of conveyors except for the transport of parts. Many enterprises have already done that. Efforts are also being made to give each worker several tasks to perform. For example, in the Red Dawn knitting mill, a careful analysis of operations has resulted in rearranging the work in such a way that the workers have greater freedom and autonomy in their daily work. Another example is the Volga automobile plant, where assembly workers have been organized into teams of 15 to 25 workers. These teams carry out a sequence of up to 20 operations. The operators are trained to do a number of different operations, and jobs are rotated among the members of the group. These arrangements are specified in a collective agreement signed between the local administration and the unions. It is important to note that worker participation in decision making at the shop floor level in Soviet enterprises is mainly exercised through the unions, which are active at all levels in an undertaking. [11]

In Japan, workers participate in decisions concerning their immediate work and work environment through workshop conferences. Workshop conferences are composed of supervisors and/or managers and workers in each workshop. In a survey of workshop conferences in Japanese firms, it was found that in 92 percent of the enterprises that had them, workshop conferences dealt with problems of work arrangement and work organization. An example of worker participation at the Hitachi Shipbuilding Company is given below:

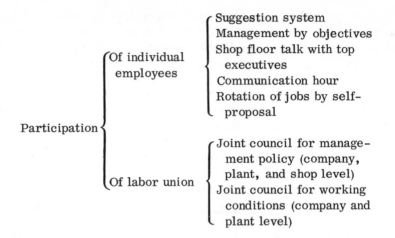

This is one of the typical examples of "management by every-one." In this company, the system works successfully. Every employee has many chances to participate in management from shop floor problems to company policy). Hitachi Shipbuilding Company is noted for its good labor-management relations.[12]

In the United States and Canada, many of the experiments in new forms of work organization have taken place mostly in nonunionized firms. However, some interest is being shown by unions in the "democratization" of the workplace. For example, in 1973 the United Automobile Workers (UAW) and employers in the automobile industry in the United States and Canada signed an agreement that provided for setting up in each of the major automobile companies a joint committee for the improvement of the quality of working life, with three members each from the union and the company empowered to study and analyze possible changes in the organization of work and to undertake experiments.

Many scholars and trade unionists in North America believe that productivity and quality-of-work-life issues can be handled effectively by union and management jointly outside the formal bargaining process. Irving Bluestone of the UAW argues that

> the goal of "humanizing" work . . . is not conducive to
> crisis negotiations. It is not the same as settling a wage
> dispute in the face of a twelve midnight strike deadline.
> Rather, it requires careful experimentation and analysis.
> While issues of economic security (wages, fringe benefits)
> and continuing encroachment on what management terms its
> sole prerogatives will remain adversary in nature, there is
> every reason why humanizing the work place and . . . the
> job need not be matters of confrontation but of mutual con-
> cern.[13]

In recent years, the U.S. National Quality of Work Center set up several joint union-management projects in order to improve the quality of work life. The Institute of Social Research at the University of Michigan was asked to undertake the role of measuring the effects such projects have on individuals, as well as on organizational performance and effectiveness. At the present time, eight such experiments are operational. Drexler and Lawler have analyzed the problems encountered in starting one of these cooperative projects, which involved one of the largest companies in the United States and a major international union representing over 20,000 of the employees who work for the company.[14]

In this case, both union and management officials felt that work could be improved in many ways by collaborative efforts that would benefit both the union and management. However, forces favoring adversary traditional type of labor-management relations were very strong. These included the different goals of the union and management; the lack of any model of, or experience with, successful cooperative problem solving; the desire of both parties to maintain a contract; the risk to both union officials and company management in changing a relationship that brought them to power; and the time and cost required to change.[15] The entry process took more than 14 months before the joint project got started. In a study of eight U.S. firms involved in joint union-management work innovation projects, Schlesinger and Walton examined the question, How do various stakeholders perceive the risks of their involvement in the initial stages? On management side the stakeholders included corporate management, local management, and supervision (in this hierarchical order) and from the union side, they consisted of the international union, the local union, and the steward. The results of their studies confirm Drexler's and Lawler's finding, that is, that various stakeholders were suspicious of each other and of the motives behind such joint ventures. Power holders in union and management organizations perceived that their involvement entailed certain career risks. The authors also found that a great deal of time, effort, and money had to be invested in allaying these fears and suspicions and in establishing a climate of working consensus before each project got off the ground. In spite of these problems, they argue that where such projects came to fruition, these joint undertakings did have a positive impact on the process of collective bargaining. Their conclusions are as follows:

1. The work restructuring activity increases the ratio of problem solving to bargaining activity compared with that normally observed in U.S. collective bargaining. This in turn places a higher premium on structuring attitudes of mutual trust and respect.

2.  Work restructuring presents some novel problems for union leaders in seeking rank and file consensus for agreements they enter into with management.
3.  Work structuring is a reflection, and in turn, will promote a trend in the U.S.A. toward "participatory democracy."[16]

Given the traditional adversary model of labor-management relations in North America, it appears that joint union-management projects in the area of work reorganization or humanization movement will not make much headway in major industries unless unions are more genuinely accepted among the employers in the private sector in North America.

## UNION AND MANAGEMENT RESPONSE TO DIRECT WORKER PARTICIPATION IN WORK REORGANIZATION AND HUMANIZATION

The new forms of work organization have so far had their impact on a very small number of workers in relation to the total labor force in the countries where such experiments have taken place. However, in recent years, union and management have come increasingly under pressure from their multiple internal constituents to reexamine the traditional adversary model of union-management relations and its effectiveness in dealing with such issues as improving the quality of working life. Management's and unions' attitudes and strategies toward quality-of-working-life projects in Western Europe and North America will be examined here.

### Management's Strategy

As costs of turnover, absenteeism, and wildcat strikes become an increasingly significant part of doing business, it is becoming clear to many managers that they must find alternate ways to attain an equilibrium between higher productivity, on the one hand, and job satisfaction and personal fulfillment of individual workers, on the other hand.

In many countries, such as Norway, Sweden, the United Kingdom, France, West Germany, Belgium, the Netherlands, the United States, and Canada, experiments are being conducted, mostly at the initiative of employers, which involve workers directly, along with members of management and technical specialists at the shop floor level, in the analysis of production problems, suggestions for improvements in the methods of work or working conditions, the development of new job designs, plans for layout of new plants, and even changes in technology and methods of production. Semiautonomous work groups or special joint committees have been set up for this purpose at various levels of the organization. It appears that in some instances, these schemes have been set up by management with a view to undermine union's influence and, in others, to forestall unionization of their employees.

Unions' Attitudes and Strategies

In view of the initiatives taken by management with regard to innovations at the workplace, it has become increasingly difficult for unions to stay uninvolved because this question is so closely related to the traditional conditions of work. Consequently, unions have been forced to develop their own strategy.

The general political climate in a country, that is, the distance or closeness between the unions and the ruling parties in the government and the underlying ideologies of each, may be the most important factors influencing union attitudes toward these issues. For example, in the Scandinavian countries, where in the past there has been a close working relationship between the government and the unions over a long period of time, it has been relatively easy for the unions to work in close cooperation with the employers' group. The very strength and pervasiveness of unionization in these countries reduce open labor-management conflict and creates a labor relations climate that is conducive to successful collaboration in quality-of-life projects.

In the United Kingdom, unions prefer to deal with changes in work organizations and work rules at work sites within the context of collective bargaining, so that they can control their content and consequences. Changes in work organization are usually brought about by productivity agreements, in which both union members and management stand to gain.

In Belgium and the Netherlands, unions are highly centralized, and bargaining usually is industrywide and takes place at the regional or national level. There is very little union involvement in work-structuring experiments at the plant level. Unions have adopted a permissive but cautious attitude toward such experiments. In France and Italy, unions suspect the employers' motives in sponsoring any new innovations in the workplace. The CGT, the largest union in France, expressed the view in 1971 that "job enriching" was more "boss enriching" than anything else.

In the French industrial relations context, "working conditions" is not a negotiable issue, and French unions have little influence over work practices at the plant level. Unions are not against humanization of work per se, but take the view that they are the only ones entitled to take initiative for real improvements at the work site. In recent years, the CGT has stressed demands in work situations that go beyond job satisfaction and that they can easily control; for example, they have asked for (1) easing the work load by limiting output requirements; (2) better protection of the workers' safety and health, (3) provision for rest period and restrooms, (4) limiting the tendency toward the devaluation of skills, and (5) guaranteed career development. The CFDT, the second largest union in France, whose ideology (opposition to capitalism) is similar to that of the CGT, is an advocate of self-management. The CFDT demands that the results of research and the knowledge of scientists, engineers, and sociologists be turned over to the workers and their unions. Only then will the workers through their unions be able to take effective action to bring about changes in work organization. Current bargaining over working conditions in France between the unions and the employers' association at the national level has encouraged and expedited the formulation of policies on these issues. These efforts have resulted in a less hostile attitude on the part of the unions to the new methods of work organization. [17]

In Italy, the ideology of the unions is not very different from the one propounded by major unions in France. However, Italian unions see work restructuring as a viable alternative to traditional job design, as long as the initiative comes from the workers. Unions in Italy took the initiative in demanding that alternative solutions to the traditional division of work be found within the framework of collective bargaining. The collective agreements concluded at Olivetti and Fiat are good examples of the unions' successful strategy. The agreements provide for a reduction in the number of categories of work, the elimination of the lowest category, and the promotion of workers from lower to higher categories, as well as training opportunities for these workers. Promotion means not only more money but also more meaningful and interesting jobs. Furthermore, Italian unions have shown a remarkable capacity to adapt their organizational structure to the changing circumstances. This was the case in 1969, when sweeping changes in labor relations in Italy brought about the gradual replacement of the existing consultative or bargaining machinery by a new type of worker representation, the "worker delegate movement," that is, representation by homogeneous work groups (workers doing pretty much the same job under identical working conditions). This movement was the means by which workers increased their control over their conditions of work through investigations carried out by the workers themselves. The right of control over the working conditions by worker delegates at the shop floor level was recognized by the unions and, later on, was incorporated in the works agreements between the employers and the unions.[18]

Some union leaders in West Germany are skeptical about the reorganization of work, while others regard it as an area where unions need to reorient their strategy from the demands for quantitative material goals to the pursuit of policies that focus on qualitative issues, such as creative work, opportunity for teamwork, social contact, meaningful and interesting work, and so forth.

It should be emphasized that European unions consider work reorganization as only one part of their total strategy for industrial democracy. The secretary of the European Metal Workers Federation in the EEC stated in an interview that humanization of work or changes in work organization presupposes the democratization of enterprises and of the economy, which means worker representation on a company's management board and greater collective bargaining rights for a greater share of the economic pie. He further suggested that since humanization of work is a task that involves workers and their representatives, union rights and freedom of speech of workers in the plants must be guaranteed and extended. Last, the changes in the organization of work and the improvement of working conditions must not degenerate into rationalization measures, with the objective of reducing employment.

For union leaders in North America, the economic issues still have top priority. Some of them believe that the growing dissatisfaction of unskilled workers is due more to inflation and the decline in purchasing power than to any feeling of alienation from work. They suspect management's motives and believe that quality-of-life experiments are just another device to prevent unions from gaining a foothold. Unions in North America exercise greater power at the work site than their counterparts in many European countries. However, they tend to regard innovation and changes in work organization as a management problem and prefer to deal with such changes within the framework of adversary union-management relations. In view of the historic reactive role of U.S. unions, it is not surprising that most quality-of-work-life projects in North America have been undertaken and implemented at the initiative of the employer, with little or no participation by the unions.

However, according to the study Work in America, there is considerable evidence that workers in jobs with little intrinsic satisfaction have begun to question the traditional role of unions. Young workers are rebelling against what they feel is "unresponsive" and "irrelevant" union leadership.[19] In recent years, union attitudes toward the reorganization of work in North America have gradually begun to change. The following statement from Irving Bluestone of the UAW is indicative of this new trend: "Just as management is be-

ginning to ponder the new problems of discontent and frustration in
the work force, so must unions join in finding new ways to meet these
problems."[20]


## Risks and Problems

The new forms of work organization have so far had their impact on a very small number of workers in relation to the total labor
force in the countries where such experiments have taken place.
From the pioneering research of Emery and Trist and the Norwegian-
Hydro[21] experiment to the recent study Work in America, there has
been a great deal of evidence in favor of improving job satisfaction,
reducing absenteeism and turnover, and so forth. The following
quote from Work in America illustrates the point. "Several dozen
well-documented experiments show that productivity increases and
social problems decrease when workers participate in the work decisions affecting their lives and when their work is buttressed by participation in profits."[22]

However, some preliminary observations can be made regarding the problems and trends resulting from these experiments. They
entail certain risks for workers and pose problems for management
as well. Changes in work organization involve reshuffling the existing power structure, which affects particularly the traditional authority
of supervisors and technical specialists. They may also be perceived
by some union leaders as a challenge to labor's solidarity.


## Problems for Workers

Although the restructuring of work may provide greater autonomy and decision-making power for rank-and-file workers, in practice, it may increase their work load. Older workers and those who
lack basic education may find it difficult to cope with the work load
associated with the changes, such as learning a variety of operations
or adjusting to an extended work cycle. Some workers may complain
of increased fatigue and mental strain due to the greater complexity
of their tasks.

The worker unable to adapt to the changes in work organization
may run the risk of being weeded out of the labor market. Work
groups may create rivalry among the various groups in an undertaking and may try to exclude from their midst less capable or weak
members. Furthermore, such groups undermine the position of
maintenance workers and may restrict or endanger their future career prospects. There are some workers who are opposed to any

change in the work organization because it disrupts the routine of repetitive jobs and requires more mental agility. They appear to be quite satisfied with the status quo.

Problems for Management

From the management's viewpoint, worker participation in decision making at the shop floor level and the introduction of new forms of work organization, such as autonomous groups, raise many problems and contradict such concepts as management's prerogatives and control management as a profession, which underlie the present management principles in market economy countries.

It is quite apparent from the results of the experiments in work reorganization that when individuals or groups of workers exercise initiative and have freedom in regulating their own working lives, the sheer amount of control exercised by management in the past must decrease.[23] Although the executives at the middle management level may pay lip service in support of changes in work organization, they may feel that these changes destroy the rules and practices they have established to maintain their control. Some of them may even perceive these changes as a threat to their position and status in the organizational hierarchy. The reorganization of work places considerable strain on supervisors. They are in direct contact with workers and are accustomed to giving orders and exercising a disciplinary function. Worker participation at the shop floor level makes it necessary for supervisors to work in close cooperation with semiautonomous work groups, which have now taken over many of their supervisory functions. It also requires the supervisors to develop skills and talents for leadership quite different from the ones they have practiced in the past.

From the experiments conducted in Scandinavian countries, it can be seen that it is both possible and desirable for managers at the middle management level to develop collaborative relations with autonomous work groups at the horizontal level. The formation of project teams to solve specific nonrecurrent problems will absorb much of the middle management capacity that was previously absorbed in performing the so-called line control functions. This type of participation will increase the autonomy of managers, the variety of their work, and their opportunities for self-actualization.

Another important but related question is whether we can encapsulate the reorganization of work at the shop floor level or whether it must inevitably lead to other changes. Successful changes at the shop floor level can only be introduced if the objective of the proposed organizational change is analyzed in its total organizational context.

There is little point in launching an experiment if it is not congruent with other developments in an organization. To give a specific example, in an organization, groups of workers assembled a piece of equipment under their own control. The department manager felt that if the workers were to be responsible for their own accounts, the accounting system should be redesigned for that purpose. After these work groups were formed, the manager also discovered that some equipment was turning out to be unsuitable due to the new method of working. It tested the ingenuity of the manager. One thing became apparent, namely, that for people involved in such projects, "there will always be consequences for training and there will always be consequences for the payment system."[24] It follows then that training schemes will have to be refined and new educational programs will have to be developed in cooperation with unions and educational authorities to bring about changes in attitudes and to retrain workers and supervisors. In the case of the workers, the objective of the training should be the rounding out of skills rather than the development of specialized skills. The emphasis on the acquisition of many and varied skills is necessitated by the fact that new forms of work organization call for the interchangeability of tasks.

Pay systems will have to be modified as well. The new wage and salary systems will have to reflect the entire process of the workers' increased responsibility and autonomy in the workplace. Furthermore, the workers must share in the fruit of increased productivity. Appropriate alternative pay and bonus systems will have to be worked out.

Problems for Unions

Changes in work organization cause particular problems for unions. The first problem is that unions tend to concentrate on establishing uniform, collective rules and protections. The redesigning and restructuring of jobs may weaken the effectiveness of unions' control over working conditions. For example, in the United States and Canada, a collective agreement defines a specific number of jobs for the duration of the contract and draws up rules under which persons may be promoted or transferred from one job to another. The effectiveness of union control over working conditions depends to a large degree on the stability of job content and the preservation of seniority rules. Anything that upsets these rules during the term of the contract would undermine the power of unions, as well as the institution of collective bargaining. In countries where unions negotiate with employers at the national level, the establishment of autonomous groups within the undertaking is likely to make it harder for them to present a united front in pressing union demands.

The second problem is that a change in the content of certain jobs, accompanied by a rise in the wages of those concerned, is liable to upset the traditional scale of jobs and wages. The unions' task will be to negotiate the workers' share of increased productivity that often flows from work reorganization. For craft unions in the United Kingdom, the United States, and Canada, which have control over apprenticeship and access to employment, job enrichment may cause particular difficulties. The accelerated training and promotion provided through job enrichment programs will be regarded as a threat by those workers who have obtained their jobs through traditional channels and lengthy training. Unions have no choice except to oppose such a program.

The third problem is that experiments in new forms of work organization may alleviate the dissatisfaction of workers with their immediate work situation and may weaken their allegiance to the unions. Workers may also espouse the values of the business organization, which will be perceived as a threat to the union movement in the long run. The fourth problem is that to keep abreast of the new forms of work organization, unions will have to change their organization structure as far as rank-and-file workers are concerned, such as an enterprise union for all employees in Japan or industrial unions in Germany. The final problem is that in new plants, innovations designed to improve the quality of working life might result in a reduction of the number of workers required for a given level of production. Consequently, the unions perceive such innovations as a threat to employment in the long run.

## CRITERIA FOR A SUCCESSFUL MODEL OF UNION-MANAGEMENT INVOLVEMENT IN JOINT PROJECTS

Based on the discussion with union and management and his own readings, this writer has come to the conclusion that a collaborative union-management venture for the purpose of improving quality of life in the workplace is viable whenever the following enabling conditions are present.

1. Union and management are two interdependent organizations with often conflicting goals and priorities. Therefore, both parties must be willing and able to negotiate and made compromises over the goals of joint projects.

2. Joint ventures should be perceived as instrumental to the attainment of goals valued by each party. For management, it should lead to increased productivity and profits and should not affect effi-

ciency adversely. For workers, it should provide practical gains, that is, they should be able to share in the economic benefits of improvement. For unions, any joint venture should not threaten or impinge upon their established rights or upon the issues subject to collective bargaining.

3. Commitment of key officials at all levels of management and union hierarchy is crucial.

4. The environmental conditions should be conducive to the collaborative venture. Experiences with joint ventures in Scandinavian countries and in particular companies in other countries indicate that enterprises with a history of constructive union-management relations offer the best prospect for success of joint projects on work restructuring and humanization of work. However, where union-management relations are based on the traditional adversary model, adequate time, effort, and money must be invested in allaying fears and anxieties of various stakeholders in both union and management before parties can engage in a meaningful collaborative problem-solving effort. It is necessary that organizational norms actively support attempts made by both parties to find integrative solutions. In other words, union and management should make sure that individual power holders within their respective organizations do not attempt to block joint efforts.

5. Both parties should make sure that needed competencies are available. An independent consultant, who is acceptable to both parties and has the ability to relate to various power holders in both organizations, could assist in designing and implementing joint projects. He or she could also help parties in developing problem-solving skills and in finding integrative solutions. However, a broad program of education and training for management officials, employees, and union officials involved in joint projects must form an integral part of all collaborative efforts.

6. Finally, there is a greater likelihood of success for collaborative ventures if joint union-management committees are established at the top level as well as at lower levels, particularly at the work site, and if the same committee structure is used in disseminating project information through union and management organizations; if decisions are arrived at by consensus; if both union and management are introduced to similar joint ventures that have been successful elsewhere; and if parties obtain success in the initial stages of the project. This will increase their commitment and will enable them to sustain innovative efforts.

SUMMARY AND CONCLUSION

The future of the direct participation of workers in quality-of-working-life projects must be considered within the context of the overall goals and objectives of management, the workers, and the unions and of the relative importance they attach to such problems and other issues connected with the new forms of work organization. There is much division of opinion among unions on the importance to be given to such issues, and therefore, it is difficult to generalize on a global basis. Most union leaders believe that the main purpose of introducing changes in work organizations is to overcome economic difficulties encountered by the employers or to resolve certain personnel problems, such as absenteeism, labor turnover, difficulties in recruitment, unsatisfactory standards of work, and so forth. Consequently, the unions do not feel that such changes should directly concern them. However, what the unions want most is to control the direction and consequences of any new moves sponsored by the employers in this area. The unions strive to impose their countervailing power within the framework of established institutions, such as collective bargaining.

It is evident from the earlier discussion that unions will be increasingly pressed by management initiatives, on the one hand, and their own desire to improve the working life of their members, on the other, to explore alternatives to the present work organization. An important lesson that can be learned from various experiments is that it is difficult to see how the goals of job improvement could be achieved in unionized undertakings without the fullest support of workers and their unions.

Involvement of union and management in the quality-of-work-life projects implies a change of attitudes and value system on the part of unions and management. According to Walton, it will require some revision in the practice and theory of collective bargaining, with its focus on representative democracy, where worker influence is exercised through union representatives in a two-party (union-management) forum. If the joint ventures designed for improving the quality of working life are to be in accord with the changing aspirations of the workers, these must be based on their involvement in matters that affect them in their work environment. These joint ventures should not only provide economic gains for employees but also new opportunities for learning and career development.

All things considered, it appears that the trend toward the redesigning of jobs and the democratization of the workplace is likely to continue. The involvement of workers, and of their organizations in such experiments, will hopefully result in better working conditions, as well as in more productive and satisfying work.

NOTES

1.  Kenneth Walker, "Industrial Democracy: Fantasy, Fiction or Fact?" The Times Management Lecture, 1970 (London: Times Newspapers Ltd., 1970), p. 24.

2.  Reinhold Weil, Alternative Forms of Work Organisation: Improvements of Labour Conditions and Productivity in Western Europe, International Institute of Labour Studies, Research Series, no. 4 (Geneva, 1976), p. 4.

3.  Work in America, Report of the Special Task Force to the Secretary of Health, Education and Welfare, prepared under the auspices of the W. E. Upjohn Institute for Employment Research (Cambridge: Massachusetts Institute of Technology Press, 1973), pp. 103-4

4.  Shin Ichi Takezama, "Methods of Work Organization" (Framework paper, prepared for the Fourth World Congress in Industrial Relations, Geneva, September 1976), p. 20.

5.  Work in America, Appendix: "Case Studies in the Humanization of Work," pp. 188-201.

6.  B. Bordrup and P. Roos, "Industrial Democracy in Denmark" (Paper prepared for the International Labour Organisation's Symposium on Workers' Participation, Oslo, 1974), pp. 7-8.

7.  D. DeNorre, "Workers Participation in Decisions within Undertakings in Belgium" (Paper prepared for the International Labour Organisation's Symposium on Workers' Participation, Oslo, 1974), pp. 2-4.

8.  International Labour Organisation, "Symposium of Workers' Participation in Decisions within the Undertaking," Background paper for the ILO's Symposium on Workers' Participation (Geneva: ILO, 1974), pp. 22-23.

9.  Ibid.

10.  Ibid.

11.  Ibid., p. 24.

12.  J. Naruse, "Workers' Participation in Decisions within Undertakings in Japan" (Paper prepared for the International Labour Organisation's Symposium on Workers' Participation, Oslo, 1974), p. 4.

13.  Irving Bluestone, "Worker Participation in Decision Making" (Paper delivered at the Conference on Strategy, Programs, and Problems of an Alternative Political Economy, Institute of Policy Studies, Washington, D. C., March 2-4, 1973), p. 9

14.  John A. Drexler, Jr., and Edward E. Lawler, "A Union-Management Cooperative Project to Improve the Quality of Work Life," Journal of Applied Behaviorial Sciences 13 (1977): 386.

15.  Ibid.

16.  L. A. Schlesinger and R. E. Walton, "Work Restructuring in Unionized Organizations: Risks, Opportunities, and Impact on

Collective Bargaining," Twenty-Ninth Annual Conference Proceedings of the Industrial Relations Research Association (Madison, Wis.), pp. 245-351.

17. For more information see Y. Delamotte, "The Attitudes of French and Italian Trade Unions to the Humanisation of Work," Labour and Society, vol. 1 (January 1976); see also R. Tchobanian, "Trade Unions and the Humanization of Work," International Labour Review, vol. 3 (March 1975).

18. Ibid.

19. Work in America.

20. See Irving Bluestone, Work in America, p. 114.

21. F. Emery and E. Trist, "The Causal Texture of Organizational Environments," Human Relations, August 1963, pp. 20-26. See also "Norsk-Hydro," described in N. Wilson, The Quality of Working Life (London: Department of Employment, 1975), pp. 35-36.

22. Work in America, p. 113.

23. Ibid., p. 104.

24. L. Klein, New Forms of Work Organization (Cambridge: At the University Press, 1976), p. 74.

# *Part II*

## Section B: Case Studies

# Case 1

## SHOP FLOOR PARTICIPATION:
## EXPERIENCES OF THREE ENTERPRISES
## (THE NETHERLANDS, BELGIUM, AND ITALY)

Alan Gladstone and Bert Essenberg

The three cases described below were presented in a
March 1977 meeting in Brussels. The aim of the meeting was to provide the opportunity for industrial relations
practitioners to discuss issues that arise for management
and unions when the introduction is contemplated or effectuated of systems of more direct participation of workers in decisions concerning the organization of their work,
their work environment, and their working conditions.
As background for the discussions, the experiences in
three enterprises, located in the Netherlands, Belgium,
and Italy, were presented in each case on the basis of a
paper by a representative of the management, which was
then commented on by a representative of the union concerned.

BACKGROUND

At the outset of the meeting, the main lines of discussion were
drawn. Participation may be direct or indirect. Often, attention is
focused only or principally on the institutional forms of indirect participation through representation, for example, worker representatives in works councils and on company boards. However, direct
participation at the job or shop floor level has increasingly become
a subject of research, inquiry, and discussion.

Shop floor participation may be considered within the framework
of improving the working environment or, in the now somewhat

Alan Gladstone and Bert Essenberg, "Note on Social Perspective Meeting—Shop-floor Participation," in Labour and Society 2
(October 1977): 440-49. Reproduced with the permission of the International Institute for Labour Studies, Geneva.

frowned upon expression, "humanization of work" (to the extent that the expression implies new forms of work organization, such new forms are not necessarily participative). Restructuring of tasks through "horizontal" job enlargement can made work more satisfying, but it does not in itself give the worker more participation in deciding on the manner in which he or she is to carry out his or her job. What is of concern here are precisely those newer forms of work organization that give the worker greater freedom in the choice of tasks and greater responsibility for controlling his or her own work. This form of "job enrichment" may be individual (in the sense that the work is done essentially independent of others) or may be characterized by work groups with a certain degree of autonomy, for example, production groups that are responsible for a clearly designated production operation reflecting an identifiable complete whole (component or finished product); these production groups may decide freely about the internal work assignments and changes in tasks, length of breaks, production targets for the group, and so forth (all within the framework of overall goals, targets, and schedules).

New participative forms of work organization are introduced for various reasons. In virtually all cases until now, it is management that has initiated the change, and the motives have generally been economic. Increasing difficulties of recruitment into routine, monotonous, and repetitive work and high rates of absenteeism and turnover attributable to such work, as well as general job dissatisfaction (leading to productivity and quality difficulties) may be cited among the motives for change. The still incomplete evidence regarding experience with newer, more participative forms of work organization seems to indicate genuine improvement with regard to these questions. Management's economic motivation for the introduction of participative work organization (in particular, semiautonomous work groups) can also relate, in some cases, to the possibility it affords for greater flexibility for rapid changes in the nature of production or the product.

It is difficult to make generalizations about union attitudes with regard to the introduction of systems of shop floor participation, owing to the many nuances of their positions, which, however, seem to be in a state of evolution toward greater recognition (particularly at the shop floor union level) of the positive possibilities of such participation. Nevertheless, it may be observed that these attitudes range from hostility to full acceptance. The hostility of some unions is based on their ideology, which seeks a radical restructuring of society—shop floor participation thus subverting the class struggle. In other union circles, shop floor participation is seen as a subterfuge or manipulative device by employers to increase worker effort and productivity and divert them from wage and other economic issues.

Still other unions have an attitude of indifference or grudging acceptance of participative forms of work organization, contenting themselves to protect members' wage levels and other interests and to bargain about certain aspects of the consequences of the introduction of such new forms. Finally, an increasing number of unions fully participate in all phases of the conception and introduction of new forms of work organization.

Regardless of what their attitude may be, unions will have to deal with situations arising out of the introduction of new forms of organization that give more room for participation of the workers. In fact, both unions and management are being called upon, jointly or separately, to resolve new issues. Some of these are protection of employment and the type of skills needed; protection of workers who do not want to, or cannot, change; wage levels and wage systems— job classification practices, incentive systems, and the equalization of skills; work loads, work tempo, and stress, particularly as regards older and disabled workers; greater identification of the workers with the firm, which may cause less interest in union activities; need for stepped-up union research efforts and for more training and education of union representatives; career patterns and limitations on upward mobility in the firm; changing role (and the obsolescence) of supervision; disciplinary problems arising out of greater autonomy of workers or groups of workers in the execution of their tasks and handling of intra- or intergroup grievances; and increased vocational training costs of management.


CASE STUDIES

The first case presentation concerned the Postcheque-en Girodienst in the Netherlands. This is a large public administrative service for the payment of bills. The case described was a sociotechnical experiment on the enlargement and enrichment of jobs in one of the code centers, which started in 1965. All the work concerning the keeping of accounts is done in small groups, which are responsible for a certain number of accounts. The work of these groups includes the following tasks: checking the payment orders, working at the punching machines, and verifying the punched cards.

In the original form of organization, the personnel was divided into three occupations, each responsible for one of the tasks. There existed differences in responsibility, attractiveness of work, remuneration, and so forth. Under the new system, the tasks are rotated among the members of the group; individual jobs have thus been enlarged, and each group has been given responsibility for the organization of the work within the group.

After a few months, the employees involved were generally much more satisfied with their job and showed a marked preference for the new form of work organization. The reactions of the supervisory staff were not, however, all positive. It became clear that certain supervisors had difficulties in adapting to the new system. The supervisors, who were production minded and rather authoritarian, were not well prepared to change the nature of their functions to one of problem solving through discussion with the groups concerned.

Difficulties also stemmed from the fact that the introduction and execution of change was imposed by the central management and was effectuated in good measure by outside researchers. The totality of changes did not seek to take into account the views and perceptions of the workers and supervisors themselves. Moreover, initial problems arose in terms of the equalization of status of people previously performing higher- and lower-level tasks. For example, the "verificators" felt that their prestige was somewhat diminished owing to the "equalization" of jobs. This task had been graded at a higher level than the other two tasks, and for a time at least, these employees perceived their status as having been diminished by the combining and "equalization" of tasks.

Although the new organization did not result in any appreciable change in productivity, the overall results were encouraging enough for the board of directors to decide to introduce the new system in the other code centers. The experience was not entirely successful, however, in the sense that it was not possible to meet the objective of the board to modify the hierarchical structure of Girodienst in accordance with the objectives of the experiment.

An additional noteworthy point is that participation of the unions in the experiment has been very marginal. They preferred to "wait and see" rather than challenge or cooperate with the central management. The unions could have played an important role in the solution of daily problems and could also have assisted in overcoming a certain underlying initial distrust of the employees with regard to management. Nevertheless, in the view of management, the new form of work organization has gradually promoted conditions that are favorable for better industrial relations.

It would appear that union aloofness was due, at least in part, to a shortness of union staff and because of the fact that working conditions were only a part of the union's range of concerns. While the unions did not feel responsible for these experiments, they did ask to be informed about developments, and on those occasions, the unions made observations and, also, suggested some changes. Moreover, union membership is very low, largely owing to the composition of the personnel of the code centers (mostly young women) and by the limited career perspectives. This fact, added to the plurality of unions representing employees in Girodienst, might also contribute to an explanation of the unions' less than overwhelming interest or involvement. The view was nevertheless expressed from the union side that key areas warranting further development related to increasing the degree of employee participation in the control and supervisory functions and, concomitantly (as alluded to earlier), further training and preparation of supervisors to function in a more participative structure.

Not surprisingly, the discussion on this case concentrated on the following points: (1) the position of the supervisors and the situation caused by an official hierarchy; (2) the position of the unions and the role they could play; and (3) shop floor participation, morale, and labor relations.

On the first point, the official hierarchy, typical of public sector or parastatal institutions, does not, as such, necessarily create obstructions to more participative work organization. It is still possible to vary responsibilities and, relatedly, to ensure an effective chain of communications to break down ingrained traditional job structures and hierarchy. However, a problem in the case discussed lies in the fact that the hierarchical order was not sufficiently differentiated and that in the final analysis, responsibility remains at the top for even relatively minor decisions. Shop floor participation can only have positive results if delegation means a real devolution of authority.

As regards the position of the unions and, in particular, their fear of being committed by a single union representative (representing the four unions involved), this feeling was not shared by the Belgian union representatives, who had experience in interunion cooperation and also, moreover, considered that any decision of a union representative could later be called into question by the other unions involved. In any event, the policy of the unions active in the Postchequeen Girodienst is changing, and it is expected that they will participate much more actively in the near future.

There was a general feeling that it is impossible for unions to leave changes in work organization to management and researchers. Unions cannot abstain because these changes are of vital concern to workers.

It is important to note that good labor relations and reasonably high morale were present within Girodienst even before changes were made in the work organization. Thus, it is not surprising that job motivation and morale did not show a significant improvement as a result of the experiments. Yet, it may be recalled that the employees by and large accepted and preferred the new system. With regard to the content of shop floor participation, the groups are at present mostly concerned with routine questions and do not enjoy that degree of autonomy whereby they are in a position to make really major decisions. It was also recognized that the system was developing, largely by learning from past mistakes, and that employees and supervisors are becoming more and more involved in the evolution of change, which is increasingly based on their perceived needs and aspirations.

The second presentation concerned the experiences of Barco Electronics in Belgium. Changes in this enterprise were based on an organization model stressing the utmost participation, both through representatives and direct means, at all levels and recognizing the essential value and contribution of each member of the organization. This manner of thinking implies: reorganization of subsystems or work communities; smaller or medium-sized operations in order that management can know and cooperate with workers at all levels; keeping as broad a functional participation as possible by delegation and decentralization; promoting deliberation and ensuring the synthesis of these deliberations at various levels of the organizational structure; and accepting coresponsibility for the assets of the company.

Pursuant to these ideas, the firm had abandoned assembly line production and, in fact, offered employees a choice between various production methods, including participative group work.

The highest organ in the company, the Supervisory Council, is advised by a Deliberation Committee, of which three worker representatives are members. The company is divided into three major departments, subdivided into branches, with a maximum of 100 employees each; every branch has sections. At each of these levels (department, branch, and section), there is an advisory council in which the head of the sector meets, at least once a month, with employee representatives or, at the section level, with all of the employees. The discussions in these meetings are becoming more and more participatory in terms of influencing basic workplace decisions and practices. One of the benefits of these contacts is that the supervisors are gaining a better understanding of the problems of the workers.

From the point of view of the unions, while they support and cooperate with the participative machinery described, they are nevertheless careful to ensure that the council system does not become a substitute for the unions. The union evaluation of the council system, which is basic to the structure of shop floor participation at Barco Electronics, is that as a means of communication, the system has been successful. A supervisor never becomes isolated, as he or she is obliged to meet regularly with the workers concerned. Negative points are that the system is sometimes regarded as a "safety valve" and that the heads of the sectors, and hence the advisory councils, have too little room for decision. Finally, the unions are also active in initiating changes in production methods, and so forth.

The most acute difficulties in the view of the unions are that the training and education of the union representatives are not sufficient and that in terms of the more active direct participation at the section level, where some employees are very active, others are not at all interested, which can weaken the functioning of the system.

As regards work organization in the firm, in addition to the suppression of the assembly line, there are now semiautonomous groups with which employees work on individual tasks and collective tasks of given duration. Interestingly, it was pointed out that changes in work organization were sometimes initiated by individual workers, even without the knowledge of the higher management. These modifications were sometimes extended to other sections or workplaces.

The future production of the company is planned at a very early stage to give the advisory councils at all levels the opportunity to discuss the consequences of new plans for their sector. The Works Council, on the other hand, discusses the overall consequences of production planning for employment, and so forth, based on the reports of the sector councils.

An interesting point is that the workers of a sector also have a say in the appointment of the supervisor for their sector. Such an appointment must be acceptable to the workers concerned, as it is considered that otherwise, such an appointment may lead to difficulties.

The third case concerned the changes at the Ivrea plant of Olivetti in Italy. In the second half of the 1960s, more tasks, including those related to quality control, were entrusted to the workers. These measures have led to better quality, simpler organization, and less indirect personnel. Due to several reasons, the traditional assembly line system was abandoned. Instead, semiautonomous groups of the "stellar" model were established, which assemble and test certain components and products. Every worker is able to execute all the necessary operations. The enrichment in the tasks of the workers involved their assuming control over lower supervisory functions. These developments both prompted and reflected union demands for the improvement of skills of the workers (in connection with improvement in working conditions). Moreover, the unions participate actively (frequently by way of negotiation) in every planned change of any importance and are kept systematically informed about the implementation of changes.

In effecting change, there was some friction between the sociopsychological services and the traditionalists in the industrial engineering (time and methods) sector of the firm. This, however, has been overcome.

It was pointed out from the union side that Olivetti has a special position in Italian industry and that the unions involved have a positive

opinion about the changes there. Changes in work organization are
one of the most important and principal demands of the Italian union
movement. That is why the unions are fully participating in experiments in participative work organization; in fact, the demands of the
unions have been one of the most fundamental reasons for change at
Olivetti. Thus, the union attitude is active to the extent of presenting demands rather than merely reacting to management initiatives.
Since a central approach to the different experiments is impossible,
the unions have greatly increased their bargaining activity at the plant
level. However, this is creating problems for union organization and
structure, since unions in Italy traditionally have been fairly centralized, particularly in their dealings with management, which had
been largely at an industrywide level.

The in-plant Italian union representatives dealing with questions
of work organization represent all the workers and are, in fact,
elected by all the workers and not only by union members. The
unions prefer to discuss planned changes in work organization before
their introduction, because once introduced, it is much more difficult
to make changes. In their view, increased wages and skills should
not be considered as incentives for accepting changes in work organization; rather, these should be seen as an essential part of the introduction of new systems, which give the worker the opportunity to
enrich the job and obtain greater satisfaction. At the same time,
because of close union involvement in these matters, workers keep
their interest in the union and in the wider problems of the labor
movement.

## GENERAL DISCUSSION ON SHOP FLOOR
## PARTICIPATION, WITH PARTICULAR REFERENCE
## TO THE SITUATION IN BELGIUM

A number of salient points arising out of the presentations and
comments were further developed.

### Union Attitudes Concerning Shop Floor Participation

A widely held Belgian union viewpoint was that democratization
and humanization of work through more participative forms of work
organization was not only acceptable but should be promoted. In fact,
in given cases, it would be desirable for unions to take the initiative
in militating for changes in work organization in order to make work
more meaningful and the workplace a forum for cooperation and collaboration rather than antagonism and conflict. Shop floor partici-

pation could be the basis for real democracy in the enterprise, but only under certain conditions: (1) changes should be based on a democratic decision of the workers themselves and not be imposed on them; (2) there should be guarantees for the safeguarding of employment for those who do not wish to, or cannot, cope with changed work organization, as well as those who do opt for the new system; (3) the experiments should fit in the system of industrial relations and not replace existing institutions, such as works councils, the union delegations, and so forth. In other words, the introduction of newer participative forms of work organization should not serve to subvert or vitiate the effectiveness of existing institutions in an enterprise.

In addition, unions had to be vigilant to ensure that shop floor participation was not used to undermine union organizational efforts and union impact on the enterprise. Unions also had to ensure that the new participative forms of work organization did not mask new systems of exploitation of the workers.

It was further pointed out that while it may be difficult to involve workers in the conceptual stage of elaborating new forms of participative work organization, it was necessary to involve them in the development and implementation of these new forms. Unions could carry out important work in motivating, stimulating, and assisting their members to actively participate in changes involving the introduction of more participative forms of work organization. For the unions, shop floor participation, and their involvement therein, was a natural and normal extension of their traditional tasks of protecting and furthering the well-being of workers.

The Relationship between Institutional Participation
and Shop Floor Participation

In the view of some union spokesmen, direct worker participation at the job level could not be divorced from wider institutionalized and representative forms of worker participation in management at all levels of the enterprise (including the company board level), and even of society as a whole. These processes should take place at the same time and in a parallel fashion. Moreover, the view was expressed that shop floor participation should lead to developing the principle of management whereby as many decisions as possible are to be taken at the lowest level possible.

Reservations Expressed

An employer viewpoint was that industry is now entering a sociotechnical phase of work organization and that the economic system was beginning to take into account the priority of the human factor. However, one had to look closely at what workers were aiming for with regard to shop floor participation. When confronted with a technically qualified supervisory staff, they could not be equal partners. Although management would be forced to go down the ladder to consult the workers, where were the limits or boundaries of participation? What would be the outcome in terms of efficiency and competitiveness of the enterprise?

## A Government View

The position of the Ministry of Labor and Employment concerning the humanization of work was explained. The ministry was in favor of humanization of work, which in its view could find expression in matters of security and hygiene, in shop floor participation, and in democratization of the structure of the enterprise. These three aspects were very strongly interrelated.

The ministry was in a position to inform those interested about the theories and experiences concerning new forms of participative work organization and to give a certain diffusion to these ideas by means of seminars, pamphlets, information, and so forth. The real change nevertheless had to come from the interested parties themselves, and to this end, it was necessary that they have trained persons capable of initiating and generating processes of change in the enterprise: these could be engineers, managers, in-plant worker representatives, and union officers.

## The Role and Position of Supervisors

First-line and intermediate supervisors have often shown an understandable resistance to the introduction of participatory work organization schemes, which often threatened their functions and longstanding responsibilities. It was pointed out that the problem of the resistance of first-line supervisors might resolve itself in the long run because of the fact that most of them come from the ranks, and after a certain time, a new generation of supervisors would be comfortable working in the context of these new, more participative structures.

## The Introduction of Shop Floor Participation and the Role of Experts and Consultants

It was emphasized, principally by some of the university scholar present, that the conditions surrounding the initiation of an experiment were very important. Many experiments had failed because the aims, purposes, forms, and possible consequences of the experiment were not clear to all the participants. Assistance of researchers and advisers may be necessary both in the initiation of change and in monitoring the effects of experiments. Universities were becoming increasingly equipped for these functions. However, it was cautioned that consultants had to work closely with, and rely upon, management at various levels, as well as the workers concerned and their representatives.

## FINAL COMMENTS

There was little doubt that generally speaking, the various participants were supportive of shop floor participation, although perhaps for different reasons. In this regard, union initiative and pressure were beginning to be felt.

At the same time, it was felt that if shop floor participation, in whatever form, were to come about on any wide scale, then it had to reflect a policy objective and political commitment. It was, however, difficult to find anything on this subject in the programs of the political parties of the country.

The idea of shop floor participation, although spreading, remains somewhat misunderstood or only vaguely known. It was evident to some that education in schools and universities, as well as participation in other social institutions, had to change and become less authoritarian, for it would not be easy to organize shop floor participation where other aspects of society remained hierarchical and non-participative. A change in mentality was certainly called for as a first step in generalizing shop floor participation. At the same time, it had to be recognized that to change the mentality and behavior of people was difficult; this was equally true for managers at all levels and for workers, their representatives, and unions.

# Case 2

## UNION-MANAGEMENT CONFLICTS OVER QUALITY-OF-WORKING-LIFE ISSUES (FRANCE)

### Henry Douard and J. D. Reynaud

This case study is divided into two parts. The first part describes the effects of power relationships in a French tool-making plant. The analysis of the problem involved has led to some changes in the organization of the plant that affect such relationships. The second part describes the way in which the power relationships are articulated between management and labor and the way in which they are institutionalized in the French system of industrial relations.

## BACKGROUND

It is increasingly assumed that conflict is a built-in aspect of organizational life. The relationships that take place among the various levels of the organizational hierarchy are power relationships, involving pressures and attempts to enlarge spheres of influence. The coordination of tasks, for example, in a specific production process cannot be considered to take place in perfect harmony. Although management is usually a party to conflict, it can act as arbitrator, making the final decision. In this context, the content of jobs would seem to be in part the result of an interplay of these power relationships.

If these assumptions are correct, the organizational structure of a plant is the result of the power struggle that goes on at the different hierarchical levels under the guise of technological constraints and efficient coordination. The creators of this structure may have

Henry Douard and J. D. Reynaud, in The Quality of Working Life, ed. L. E. Davis et al. (New York: The Free Press, 1975), 1: 393–403. Reproduced with permission.

a rather large range of choices: for example, between various mechanisms of control that are more or less centralized or participative. Their decisions may mean different criteria for job design and control methods at the various levels of the organization; any dysfunction, therefore, could be considered to reflect the nature and purpose of these decisions.

French unions have had a rather weak hold on work practices and thus emphasize the more easily controllable aspects. In the French system of industrial relations, working conditions are not a negotiable issue, and bargaining is generally conducted on an industrywide basis, not at the plant level. The consultative but nonbargaining (by law) role of the works committee is not satisfying to the unions. The practical solutions to enhance quality of working life as an industrial relations issue in France still have to be found, although some advances have been made since 1968. Management's freedom of action has led, at the plant level, to a piecemeal approach rather than a systemic treatment.

## A CASE STUDY IN POWER RELATIONSHIPS

The general management of the firm was faced with a foremen problem in a tool-making plant. In a recent work stoppage over a minor matter (a disagreement over the assignment of parking places), the foremen had sided with the workers, taking part in the stoppage —a very unusual step for men who are considered the lowest level of management.

At first, management thought this action merely reflected some general underlying discontent. It asked for a study to learn more about the opinions and attitudes of the first-line foremen, expecting that the findings would recommend some kind of human relations training or improvement of the communication and information network. However, the study took a different direction. It became clear at the outset that the foremen were the victims of a very complicated distribution—or, better, stratification—of roles and that dysfunctions were built into the system. Management had created a complicated network of power relationships to enhance its right of intervention, and this was largely the reason why conditions of work were felt to be deteriorating in the plant and why the situation was in some respects a stalemate.

The plant produced tools on a unit production basis, performing all the processes from casting to finishing. On the average, 1,500 hours of work were required to make a tool, each with its own characteristics and each having different specifications and sequence of operations, the opposite of an assembly line production.

The plant employed about 350 very highly skilled toolmakers with long experience. Such men were very hard to find in the labor market and were highly unionized. In view of the nature of the work and the experience and skill of the workers, one would assume that a minimum of supervision and coordination was needed, that is, the men would have a very large degree of autonomy. In practice, however, the opposite situation obtained: the organization put very tight controls on these workers.

The plant situation was as follows: customer orders arrived irregularly, with very strict deadlines for completion. Planning was very difficult, and it was practically impossible to have a steady flow of work. The planning department staff were not too familiar with the problems of production and always sought to satisfy delivery requirements of customers, backed by pressure from general management. Many conflicts arose between them and the shop, which management had constantly to resolve.

A time study office defined the sequence of operations required and allocated work times to each, distributing the work load among gangs. As may be inferred, conflicts at this point were at their worst. The time study people were confronted by powerful opponents—foremen and highly skilled workers; their decisions encroached directly on the autonomy of both. It might be worth noting here that the time study office was next to the manager's (with glass windows). Quite clearly, their work was guided by a technological rationality, but it also had a strategic purpose—to force upon the workers management's view of the best technical method, time needed, and so on to do the job. These were the points of greatest discontent in the plant, the place where most disputes arose. The times allocated—always considered too long or too short—were the focus of controversy. The choice of the machines was also criticized by the workers, who believed they were the only ones who knew which were best.

A small group of inspectors, reporting to another plant doing later processes, checked the different parts of tools before assembly. The organizational gap between inspection and production made the settlement of disagreements very difficult (for example, tolerances not kept). The disagreements were often appealed to the top. All daily technical problems were referred to the technical engineer, who had a monopoly over technical knowledge.

As to the foremen, their situation can be summarized as follows: When work loans were not too heavy and rather steady, they could get along with their job. However, when there were difficulties, the weakness of their status became apparent. First, their responsibility consisted exclusively of distributing work and inspecting performance. They took no part in its execution (though they were former workers) or in the decisions, which were left to the time study office.

They felt their tasks were routine, promoting lack of interest and isolation. Like the workers themselves, they felt they were losing their skills. The decision-making power seemed to them widely disseminated between noncommunicating groups—shop superintendent, plant management, general management, inspection, planning department, and time study—and when a problem arose, they did not know where to report. On the other hand, foremen had very few authority problems and very few conflicts with their men. They had common interests and a similar training and work background. The chain of command was very long. At plant level, there were six levels in the hierarchy, going down from plant manager, to technical engineer, to shop superintendent, to foreman, to gang boss, and, finally, to the worker. Above the plant were those levels, from general manager through manager to assistant-to-manager. Additionally, inspection and planning reported to the manager at firm level, and time study reported to the plant manager.

## INTERPRETATION OF PROBLEM IN
## TERMS OF POWER RELATIONSHIPS

At first glance, the difficulties of the plant would seem simple to understand. The firm's organizational structure shows an effort toward rational use of capacities along the accepted lines of planning: time study and inspection, with technical testing control at the level of the engineer. Although very complicated and with an excess of hierarchical levels, this organization faithfully follows the principles of scientific management. Following the efficiency dogma has led to some dysfunctional consequences. Part of the current discontent could even be explained by the nostalgia for craftsman-type methods of production.

However, even the overview just given makes this interpretation quite untenable. The foremen were in a situation in which they could not get a clear idea of the total process. They could not settle minor conflicts, having to search for the appropriate decision maker, because of the rules of the functional departments or the complications of the hierarchy.

The entire organizational structure seemed to deny a full grasp of the process: the planning department, sensitive to customer demands, did not know much about production problems; the time study staff (incidentally, staffed by people of the same training as the foremen) decided the details of execution but was kept away from the machines; the inspectors could reject the finished work, but could not specify in advance what was desired. The many conflicts that arose seemed embedded in the definition of the tasks. This rigid hierarchy favored the centralization of all decision making and adjudication, which means that all decisions, differences, and disagreements are handled at the top.

The organization works as a system of mutual controls (planning and production, time study and production, inspection and production), with the engineer and the manager exercising control (which is reinforced by the very high number of conflicts that arise from any incident). The firm's manager explained, for instance, that the old craftsman system was uncontrollable because the absence of a worker halted all work on his tool. Though superficially sound, this argument seems more a rationalization than an explanation, given the difficulty of delivering orders on time in the present system. In fact, however, the ongoing conflicts are not unforeseen consequences of a rational organization: they are the basis of a strategy of extreme centralization of power.

The foremen's situation emerges significantly as a result of this strategy, leading to their feelings of powerlessness, or encroachment from different groups, and of loss of interest in their jobs; all these point to the same fact—the conscious strategy of management to retain all control in its own hands.

Conflicts, consequently, would not disappear with the introduction of human relations training; although temporarily useful, it would not change the constant recourse to arbitration at the top. However, a new plant manager tried to change the direction by working not on behaviors and attitudes but on the organizational structure itself and on the very definition of the work roles. For instance, he decided to rotate jobs between foremen and time study people; he made various changes to shorten the chain of command; and he organized study groups on product quality, bringing together foremen and inspectors, and, in some cases, representatives of customers' plants. He held regular consultation and orientation meetings on organizational structure. While rather modest in themselves, these steps—which should be followed by others—tended to enrich the jobs of the workers; to build a bridge between the functions of foremen, time study, and inspectors; and to enrich the jobs of the foremen by widening their responsibility. At the same time, management was no longer totally occupied with resolving minor conflicts and had more time to attend to customer demands, technological innovations, and personnel administration. Without changes in technology and product and in the general context of the firm, there is the prospect of a gradual change in the work roles, which will result in a different distribution of power.

Initially, the organization defined each function with very restricted responsibilities. This was not the result of a rational division of work, but was designed to ensure dependence on higher management. The conflicts arising out of the incapacity of each member to grasp the total process were built into the structure (in favor of continuous arbitration and control from the top). The new changes, in contrast, attempt to enrich the functions of the workers and the foremen and to facilitate direct coordination among planning, time study, and inspection. This changes the locus of operative decisions; their enhanced autonomy is closely linked to a new and different distribution of power.

A CASE STUDY IN INSTITUTIONALIZATION
OF POWER RELATIONSHIPS

In this section, the manner will be described in which the power relationships outlined in the preceding section affect labor-management relations in France.

The power relations analyzed thus far are largely implicit; they provide a perspective for organizational solutions and are useful as a hypothesis to explain them, but they are only implicitly involved. A case of conflict at the shop floor level reveals a more explicit relationship.

In the provincial plant of a large electrical appliance firm, the semiskilled operators voiced many grievances about working conditions. Management decided to seek a study of this from a group of academic researchers in ergonomics, or work physiology. It should be noted that the request was made by the works committee, through its chairperson, the plant manager. Thus, the initiative for the study was a joint one, coming from a conflict situation.

The study was completed after one-and-a-half years, and the results were made available to all members of the plant. The unions found them so palatable that the CFDT local used them very extensively in a pamphlet calling for organized action. Though the initial problem had been mainly nuisances and discomfort on the job, the rationale of the pamphlet has a much larger significance, which will serve as an example.

Relying heavily on the study by the ergonomists, the pamphlets made a general attack on poor working conditions; badly designed jobs, requiring heavy physical effort that could be avoided; excessive mental pressure because of strict work pace; inequity of work load and effort among jobs; and so on. The critics were not just denouncing the planning department. They were questioning the so-called scientific basis of rationality of the planning department, not only because it did not recognize individual differences in capacity and skill among the operators and combines in the same job heavy physical effort and precision operations but also because the accurate determination in advance of all operator movements is deemed an impossible task. Criticized is the so-called scientific management of work, which disguises arbitrary decisions as "technical reasons." This is reinforced by the fact that the planning technicians under scientific management have no training in adapting jobs to people. At stake are not only the criteria of the decisions but the distribution of power to make them.

What follows are logical conclusions. The pamphlet cites all the cases where operators have to take the initiative and change the prescribed ways of working so as to make for effective production, where they have to improvise because of variances or material defects, where they help one another to solve problems, and where they themselves train newcomers. The conclusion is that the semi-skilled operators are really responsible for effective production and that management has to draw upon their "knowledge" and "work skills" to ensure that jobs are well done.

The criticism is interesting on two accounts. First, it sheds light on what is left of initiative and responsibility in jobs that seem very poor in content and strictly determined from above. In itself, this notion should come as no great surprise for time-and-motion study technicians, at least those who are conscious of the limits of their planning. But it is used here to demand "an improvement of the status of semiskilled jobs." The context makes it quite clear that the demand is for a higher classification and higher wages, but not only for that—it is, too, for job enrichment, using as a point of departure the daily working practices, and it is articulated as a grievance.

Second and more important, what is left of the initiative and responsibility is used in argument—that the semiskilled operators have some power in bargaining with management. The pamphlet considers the possibility, among others, of using "working to rule": "If we did the work exactly as it is prescribed," it reads, "that would stop production." In other words, the operators already have some autonomy in their work, unskilled as it is, and this autonomy could be a source of power in case of open conflict.

This rather detailed account of the pamphlet is an example of how the analysis of work can be used in a conflict situation. However, it provides few details on how these grievances can be resolved and states the objectives in very general terms. The reason is a basic one: there are difficulties in translating the gripes and feelings at the shop floor level into union strategy.

WORK CONDITIONS AND UNIONS: THE CASE OF THE CGT

The problem of working conditions came to the forefront in the major strikes of 1968 and in several minor ones in the following months, when it was articulated, but often not in its full implications (work pace, work load, workweek, and shift work). The left-wing groups of the unions tried for some time to identify the problem with their cause. What was new, in fact, was not the topic itself but its very strong expression and the radical aspect of some grievances.

The problem has been a traditional concern of the unions, and they integrated it very easily into their programs. Each federation did it in its own style (and this style was influenced by their respective relations with their left-wing groups). Some conclusions may be drawn from the case of the General Confederation of Labour (CGT).

The confederation's paper printed the report of a study in February 1972 calling "for working conditions in keeping with the human needs of our time" and concluding with a list of demands. The main conclusions are stated in the "action program," called for by the Federal Congress of April 1972. At that congress, a shortened version was given in the report of the Federal Executive Council, presented by its secretary-general, Georges Seguy.

These reports develop the confederation's position on the problem of working conditions. This time, the term has a more inclusive meaning, incorporating work pace and schedules, as well as interesting work and opportunity for advancement. Some elements of this union strategy are discussed below.

CGT Attack against Employer Initiatives

At the outset, the CGT launched a very strong attack against employer initiatives. Job enrichment and improvement of work on assembly lines (it also added participative management) are cited as being "a wide maneuver in ideological demagoguery." The employers, "faced with well-grounded demands by their workers, try to deceive and trap them into class collaboration." Their purpose "remains the same: to go on with and strengthen capitalist exploitation."

This sweeping attack does not imply that no problem exists. On the contrary, the union's program states as an objective that it is necessary to "improve the quality and variety of the tasks for everyone" and to "give the workers a better share in initiative and responsibility"—a formula that could serve as a rather sound definition of job enrichment. The purpose of this attack is, then, to discredit the initiatives (as exclusively the employers'). In this way, the unions are the only ones entitled to take initiatives for real improvement. Moreover, having proved to its own satisfaction that nothing is new in this problem except "technical and economic conditions," the CGT is not faced with any basic reappraisal. The problem of working conditions has been brought back to the classic conflict situation between labor and management.

## The Basic Problem

To make quite clear that the basic problem is an old one, though the economic and social context makes it more acute and pressing, a good part of the discussion is spent on classic topics, like the pace of work or the deskilling process as logical consequences of capitalist exploitation. The current issues, though they deserve to be studied for their own sake and are granted a special chapter in the action program, are the natural result of previous conflicts, articulated in a language congenial to the activists.

## Main Difficulty

The main difficulty, however, is to make operative these general demands, that is, to articulate objectives that are controlled by union delegates or elected representatives of the employees. It should be recalled that French unions have a rather weak hold on work practices and that their powers have to be extended if they are to control them. This is the reason why the list of demands stresses, within the work situation, the more easily controllable aspects. For instance, the CGT asks that work pace, manning, and work loads be posted in the shop; it asks for rest periods and rest rooms; and it demands that employees, worker representatives, and union delegates be notified in advance of any change in the work procedure. Concerning training and promotion, it asks for "guaranteed career development" and for the right for all semiskilled operators to be placed in a new job after one year's experience. In this effort to make demands operative, interest in the variety of work, in responsibility, and in initiative is no longer mentioned for very obvious reasons.

## Formulation of Demands

Lastly, care has been taken to give these demands as broad a formulation as possible in order to involve the largest number of union members and nonmembers. A striking example is the report of the Executive Council, which, after giving a systematic view of the problem of working conditions, returns to a very simplified statement, insisting only on the shortening of the workweek and earlier retirement. Step by step, the complex content of the report is "simplified" in the action program, and from the action program to the Executive Council's report, and not without reason. This process is indicative of the difficulty surrounding the problem in the traditional context of industrial relations.

Is There a Management Strategy?

This question is better understood in the light of some statements from the employers' side. The National Employers' Association did not take a stand as such, but it printed the conclusions of a
study group that, while not acting on behalf of the association, speaks
in an official capacity. The study group consulted several experts
and made a very broad analysis of the "problem of semiskilled workers," discussing wages, classification, status in collective agreements, and a time and motion study.

The main purpose of the report was to remind the employers of
their responsibilities and to invite them to action. But it cannot be
said that in so doing it would close the door to collective bargaining
and ignore the unions. For instance, when discussing the possibilities
for training and advancement, it makes explicit reference to the interindustry agreement on training of July 1970. Moreover, it considers the opportunity to negotiate some of its proposals; promoting
a better classification of semiskilled workers, it mentions the current negotiations in several industries on classification. In the same
spirit, it stresses the value of the "monthly salary" agreements,
which have been signed in different industries since 1970, and it proposes several provisions directly inspired by the intent of these agreements. It is fair to say that the stand taken implies no aggression
toward unions and no systematic avoidance of bargaining.

In other respects, however, there is a different attitude. Wages
are a good example. The employers' committee intends to improve
the relative level of compensation for semiskilled workers and concludes: "It would be a very good thing if the law of supply and demand
could operate more freely in our country." Limiting the effect of the
market is public regulation, the example of the public sector and "a
tendency to follow the pattern of civil servants." The committee
plans, as a first step, to distinguish between the scale of take-home
wages and the scale of minimum rates and to provide "complementary
compensation" for less attractive jobs—no innovation, since such a
practice is currently in force. However, it must be remembered that
the difference between effective wages and minimum rates, and even
more between the scale of both, is one of the matters unions complain
about.

More generally, the employers' association's report sees in
agreements already concluded or in prospect an opportunity for more
managerial initiative. The national agreement on training could be
used as a basis to promote semiskilled workers. However, such
promotion is not guaranteed by the agreement and is not a negotiable
matter. Likewise, changes in time-and-motion study methods for the
purpose of improving comfort and interest on the job rest on "a steady

effort of higher management to change the attitudes of shop management. "

In other words, if progress is possible in this field, it must depend on managerial initiative, and while this would not disrupt the pattern of collective bargaining, it would not broaden it. Although "workers' grievances" about working conditions are mentioned, this area is defined as a mangerial prerogative, a natural attitude in a system of industrial relations in which the work practices are not a legitimate object for bargaining: it would be surprising indeed if the employers offered to include them in negotiation. In this context, then, it becomes clear why the CGT, before discussing substantive issues, starts with a massive attack on possible initiatives of the "enemy."

Working Conditions and the
System of Industrial Relations

The basic stumbling block is rather easy to define: In the French system of industrial relations, working conditions, in its inclusive context, is not a negotiable issue. Only in very exceptional cases does bargaining, properly speaking, take place at the plant level; it is generally industrywide (for a region or for the whole country). It can easily accommodate the workweek or special compensation for shift work, but it can hardly concern itself with problems of job content.

The works committee, by law, has a consultative role with respect to working conditions that does not include bargaining. Moreover, the unions feel reluctance toward the increasing role employers have been willing to give them during the last few years (it is very significant that this is not even mentioned in these CGT reports).

The grievance procedure, handled by employee-elected representatives, would be a more appropriate framework, but is not adequate; it is in most cases strongly centralized because the representatives are elected at the plant and not at the shop floor level and because it is generally not a step-by-step procedure (most issues go directly to personnel managers). With final and binding arbitration not available, the outcome of a grievance rests largely on worker action, and the procedure tends to discriminate in favor of those grievances that can be most easily generalized.

This overview does not mean that there are no solutions but that the practical solutions have yet to be found. Industrial relations in France in the last four years have left much room for innovation. The current uncertainty explains the cautiousness of the unions, as well as the very unobtrusive way in which employers experiment along this line. Results are few, but they exist; however, in most cases, management avoids publicizing what it is doing.

In a paradoxical way, this situation, which seems to leave total freedom of action to management, is a real hindrance to the development of enhanced quality of working life. At the plant level, it favors a piecemeal approach instead of systemic treatment; prudence suggests seizing local opportunities rather than facing the general problem. Moreover, the diffusion and public discussion of experiments are very limited, and successful attempts have had little influence.

Improving the quality of working life implies a change in the principles of job design, that is, eventually a change in the value system of management. In the conflict context of industrial relations, however, a value system does not arise out of faith but out of compromise. Changes are possible when they are needed and when institutions are available to develop such compromise. The current problem in France (and perhaps in other European countries as well) involving conditions of work and the quality of working life is not their stake in industrial conflict; rather, it lies in the difficult institutionalization of conflict.

# Case 3

## EXPERIENCES OF AUTONOMOUS WORKING GROUPS IN A SWEDISH CAR FACTORY

### Sigvard Rubenowitz

This is a case study of one Swedish auto manufacturing plant—Saab-Scania—which experimented with autonomous work groups as an alternative to the traditional assembly line production. This study outlines the changeover and new production system. The merits of the "line out" system are portrayed, particularly in regard to productivity gains and increased job satisfaction.

### BACKGROUND

In 1975 most of the assembly lines at the body department of the Saab-Scania plant in Trollhättan were replaced by work stations where eight workers carry out the final welding, grinding, adjustment, and inspection, while the auto is stationary.

The reason for the transition was the various problems linked to the assembly line's human costs. When the employee turnover rate amounted to more than 50 percent in the beginning of the 1970s, and the absenteeism grew to about 25 percent, the company began to investigate changes to the work environment. In 1971 Saab had scrapped the assembly lines at the engine factory at Södertälje, and on the whole, this experiment had proved to be successful.

By abandoning the assembly line, the possibilities for each employee to influence his or her own work situation would be enhanced. Another objective was to render the various production tasks more attractive and meaningful. A further aim was to reduce susceptibility to disruption and to increase production efficiency by greater flexibility and adaptability. Thus, in sum, the object was to strive for increased productivity accompanied by higher job satisfaction.

---

This study was conducted by Sigvard Rubenowitz, Göteborg University, Sweden.

## LABOR RELATIONS CLIMATE
## IN THE PLANT AND THE ENTERPRISE

As in most other Swedish plants, the collaboration between the management and the unions was good. In the course of time, and backed by a lot of basic agreements between the Swedish Employers' Confederation and the Swedish Trade Union Confederation, a valuable mutual trust had developed between managers, foremen, and worker. This "confidence capital" proved to be most helpful during the transition period.

## THE CHANGE PROCESS

The initiative toward the work organization change was taken by the department manager, who established a steering group, the members of which were the production director, two other management representatives, and two union representatives. At the shop floor level, production groups with foremen and the affected workers were established. The steering group was responsible for the policy question pertaining to the work organization, while the production groups were more involved in the practical job task questions.

The changeover was accomplished during the summer holidays (1975) at a cost of about U.S. $2.5 million.

Even if there was some suspicion to overcome, not least from the foremen's side, most people at the department, from the shop floor to the department manager, worked with commitment for the change once the decision was made. Involving the workers affected by the change in the planning of it tended to mitigate the feelings of insecurity workers had when established work methods had to be changed for untried ones.

## THE NEW PRODUCTION SYSTEM

Before the change, the car bodies were made on a traditional assembly line with a cycle time of three to six minutes. The workers were directly steered with a detailed control system and without individual responsibility for the quality or other parts of the job.

The autonomous groups (or self-controlling groups, as they are called by the Saab people) have several types of jobs within their responsibility. At the work stations, where the bodies are stationary, the production group members are carrying out welding, grinding, and adjustment, and in addition to these production tasks, they are responsible for equipment maintenance, transport, and the cleaning and controlling of their own work area and administration. The cycle time is about 45 minutes.

Dependent upon the technological structure of each group, the proportion of the various tasks can vary from group to group. In principle, each individual group member should be able to work at any of the tasks of the group.

The coordination of the tasks is made by one of the group members, "the contact man." This function, which rotates between all group members, is normally of one week's duration. Most of the coordinator's time is devoted to administration, but also to transport and equipment maintenance. The coordinator also has to visit the following production section in order to estimate the production quality of the group in relation to the demands of the following section.

The goal for the group is to produce 52 bodies a week, and since a higher production rate does not give a higher wage, the group need not experience the stress arising from piece rates.

The responsibilities of the group can be summarized in the following way: planning and accomplishment of the production program, control of arriving material, transport, maintenance, cleaning, introduction and teaching of new members, permission for absence (one day maximum), control of the product, feedback of sample control of the product, and budget. The groups have, together with the foreman, worked out rules for the behavior inside the group. These rules have been confirmed by the groups and the steering group (management and the union). Formal rules exist for all groups on such matters as the role of the coordinator, rules for recruitment (the groups have veto rights), job rotation, control, and so forth.

## EMPIRICAL FINDINGS

### Productivity

What gains and drawbacks have been registered since the new organization was introduced four years ago? Has the new organization, offering an increased possibility for people to decide on matters that directly affect them, resulted in increased job satisfaction and increased or retained at least the same productivity?

As to the productivity, it can first be noted that considerable production gains have been made. When the new system was planned, Saab estimated a payoff time of the investments at 3.8 years, but the goal was reached after only 2.63 years.

It is a general opinion that the modern scale of car production makes assembly lines necessary from a profitability point of view, even if it might be disastrous for the physically and psychologically

TABLE 10

Time Losses in Different Technological Systems
(in percent)

| System | System Losses | Balance Losses | Handling Losses | Total |
|---|---|---|---|---|
| Old welding and grinding assembly line | 45 | 16 | 0 | 61 |
| New line-out system (autonomous group system) | 15 | 2 | 4 | 21 |

Source: Compiled by the author.

isolated assembly line worker. The experiences from Saab-Scania contradict this widespread opinion. From the human or the technical-economical point of view, the line system proved to be inferior to the autonomous working group organization. A comparison between the two systems as to efficiency losses clearly is in favor of the new system, according to thorough analyses made at the plant. In a production system, there are always efficiency losses in the sense that more time is needed than would be theoretically necessary. First, there are system losses—time needed for control and adjustment. Then, there are balance losses due to the fact that it is impossible to keep all operators busy to the same degree. On an assembly line, these losses can be of a considerable size, about 20 percent is not unusual. Then there are handling losses—handling of tools and material can be considerable in comparison with assembling and fixing time. In Table 10 some figures on the losses at the traditional driven assembly line at Saab and the new line-out system (the autonomous groups) are given. The figures are based on careful and reliable measurements at Saab.

As Table 10 shows, the total time losses at the new line-out group system proved to be 21 percent of the necessary production time, compared with 61 percent for the old lines. The large difference between the two systems is mainly due to the diminishing number of quality controllers in the line-out system. At a production rate of 60,000 bodies per year, a saving of 15 controllers is obtained. A statistical sample control on about 5 percent of the finished bodies is still applied. According to this, the quality has increased significantly since the change.

Among other production gains, it can be mentioned that unplanned stoppages have proved to occur much less frequently in the new line-out system than previously.

On the debit side, it can be mentioned that there is an increase in the expenses due to the need for relatively large buffers, for changes in the technological structure, and for the considerable training investments. However, according to the financial calculations, the production gains outweigh these expenses by far. As the department manager puts it:

> A common view on work organization changes toward
> autonomous groups is that this is something that you
> can take up under good times, when you can afford some
> money in order to increase the job satisfaction. Had it
> not been profitable with autonomous groups, it would have
> been beyond our means to carry on with such activities.
> Fortunately the fact is that if the activities are run in the
> right way, it is a profitable investment.

Job Satisfaction

Three different measures were used in order to get a view on the general job satisfaction among the employees working in the autonomous groups: the absenteeism, the turnover, and attitude surveys.

As far as absenteeism is concerned, the figures for 1976 and 1977 can be compared between workers in the autonomous groups and workers at the traditional assembly line (see Table 11).

It appears from Table 11 that the total absenteeism is clearly higher at the assembly line than at the line-out unit. However, it also appears that sickness accounts for the differences. Absenteeism "for other reasons" proved to be of the same magnitude. As mentioned previously, the members in the production groups were allowed to give each other permission for absence for personal reasons. This possibility for leisure time is highly regarded and also utilized in a planned way.

As regards turnover, it was hoped that a substantial decrease would appear among the workers in the line-out system. The expectation was already fulfilled within one year of the change; after that, the turnover continued on a low level. However, the oscillations in the state of the market and changes in shift work, of course, affect the turnover figures. Perhaps one of the most interesting items to note is the direction of the manpower flow. When workers leave the traditional units, they either go to the autonomous working groups or

TABLE 11

Absenteeism at New and Traditional Units
(in percent)

| System | Absenteeism for Sickness | | Absenteeism for Other Reasons | | Total Absenteeism | |
|---|---|---|---|---|---|---|
| | 1976 | 1977 | 1976 | 1977 | 1976 | 1977 |
| Old welding and grinding assembly line | 15.5 | 18.4 | 10.3 | 10.0 | 25.8 | 28.4 |
| New line-out system (autonomous group system) | 12.0 | 13.7 | 10.7 | 9.0 | 22.7 | 22.7 |

Source: Compiled by the author.

to other companies. Among workers leaving the autonomous groups, hardly any go to the traditional units. They either go to qualified service departments within the Saab plant or, to a lesser degree, to other companies.

A view on job satisfaction was obtained through group discussions and attitude surveys. According to the group discussions, job satisfaction is considerably higher in the autonomous groups than at the line. However, in the changed work situation, it is not the individual job content that is of greatest importance. It is rather the general job conditions that lie behind the increased satisfaction, especially the possibility to choose one's working pace and the feeling of group cohesiveness. If one compares the difference between the minimum time needed to perform a day's job and the time available, there is no difference between the line and the line-off systems. In both cases, it amounts to about one hour and a half a day. But the important difference is that at the line, you are paced by the system and forced to take the time off repeatedly in fractions of minutes. In the line-off system, you are free to dispose of this time at your own convenience. In many groups, for example, the workers would work eagerly in the mornings in order to get an hour off in the afternoon to rest before leaving the plant. An important technological prerequisite for the relatively free time disposal is sufficiently large buffers before and after the production group.

A quantitative way of measuring job satisfaction is to use attitude scales. Some results are shown below that were obtained when several well-standardized questions were given to both assembly line workers and autonomous group workers within different production systems at the Saab plant in Trollhättan. The scale measures individual job satisfaction ("How interesting and stimulating do you regard your work to be?" Do you like the work you are doing in this plant?").

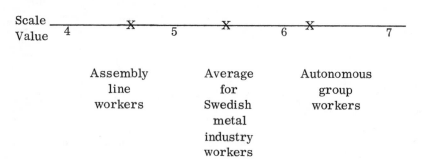

It is obvious that the attitude survey results support the general picture obtained from other data.


The Changing Role of the Supervisors

It is often (and sometimes with good reasons) feared that the foreman group will get into a problem as a result of organizational changes from the traditional to a more participative pattern. How did the foremen react during the change process at Saab, and in what way did their role change?

From the beginning of the discussions concerning alternative organizational changes, the foremen affected were directly engaged in the planning of the project. They soon changed from a wait-and-see policy to a more positively active attitude. As a matter of fact, many of them acted as eager change agents during the transition period. They were not dismissed but, rather, played a new and more stimulating role. In the new group organization, the supervisors must be prepared to discuss all changes or adjustments, very often with group members with a considerable theoretical and practical knowledge. In order to meet the new role, the supervisors received a wide training within the fields of organization, personnel administration, production technology, economy, and so forth.

It may be added that the majority of the foremen were in favor of this new role, but there were some exceptions, primarily among older supervisors.

CONCLUSION

In summary, the autonomous production groups, in the way they are planned and function at Saab-Scania in Trollhättan, have proved to be an economically profitable alternative to the traditional line. The change has resulted in both increased productivity and increased job satisfaction, and the new organizational principles are expanding more and more within the company, in spite of some drawbacks and problems. These are primarily linked to the costs of rebuilding the technological production system, to increased costs for training, and to capital costs, which are connected with an increased number of buffers. The material handling problems were not great at the body shop, but have proved to be considerable at the end assembly of the cars.

On the positive side, there are decreased costs for quality control, fewer and shorter stoppages, more reliable material handling, decreased costs for instructors, decreased turnover, and decreased rationalization costs. Also, since the personnel can be more usable in various jobs, they tend to become more positive and engaged in their work and offer opportunities for increased organizational development.

What has been described is the experiences in a plant unit where all main demands, which according to general findings are necessary for successfully functioning autonomous groups, are satisfied.

These demands might be summarized in the following way:

1. The production group should work within a well-defined and limited work space.

2. The production group should have a well-defined common production goal.

3. The members of the production group should, if possible, have the competence to carry out all kinds of tasks.

4. The wages should be the same for all members; any differentiation should be linked to competence rather than to individual productivity.

5. The group should have the chance to have a say over its own composition, for example, over the recruitment of new members.

6. The work pace should not be linked to a production rate steered by the surrounding technological system; the group should, in other words, have a certain autonomy in relation to the production system, which implies considerable buffers at both sides of the production.

7. The group should also have a certain autonomy in relation to the administrative system, including, among other things, responsibility for the quality, economy, and work assignment—a prerequisite for this is a well-functioning system for feedback concerning the productivity.

8. There should be a variety of tasks for the group.

9. If a coordinator is needed, the position should circulate between the group members.

10. The level of production goal should allow a good collaboration without risk of ostracism (thrusting out members who do not have a high working capacity).

## SOME USEFUL FINDINGS ON THE CHANGE PROCESS

In a large number of plants, more or less successful attempts have been made to establish autonomous production groups. Is it possible to find some general characteristics in the process of enlarging the work content of the individual, either separately or by creating autonomous or semiautonomous work groups? Yes, at least according to experiences in Swedish plants, among all factors, the change agents probably play the most important role. In plants where line managers, supervisors, and well-qualified skilled workers assume an active role in the change process, it has been much more successful than in plants where the innovations have come primarily from external consultants, or where the reorganization has been planned by staff members or by representative groups working as separate adjuncts to the established organization. The expanded scope for employees should take place entirely in the work organization itself.

The most successful attempts have been made according to a program that has begun on a small scale in one or more foreman areas or departments where there has been found a willingness to try new ideas, rather than on a large scale, covering a whole plant and according to a strict timetable.

Besides, on the whole, it has been found that the possibilities of achieving comprehensive changes in the existing job design is more limited by technological and economic considerations than is expected by most people. Thus, possibilities for more radical sociotechnical solutions are most often applicable in new plants.

Another problem in the change process is linked to the traditional attitudes at the working place. If a relatively tough authoritarian atmosphere has been prevailing in a workplace for years, the likelihood that the workers will collaborate in autonomous groups is relatively small. Nor can you expect a positive attitude without any question toward job enlargement from workers, who for years have had individual tasks of the same kind. In such cases, it is better to organize limited self-steering groups with an authorized leader at the beginning. If, however, newly hired workers, especially when they have a relatively solid education, are required to be prepared to accept responsibility for several associated tasks, gradually, you will probably be able to get efficient autonomous production groups.

# Case 4

## THE QUALITY OF WORKING LIFE: THE JAPANESE EXPERIENCE

### Shin-ichi Takezawa

This study describes the background and nature of quality-of-working-life projects in Japan. It examines the experiences of workers, unions, and management in four Japanese enterprises that have experimented with quality-of-working-life projects and draws the lessons from such experiences for the future.

### INTRODUCTION

What constitutes a high quality of working life may vary in relation to both the worker's aspirations and the objective reality of his or her work and society. Whether it primarily means security, equity, individuation, or democracy, one thing seems clear.[1] The quality of working life is ultimately defined by the worker himself or herself.

### TRADITIONS CONCERNING THE QUALITY OF WORKING LIFE

In every industrial society, working people have traditionally considered improved employment conditions to be one of the basic requirements of a good quality of working life. After World War II, Japanese labor and management reached the mutual consensus that their economic well-being was to depend not only on equitable dis-

Shin-ichi Takezawa, "The Quality of Working Life: Trends in Japan," in Labour and Society 1, no. I (1976): 29–48. Excerpts reproduced with the permission of the author and of the International Institute of Labour Studies, Geneva.

tribution but on the growth of income itself through increased productivity. As was usual in a labor surplus economy, Japan's goal was to raise the level of productivity and wages to that of advanced industrial nations, while maintaining the fullest possible employment. From 1960 to 1972, individual wages registered a 111.1 percent increase in real terms, while the annual unemployment ratio was kept stable between 1.1 and 1.5 percent. * In a way, the economic goal set forth in the 1950s has been more or less achieved. Even though the social stock still needs substantial enrichment, industrial money wages nowadays compare well with those of many European workers. As the five-day workweek becomes a rule, Japanese workers will also have more time to think. The real question then is what to think about.

Perhaps the age of single-minded economic growth is already over, as suggested by Masumi Tsuda, labor economist. According to him, gone is the national consensus of the 1950s and 1960s, and in the 1970s, we must switch to a low growth in search for better quality of life.[2] Does the substantial revision in old-age pensions that just began in 1973 really symbolize a shift in social policies? Is a parallel change in emphasis occurring in corporate management and union attitudes? Last but not least, are the values of workers really to undergo a change? In a previous article, I pointed out that predominant workers' values still centered around economic issues, with the possible exception of young workers.[3] Are meaningful work and participation gaining further importance among young Japanese workers?

At least the basic quality of Japanese corporate life, which Dore once referred to as the "welfare corporatism," has shown little evidence of change.[4] Career employment security until retirement is still the rule and is taken for granted by the mainstream of the work force. † In private industries, enterprise-based labor unions are hard

---

*Even around 1960, substantial make-work must have existed when viewed from the present level of productivity. If the 1972 productivity level had prevailed in 1960, 13.6 million workers, or 57 percent of the 1960 employed work force, would have been jobless without loss to the 1960 economy. Calculations are based on statistics from Manpower Survey (Prime Minister's Office) and National Income Statistics (Economic Planning Agency), Tokyo.

† Even though the 1970/71 recession hit the two countries somewhat alike, the half-year rate of separations for "employers' convenience" in Japan never exceeded 1 percent; whereas in the United States, the half-year layoff rate fluctuated between 8 and 12 percent levels during the period. Japan, Ministry of Labour, The Analysis of Labour Economics, 1973 (Tokyo: Government Printing Office, 1974), p. 100 (in Japanese).

bargainers in wage negotiations, but they also keep a close eye on the
future corporate growth. For all classes of workers, age, which almost equals the length of service, remains the principal parameter
of income differences; even education counts less in Japan than in the
United States. Almost everybody has become a supervisor or manager by the time of compulsory retirement. Such elements of security
and equity, hard won over the past three decades, are very unlikely
to be forgone even in the future. Although none can excuse the social
evils of the dual economy and the discrimination against talented
women and the aged, the balance in these areas has also been somewhat redressed.

In any enterprise, public or private, voluntary interorganiza-
tion turnover is still virtually nonexistent among managers: this fact
makes the human bonds exceptionally solid in Japanese organizations.
Most of the top managers of large corporations have made their way
through successive promotions within their own firms. Just as the
present-day university graduates have to do, the senior executives
also once took the entrance examination and started their work as
rank-and-file employees. Most of the middle managers today held
union membership until they reached the management level, and not
a few have even served as union officers. The present-day foremen
are likely to have been senior colleagues of many of the current young
executives. All of these statements apply equally to specialists in
Japanese organizations; the difference between a manager and a specialist is a matter of work assignment and, quite often, a coincidence
in the process of corporate manpower allocation and utilization.
Hence, overall personnel practices make it difficult for functional
and class divisions to be perpetuated in Japanese organizations.

This characteristic nature of Japanese organizations may have
much to do with the managers' expressed interest in behavioral theories of management ever since the days of the human relations
movement. The literature in behavioral sciences, such as the works
of Maslow, McGregor, Herzberg, Likert, and Argyris, are widely
circulated in translation, and their popularized versions are also used
in foreman training courses. The behavioral science model of management, however, is not perceived as an antithesis of the organizational reality, as it might be in the United States. Instead, Japanese
managers tend to accept the model as an idealized goal, which essentially lies in the same direction as their own behavioral orientation.
Often, they are puzzled to find out that U.S. management in practice
fits the scientific management model far better than the behavioral
model.

Around 1960, the interest in worker expectations and reactions,
inevitably shared by managers and labor leaders, took the new form
of growing popularity of worker "consciousness" studies, as funds

and computers became rapidly available due to Japan's economic prosperity. Previously, only social scientists had been engaged in job satisfaction studies, but in the later 1950s, management also took an interest in studying workers' morale and attitudes. * Labor unions and government joined later in this trend.

The preceding paragraphs should not be interpreted to mean that the quality of working life is already considered to be adequate in the Japanese scene. Increasingly, there is a recognition that workers' values—their preferences, reactions, attitudes, and consciousness—constitute a legitimate and important constraint in management, union, and governmental policy formulation. However, the internal industrial environment, structured mainly to meet the accelerated productivity demands of the 1960s, has often been incompatible, socially as well as physically, with the necessary shift in policy emphasis. On the contrary, in many large capital-intensive firms, organizations are being further subdivided, skills are undergoing profound changes, and specialists' roles are gaining more importance; the autonomy of each workplace is still being reduced. What, then, are the patterns of workers' reactions to the reality of Japanese organizations?

## PROTESTS IN QUEST OF BETTER QUALITY OF WORKING LIFE

The first wave of protests from labor during the postwar upheaval was directed toward the "democratization" of enterprise management. Under the revised legal framework, the newly organized labor unions first institutionalized the system of collective bargaining. Then, in addition to "livelihood wages," unions demanded the removal of various status distinctions that had sharply separated the blue and white collar workers until the war's end. Some of the imposed distinctions were trivial but irritating and humiliating. For example, one company prohibited the use of coats and ties by production workers, even in their private lives. The unions succeeded in eliminating most of such authoritarian discriminations, including, in many cases, the division of daily wages and monthly salaries. Egalitarianism is by no means exclusive to Japanese labor unionism, but its contribution

---

*Since 1955 the NRK Employee Opinion Survey, a standardized questionnaire concerning the morale of workers (most widely used in Japan), has been administered to over 2 million workers, according to the Japan Personnel Research Association, its sponsoring institution.

to the equity goal is evident not only in the working life but also in society as a whole. (For example, education is increasingly losing ground as a prime determinant of differences in career income among the employed work force.)[5] There is one area in the work life, however, that remains largely untouched by the unions: work itself.

Japanese unions are divided as to whether they should confine themselves to collective bargaining or whether they should participate in "management" issues, including organization and work problems. During the early postwar years, the mainstream of labor unionism almost unanimously supported the eventual socialization of industry. This position has since been inherited mainly by the largest national labor centers, Sohyo (General Council of Trade Unions of Japan), whose major affiliate organizations come from the public sector. Sohyo still maintains its official position that social ownership is its ultimate goal and is highly skeptical of labor's formal participation in management. Collective bargaining, or participation by protest, then, becomes the only legitimate form of union interaction with management. As to the union's role in the quality of working life, General-Secretary Shogo Ohki of Sohyo does not rule out youth's possible discontent with work monotony. But he believes that longer and more frequent rest periods and the enrichment of the material basis of off-the-job life will be more effective as countermeasures. In all likelihood, he will not press for job enrichment or job rotation.[6]

However, many unions in the private sector, which experienced tremendous growth during the 1960s, seem to hold a different view toward the quality of working life. Union participation through joint consultation has already become a reality in most private firms. Union leaders view their role as being an agent for the maximization of both immediate and long-term interests of workers in the market economy; collective bargaining, in their view, serves to achieve only immediate interests. The quality of working life is also looked upon as a genuine concern to workers. Soichiro Asano, president of the Federation of Daihatsu Workers' Union, Confederation of Japan Automobile Workers' Unions (JAW), stated while visiting Saab-Scania and Volvo in late 1973:

> The rapid industrial development has enriched the material lives of workers (in Japan), only at the expense of our psychological peace. While wages, holidays, rest-periods, safety and hygiene also need improvements, it is essential now for every worker to have an opportunity to develop himself and to be able to participate in the search for better hatarakigai (quality of working life) and for better ikigai (quality of life).[7]

Behavioral scientists accumulated data during the 1960s on alienation and monotony, sometimes under the auspices of the Ministry of Labor. One ministry study analyzed the reactions of 2,451 workers who held repetitive, surface-attention jobs in production, inspection, business machine operation, and instrument control.[8] The study clearly showed, in comparison with 1,387 workers on non-monotonous jobs, the adverse effect of monotonous work on job satisfaction. The study concludes, however, that long-range social measures, such as the development of multiple skills, autonomous groups, and career progression channels, may be more potent measures than short-term technical rearrangements.

How urgent are problems of the quality of working life to Japanese managers? The Japan Quality of Working Life Committee surveyed in 1973 the reactions of personnel directors at 201 plants in electrical, car, and shipbuilding industries.[9] The major management problems reported included the difficulty in recruiting, increased turnover, and increased worker complaints. The respondents answered that accidents, work rejects, and absence without leave had decreased over the previous decade. Nonetheless, the personnel directors believed that there was a great need for effective measures to cope with worker alienation, working from both the technical and social ends. Together with skill diversification and job posting, one-man production, job enrichment, and group production schemes received endorsement as potentially viable measures.

## WORK REORGANIZATION EXPERIMENTS

Like most technological innovations, modern management theories also travel fast, crossing national boundaries. On the one hand, we know that sociocultural backgrounds affect the nature of work-related problems, methods of investigation, the decision-making process, and even the means used to solve similar problems.[10] On the other hand, we realize that innovative approaches, regardless of their national origins, represent a new addition to the reservoir of available resources and that it would be absurd if management in any country tried to shut its eyes to such new developments.

The sociotechnical approach has also found its applications in Japan over the past decade, some on a permanent basis and others in the form of experiments. Initially, the apparent preoccupation of management was worker motivation: the approach was interpreted only as another means of motivating workers for higher productivity. Authority was drawn from such theories as the "Need Hierarchy" by Maslow, "Theory Y" by McGregor, "Hygiene Factors vs. Motivators" by Herzberg, and "System 4" by Likert. Since some of the technical terms did not find ready counterparts in the language, new phrases were coined for the concepts, such as "job enlargement," "job enrichment," "work-structuring," and "job design."

The current interest in the sociotechnical approach first arose among industrial engineers. Together with their exposure to Western literature, their role itself may have induced them to try the new approach to organizational structuring. Although they, too, are not immune from the organizational climate of Japanese enterprises, which is not quite compatible with "human experiments," industrial engineers have managed to come up with some concrete findings from their experiments, at times with the assistance of psychologists.

## Mitsubishi Electric

A diversified manufacturer of electrical machinery and appliances, Mitsubishi Electric employs 55,000 workers. Since 1968, the firm has been striving for the humanization of work throughout its scattered plants, under the leadership of Naomi Yamaki, managing director. This firm combines job enlargement, job enrichment, and autonomous group and job rotation in its approach, even though the overall project is often referred to as "JEL" (for job enlargement). The following experiment was conducted at Fukuyama Works in collaboration with Hiroshima University psychologists under a grant from the Ministry of Labor.

### Methods

A nine-position conveyor line was reorganized into a three-position work unit through job enlargement. Under the new system, the conveyor was used only for transportation purposes. The number of workers was reduced from nine to seven. Workers received monthly and weekly production goals, but they set more immediate targets for themselves. Both initial inspection and parts supply became the responsibility of the work group.

### Results

Performance improved by more than 50 percent, while work errors showed a substantial decrease. Workers reported satisfaction with the new system.

## Kanto Seiki

Kanto Seiki, an auto parts manufacturer with 2,800 employees, adopted small-group modules at its speedometer department. Engineers first noticed that belt-conveyors were not always resulting in expected productivity in many departments. Also, having realized that conveyor lines were incompatible with the stated company policy to promote individual creativity and autonomy, the engineers conducted work-restructuring experiments in seven departments. The following case comes from the speedometer panel assembly department.

## Methods

Originally, speedometers were assembled by 17 workers per line along a conveyor belt. Experiments were conducted on seven-worker, four-worker, and three-worker modules. The three-worker module proved most satisfactory, and it has since been put into operation in addition to the regular conveyor line.

New recruits are first placed on the conveyor line and then moved to the training module of four workers. They eventually work as a module of three.

## Results

Productivity increased by 70 to 90 percent during experiments. The three-worker module also proved superior to the regular line with respect to worker turnover and absenteeism.

## Nihon Radiators

Nihon Radiators (2,800 employees) also manufactures auto parts. Experiments were conducted at its Sano plant (500 employees) on various reorganization schemes at the initiative of its plant manager, Seiichi Kawanabe, once a labor union officer himself. One-man production, facing-pair, and small groups (eight-worker, six-worker, and four-worker modules) were tried out in various departments. On the basis of such experiments, the plant organization was restructured to meet both production needs and worker preferences for various arrangements.

For example, a new car-heater line was installed with modules of four and six workers, which required an initial capital outlay five times the cost of conventional conveyors. Plant management estimates that production increased by 20 to 30 percent, rejects decrease from 3 to 0.5 to 0.6 percent, turnover was reduced by half, and absenteeism dropped from 4 or 5 to 2 or 3 percent.

TEAC

TEAC (1,400 employees), a high-quality tape-recorder maker, was among the first companies to replace conveyors by round benches. Its Toyooka plant removed belt-conveyors from its magnetic-head department and installed six round worktables, each having five operating positions and one position with inspection tools. Five girls assigned to a table now have autonomy in work distribution and inspection. The new method resulted in greater productivity, fewer rejects, and higher attendance records, although management had held little concern with these aspects from the beginning. In each case, workers were asked to write freely up to three comments about when they felt satisfied or dissatisfied on the job. Comments were then classified and tabulated. The new method apparently improved human relations, but more important, it did not lessen work monotony.[11]

QUALITY OF WORKING LIFE—NEW DIRECTIONS

In addition to those firms represented in the preceding section, a number of other companies have been active in work reorganization, including Toyo Communications Equipment, Nihon Atsudenki, Mitutoyo Manufacturing, Temmaya Department Store, and Dentsu Kiko. Although not an experiment, the work-restructuring program of Tokyo Gas Company should also be mentioned, which reduced 450 job grades to 250 through the participation of 12,000 employees.[12]

In Japan, however, the first round of the work redesign "boom" in which experimental "technology transfers" in job enlargement and job enrichment played a central role seems to be over.

Quality of Working Life for Whom?

Early experiments in work reorganization, carried out mostly by industrial engineers, placed a heavy emphasis on productivity improvement as the ultimate criterion. The improved worker motivation triggered by better work environment (the hypothesis went) would lead to higher production, better quality, less turnover, and less absenteeism. Gradually, however, there has emerged a sign of change in management logic. The quality of working life is now being defined more in terms of immediate, as well as long-range, interests of the workers involved. Naomi Yamaki of Mitsubishi Electric states:

> Job enlargement [in a broad sense, that is, in his company]
> means reorganization of work in order to meet the changing

values of highly educated workers. In this society mass-
production still tends to lead to further work simplification. The real issue is the solution of a human problem.[13]

Experiments also prove that the involvement and cooperation of
labor unions are essential ingredients of successful programs for improving the quality of working life. At Kanto Seiki, the understandings
and cooperation of the union were secured through thorough discussions of the objectives in advance and of the research data as they became available. There was a prior firm consensus between Tokyo
Gas and its union before the company launched its work-restructuring
program. At Isetan Department Store, the union went a little further:
it set up a residential workshop for volunteer managers to discuss
topics, including the quality-of-working-life problems. At least,
labor unions should be able to see to it that proposed programs will
not work against the best interests of their members.

Quality of Working Life by Whom?

During the experimental stage, industrial engineers took an active role in determining, at least tentatively, what was good or bad
for the quality of working life. In many cases, hypotheses as to worker
needs and motivations were based on the experiences accumulated in
other countries. The active involvement of experts is a vital element
in the pursuit of better quality of working life, but their limitations
must also be appreciated. After an experiment involving job enlargement at Tago Works of Hitachi, the participating workers unanimously
disapproved of any further extension of job enlargement.[14] At Mitsubishi Electric, one-worker production had to be dropped, even though
it had proved successful during the experiment. The workers pro-
tested that the method was too "individualistic and competitive." The
method involved an electronic counter that fed back to the worker her
production records against her self-imposed goal. The neighboring
workers soon became excessively competitive with one another.

It seems too obvious that the quality of working life must be defined by the workers themselves, or at least with the participation of
the affected workers. Not only the end results but also the change
process must be meaningful to those for whom the end results are being sought. In the case of Tokyo Gas, work restructuring was one of
the subsystems of the overall change in the personnel program on
which management and the union had agreed. As to the work-restructuring phase itself, each of the rank-and-file workers, or the bulk of
12,000 employees, first completed a job questionnaire (job description) with his or her suggestions for organizational change and work

assignment. Then, the workers and managers of each work unit held
a series of intensive discussions at workshop meetings, which took
place outside the workplace, during off-hours, with pay, in order to
develop the best possible organizational setup for the work unit. During this process, according to Koichi Yoshida, the manager responsible for the entire project, "It was the principle that the discussion
would be held until unanimous agreement was reached."[15] While
union participation can check abuse and misuse of the means, the
best assurance of success in the quality-of-working-life program
seems to lie in the participation of workers themselves.

Choice in Working Life

Another lesson from our experiences is that the quality-of-
working-life program needs to be designed with sufficient allowances
made for workers' individual differences. The 1.9-minute work cycle
may be more rewarding than the 62-second work cycle on an average,
but the latter cycle may be considered optimal by the workers who
want to minimize energy expenditure at work for whatever reasons.
It would be a tragedy, if not a comedy, should we overlook differences
in individual needs in our effort to redress damaged individuality. In
an age when claims for greater individuality are made more strongly
than ever, the quality-of-working-life program should aim to cultivate
opportunities for individual choice, whenever possible, so long as the
fulfillment of the equity criterion is being assured.

As for production workers, there seems to be too little individual choice or individual consideration in the Japanese personnel and
organizational system. However, the relative absence of job and incentive rates in itself becomes an advantage in Japan if management
wishes to widen the scope of individual influence available to production workers with respect to work assignments and career patterns.
At Nihon Radiators, this background was fully utilized: workers were
given as much free choice as possible to shift between different departments and work methods. In the survey cited previously, personnel
directors also predicted that the individual workers' self-assessment
(jikoshinkoku) would gain considerable importance in placement and
transfer decisions in the future.[16]

Autonomy and Autarchy of Small Groups

One well-known development in the quality of working life in
Japan has been the proliferation of small groups since around 1960,
as pointed out by Davis and Trist, the most representative move be-

ing known as "quality control (QC) circles.[17] Some cases were undoubtedly touched off by behavioral science theories of the West, but
the true driving force behind the QC circle phenomenon seems to have
been the fact that group behavior appeals strongly to the Japanese.[18]
If so, the present interest in small groups will not wither away easily
among either workers or management. Instead, the small group move
ment in Japan may develop further implications along the following
two lines.

One line is the development of immediate supervisors as effective leaders, as in Likert's system 4 model.[19] Dysfunctional supervision arises in Japan not so much from the arbitrary exercise of supervisory authority as from the supervisor's inability to influence
management decisions in the direction of human and technical needs
of the workplace. Consequently, any scheme leading to effective enrichment of the first-line autonomy of supervisors will have only good
effects upon the quality of working life of the rank-and-file worker.
For example, the following set of schemes seem useful in enhancing
the degree of autonomy available to each work-unit in an organization
and, hence, conducive to the quality of life at work: decentralization
of authority to supervision, meritocracy in supervisory appointment,
training in group leadership, and supervisors' intensive involvement
in subordinates' groups.

The other implication is primarily social in the Western sense,
and yet its significance cannot be ruled out in the Japanese context.
When workers are otherwise satisfied in their organizational life,
they expect both management and the union to provide assistance in
their social functions. That is, the more cohesive and close the
work group, the more "autarchy" it tends to demand as a human community. The "assistance" sought nowadays may not extend beyond
optional sports activities and recreational coaching services, whether
rendered by management or by the union. Nevertheless, when in demand, socialization within the work group will become an integral
element in the quality of working life in Japan.


Technology versus Career

Still another experience was the insatiable nature of certain
needs of workers on the job. Sociotechnical changes often succeeded
only in producing a temporary "honeymoon" effect on the workers;
their aspirations soon exceeded the capacity of technical rearrangements. The women at Nihon Radiators, for example, were not much
impressed by the reduced monotony achieved by way of simple round
tables. This realization of the limited effect of technical changes, a
truism indeed, should not, however, lead to pessimism. It may even

direct Japanese management toward a search for more comprehensive breakthroughs in technology, as it did in some other countries. Once started, the pursuit of better quality of working life becomes a continuing process.

Still further improvements in working life may be realized through a series of arrangements designed to assist a worker's growth throughout his or her career. Though many Japanese firms already provide training programs geared to various stages of workers' lives until retirement, Honda Motors' case has some unique features. Honda tries to provide as many equal and meaningful opportunities as possible for individual growth throughout a worker's career. Everybody starts his career on the assembly line at Honda, including management trainees and graduate engineers. Each worker then has several complementary ways to demonstrate his potentialities and to switch to the jobs of his preference while in the company. For example, not only management but elected fellow workers as well review the records of each worker and make recommendations. When a worker stays on production jobs, he goes through intensive on-the-job-training programs and follows a job rotation plan of his choice. Hajime Okamura, former director of personnel, said, "A man demonstrates the best of his abilities on the job, in union activities or in play. Whatever it is, and wherever he goes, it is an important human asset of his own. We try to provide opportunities so that everybody can make the most of his best."


CONCLUSION

In all likelihood, the issue of the quality of working life will gain further importance in Japan in the coming years. The data from a Ministry of Labor study conducted in late 1972 seem to substantiate this point. The study was addressed to some 700 influential leaders who were knowledgeable on labor problems (drawn from labor, industry, government, and learned institutions). Using the Delphi method, the study asked experts to forecast probable labor problems in the coming 1980s.* One question asked respondents to assess the degree of concern among workers about certain aspects of working conditions,

---

*A survey technique for technological forecasting developed in the United States for military purposes, the Delphi method has been turned to positive use by social researchers. It operates on a principle of "controlled feedback" in which respondents are successively asked to reconsider earlier answers in the light of new information received from other respondents.

now and in the 1980s. Both labor and industrial leaders came to the same conclusion independently: wages and salaries would lose importance, whereas job satisfaction would gain importance. If so, the quality of working life will become a major labor issue in the future, even more than wages and salaries, according to management predictions, unless actions are taken in time. At least it is gratifying to note that the existing differences between labor and management groups do not seem substantial enough to prevent the likely emergence of a consensus for action between the two parties.

The Japanese experiences summarized in this case study may not be very unusual, as in this industrial age, experiences are bound to overlap among different countries. International exchange on the quality of working life becomes all the more meaningful when the problems and solutions are commonly shared by the participating societies. Nonetheless, one can predict that some unique features will inevitably accompany the experiences of each country in the search for better quality of working life. Indeed, the scope for individual differences may even expand further, as the increased resources in each society are likely to enlarge the scope of options available. It will be even more probable, then, for each society to strive for its own idealized model of work, partly drawn from its cultural heritage, but still compatible with the modern age. In the case of Japan, the preference of people for association with an enterprise as a career and their predisposition for group behavior may prove to be the basis of which a better quality of working life will be sought in the future.

NOTES

1. From Neal Q. Herrick and Michael Maccoby, "Humanization of Work: A Priority Goal of the 1970's" (Paper delivered at the International Conference on the Quality of Working Life, New York, 1972); see also Richard E. Walton, "Criteria for the Quality of Work Life" (Paper delivered at the International Conference on the Quality of Working Life, New York, 1972).

2. Masumi Tauda, "The Environment Change Underlying Managerial Labour," in The Managerial Labour Problems in the Changing Era (Tokyo: Japan Society for Personnel and Labour Research, 1974). pp. 3-27 (in Japanese).

3. Shin-ichi Takezawa, "Changing Worker Values and Their Policy Implications in Japan" (Paper presented to the International Conference on the Quality of Working Life, New York, 1972).

4. Ronald P. Dore, "Commitment to What, by Whom and Why?" in Social and Cultural Background of Labour Management Relations in Asian Countries, Proceedings of the 1971 Asian Regional Conference

on Industrial Relations (Tokyo: Japan Institute of Labor, 1972), pp.
118-19. Dore maintains the following:

> These terms [the corporate paternalism, or better, the
> welfare corporatism of a modern large Japanese enter-
> prise] seem preferable to "managerial paternalism" as
> used by Clark Kerr et al. (Industrialism and Industrial Man,
> pp. 150-51). The point of difference is that managerial
> paternalism in their conception of it is still "patrimonial"
> —an expression of managerial authority. Welfare corpora-
> tism on the other hand is rule-bound; in Weberian terms
> it belongs less to the "patrimonial than to the legal-ra-
> tional mode of authority."

5. Japan, Ministry of Labor, The Analysis of Labor Economics, 1969 (Tokyo: Government Printing Office, 1970), Reference sec., pp. 46-49 (in Japanese).

6. Shogo Ohki, "An Interview," IE 16 (1974): 28-29 (in Japanese).

7. Confederation of Japan Automobile Workers' Unions, "Report on the Work-Reorganization Seminar at Saab and Volvo" (Tokyo, 1974), p. 23 (in Japanese).

8. Japan, Ministry of Labor, Labor Standards Bureau, Monotonous Work (Tokyo: Romugyosei Kenkyujo, 1970) (in Japanese).

9. Takao Kondo, "How Much Progress in the Quality of Working Life?" Management Today 18 (November 1973): 20-27 (in Japanese).

10. Arthur M. Whitehill, Jr., and Shin-ichi Takezawa, The Other Worker: A Comparative Study of Industrial Relations in the United States and Japan (Honolulu: University of Hawaii Press, 1968).

11. Mitsuo Nagamachi, Job Enrichment Designs (Tokyo: Daiamond-sha, 1973), p. 188 (in Japanese).

12. Koichi Yoshida, "Work-Restructuring in Tokyo Gas Company Ltd.," unpublished report (1973).

13. Naomi Yamaki, "An Interview," IE 16 (1974): 27 (in Japanese).

14. Shigeru Ono, "Jobs Must Be Redesigned from Workers' Viewpoints," IE 15 (1973): 51 (in Japanese).

15. Yoshida, "Work-Restructuring."

16. Kondo, "How Much Progress?"

17. Louis E. Davis and Eric L. Trist, "Improving the Quality of Working Life: Experience of the Socio-Technical Approach" (1972), pp. 53-57.

18. For recent analyses, see Chie Nakane, The Japanese Society (Berkeley: University of California Press, 1970); Isaiah Ben-Dasan, The Japanese and the Jews (New York: Weatherhill, 1972);

and Takeo Doi, <u>The Anatomy of Dependence</u> (Tokyo: Kodansha International, 1973).

19. Jyuji Misumi and Tamao Matsui, both members of the Japan Quality of Working Life Committee, are engaged, respectively, in research and diffusion along this line.

# Case 5

## IMPROVING PRODUCTIVITY AND QUALITY OF WORKING LIFE: THE U.S. EXPERIENCE

### Stephen X. Doyle

This case study examines the experiences of labor and management in two large labor-intensive corporations, one unionized and one nonunionized, in the United States that have experimented with quality-of-working-life projects.

PURPOSE AND FOCUS OF CASE STUDY

The following case study was undertaken in order to (1) identify the various behavioral factors that affect productivity and quality of working life and (2) conduct an empirical, longitudinal inquiry into the effectiveness of a comprehensive human resource strategy based on those factors.

The rationale and scope of the study were shaped by the following considerations:

1. As compared with capital investment as a means to increase productivity, behaviorally oriented human resources approaches offer the distinct advantages of increased latitude for worker participation, providing greater potential for worker acceptance and satisfaction; equal or greater potential cost effectiveness; greater flexibility as to both specific methods and objectives; and wider scope for exploration and discovery.

2. The success of human resources approaches to productivity and worker satisfaction has been limited by the frequent failure to address more than one behavioral variable, compounded by the failure to do even that much empirically and longitudinally.[1]

3. To provide fruitful, significant data, an examination of the effects of the various behavioral factors on productivity and worker

---

This case study was conducted by Stephen X. Doyle, Iona College, New Rochelle, New York.

satisfaction would not only have to be empirical and longitudinal but would require both a union and a nonunion setting where most or all of the behavioral factors were present and easily measured.


## BACKGROUND

Two large, successful corporations provided the settings for the case study. One of the companies is in transportation service (freight) with annual revenues in excess of $150 million; the other manufactures and sells corrugated containers and has annual revenues of about $15 million.

The freight industry is highly competitive. With 200 terminals and high profits, the company involved in the case study is known as a high-performing industry leader. The container company, although it is considerably smaller, is also a recognized high-profit leader in a very competitive industry. This quality of aggressive and success-ful industry leadership proved to be a significant factor in the success of the program, since top management in both firms were able and willing to take the risks inherent in providing a guarantee that no lay-offs would take place as a result of increased productivity.

Workers in the freight company sorted, labeled, and loaded freight. The dock workers performed all tasks, cooperating to meet deadlines. These deadlines were important, because a missed dead-line meant a delay in transit. Average gross pay was $6.90 per hour.

The work in the container company was different, both in nature and in structure. Here, the work was performed on an assembly line manned by 11 workers, each performing a given repetitive task. Lift-ing, stapling, and driving nails were essential elements of the job. The work required less skill than that at the freight company; new workers could be adequately trained in about a half hour. Average gross pay was $3.96 per hour.

In both firms, first-line supervisors had risen through the ranks. They were task experts, who knew how to solve production problems when they occurred. As such, they were respected and trusted by their subordinates and by management.

The differences in size and function between the two companies were minor, for the purpose of this study, compared with the fact that the freight company workers were unionized and those at the con-tainer company were not. Besides enjoying higher pay (mainly a func-tion of higher skill level), the unionized workers had better job se-curity, more formal and more effective grievance procedures, and better fringe benefits.

These advantages reflect the nature and extent of worker partici-pation typically sought by unionized workers in the United States. This participation, almost wholly limited to representing the workers' interests on issues of standard of living and working conditions, is effected through collective bargaining (to negotiate the terms of each new contract) and through day-to-day representation of workers' interests and policing of contractual compliance by elected union officials at the shop and plant level. The union in the freight company was typical, evincing little or no interest in other kinds of participation, and, indeed, was initially hostile to the participation required by this study, on the grounds that it would undermine the equality of the workers and lead to layoffs.

Within the U.S. context of the nature and extent of participation by union and nonunion workers, there was nothing striking or atypical about the climate of labor-management relations in either company. In the freight company, union leaders and management respected the magnitude and legitimacy of each other's power and pursued their respective interests aggressively but responsibly. This healthy labor-management climate, along with the growth-oriented vision of management, made it possible to overcome the union's initial resistance to participation in the study through negotiation, with very little friction.

In the container company, although the workers enjoyed relatively less job security and although a number of attempts had been made to unionize the workers, the climate of labor-management relations was, like that in the freight company, essentially open and untroubled.

RESEARCH METHODOLOGY

Given the stated purpose of the study—to identify the various behavioral factors that affect productivity and quality of working life and to conduct an empirical, longitudinal inquiry into the effectiveness of a comprehensive human resource strategy based on those factors—the first step was to obtain the assistance of top management in each company in designating the factors that would be relevant to the study. The following five factors were chosen: (1) worker participation in goal setting, (2) redesign of communications systems to provide timely feedback to participants in the program, (3) group problem solving to tap the knowledge and creative potential of hourly workers and first-line supervisors, (4) direct rewards for performance improvements owing to the program, and (5) guarantees of job security. It was further agreed by management that (1) hourly employees and first-line supervisors would be involved in all decisions regarding implementation, (2) that participation in the program would be voluntary, and (3) that all relevant information on the program would be made freely available to all prospective participants. These eight factors provided the framework for the design and implementation of the program.

## Design

The research design was a straightforward experimental/control model. Although seven supervisors volunteered their departments for the study, the companies elected to confine the initial stages of the program to one department of the New York City facilities of each firm. Management in each of those offices selected experimental and control groups, based on criteria of roughly equal average performance, length of service, age, and skill between the experimental and control groups in each plant.

The program, which involved only the experimental groups, consisted of four components: participative goal setting, feedback systems, rewards, and problem-solving training for supervisors.

For the purposes of measurement and evaluation, two outcome areas (dependent variables) were designated—productivity and worker satisfaction. Because of the different kinds of work performed, productivity was measured slightly differently in each firm. Basic to both was labor cost and percent of deadlines met; percent of damaged freight, in the freight operation, and percent of scrap, in the container operation, measured roughly equivalent performance variables.

Worker satisfaction was measured using a questionnaire based on the well-tested Likert scale, which obtained information on such areas as, for example, "extent to which immediate superior in solving job problems generally tries to get subordinates' ideas and opinions and make constructive use of them."

Evaluation of the program, in terms of both productivity and quality of working life, was to be effected through pre- and postmeasures. In the productivity areas, this consisted of establishing baselines against which to compare subsequent monthly measurements. In the area of worker satisfaction, evaluation was based on administration of the questionnaire once, before implementation of the program, and again at 12-month intervals.

## Implementation

### Component Number One: Participative Goal Setting

The experimental group in each company elected three workers to a committee charged with responsibility for goal setting and feedback system design. The first-line supervisor, and, in the case of the unionized freight company, the shop steward, also served on these committees. Inherent in the goal-setting task was the collection of base-line data in each productivity area. With these data in hand, the committees established a specific performance goal in each productivity area. With these data in hand, the committees established a specific performance goal in each productivity area. This phase of the committees' work was accomplished in five three-hour sessions in the freight company, and in four three-hour sessions in the container company. The goals established by each group are shown in Table 12.

TABLE 12

Participative Goal Setting: Goals Established by Each Group

| Container Company | | Freight Company | |
|---|---|---|---|
| Goal | Target | Goal | Target |
| Reduce labor cost | $1.10 per unit or lower | Reduce labor cost | 25 percent reduction in shipment handling cost |
| Reduce scrap | 1 percent waste factor or lower | Reduce damaged freight | 0.2 percent damage factor or lower |
| Meet production deadlines | 98 percent of the time | Meet dock deadlines | 95 percent of the time |

Source: Compiled by the author.


Component Number Two: Feedback Systems

Each representative committee was asked to review the performance feedback system that had been in use in its company, based on the following guidelines: (1) information on production results should be rapidly returned to the individual workers doing the job; (2) the information should be measurable and precise; (3) the feedback system should emphasize self-measurement; and (4) weekly results should be summarized and forwarded to management. The committees' task was structured with such obvious guidelines because the author had found that in both firms, as in many others, even such rudimentary considerations had been largely overlooked, and thus, even employees highly motivated to contribute to improved productivity were thwarted by the lack of appropriate information.

## Component Number Three: Rewards

A great deal of effort was spent in the design of the appropriate incentives, since poorly conceived incentives have been demonstrated to increase labor costs without improving productivity and, in some instances, to actually reduce worker performance. Whyte found that informal work groups often force individual employees to restrict their output when working in a piece-rate type of incentive system.[2] As Kopelman has pointed out, in many instances, rewards have been found to be ineffectual because they have not been based on actual individual or group performance.[3]

For these and other reasons, three factors were considered essential to the successful design and implementation of an incentive system: (1) rewards would be selected that "fit" the needs and values of the employees; (2) management guarantees that there would be no layoffs as the result of productivity gains produced by the program; and (3) timing of rewards to coincide to the maximum extent possible with measured productivity gains.

To determine the specific incentives valued by the workers participating in the study, questionnaires were administered. In both firms, employee preference for money and recognition led to the adoption of monetary rewards. These rewards were designed as group incentives, because this approach encouraged group problem solving and cooperation rather than individual performance and competitiveness.

The incentives in both firms were designed to be self-financing in that bonuses would be given only if there were measurable productivity gains, in which case the workers involved would split equally a group incentive amounting to 40 percent of the savings produced by their increased productivity.

## Component Number Four: Supervisory Training

The performance of the first-line supervisors was seen as instrumental in the success of the program. However, the traditional role of these key individuals had been significantly altered by the involvement of the work groups in goal setting. Instead of functioning as directive task experts, the supervisors were now expected to encourage their crews to review their own performance and to develop solutions to production problems. Since such major role changes can cause anxiety and elicit resistance, several steps were taken to reduce any tension stemming from the new supervisory responsibilities:

1. Supervisors themselves made the choice of whether or not to participate.

2. Supervisors were promised that they would not lose their jobs, no matter what the outcome of the study might be.

3. On-the-job coaching was provided by their own managers.
4. A training program was designed for the supervisors.

The components of this training program included explicit consideration of the expectations of all concerned—management, supervisors,
and workers; role playing; and group problem solving. The last component involved training in specific problem-solving techniques, as
well as weekly planning and review sessions for all group members,
workers, and supervisors, in order to review the week's results and
plan for the coming week. These discussions utilized the vast amount
of production know-how of individual employees to develop action
plans aimed at improving group performance.

These training programs and intangible incentives were provided to supervisors in both companies. In the later stages of the
study, the container company complemented these efforts with a system of monetary rewards for supervisors.


RESULTS

In terms of productivity, the initial results of the experiment
(for the first year and a half of implementation, planned for five years'
total length) were strongly positive in both experimental groups.* In
the container company, unit output of the experimental group more
than doubled, far surpassing the targeted 40 percent reduction in unit
labor cost. This reduction of labor cost amounted to an annualized
total of more than $30,000. Delivery dates were met 91 percent of
the time, up from the base-line figure of 75 percent. Scrap was reduced from 5.5 percent to 2.1 percent—an annualized savings of close
to $25,000.

Similar productivity improvements were achieved by the workers in the experimental group at the freight company. Shipment handling costs were reduced by 41 percent, the incidence of damaged
freight declined, and percent of deadlines met increased from a base-
line 68 percent to 87 percent. The reduction in labor cost alone represents an annualized contribution to profits of more than $130,000.

In terms of quality of working life, the results in both groups
were similarly encouraging. Questionnaires administered showed
significant positive shifts in worker attitudes. The following comment,
from a member of the experimental group at the container company,
typifies the group's shift in attitude: "All the guys like this program,

---

*For experimental groups, in all cases, as compared with no sig-
nificant changes in both control groups.

. . . We are proud of what we have done. . . . I brought home my first bonus and it was over $400! . . . My wife couldn't believe it."

At the freight company, the positive shift in worker attitudes is accurately represented by the substantial distance between the initial negotiated acceptance of the program by the Teamsters' Union local and the following comment, typical of the dock workers' responses to the questionnaire at the year-and-a-half mark: "It is unbelievable how our group is turned on. We are hustling. . . . Guys are coming up with ideas on how to improve things."

## CONCLUSION

The results of this study demonstrate that management can significantly increase productivity and improve the quality of working life through programs similar to the one studied. This involves (1) worker participation in both goal setting and design of feedback systems, (2) financial and nonfinancial rewards contingent upon productivity gains, (3) effective supervision, and (4) procedures for group problem solving.

For managers in the United States and in other industrialized nations whose productivity is declining at an accelerating rate amid large gains in productivity elsewhere, these findings are especially significant. Traditionally, managers have relied on investment in capital improvement in order to increase productivity. However, as the results of this study demonstrate, this definition of rising productivity as a function solely of capital investment is no longer valid—if, indeed, it ever was. Today, human-resources-oriented programs offer managers a less costly, more flexible strategy that not only increases productivity but improves the quality of working life and the attitudes of workers, even those initially opposed to any kind of productivity plan. More effective management of human resources is, moreover, especially attractive in today's vexing and unprecedented economic and regulatory climate, since it offers not only increased productivity but increased profits and an effective weapon against inflation as well.

## NOTES

1. Gene W. Dalton, Motivation and Control in Organizations (Homewood, Ill.: Irwin, 1971), pp. 1–35.
2. W. F. Whyte, Money and Motivation (New York: Harper, 1965).
3. R. E. Kopelman, "Organizational Control System Responsiveness" (Working Paper), mimeographed (New York: Baruch College, City University of New York, 1975).

# Case 6

## THE SHELL CHEMICAL PLANT AT SARNIA (CANADA): AN EXAMPLE OF UNION-MANAGEMENT COLLABORATION

### D. A. Ondrack and M. G. Evans

This is a case study of a new chemical manufacturing plant that was planned from the start to offer an enriched quality-of-working-life environment. A task force was established four years prior to the start-up of the plant to plan the new system and implement the necessary job designs and managerial practices to achieve the quality-of-working-life objectives. In addition to the unusually long lead time for planning, other key factors in the case were the involvement of union representatives in the task force almost from the onset; changes in some aspects of the design of the new plant to enhance quality of working life; and significant investment in training and preparation of the new work prior to start-up. The authors conclude that the case is an unusual example of union-management cooperation and an unusually well-planned and implemented quality-of-working-life system.

## INTRODUCTION

Shell Canada has constructed a new $200 million chemical plant near Sarnia, Ontario, to produce polypropylene and isopropyl alcohol. These products are used as raw materials for the manufacture of other petrochemical consumer products, such as thinner solvents, carpets, ropes, and containers. The plant, which expects to begin production in the spring of 1979, will employ approximately 150 employees. The new plant is also located in close proximity to a Shell

This case study was conducted by D. A. Ondrack and M. G. Evans, University of Toronto. Research for this project was sponsored by the Canada Department of Labour.

oil refinery, which as been in operation since 1952. The work force
of the refinery and the chemical plant are completely separate, and
although the workers are represented by the same union (Oil, Chemical and Atomic Workers International Union [OCAWIU]), there are
vast differences in the working arrangements between the two plants.

The new chemical plant is a departure in many ways for Shell
Canada. It is the firm's first venture into a new type of petrochemi-
cal technology, and it is a plant with considerable design changes, intended to improve the productivity and the quality of work life in the
plant. It is also a departure in that a special task force was set up
years prior to the start-up of the plant to plan for and implement a
new style of management and design of work in the plant, with the objective again being to improve the quality of working life. Finally,
a significant departure has been the decision of the firm to recognize
the union in the neighboring refinery as the representative of the
workers in the new plant and to invite the union to participate fully in
the task force. The ultimate objective of all of these departures is
to have a chemical plant that is competitively superior in its operations; one competitor has remarked that if Shell achieves its system
utilization targets for the new plant, "they expect to be able to under-
bid any competitor on a worldwide basis."

For all of these reasons, the new Shell Chemical plant has at-
tracted a high degree of attention from academics, competitors, and
the general public. In this case report, we are not yet able to describe
the performance results of the innovations at the chemical plant because the plant has not yet started up. However, we are able to describe the historical process of the planning for the plant, the nature
of the design of the new system, and the process of implementation.


EMPLOYEE RELATIONS PHILOSOPHY
AT THE SHELL PETROCHEMICALS PLANT

The philosophy statement developed at the chemical plant is a
seven-page document. It reflects a deliberate attempt to examine the
current operations of management in the company and to see if alternative ways of managing the human resources of the organization might
be appropriate and feasible. As such, it represents a departure from
the current philosophy of line management in the organization.

The introduction to the philosophy statement makes the following general statement:

The Company recognizes that, in order to achieve its primary objective, it is necessary to give appropriate consideration to the design and management of both the social and

technical aspects associated with its operation. The former is related to employees and encompasses such areas
as organizational structure, levels of responsibility and
authority, supervisory roles, communication networks,
interpersonal relationships, reward systems, etc. while
the latter deals with the physical equipment—its capacity,
layout, degree of automation, etc. Although our operations involve a high degree of sophisticated technology
which can be exploited to improve efficiencies, it is only
through the committed actions of our people that the full
benefits can be realized. The social and technical systems are interrelated and must be jointly taken into account to achieve overall optimization. [1]

This is followed by spelling out some key consideration of the
technical (informational) and social systems. The key technical consideration is around information to make decisions:

The nature of our industry is such that delay in recognizing
errors or need for operational changes, and taking corrective action is likely to result in substantial costs. . . . Accordingly, information should be directed to the individual
capable of acting most promptly and for that individual to
have the authority to take action and to be internally motivated to do so. [2]

About gaining individual commitment to the system, the following points are made:

[Individual] commitment . . . can only be expected to develop if . . . other needs such as the following are met:

1. . . . the content of the work to be reasonably demanding of the individual in terms others than those of sheer
   endurance, and for it to provide some variety.
2. . . . for an individual to know what his/her job is, how
   he/she is performing in it, and how it relates to the objectives of the company.
3. . . . to be able to learn on the job and go on learning.
4. . . . for some area of decision making where the individual can exercise his/her discretion.
5. . . . to know he can rely on others in terms of needs
   and that his/her contribution is recognized.
6. . . . to feel that the job leads to some sort of desirable
   future. . . . Allowance must therefore be made to ac-

commodate individual differences [in significance of their needs].[3]

Finally, some of the desiderata of a new sociotechnical design are listed:

Policies should reflect beliefs that:

  i) employees are responsible
  ii) individuals are capable of making decisions
  iii) groups can work together effectively . . . with minimal supervision

—Employees should be permitted to grow, advance, and contribute to their fullest potential
—Compensation should be on a basis of knowledge
—Communication should be open
—Information flow should expedite action
—Whole jobs should be designed
—Feedback should be designed to maximize individual self-control
—Artificial departmental or functional barriers should be eliminated
—Shift time should be minimized
—Climate should encourage problem solving, learning from errors rather than punishing the errant
—Status differences should be minimized.[4]

From these extracts, it is clear that the philosophy represents a human resources approach to managing people in organizations. In other words, people can best be utilized by arranging for the best use of their technical skills, by the development of new technical skills, and by allowing and encouraging each employee to use and develop decision-making skills by arranging for the majority of operating decisions to be made in the shift group.

DEVELOPMENT OF THE PHILOSOPHY

The development of a philosophy and the design of a new management/operating system went hand in hand. Initial (rather vague) concern about finding a better way to manage resulted in a wide-ranging search during 1973 by a two-man team into the operation of many quality-of-working-life experiments in the United States and Europe. This resulted in a report to top management (in January 1974) suggesting that Shell consider reevaluation of the traditional ways of operating without necessarily copying what others had done. The problems uncovered in their exercise included underutilization of human resources, overcontrol of employees, inability to respond quickly to problems, employee dissatisfaction with shift work, limited opportunity for growth, poor communications, artificial status differences, and attrition (turnover). In addition, it was believed that these problems would become worse in the future as a result of changing employee values and attitudes (especially among newer, younger employees).

It appears that this new philosophy was somewhat of a shift for all employees in Shell. Evidence for this is found in the insistence that this philosophy could only (or at least more easily) be implemented in a "green field" site, where careful selection of both managers and employees would ensure that not too many traditional values and ways of operating would interfere with the implementation. It is fair to add that these traditional values are to be found among both workers and managers.

The insistence on a fresh start at a new site was reinforced by Shell's experience at the Sarnia refinery. In 1975 a Union/Management Joint Committee tried to develop a plan with the major goal of reducing the amount of shift work in the refinery. Their solution to this was to develop some multiskill capacity in operations so people would work at skilled trades jobs on the day shift. This plan was rejected by the union membership in the refinery. As we shall see later, some of the ideas developed here turned out to be quite similar to those developed later for the chemical plant.

The next step (taken in early 1975, some four and one-half years before the planned start-up) was the formation of a six-man team, made up of the designated top managers of the new chemical plant and members of the Employee Relations Department. This resulted in the development of the philosophy statement outlined above.

Following the development of the philosophy statement, a meeting was held with the senior management of Shell Canada (October 1975) in order to (1) acquaint them with the philosophy, (2) spell out for them some of the practical implications for the management of the plant and of the relations between the head office and the chemical plant, and (3) obtain senior management commitment to the philosophy and to the implicit managerial behaviors.

After the top management had given their commitment to the idea of designing a plant to operate in accordance with the philosophy statement, the six-man team developed into a task force, which was appointed to translate this idea into practice.

Composition of the Task Force

This task force consisted initially of the core group that was involved in the development of the philosophy, together with a consultant, Louis Davis, of the University of California-Los Angeles (UCLA), who had worked with the team since mid-1975.

Following a decision to voluntarily recognize OCAWIU as the bargaining agent for the chemical plant, union representatives (that is, the president of Local 9-848) were invited to the task force in January 1976. In addition, the union president and the local international representative have been involved both in collective bargaining activity and with the design team. As new supervisory and technical staff were appointed to the chemical plant, they were also automatically appointed to the task force. The sequence of events is summarized below.

1972—There is a general study of human resource policies for manufacturing ("Must Be a Better Way" report).

1973—Research team studies quality-of-working-life applications in North America and Europe.

1974—There is a report to top management on quality-of-working-life study.

1975—January-February: task force formed for new Sarnia chemical plant; Union/Management Joint Committee formed for Sarnia refinery; proposals for shift work revisions are rejected by union membership; mid-1975: Louis Davis of UCLA joins task force; and late 1975: top-management approval secured for task force plans for chemical plant.

1976—January: OCAWIU representatives invited to join task force; site clearance begins; planning, policy development, design modifications, and visits to existing Shell chemical plants in Europe and elsewhere by task force; August: construction begins; and new management staff appointed to chemical plant are incorporated into task force.

1977—January: union contract signed; recruitment and selection of team coordinators begins; mid-1977: training of team coordinators begins.

1978—Team coordinator training continues; managerial staff trained as trainers; orientation sessions between chemical plant staff and interacting groups in other parts of the organizations; recruitment and selection of first group of operators; mid-1978: training begins of first group of operators; recruitment and selection of second group of operators; late 1978: training begins of second group of operators; initial formation of shift teams based on sociogram choice; and late 1978: development of team norms.

1979—Technical training of teams to start up in spring of 1979.

Role of the Union

The question of union involvement was critical, as some of the elements of job redesign and the dropping of jurisdictional boundaries to allow for some multiskill operating had already been rejected by the union membership in the refinery. A number of options were considered by the task force: (1) consider the chemical plant as a "new" site and go ahead and design the plant the way management wanted (force the union to battle for recognition); (2) give the union recognition, but take a strong management's-rights position concerning the design of jobs, organizational structure, and control and reward systems; and (3) give the union recognition and collaborate with the union on the whole design. In order to maximize the potential for success, the third option was taken; approaches to the union were made at the national and local levels so that internal union pressure might provide support for the project. As it turned out, this has appeared to be a successful strategy so far.

The union membership on the task force played a positive role: they were not there simply as guardians of the union position with veto power to block any development that they judged undesirable; rather, they contributed to the development of the ultimate task structure. This was attributed to the willingness of the union representative to take considerable risks with his position; an elected representative is much more vulnerable than an appointed manager.

The Union Contract

The company/union contract is a brief six-page document. It is noteworthy for what it does not specify. The contract is quite specific in the following areas: duration of the contract; recognition of the union and the role of the union plant committee; deduction of union dues; seniority rights in layoffs and recalls; payment systems, overtime, and changes in schedules; and vacation and statutory holidays. The contract deals with the following issues in the most general terms: grievance procedures, work schedules, and safety and health. The contract says nothing about work assignments, role of supervision, management rights, and technological change.

The company/union contract is unique in that very little of importance is specified. Only the skeleton framework to guide relations between management and workers is provided. Management retains flexibility in work assignment and scheduling; payment systems on the basis of acquired skills are defined; and the union gets dues checkoff rights (Rand formula). Clearly, both sides have to trust the other not to take advantage of the lack of specificity in the document on a number of citation issues (for example, task assignment and grievance procedures). While participating in a discussion of the contract by unionists and managers from other sectors of the country, both groups expressed the view that either side would be hurt if "the opposition" chose to betray that trust. It appears that a high level of collaboration will be necessary to work within the contract.

Role of the Consultant

In mid-1975, Davis was appointed as consultant to the chemical plant task force. It was pointed out that other consultants had been considered; however, Davis was chosen because of his style—he was willing to let the task force come up with its own solutions to the problems of plant and social system design. Some of the other consultants had their own pet ideas that they wanted to impose upon Shell.

The Role of the Task Force

Essentially, this group took a very tentative "minimum specification" approach to the design of the organization. This meant leaving as many options open in the design until as many people as possible would be involved in the decision.

The argument was that each decision—technical or managerial—had the potential of closing off a variety of other sociotechnical alternatives, which might later prove to be desirable options to pursue; this resulted in as many decisions as possible being delayed until the last possible minute so that these alternatives (at present unknown) might have a chance of surfacing and being considered.

It should be noted that such a strategy did not mean that the philosophy was kept at a "motherhood" level as a set of vague, nice-sounding statements. In some areas, some very practical implications were spelled out very early (for example, the decision to place a quality control laboratory in the chemical plant site rather than having quality control for the chemical plant performed at the refinery laboratory). However, other decisions (for example, whether to go to 12-hour shifts) were not made in advance, as not all those to be affected were on site yet; even now, a task force (made up of management and shift team members) is working on this unresolved issue.

One important function for the task force was to manage the link between the plant and head office. The planning task force was made responsible to a four-man general managers' committee. This group cleared major initiatives by the task force, was looked to for help and support by the task force, and generally acted as a buffer between the task force and the rest of the organization. For example, the task force cleared the touchy issue of union recognition with the committee; in addition, the new pay system, the multiskill concept, and other major policy departures were cleared with the committee.

### Comprehension

The philosophy and its implementation seem well understood among the inner circle—we have no data on anyone else. The selection and training processes are designed to ensure comprehension at all levels (see later sections of this case study) in the chemical plant.

## GOALS OF THE QUALITY-OF-WORKING-LIFE ACTIVITY

The philosophy statement indicates as its major goal the following: maximum return on investment for both technical and human resources, consistent with being a responsible firm in the community and a firm responsive to employee needs.

As an additional pressure toward a new organizational form, it was suggested to us that as the technology is relatively new (at least to Canada) and as the production of the product is relatively tricky, it is important for operating decisions to be concentrated close to the work flow (that is, among the operators). This means that operation of each shift has to contain an appropriate mix of technical and decision-making competences.

## NATURE OF THE SYSTEM

The basic functions to be performed in a chemical plant include (1) process operations (including tank farm); (2) laboratory—testing and quality control; (3) maintenance—mechanical, electrical, instrumental, and pipe fitting; and (4) warehouse—receiving, shipping, and scheduling. In a traditional chemical plant, these are set up as different departments, and in each department, individuals specialize in particular jobs.

At the Shell chemical plant, a different perspective is taken. Each function has to be performed, but all functions are the responsibility of a team of individuals operating as an autonomous group in a department.

In particular, in a conventional polypropylene/isopropyl alcohol (PP/IPA) plant, the two products are produced on separate chemical

process lines, each being controlled from its own control room. At
Shell, both lines will be run from a single control room. Furthermore, in a conventional PP/IPA plant, each line is operated by its
own group of operators, who are responsible for only the operating
activities, such as control room, operating valves and pumps, checking instruments, tank farm, and so forth. Usually, each individual
occupies a single role: boardman, pumps, and valves located in a
particular area of the plant and so forth. At Shell, three major
changes are contemplated: first, within each line, individuals will
carry out many different tasks. At one time, a person might be on
the board; at another, he would be out in the plant tending valves and
pumps or checking instruments. Thus, within each line, there would
be flexibility of assignment. Second, there would be flexibility across
the two production lines of polypropylene and isopropyl alcohol. As
these two processes are very different, this means quite different
knowledge about products and processes are required. This implies
that each individual will need to develop a wide variety of skills.
Third, as discussed below, each individual will be responsible for
one support function (maintenance, warehousing, and so forth). This
again implies the development of additional skills in comparison with
an operator in a traditional plant.

The basic group in the Shell chemical plant is the shift team.
Six teams are planned. This shift team is headed by a shift coordinator and will consist of 18 people. Among these 18, it is expected
that initially the following skills (and numbers of workers) will include
two instrument technicians, one electrical technician, three pipe fit-
ters, three millwrights, two quality control analysts, three laboratory
specialists, and four warehouse/inventory, control/scheduling specialists. It is not expected that each shift team will have journeyman
competence for each skill; rather, the skills in the team will be at a
level sufficient to deal with common problems/tasks that arise within
each specialty. When the shift reaches a mature state, it is expected
that within a team, perhaps shared among different members, there
would be significant competence in each shift, but not at the journeyman level.

In the plant, there will be six of these shift teams, backed up by
a group of 14 journeymen specialists in the technical maintenance
areas. This latter group will be responsible for solving difficult technical problems and training team members. They will work predomi-
nately on the day shift.

At present, it is planned (though in the light of the principle of
minimal specification, it has not been ultimately decided) to run the
plant with three eight-hour shifts (an alternative would be two twelve-
hour shifts). The eventual system will be decided in the light of experience, but probably not until the confusion and problems of start-up

have been solved. The task force has decided in favor of eight-hour shifts on the following grounds:

1. Many new employees do not have any shift experience at all; it was thought necessary to have them experience the less demanding (physically and mentally) eight-hour shifts.
2. The plant or the company has had no experience yet in manufacturing polypropylene and isopropyl alcohol. It may be a very demanding process in terms of even highly experienced shift team members' physical and mental capacities; if this is the case, the eight-hour shift will probably remain.
3. Finally, start-up procedures are more demanding than normal running, so any change will not be considered until start-up is largely past.

The preceding account has described the steady state of what the team does, but individual assignments are much more fluid. Prior to start-up, each team member will be given technical training in plant operations and in one of the technical specialty tasks, such as instrument maintenance. During start-up, it is expected that each individual will stick fairly closely to his/her major area of competence. Over time, full multiskill abilities will be developed. This means that each individual can operate all the process jobs on both production lines and have significant competence in one speciality: for example, quality control; electrical, millwright, or instrument maintenance; or warehousing and scheduling. Each individual will proceed at his or her own pace toward multiskill competence without any time constraints or pressure. There are, however, likely to be two incentives pushing the employee toward rapid multiskill acquisition: (1) the payment system, which improves the payment according to the number of skills mastered (as opposed to job done), and (2) group pressure to be a flexible group member able to do a wide range of tasks, as failure to do them results in another team member carrying this individual. Opportunity must be provided to ensure the system's development by scheduling training and job rotation activity.

An important aspect of the technical system is the plant's control system. To understand what is involved here, some comment about the nature of the product must be made. In the jargon of chemical processing, polypropylene and isopropyl alcohol are "performance" products (as opposed to "specification" products).* Each customer

---

*A specification product is one whose characteristics depend solely upon its physical and chemical specifications. In other words, such factors as density, melting/boiling point, and chemical/molecular

needs raw materials that will "work" in his or her facilities. A performance product is more tricky to make to customer requirements, as the technical specifications of the chemicals are not the only information required to produce for a particular customer. Output from the same batch will behave slightly differently for two different customers, depending upon their own plant facilities and the products they are making. To produce the appropriate product for a customer, therefore, requires close contact and feedback from the customer to the chemical plant so that the chemical plant knows what is required for each customer. In a very real sense, each product has to be tailored to meet the individual customer's requirements, based upon that customer's experience with the product.

As a consequence of this, each shift team, especially those involved in warehouse and shipping, has to keep in mind general product specifications and the requirements of each customer. The team will then be in a position to make shipment decisions of products that are unacceptable to one customer but quite acceptable to another.

A second technical concern is the scheduling of different grades of product (up to 20 can be made at the plant). Essentially, products with different operating characteristics are run continuously as a set of batches. Technically, one is likely to get "cleaner" batches if only small differences are made in the composition of adjacent batches. Too large a jump (say, in melt index) leads to a large amount of intermediate/boundary product with unknown characteristics. In addition, larger runs of a particular batch result in a more stable batch and a lower proportion of boundary products. It is therefore important that the production run be carefully planned and that the consequences be known of deviating from the plan in terms of potential unusable product.

The grade of product is varied by differences in various operating characteristics of that plant—temperature, pressure, speed of flow, and so forth. These parameters are controlled in the plant control room. The information system has been designed to allow operators to get feedback in the implications of different actions that they may take with regard to (1) the type of product that will be produced and (2) the economic efficiency with which a particular product can be produced.

For any particular product, tolerance limits for each parameter, such as temperature and pressure, are established. Traditionally,

---

structure are the major determinants of how the product will behave during future processing. A performance product is one whose physical/chemical characteristics interact with characteristics of the customer's plant and equipment to determine how the product behaves during future processing.

control room operators make the necessary adjustments to the controls when deviation from these limits threaten (or show a trend) to become intolerable. In such plants, one cannot wait until the limits are breached because of the lag time in system response to any control activity. At this plant, additional information will be made available to workers, such as costs of each deviation in terms of plant efficiency and potential product loss. This allows the operator who is confronted with several mild deviations from optimal efficiency to choose to work on correcting those that have the greatest potential for increasing overall operating efficiency, as well as to give the team members insight into the significance of their actions. This feedback of cost information is expected to increase the operators' felt responsibility for the operation of the plant.

## DEGREE OF REVERSIBILITY

Technically, it would be possible to operate, maintain, and manage the plant in a conventional manner with specialization of maintenance, laboratory, and warehouse/distribution staff and with minimal rotation in the operating crews. However, the processes of planning and implementing the new design, including careful selection and training, would make it unlikely that such a management system could be effectively implemented with the existing staff. Too much has been invested in preparing the organization for the new system of work to allow a reverse in management philosophy without creating a crisis of unsatisfied expectations.

## PLANNING PROCESS: SUMMARY

1. There was a careful sociotechnical design, using minimum specification guidelines.
2. There was an initial five-man management team; then there was added a consultant and union representatives; then each new member of plant management was added to the team.
3. Sociotechnical design from the first stages (it should be noted that significant design changes in the technical system were made by the task force) included the development of a two-control-room plant, one for isopropyl alcohol and one for polypropylene (the task force concept required a single control room, and the plans were changed; the concept that quality control could be performed in the refinery laboratory (this ran counter to the multiskill concept of job design, and a laboratory was built next to the control room); the development of computer software systems, to provide cost information about deviations from standards; and automation of the bagging operation.

4. Management, the consultant, engineers, and the union all had high involvement in the task force.

5. There was a high degree of planning for plant design, job design, timing of hiring, training, and so forth.

## SELECTION OF PERSONNEL

Because the task force worked with a green field site (albeit adjacent to an existing Shell refinery), they were in the position of being able to select those potential employees and managers who might be compatible with the proposed management and operations systems.

### Management/Supervisory Selection (1977 and Earlier)

To fill these existing jobs, including the key role of team coordinator, a three-stage selection procedure was established. First, jobs were posted throughout the Shell organization. For team coordinator, some 70 applications were received. All were interviewed by the plant superintendent. This reduced the group to 22; then two or three previously appointed managers interviewed the applicants with employee relations representatives; finally, the applicant was interviewed by an external consultant to focus on interpersonal skills. From this procedure, seven applicants were chosen (selection ratio: one out of ten).

### Employee Selection (1978)

The selection procedure was explicitly seen as involving mutual choice. The individual had to want to work in the new plant environment, and the company had to judge him as capable of fitting into that environment. Accordingly, Shell made an extensive effort to indicate the nature of the work environment both through written material and extensive audiovisual and question and answer sessions with prospective applicants. In addition, intensive publicity was generated both in-house and nationally.

As a result, some 2,000 application forms were received for 108 jobs (selection ratio: 1 to 18); the applicants then were screened, and 450 candidates proceeded to the next stage of being interviewed by an employee relations officer and a team coordinator (all team coordinators took part and received prior training in interviewing techniques). Both the application form and the interview schedule focused on interpersonal skills, as well as on technical skills. From this group, 66 male operators were selected. In late 1978, a second group of 46 operators was hired by a similar process.

## TRAINING AND SOCIALIZATION

### Managers and Team Coordinators

A training program on both technical and social aspects of the plant's future operations was initiated in mid-1977. Technical training includes extended periods in Europe, where Shell PP/IPA plants are in operation.

The first formal skill-training session took place in October 1977. This was essentially an orientation session, with little actual skill training, rehearsal, and coaching. It should be noted that many of the managers and supervisors who took part in this had also (from their time of appointment) served as members of the task force.

The October 1977 session was designed to (1) reinforce people's awareness of the philosophy statement and its practical implications; (2) help people clarify the roles they were to play in the organization, the expectations they had of others, and the expectations others had of them—some role-playing exercises were specifically developed to aid in this process; and (3) enable people to understand the multiskill concept and the managerial problems it would create—for example, scheduling constraints for full-skill manning on each shift.

In January 1978, team coordinators were given training to prepare them for the role they were to play in selecting team workers. This was a short workshop in selection and interviewing skills; in particular, this emphasized the kind of selection criteria that were to be used (technical and social skill competence) for selecting team members.

In February 1978, the managerial staff was given training in training techniques. This was done to prepare them for the entry of operators into the system. The managerial staff was to act as trainers for the technical training in plant operations, safety techniques, and social skills. The essential purpose was to clarify the roles each would play and the different types of operating and social norms that existed in each group. Second, a one-day session was held that linked the chemical plant to the head office Chemicals Division, which provides technical support and the sales function for the plant.

Finally, a number of union/management sessions have been held to orient a new union executive to the chemical plant philosophy and to continue the collaborative relationship built up in the task force, as the task force was gradually moving from a planning and design function to a managerial function. One outcome of the union/management meetings was the development of an <u>Employee Good Work Practices Guidebook</u> (to be discussed below).

In May and June of 1978, sessions were held to help build the links between the chemical plant and other parts of the Shell organization. A two-day session linked the chemical plant to the technical (engineering) group in the refinery, who were to provide technical back-up to the operation.

### Operators/Team Members

For these employees, too, a mix of social and technical training is being provided. So far, there have been two groups of entrants, 66 members in June 1978 and 46 members in October 1978. As soon as the first group was hired, an intensive training program, both in technical and social skills, was undertaken. Technical and social training took place concurrently—a morning might be spent in social skills, an afternoon might be spent on technical skills, and vice versa.

The first phase of the social skill training took about 30 hours in total. This training was done prior to the formation of shift teams; the training groups consisted of diagonal slices from the organization, that is, operators, team leaders, and supervisory staff. The program started with an introduction to the philosophy statement and the multiskill concept (reinforcing the socialization procedure). Then, the skills required to operate the multiskill teams effectively were identified, and skill training was provided in communication, negotiation, self-management, role definition and expectations, feedback, observation, collaboration and competition, and group problem solving. Specially developed relevant role plays and cases were used in the training.

The next stage (July 1978) involved the formation of the shift teams. Each individual selected his first and second choices of initial skill specialization and his first, second, and third choice of co-worker. Teams were then partially made up by a committee (made up of team members and three shift coordinators), bearing in mind the constraints of full multiskill capacity, age, and experience of worker. Only partial teams were created, with gaps left to be filled by the second group of workers hired.

In July 1978, following appointments to teams, the technical training was supplemented with team training and the development of group norms around issues of internal team discipline; adherence to multiskill progression (When can an individual decide that he has learned enough?); collective agreement interpretation; and interpretation of philosophy statement.

As a basis for norms, an Employee Good Work Practices Guidebook was presented to all teams. This deals with such issues as overview of philosophy; personnel policies regarding pay, hours of work, benefits, absence, overtime, shift swapping, vacations, safety, medical facilities, and alcoholism and drug abuse; and discipline.

This material was used as input to the teams as they discussed the formation of explicit group norms. Some groups found, and find, the concept of consciously making norms strange, not to say confusing. Process consultation by a member of the task force is being used to help some of the teams in these discussions.

In order to ensure some consistency of norms across the organization, a Norm Review Committee of elected representatives from each team has been established. This committee will review the explicit norms established by each group and try to ensure that they are congruent with the operating philosophy and code of good work practices. In one sense, social training is an on-going phenomenon, as people learn to develop norms, learn the limits on their behavior when compared with the norms set by the team, and try to work within these guidelines.


CONCLUSION

The program for organizational design developed at the Shell chemical plant at Sarnia has been a well-thought-out and, to date, well-implemented program. A key feature has been the degree of union/management cooperation and decision making in the planning and implementation of the program. The union representatives have contributed valuable inputs to the planning, and perhaps more important, their participation in the task force has legitimized the new system in the minds of the workers. Probably, management could have achieved much the same design and program decisions without the participation of the union, but the legitimization of the new program is greatly enhanced by the union involvement.


NOTES

1. Sarnia Manufacturing Centre Philosophy Statement (Sarnia: Shell Canada Ltd., Chemical Plant, n.d.), p. 1.
2. Ibid., p. 2.
3. Ibid., pp. 2–3.
4. Ibid., pp. 4–6.

# Case 7

## ACTION RESEARCH AT MACKENZIE: EXPERIENCES OF EMPLOYEE PARTICIPATION IN DECISION MAKING

### B. C. Painter

This case study is a review and evaluation of a year-long development of a participative process that involved workers and managers in joint decision making at the plant level. The report gives special emphasis to the personal experience of that participative process, from the points of view of both managers and workers, relying extensively upon excerpts from tape-recorded interviews with "C" Mill personnel. The report has also provided the researchers with an opportunity to reflect upon their own role and effectiveness in helping to develop action research capabilities within work organizations.

### BACKGROUND

Action research began in Mackenzie with the joint resolve of a company, a union, and a research organization to find and implement solutions to a problem of labor and community turnover experienced throughout the British Columbia Forest Products (BCFP) Mackenzie Division. Mackenzie, in north-central British Columbia, is the site of one of the most northerly sawmill–pulp mill operations in Canada. It is also one of the most modern and now includes three sawmills, one large pulp mill, and an extensive logging operation. Adjacent to the sawmill–pulp mill complex is an "instant town," developed in an attempt to overcome the problems of a transient labor force so typical of old-style frontier operations and of many parts of the wood product industry in particular. In spite of all this, labor turnover in the Mac-

This chapter was prepared by B. C. Painter of the British Columbia Research Council and is sponsored jointly by British Columbia Forest Products and the Canadian Department of Labour. Reproduced with permission.

kenzie sawmills was running at an annual rate of 200 percent in the period 1973/74.

In early 1974, the company and unions involved in Mackenzie (including the Canadian Paperworkers Union and the Pulp, Paper and Woodworkers of Canada) collaborated with the research team from the Tavistock Institute of Human Relations (London) and B.C. Research in a diagnostic study of the labor turnover with the Mackenzie mills. In brief, this study found that job-related factors had a most pronounced effect on labor turnover. The work itself, the tasks that people did, and the ways in which they were managed were all major determinants of labor turnover.[1]

A Tavistock-B.C. Research proposal suggested a program of action research, consisting of job design projects and supervisory skills development, to be conducted over a 12-month period, but with the option of terminating the work after a review point at 3 months. BCFP agreed to support this proposal, at least to the review point. However, as a result of a series of setbacks, including a major reorganization and a strike, the action research program was postponed several times throughout 1975.

A DEMONSTRATION PHASE

In January 1976, a year later than originally planned, a demonstration phase of action research was finally launched in the Mackenzie sawmill division. The program was coordinated by a steering committee, which was representative of the company, the union, the research organizations, and the federal government manpower department, which had provided financial assistance. The committee advised on many aspects of the program. It also provided a constant safeguard to the respective interests of management and union, which could, by the withdrawal of their support, exercise a veto and terminate the program.

During pilot and review phases of three months' fieldwork, the two-man Tavistock-B.C. Research team worked with employee-management groups to analyze problems of the workplace, to implement proposed changes, and to monitor results. As a demonstration of the action research process, work was concentrated in one mill, "B" Mill, and with one "experimental" shift, which consequently showed significant improvement in morale and productivity.[2]

Review of the pilot program continued for several months within the Mackenzie wood products division. It was an opportunity for union and management representatives to make an informed judgment as to whether action research was indeed an approach they wanted to use in their operations. In discussions at the steering committee level, local union representatives now expressed positive support for the continuation of the program, after an initial wait-and-see attitude. Of the three sawmill managers, one withheld his commitment to the program on account of his sudden promotion to another division of the company; a second manager made a decision not to implement action research within his organization because of plans for major personnel changes, which he did not wish to disrupt. The third manager, from the newest of the Mackenzie sawmills, "C" Mill, approached the research team with a proposal that the action research process be employed in a different and more extensive way in "C" Mill as a form of employee-management consultation and decision making at the plant level. The work force, supervision, and mill management would participate jointly in the analysis and solution of day-to-day problems in the work of the mill.

It would be more than a matter of "getting people together." The action research process would involve mill supervisors, superintendents, the mill manager, and the crew working as a group, with the shared task of finding and implementing solutions to get the mill running as smoothly as possible. It is important to realize that specific objectives were developed, experimental changes were agreed upon for trial implementation, and methods of evaluating results were developed. This was not done by the crew alone, nor by the manager himself. It was done jointly, and there was seldom any doubt in anyone's mind about what changes were being made in the mill or why.

## THE PARTICIPATION PROJECT IN "C" MILL

Before anything could be done, however, the mill manager and the action researcher had to talk about their own expectations for this implementation phase. In the words of the mill manager:

> I had become frustrated with the hierarchy. . . . I would ask people to do something; sometimes they did it, sometimes they didn't. Not a lot seemed wrong with the mill itself, and the people seemed okay, but I knew we could be doing better.
>
> Through the action research, I began to understand more of the motivation of people and their feelings about the job as undesirable work. People weren't looking at their job in context: when you look at the sawmill as a "total" thing, it is an interesting place. And yet, the "system" doesn't let people in the mill see it that way.
>
> The purpose of the action research program was to get the crew and ourselves to work as a group towards an objective that we could all agree was a good one.

From the perspective of the manager, action research appeared to be a way of solving problems that had been insurmountable in the past. The expectation of the mill manager was that participation by employees could generate an improvement in all aspects of performance, including safety, quality, cost control, and production. The feeling at the outset of the project was that "C" Mill was not performing as it could.

As well as his basic concern for the level of production, the mill manager expressed his conviction that "working in the sawmill should not be like a jail sentence that we endure in order to live. . . . [It] should be something that we enjoy doing and get some satisfaction or feeling of accomplishment from."

The value in the quality of life on the job was closer to the researcher's own expectations that participation would provide workers with greater control over their tasks and the opportunity to relate those tasks to the work of their fellow employees. At the same time, improved performance was not irrelevant to the researcher's expectations. Insofar as performance could improve from participation, previous research has shown that such achievement is a source of significant job satisfaction. One of the main research findings from the pilot program in Mackenzie has indeed been the high correlation between workers' own feelings of job satisfaction from a given day's work in the mill and the simple measure of output (in board feet of lumber) for that given day of production.[3] In discussion of this data, the experimental shift of "B" Mill concluded that both their performance and satisfaction on the job were being critically affected by downtime in one of the key work areas. The reduction of this downtime by a specific and appreciable amount became a target set by the operators themselves in cooperation with their supervisor.

THE RESEARCH PARTNERSHIP

From this example of the earlier pilot program in "B" Mill, the researcher and manager of "C" Mill now identified downtime in the operation of the mill as the general problem on which they could effectively collaborate. Downtime was a factor that had very significant consequences for production at the same time that it affected the satisfaction of workers on the job through the disruption of the even and controlled flow of work. This was an objective that appeared to have an evident payoff for both the work force and management. Through this process of problem identification, the partnership became established between the quite different perspectives of the researcher and mill manager. They were able to form a collaborative relationship based upon a respect for each other's distinctive competence and acceptance of (but not necessarily agreement with) each other's values.

The initial anxiety felt by a manager in approaching the work force on a collaborative basis often arises from the question of whether people in the organization are really "with us." However, if there is a sufficient degree of openness and trust between researcher and manager, action research can be regarded as a means for a manager to inquire into and respond to this question of commitment. The support that a manager and researcher must offer one another in the course of the research also serves as a continuous experience from which both parties can learn more about the management function in a collaborative process.

Already, the "C" Mill manager had begun to redefine his role, so that he became more of a researcher and resource person himself, using the knowledge and power of his position to support and involve others in the solution of problems. This was the first step in the process of establishing action research as an integral, ongoing part of life within the organization, instead of as a temporary "outside" intervention.

The mill manager and the outside researcher (on site ten days out of a month) now functioned as a new research team. During the following months, the manager and researcher worked closely together, planning and reviewing the research and jointly leading meetings with staff or the action research groups. At this early stage, however, the essential requirement for the research team was to obtain sanction to conduct the action research from key parties within the organization. The research team therefore met with "C" Mill union representatives and members of the superintendent and supervisory staff to develop a steering committee that would oversee and help coordinate the action research. (The eventual membership of the "C" Mill steering committee included two union representatives, two superintendents, and the mill manager and the researcher.)

The mill manager explained to the steering committee his objectives for the improved performance of the mill and his desire to involve the work force and supervisory staff in the solution of problems in the day-to-day operation and maintenance of the mill. He proposed that the process of action research demonstrated earlier in Mackenzie be adapted in "C" Mill to provide the instrument for this shared decision making and planned change. He asked for the committee's support and guidance on how to proceed with the implementation.

Union representation in the committee included the president of the union local for the total Mackenzie sawmill division, which had already given its support to the action research program. Among the company's supervisory group, sufficient understanding of the action research process had been gained from the pilot program that they could also offer initial support to the implementation of action research in "C" Mill. As a committee, the steering group recommended that a general meeting be held with the total work force and salaried staff to launch the project. Agreement was also reached on some essential housekeeping items. Workers were to be paid for their participation in any meetings outside of normal shift work hours, while foremen were to be granted compensatory leave in lieu of payment. However, participation for everyone was to be clearly voluntary. (To the present day, these terms and conditions of participation apply in "C" Mill.)

All of this preparation took time, but it was necessary to consult with the various organizational levels and interests in order to develop a consensus that would enable the research team to construct a new kind of institution within the organization. The institution was the action research group, which brought individuals together on a nonhierarchical basis to complete a joint action research task. The final part of the organization, which had now to be contacted, was the mill work force, where one of the very reasons for this new approach was the general difficulty of communication among a crew and between supervisors and the crew, who were spread out across a large, noisy shop floor.


DEVELOPING THE ACTION RESEARCH TEAMS

At four o'clock on a hot afternoon in July 1976, the heavy machinery in the sawmill of the "C" Mill at Mackenzie was shut down between shifts for an extraordinary general meeting. Approximately 100 machine operators and maintenance workers were gathered with their chargehands, shift foremen, and superintendents into a crowded lunchroom above the shop floor. It happened to be the first time that the people of the sawmill had met in the work context as the one large group that was charged with the responsibility of running a mill.

The crew is usually divided into two shifts of production workers and three shifts of maintenance. On the job, individual production workers are scattered along several hundred feet of heavily mechanized production line. Finally, this total group of sawmill workers is separated from the rest of the "C" Mill population (another 100 persons) by a physical division of the overall production process into the sawmill operation, dry kilns (where the rough, green lumber is dried), and a planermill (where boards are made into finished lumber).

The meeting of July 6 had been called by the "C" Mill manager to announce an agreement between the union, the mill management, and Tavistock-B.C. Research. The agreement was to develop a process by which the work force could participate with management in the diagnosis and solution of work problems in the mill. The process was referred to as "action research." The objective, as stated by the manager, was to get the mill running as smoothly as possible.

The mill manager had defined a new task for the organization and a new way for the organization to go about its work. He proposed to give the work force an opportunity to participate in the management of the mill. It would provide a chance to learn about all aspects of the mill. The mill manager would still be the accountable leader of the organization, but there would be a spreading of responsibility. The question was whether members of the work force would choose to assume that responsibility. In other words, would workers see this new way of relating as something in their own interests?

Clearly, there were differing views and expectations. Most workers were bewildered by the opportunity:

> Before this, the company never turned to the people. If our machines weren't running like they should, unless they completely broke down, that was our tough luck. So, no one cared, and so, the company never really found out what was going on.

> It was a surprise to me that they wanted us to get involved.

> As a chargehand, I didn't know what to expect. . . . I went along as an observer.

> It was a chance to work on problems that we were having day after day, but which got taken for granted.

> The people who got involved were those who wanted a challenge.

Some workers were frankly suspicious:

> I had trouble with the idea that the company was all of a sudden going to do things in a cooperative way.

> Production is the company's business— . . . problems are for the higher-paid help to solve.

> A lot of people took part just for the overtime pay.

During the next few weeks, representatives of the steering committee met with the various departments of the mill organization, that is, sawmill and planermill and maintenance and production and various shifts of workers and foremen within departments. From these meetings, the committee was able to reach a consensus that the action research ought to start in the log-infeed area at the front end of the sawmill.

This was an area where it was felt that the most critical disruptions occurred in the work flow. The specific limits of this work area were defined by a set of operations that seemed to form a "whole task of transforming the raw material, tree logs, into rough lumber (which is trimmed and edged by another part of the mill to make a board of quality length and width). Several months later, the committee did extend the action research into another apparently self-contained work area, the planermill.

Within the log-infeed areas of the sawmill, the committee now identified two groups, one from each production shift, to work on action research at the plant level. Each group involved the work force (eight machine operators from the log-infeed area), one production supervisor and a chargehand, the two mill superintendents representing production and maintenance departments, and the mill manager and the outside researcher as leaders of the research team. Invited to join this group were individual members of the sawmill maintenance crew, who worked on a shift schedule that was different from that of the production workers. The rate of actual participation was such that each action research team usually met as a group of 12 to 14 persons. Meetings were held for approximately one hour, immediately prior to or just after the work shift.

The teams were designed to be effective problem-solving groups, with the "vertical" involvement of management providing a full scope of authority and knowledge of the organizational requirements of any change, while the combination of production and maintenance departments allowed for an examination of social and technical aspects of problems. When it was later discovered that a particular lower-paid production job was also critical to problems faced by operators in the front end of the sawmill, the worker on this job was invited to join the research teams.

The first task of the action research teams was to develop a clearer definition of the problem. "Lost-time" records had traditionally been filled out by operators on each shift, although workers made no use of the records themselves and wondered if anyone else did. Many workers did not understand the old forms or found them difficult to use on the job. At this stage, there was a good deal of impatience on the part of both workers and supervisors with regard to use of the old records (which were considered inaccurate and invalid); there was a desire to move on to specific problems that were believed to be causing disruptions and annoying stops and starts in the work. The responsibility of the mill manager and researcher as resource people was to indicate to the group that without reliable data on downtime, it would be as difficult as it had been in the past to achieve a real understanding of the importance and cause of specific problems.

Over a period of a month, meeting once every two weeks, the research groups developed a procedure for recording problems and commenting on their possible causes. It was a procedure that the operators could understand and use in working toward a solution of their own problems. The time spent in this original design of the research allowed people in the mill to develop "ownership" and, therefore, commitment to the task. (Significantly, in the planermill, where pressure to start the research prevented the same time and care in developing a record-keeping procedure that "belonged" to the crew, commitment to the research task took longer to become established.)

The work of the action research teams in the sawmill now came to involve much more than participation at the group meetings. In the role as a resource person to the research teams, the outside researcher spent time in the mill and outside work hours, helping people identify from their own experience what might be the possible causes for many of their problems. These informal discussions were supplemented by the operators' own daily record of problems, which helped workers identify more clearly what was happening on their job: for example, "The records made you look for things," and "We were more conscious of what was happening. Without the records, problems used to get lost."

The opportunity to express freely their ideas and complaints about some long-standing problems may have appeared to some workers like a new kind of "game" at work. However, workers began to understand that they were becoming involved in a new kind of work, which required careful thought and the development of cooperation with fellow workers and management personnel.

> We began to realize that what was going to make this thing tick was ourselves.

> At first, some people held back because of misunderstanding among fellow workers, but soon we were learning from one another about one another's jobs.

Suddenly, the priorities of the mill began to change. More attention was given to the apparently "little problems" of operators.

> We started to let loose with our ideas . . . things we knew had been wrong for a long time but nobody had listened to.

> Maybe they were little things that no one saw because they didn't seem to hurt production. . . . They just hurt the guy who had to fight the machine every day.

> The important thing is that these were the crew's ideas.
> We had a chance to express ourselves.

While the machine operators were becoming increasingly involved and able to use the research to their benefit, only a few of the sawmill maintenance workers continued to participate actively. The study and solution of problems in one specific area of the mill did not directly coincide with the interest of maintenance workers, who were responsible for the care of machinery in the mill as a whole. More important, sawmill maintenance crews did not rotate on the same shifts as production workers and did not, therefore, share the problems of a specific operating crew.

What may often be overlooked is the fact that participation is a process that takes place within a group in whose objectives members must be able to share an interest. Maintenance workers did not, however, see themselves as participants in the groups defined by the original action research teams, since the objectives and concerns of these groups were not theirs but, rather, the problems of production workers. Yet, once action research began within the maintenance department itself, maintenance workers started to participate actively regarding problems that they "owned" and had a clear interest in resolving.

## PARTICIPATION OF MANAGEMENT PERSONNEL

Though in its origins, the "C" Mill project may have concentrated upon the development of employee participation, the wants and needs of management personnel were also critical. The new initiative of the work force did indeed present a new experience for the management group, some of whom in this early period of the research began to question their own commitment to the process.

I didn't realize how much time would be involved. . . . I was also unprepared for the initial meetings which seemed like "bitch" sessions.

The crew seemed to expect that we could act on all these problems at once.

No matter how strong a leader you are, it is difficult to face the fact that people don't necessarily think you're doing a good job.

Many of these feelings were shared by the mill manager himself, though he had initiated the process; he was perhaps more prepared for the experience than some of his supervisors and superintendents, who felt the pressure of a shift in the "balance of power" within the organization. In the words of one supervisor, "Management had to put up or shut up."

Many of the supervisory-superintendent group remained puzzled and genuinely disappointed by the fact that the problems of workers had not come out before the use of action research:

> They should have gone through the proper channels. . . . There is no reason why they should have to come out in a meeting. People are just not willing to take the responsibility to go themselves and get action on their problems.

The stress of confusion felt by members of the management group was primarily due to the change in leadership style implied by the participative process. One of the major concerns for management personnel was the amount of time involved in reaching decisions through a consultative approach:

> It took a while to get used to the time it takes to listen to people, but coming through the action research, I learned the priority of listening. . . . Without listening, you don't get the real cooperation; you don't know what's going on.

> The old traditional way is that the supervisors-superintendents-managers are the bosses. The operating people run the mill the way that management wants it run. . . . Rarely, and in some plants never, are the crew, foreman, superintendents and managers present to discuss general problems to do with the running of the mill. If such a meeting is held, the manager usually makes a speech, and there is little if any two-way communication. . . . I think we've changed that in "C" Mill. I think the mill is being run with the cooperation of people because they have a lot to contribute.

What was often learned in the course of the action research was that joint decision making can develop the kind of commitment that is more likely to make decisions lasting and effective in their implementation.

> I had to program myself to go with the action research rather than against it. I used to think that I didn't have time for all the meetings and discussions, and then I began to think that maybe my job had more to do with action research than some of the other things that took up my time.

> I didn't think I was losing control as a supervisor, but I was finding out a lot more about the problems that people had and that were never out in the open.

Even in the early stages of the program, it became clear that the quality of participation of the work force depended greatly on the participation of management through their style of leadership. Participation is indeed a joint undertaking of management and employees.

> At first, we didn't know if the managers really cared about the action research, but later they started to ask the right questions. . . . We got more involved because we knew they were more involved.

> The managers started to open up. . . . They admitted their problems, too, and because of that, I gained a lot of respect for some of the managers.

However, as one worker cautioned:

> The change in behavior is only starting. The managers are becoming involved with the crew, and the crew is only becoming more relaxed and confident in their jobs because they can feel a more definite communication with management. . . . But really, you don't see fantastic changes at once. This kind of thing has to go long enough for people to program themselves differently.

The rewards to be gained from this change perhaps came more slowly for most supervisory staff than for the work force. As one first-line supervisor commented:

> I wasn't impressed at first, but eventually the research created a more workable atmosphere. Both supervisors and production people came to understand each other better, not individually perhaps, but as a group.
> As a supervisor, I'd say it brought top management down to earth.

## CONSENSUS AND POWER SHARING

Summaries of the records kept by operators were compiled by the researcher once every three weeks. The mill manager then decided upon the time to convene a meeting of the action research teams in order to conduct a shared analysis of the documented problems and to search for consensus on the possible solutions. If consensus was not possible, no action was taken. If, as in one instance, a trial change did not prove beneficial, conditions were returned to their original state.

Existence of actual data on the frequency of problems and the lost time provided a common basis for discussion and decisions on priorities. The requirement that ideas be tested by trial implementation afforded another degree of objectivity and sense of fairness that freed further expression of ideas. Ideas were no longer judged essentially by the authority or personality of their proponent but, rather, by their proved value.

When asked who made the decisions within the group, most persons felt that decisions had "emerged" or "evolved" from the discussion. Some workers did feel, however, that they had determined what actions were taken:

> The problems we solved were our problems that had been frustrating operators for a long time.

> The managers could say no to a change, but then they also had to give their reasons.

Equally, some management personnel felt that they had steered the discussion: "It allowed me as a manager to do a lot more." In fact, the requirement of consensus within an action research team that combined all levels of management and all areas of knowledge and skill appears to have made this into a new situation of power sharing, where different interests could be jointly satisfied.

Exercising power in this new way was a significant experience for workers and managers alike. For workers, there was the revelation that given the opportunity, they could influence decision making in a way that benefited themselves, as well as the company. For managers, there was new evidence that by providing such an opportunity (that is, by sharing power), they could actually generate improved performance from the work force. This new experience of power conflicted so dramatically with the years of learning spent in the conventional roles of management and worker that there was often a tendency to deny the fact of power sharing. Nevertheless, this was the real source of both the apprehension and the excitement for those who became involved in the action research. It is power that makes things happen, and it was the new use of power that made new initiatives and solutions possible in "C" Mill.

The role of the action researcher was to support workers and managers in their exploration of this new experience and to facilitate the expression of their thoughts and feelings without the threat of retribution or loss of authority. The researcher helped individuals and the group develop their ideas as research hypotheses that could be tested by trial implementation. This commitment to the research task was the focus that could allow different interests to interact creatively and positively. It required a trust in the researchers on the part of both workers and managers, and even then, the sharing of power was something that individuals had to do often enough that they could come to realize its benefits.

## THE CRITICAL ISSUE OF EFFECTIVENESS

From the point of view of both management and the work force, the most significant force in developing participation was the achievement of positive results. Changes were made in most aspects of the organization, the technology, work procedures, and organizational roles and structure.

Action research was a good thing, provided something got done. . . . Otherwise, it wouldn't be good for anything.

What appealed to the crew was that there was some action and not just idle talk.

When positive results came out of it, that's when my attitude changed.

The kinds of technical change ranged from the simple reduction in speed of some machinery to the complex and costly installation of closed-circuit television monitors (to provide sawmill log-deck operators with greater control of their machine out-feed and to establish effective communication with the interior of the mill). Most design changes have been small in scale but quite large in effect, as with the rebuilding of a hydraulic hoist to enable operators to run a machine at variable speeds and prevent frequent bothersome jam-ups in the unstacking of lumber.

Some of the more far-reaching changes were not technically complex. They were simple procedures devised by operators to smooth the work flow and improve the transfer of logs within the mill. The change that may yet have the greatest effect was the work of a group of sawmill maintenance and production workers in the joint development of training manuals and procedures to provide operators with instruction in the basic mechanics and electronics of their machinery. Implied in these procedures are new roles for maintenance employees in the training of production workers, who, themselves, assume a new responsibility for the inspection and preventive maintenance of machinery.

The cumulative effect of these social and technical changes has been a significant reduction in stoppages and interruptions in the work flow. The solution of problems has been reflected in sustained improvement in production, which has steadily increased from 350,000 board feet of lumber per day to over 410,000 board feet. During this same period of productivity improvement, the "C" Mill safety records show that no accidents were recorded in the whole of the sawmill operation. As an indication of how people now feel about their work, the rate of absence in "C" Mill has fallen by over 50 percent, and turnover has been reduced to an annual rate of less than 30 percent.

One of the unintended consequences of improvement in the sawmill was the aggravation of problems further along the production line, namely, in the area of the planermill, where rough sawmill boards are transformed into various dimensions of finished lumber ready for sale. In January 1977, the steering committee extended the action research into the planermill at a time when the crew had developed strong feelings of bitterness and frustration about what appeared to be the virtual impossibility of accomplishing a good day's work in the planermill.

Since January, the improvement in the planermill has been from a level of less than 50 percent efficiency to a sustained level of 70 percent or more. An equally significant indicator of the kind of change that has occurred in the planermill is the decline in the rate of absence from work, which has fallen from a rate of two absentees per shift to a rate of one absentee on the average of every two shifts. (At the same time as this change was occurring in "C" Mill, the absentee rate in another comparable planermill on the Mackenzie site increased by almost 100 percent.

THE PROCESS OF INDIVIDUAL AND
ORGANIZATIONAL LEARNING

As well as an improvement in performance, there has been a process of learning at the level of the individual and for the organization as a whole. This is most evident in the experience of action research in the planermill, where there were more problems in the organizational structure, as opposed to technical or procedural problems.

Change in organizational roles and structure was not an initial focus of attention in the action research. The problems first identified by the work force were individual "maintenance" issues, concerning the condition of their machinery, the evenness of the work flow, and the general quality of the work experience in their own particular work area. However, as participation developed, issues of "coordination" arose: between individual operators on the same production line, between production and maintenance workers in general, or between the sawmill and planermill as two related parts of one total production system.

It is an indication of how skills and understanding develop through participation that workers and managers were now able to tackle the complexity and challenge of involvement-in-change of their own roles (and, possibly, status) within the organization. For example, workers rotating on a particular job in the planermill diagnosed the problem of repeated jam-ups to be the result of their own lack of operator skill and training. However, so long as this job was grouped in a rotation pattern with a number of significantly less demanding jobs, it was unlikely that the skill and training of operators would improve at that job. A trial run to remove this key job from the rotation pattern eliminated many of the production problems and personal disputes among crew members. The job has since been made part of another job grouping that includes more skilled work (paid at a higher rate).

However, the problem that showed up most significantly in the research team's analysis was referred to as "the maintenance problem." It was a case of strong personality differences among maintenance workers (planermen) being aggravated by a form of organization that made individual planermen responsible to separate production shifts that tended to be in competition with one another. Pressure was placed upon planermen to avoid stoppages for maintenance work that was not absolutely required for the performance of their own shift. As a result, much necessary maintenance work was left undone, and planermen were blaming one another for problems that were inherited from previous shifts.

In a situation that was the complete opposite of that in the sawmill, maintenance workers in the planermill suffered from being too closely integrated with production crews. On the encouragement of the mill manager, a diagnosis of the problem by the planermen, together with the help of the researcher, led to the definition of some maintenance objectives and a division of labor, with a new shift schedule of maintenance work based upon the special abilities of the different planermen. This new maintenance organization overlapped with the organization of the production shifts so that its implementation required consent from the production superintendent, planermill foremen, and the "C" Mill manager, all currently involved in the management of the planermill.

About the same time, the need for change in organizational roles was beginning to affect the management group itself. The action research had indicated some problems and confusion from the overlap and redundancy of the various levels of authority within the small planermill department. The need for change arose also from the new initiative of the work force, who were now seen to require less constant direction and control. As one supervisor reported: "My job has become easier since the crew started to work together as a group. . . .

Guys now go help one another, instead of me having to tell people to go help."

This was a period of serious and somewhat difficult self-evaluation by the management group. It led, however, to changes that relied on initiatives by the staff themselves. The key decision was taken by the "C" Mill production superintendent to relinquish many of his responsibilities in the sawmill in order to assume sole supervisory and management authority in the planermill. This one initiative enabled other changes, which have combined to shorten and simplify the levels of authority in both the planermill and sawmill.

Participation in the development of these changes has provided workers and managers with a greater understanding of the nature of their organization and of the possibilities of their own individual development as members of that organization. For example, action research into specific problems of rotation among various jobs has produced a better understanding between management and the work force about some of the conditions for effective job rotation. These ideas were applied in the negotiation of the most recent collective agreement, which designated some new patterns of job rotation in "C" Mill. Another aspect of the organization that has become more clearly identified is the extent to which the two apparently separate parts of the operation—namely, the sawmill and planermill—actually form one technical system. Understanding of this fact has helped lead to an adjustment in the corresponding social organization, with more coordination between the mills on matters of quality control and maintenance, and these initiatives are likely to develop further. From the start of the action research, there has been concern with the possible integration of production and maintenance functions, which, otherwise, are often experienced as being in conflict with one another. In both the planermill and the sawmill, experiments have found various kinds and degrees of possible overlap between the functions (that is, in training roles or operating maintenance crews). Insofar as these changes developed, maintenance and production workers began to experience an improvement in their relationships on the job.

Through the process of participation itself, supervisors and managers have learned that they could achieve greater understanding and closer contact with their crews. In most cases, management personnel also derived a sense of achievement from the significant improvement in productivity. For some individuals, the group setting of the action research process provided a forum in which they could finally function as leaders.

From the workers' standpoint, the experience of participation has provided a sense of belonging, a greater awareness and control of change in the work environment, a sense of achievement and self-respect, and above all, an opportunity to express oneself.

I learned that I had a part . . . not just management or the big shots.

We got rid of a lot of little problems that really bothered people on the job.

Above all, we learned that you can get the orange hats and the workers together.

A person was giving more of himself. . . . You felt pride; you felt that you cared.

What I learned most of all is that things can get done, and I got satisfaction out of seeing them done . . . and out of realizing that I helped make them happen.


## THE BATTLE TO KEEP THE PROCESS GOING

From the original concept of the joint leadership of the action research, between the "outside" researcher and the mill manager as a permanent "internal" researcher, a stated objective of the participation project in "C" Mill has been to establish action research as an ongoing process led by a research capability internal to the "C" Mill organization. The various approaches taken to try and sustain the process in "C" Mill have embodied the essential spirit of action research itself, in the willingness "to look into what one is doing and to regard this in some measure as experimental rather than based on proven fact or incapable of investigation."[4]

Six months after the start of the action research in the sawmill, the mill manager assumed sole leadership of the program in the sawmill, while the researcher concentrated on the development of action research in the planermill. What was discovered, however, was that other priorities soon absorbed the time of management personnel in the sawmill, including the mill manager, to the detriment of the action research program.

Even with the best of intentions, supervisory and management personnel found it difficult in practice to give continuing attention to the research task and the satisfaction of human needs, in the face of the demands of the normal work schedule: "Action research often seemed to be something 'extra,' beyond the normal day's work. After all, we have a mill to run."

It is probably true that participation will not be regarded as the real work that it is until it takes place within the "real" time of normal working hours—and not after shift or during days off work. However, the greater difficulty for management personnel in maintaining their involvement in a participative process was probably the persistent tradition of the "star" supervisor or manager who successfully makes the key decisions on his own. Recognition is as much a concern to the management person as it is to the individual worker, and managers and supervisors often feared a loss of status more than they felt satisfied by the new rewards of a still unaccustomed style of participative leadership. Any deep concern with status may also have been related to a lingering perception of the work force as people "who are not really with us."

A positive outcome of this experience was nonetheless the willingness of the steering committee to try a new approach in the planermill, where after several months, the outside researcher withdrew from an active role, to be replaced by a new joint research team, composed of the "C" Mill manager and an employee of the planermill, who as shop steward had achieved a reputation for personal effectiveness with both management and the workplace. The employee selected by the committee has remained an hourly paid member of the work force, performing her regular job as a mill grader, but with provision for relief from this job in order to consult with all crews and management personnel in the mill, assisting them in the follow-up to problems or the diagnosis of immediate issues, while also collecting new data and working with the mill manager on preparations for action research on longer-term problems. The employee and the mill manager have also jointly led the meetings of the planermill action research teams.

This new form of joint leadership was designed by the "C" Mill manager and action researcher to assist the mill manager in making the necessary time commitment to the action research, while at the same time giving added force to the consideration of the needs of the work force through their representation on the research team itself. During several months of collaboration in the planermill, this joint leadership does indeed appear to have functioned quite effectively; it is a definite improvement over the previous arrangement in the sawmill.

What has become evident, however, is that the employee as coresearcher has felt constrained by some doubt as to her actual authority. This sense of personal uncertainty appears to reflect an ambivalence in the commitment to the participative process by the general work force itself. The fact is that the members of the work force have only begun to see the possibility that they can benefit themselves through their work experience. There is still a conventional wisdom that anything that might contribute to the welfare of the company is unlikely to benefit the worker as well.

It is this kind of ambivalence or resistance from workers and managers alike that has led people in "C" Mill to refer to the "battle" to keep action research going. The conclusion drawn by some workers and managers is that continued intervention by an outside researcher is required to sustain the participative process. Yet, the development of participation is obviously such a long-term and continuous process, affected by constant changes in organizational membership and in the external environment, that this suggestion appears impractical. More than the matter of practicalities, however, the concern of the researcher would be that continued intervention is likely to conflict with the ultimate objective of developing within people themselves the capability for personal and organizational change.

People within "C" Mill have already learned a great deal from the process of participation. The organization itself has changed. Some management personnel have been particularly successful in applying a more collaborative approach throughout their work. Among the work force, individual workers have emerged as spontaneous leaders in the mill. As another outgrowth of the action research process, workers have collaborated with the mill manager in developing a plant safety program effectively administered by the crew themselves. (One year ago, "C" Mill Mackenzie had one of the poorest safety records in the whole of the company, whereas today, it holds one of the very best in all of the British Columbia forest industry.)

The capability for the further development of participation in the "C" Mill organization depends upon the willingness of people to inquire into and understand the nature of present resistances to change. To this extent, the realization that the development of participation is indeed a battle serves as a liberating insight for workers, managers, and action researchers alike. What is apparent at the very least is that the resistances felt by the work force and management, respectively, are noticeably interdependent. Individual supervisors or managers who may harbor the belief that the work force is not entirely with them can only be helped by the evidence of commitment from workers themselves. Similarly, any belief on the part of employees that work cannot be a source of personal fulfillment will be overcome only by the visible initiative of management personnel to invest in the development of their employee group.

The development of the participative process must therefore become truly collaborative, not just between the researcher and the organization as a whole, as was the case in the initial research partnership, but, most significantly, between management and the work force within the organization. The leadership that most explicitly embodies this collaboration in "C" Mill is the union-management steering committee. Although originally a creation of the researchers, the steering committee itself is now the most appropriate group to do the planning and reviewing of the action research led by the mill manager. Reference to an outside researcher might be limited to periodic consultation with the steering committee at its request. For what is essential is not the role of the researcher but, rather, the spirit of openness to people and to new ideas, which a researcher from the outside can help establish in the organization as a whole.

The battle to develop a participative process is really a creative battle. It is the struggle to create a common experience of work within an organization that is most often divided by levels of hierarchy, fragmented jobs, and the diverse economic interests of management and the work force. The different interests of management and worker are real and substantial within our political and economic systems, but what we have lacked are sufficient means for these interests to interact collaboratively, as well as through organized conflict. We have been left with a quality of life in the workplace that is often dissatisfying to worker and manager alike.

Action research has been a way for people from different parts of the social and technical system of "C" Mill to study the effects of those old divisions in their workplace and to act together creatively to change both the system and themselves. As people in Mackenzie continue their involvement with this process, they will be contributing to an inquiry that extends far beyond the borders of their community. It is the development of a new culture of work that has a human value as well as an economic significance.

## NOTES

1. A. Alexander and D. Bryant, "Labour Turnover at Mackenzie," mimeographed (Vancouver: B.C. Research, November 1974).

2. D. Bryant and B. Painter, "Action Research at Mackenzie, Report No. I: The Process of Action Research," mimeographed (Vancouver: B.C. Research, October 1976).

3. D. Bryant and B. Painter, "An Action Research Approach to Organization Design," mimeographed (Vancouver: B.C. Research, June 1977).

4. E. L. Trist, "Action Research and Adaptive Planning," in Experimenting with Organizational Life, ed. A. W. Clark (New York: Plenum Press, 1976).

# Case 8

## AN AMERICAN APPROACH TO SELF-MANAGEMENT

Michael A. Gurdon

This case study deals with an employee-owned medium-sized textile mill situated in New York State. The author examines the benefits and problems of self-management in an employee-owned company in a North American setting.

The Yugoslav system of self-management has provided a good deal of food for thought for organizational theorists concerning the multiple types of institutional arrangements that are possible and that are neither owned and operated by government nor managed in the interests of private investors. In North America, one novel approach that is worthy of analysis is the increasing incidence of industrial enterprises in which there is worker ownership of equity.

There is some tradition of employee ownership in the United States. One of the earliest recorded examples was a joint-stock company formed in 1847 by 20 members of a Cincinnati union of iron molders following an unsuccessful strike.[1] The establishment of other industrial cooperatives, as with the above case, generally coincided with periods of economic depression and unemployment. The onset of the twentieth century, with the rise of a national trade union movement hostile to localized cooperatives and with a high rate of failure among those enterprises, saw few further experiments. However, since 1973, a significant number of totally or majority employee-owned companies have begun to appear again. The immediate stimulus seems similar to that of a century earlier—an economic downturn in which relatively small units are abandoned or put up for sale by parent corporations and from which flows the threat of large-scale unemployment. The size and type of these enterprises are quite re-

This study was conducted by Michael A. Gurdon, University of New Brunswick, Canada.

markable, ranging from the 14,000-strong Chicago and Northwestern Transportation Company to firms with a few hundred or only a few dozen workers in machine tools, frozen foods, plywood, and insurance

Such an institutional arrangement brings into focus the issue of the locus of ownership of industrial property in society. The traditional radical approach to this question has been to call for the government ownership of industry, but over the past two decades, there has been a growing disillusionment with the effects of nationalization on the part of socialist theoreticians.[2] Furthermore, as has been demonstrated by the experience of the Histadrut-owned enterprises in Israel, of which all Histadrut members are theoretically coowners, representative ownership is a meaningless concept for individual workers. Yet, how can the concept be invested with meaning? One answer is possibly provided by the Yugoslav system, in which enterprises are defined as social property, thereby permitting the workers, who do not have personal ownership, to possess certain inalienable rights of influence within their place of work. Another answer, and one that is more appropriate to North American history and cultural values, may be the kind of employee-owned companies described here. After all, the status of employees as shareholders certainly grants them rights to information on the present and future development of their enterprise, and it should reinforce the legitimacy of their increased participation, precisely the objectives that have been achieved through legislative means in a number of European countries.

This case study will confine itself to analyzing in some depth one of these cases, a medium-sized textile mill situated in New York State and will attempt to elicit some lessons for practitioners and other interested parties from what are perceived to be the benefits and problems experienced in this system of employee ownership.


THE COMPANY

The textile mill is a knitting, dyeing, and finishing operation that produces high-quality fabric, mainly nylon and Dacron, for the lingerie market. It is located in a politically conservative community of 25,000. In 1960 the company, along with an associated sewing mill, had been the largest industrial employer in the area, with 700 employees. Eight years later, the corporation that operated the mill and 15 other plants throughout the country was taken over by a $500 million conglomerate. A period of gross mismanagement ensued, primarily in the merchandising of what was a new line of products to the recent buyer, and sales declined dramatically. This brief era of more extreme absentee ownership, with an insensitivity to the needs and working conditions of the employees, saw a worsening in the labor relations

climate. Three strong but unsuccessful attempts were made to unionize the plant on behalf of the United Textile Workers.

At the beginning of 1975, the conglomerate's board of directors
approved a decision to sell the plants acquired in 1968. Several offers
were tendered on the New York mill, but they were apparently at too
low a level to be entertained. Head office management then opted to
obtain the tax advantages available for shutting down a facility and
claiming a loss. The general manager of the mill (who was to become
the president of the new company) was asked to prepare a plan for
closing the plant entirely. He was incredulous. He knew from the
production figures that the mill was a money-maker in itself, and yet,
he was being asked to put 140 personnel, many of whom possessed
over 20 years' service, out of work. Moreover, with an unemployment
rate of 10 percent in the local labor market and a historically declining manufacturing base, the prospects for reemployment were not
good. Under these circumstances, it did not take long for the idea
of "Let's buy the place" to arise. In the words of the general manager:
"We knew we had a plant which was old but was competitively operational, a lot of highly experienced people, and we made a good product.
There was no reason why we shouldn't be able to go into business on
a competitive basis."

The necessary connections were quickly established. The general manager immediately "went political," contacting the local assem-
blyman, since the state might be a possible source of funds. Then,
together with a local banker, he arranged a meeting with the New York
Business Development Corporation, a semipublic concern owned by
the state's banks and utilities and designed to handle loans that would
not normally qualify as standard commercial loans. (A loan was
eventually to be obtained from this source, guaranteed to the level of
90 percent by the Small Business Administration of the federal government.) It was ascertained at this meeting that a viable financial pack-
age could be worked out provided that approximately $150,000 was
raised internally. A conference of the 70 remaining employees who
were engaged in finalizing orders was called, and from this group of
low-paid textile workers, over $100,000 was collected within a week,
in amounts ranging from $100 to $10,000. In addition, 26 local businessmen bought about $45,000 of stock.

The new employee-owned company rapidly developed a clientele
of between 30 to 40 clothing manufacturers, seven of which are major
national customers. It now holds 2 percent of the nylon market in the
United States and produces in excess of $10 million worth of cloth an-
nually.

## THE OWNERSHIP STRUCTURE

The employee-owned company became a legal entity in June 1975
The internal ownership structure can be described as follows. There
were 41 employees who had invested in the new organization and who,
therefore, had immediate shareholder rights, influence at shareholder
meetings being proportional to the number of shares owned. With the
rehiring of workers who had been laid off temporarily, however, in
addition to new hiring, there was soon a majority of nonowners working in the mill. The potential dangers of this contradiction were
quickly realized. Consequently, the mechanics of an Employee Stock
Ownership Plan (ESOP) began to be worked on. The ESOP had been
given impetus by its inclusion in the Employee Retirement Income
Security Act of 1974. This flexible instrument can also be used as a
financial mechanism designed to attract external capital, which can
be repaid with pretax rather than aftertax profits.[3] ESOPs have actually been utilized in some instances to enable employees to purchase
their threatened workplaces. Here, the bank making the loan holds
the shares, which are released to the employees as the loan is re-
deemed. In a varying number of years, the employee group comes to
own a majority of the stock. There are also examples of existing
unions, particularly where they have trust in the new management,
that agree to give up their negotiated pension plans for the unique
advantages that the ESOP provides for the company.

In the case of the textile mill, the stock ownership plan was designed to give to all employees both pension benefits and voting rights
after a vesting period. The amount distributed to an individual's account would be based on the number of points the individual had accrued. The point system was calculated on one point for every $100
of annual salary, plus a point for every year of service with the new
company. Thus, an employee earning $7,800 with two years of ser-
vice would have accumulated 80 points (78 + 2) for the year. The actual amount he or she would receive would depend on the value of each
point, that is, on the total distribution for the year (which was
$120,000 in the first year) divided by the total number of points in
the system. The benefits in an account are vested according to an
established schedule—40 percent after four years, rising to 100 percent after 11 years. Only fully vested shares can be individually voted
by the participants (that is, after 11 years). Until that time, both the
vested and unvested portions are voted by a Trust Committee, composed of three board-appointed company officers. Employees who retire receive their benefits in the form of shares, which can then be
repurchased by the Trust Committee for cash. (The Trust Committee
is designated as the only body with the prerogative of at least first
refusal on buying back stock, whether from outside shareholders, em-

ployee shareholders, or retirees. This is to ensure that control is retained within the company.) Employees who leave the company receive only the amount vested. In other words, they receive nothing if they quit before four years, 40 percent of what is in their account if they leave with four years' service, and so on. Any portion of the final balance of an account that does not become part of an individual's plan benefit is called a "forfeiture." All such forfeitures are reallocated, along with the company contribution and accrued interest, among the remaining participants for that year. The amounts allocated to individual accounts for 1976 ranged from several hundred to several thousand dollars.

## RESEARCH METHODOLOGY

There were two distinct stages of data collection in the study of the textile mill. An extensive questionnaire was administered on company time in June 1976, just 12 months after the employee purchase. Employees were encouraged to take the questionnaire, but were not compelled to do so. In all, 90 percent of the work force returned usable questionnaires. The written instrument was supplemented by a random series of semistructured interviews. A sample of managers and workers was selected from every department and from all shifts, and a total of 32 persons, or nearly a quarter of the work force, was interviewed. The second stage of the study involved a readministration of the questionnaire in June 1977 in order to ascertain the impact of a longer-term experience with employee ownership and whether any discontinuities were coming to light. In addition to these formal methods of data collection, the author sat in on meetings and observed task and interpersonal activity in the course of several plant visits.

## PERFORMANCE AND MORALE MEASURES

In an employee-owned enterprise, it is suggested that ownership to some extent legitimizes rank-and-file inputs (supervisors and managers accept input because the rank and file are also owners), a situation that is not to be found in even the most enlightened participative corporations. This proclivity is undoubtedly reinforced by the very involvement of workers and/or union leaders with the local management in the campaign to save jobs. It can be assumed that this experience of working together as a unified team will produce a convergence of interests within the employee-owned firm. Since ownership in any case legally guarantees the right to participate in a company's critical decisions, we can draw upon much of the research that has been done on participation in group decision making and planning and predict that there will be feelings of increased satisfaction and, perhaps, improved productivity.[4] In relation to the latter aspect, it might be useful to make the conceptual distinction in cooperative situations that Whyte makes between passive acceptance and active cooperation on the part of employees: "We would expect to find restriction of output prevalent under passive cooperation. We would expect to find the lid taken off production under conditions of active cooperation."[5] The case of Walt Flemm, presented by Garson, persuasively demonstrates what happens to a man's motivation and behavior when it is palpably made clear to him that the mill is not _his_ mill and never was.[6] Conversely, employee ownership can be expected to generate active cooperation. Moreover, Bakke shows that one of the most important needs of workers is to enlarge those areas of their lives in which their own decisions determine the outcomes of their efforts.[7] To the extent that part ownership of the company meets this need— and in doing so reinforces the self-image of "producer"—employees should be more satisfied. The above theoretical assumptions will be tested by an analysis of some of the research findings flowing from the mill study.

Each employee who had worked at the mill when it was operated by the former conglomerate owner was asked to complete a list of statements designed to elicit the individual's feelings about the value of the new system of ownership as it impinged upon him or her. The statements measured real, subjective change, since the individual was comparing his or her present feelings against his or her own baseline standards, and thus, any reported change stands as a change irrespective of the level (be it positive or negative) of the original pre-purchase feelings.

One year after the employee purchase, there was a widespread feeling that things had changed for the better. The majority of workers stated that their overall work satisfaction had increased (64.0 percent), felt more secure in their jobs (59.0 percent), saw their own productivity as markedly increased (76.5 percent), were likewise putting more effort into their jobs (70.0 percent), and saw the effort exerted by others as similarly increased (66.0 percent). This general satisfaction possibly existed because they perceived their own skills and abilities as being better utilized (59.0 percent) and thus were more interested in what they were doing (62.5 percent). Certainly, there was a dramatic increase in the general concern with financial results (73.0 percent), which accords with what might be expected in an employee-owned firm, and whatever alienation there might have been from the product had largely disappeared (79.0 percent felt a greater pride in the product that they were producing). It is a significant fact that the majority (55.0 percent) were favorably oriented to even more change in their workplace.

A critical question to be answered is whether the positive feelings displayed were translated into actual behavior. We know that in 1974 the mill had been operating at about half of its capacity, and thus, in addition to incurring a $500,000 loss for that year, there was much production machinery lying idle. Following the employee purchase, the output of the mill quickly became restricted only by the capacity and quantity of the machinery available to meet the demand. In its first ten months of operation, the company accumulated a net profit of $257,000, and the book value per share of common stock had risen from $100 to $191. There is other evidence of a change in behavior. Prior to the change of ownership, employee pilferage was serious enough to warrant a guard service. This service was terminated following the purchase, and yet, the incidence of pilferage was almost nil. Another measure of employee care and attention is the cost of redyeing batches of cloth. An improved quality consciousness was maintained throughout the first year to the extent that redyes represented only 0.6 percent of total manufacturing cost compared with 3.0 percent under the former owner. A final objective measure of morale is the amount of voluntary quitting that takes place. During the last "normal" comparable period under absentee ownership, from July 1973 to June 1974, the quitting rate was a 4 percent monthly average, which was on par with the national average for knitting mills. The comparative figure at the mill for the July 1975 to June 1976 period was 1.7 percent, an improvement that represents a significant difference at the < .05 level.

Data from another employee-owned firm—a trucking company in Alberta with 165 workers—add further credence to the above account of an improvement in performance.[8] After two years of employee ownership, the share prices of this Canadian company had increased by 300 percent. The amount of customer claims for freight damaged or lost, reflecting the care displayed by freight handlers and drivers, declined by 60 percent. This higher quality of output per man-hour did not come at the expense of quantity of output—pounds loaded per man-hour increased by 5 percent. As for turnover, it had declined by 30 percent, the great part of this reduction occurring among the shareholders (70 percent of the work force) who had a quitting rate of less than one-third that of the nonshareholders.

The very last piece of data suggests yet another way of measuring the impact of becoming an employee-owner. The fact that the work force at the textile mill is also composed of both owners and those who cannot experience the rights of ownership for several years (and are therefore effectively nonowners) permits us to assess the impact of ownership by dichotomizing and comparing the responses of these groups. Three of the variables used to measure work-related attitudes are presented here.

1. Job satisfaction: Feelings of satisfaction were measured by three items constructed with a seven-point scale. The items asked to what extent the individual liked his or her job, how often he or she thought about quitting, and whether the company was a good place to work. The reliability of this measure was 0.76, estimated by the Spearman-Brown formula. [9]

2. Institutional commitment: The extent to which the individual felt committed to or alienated from the firm was measured by eight items on a five-point scale. Examples of the items utilized included the following: "I sometimes regret that I joined the Mill" and "It's all the same to me whether I work for the Mill or for some other firm." The reliability of this measure was 0.92. It was anticipated that shareholders would feel more attached to their employment because of both the financial incentives and the greater degree of personal influence involved.

3. Prounion: This measure was constructed out of three items based on a seven-point scale. The items sought to elicit the belief in the necessity of a union at this time, whether employees could get fair treatment in its absence, and if union representation was the best way of achieving worker influence in decision making. The reliability of this measure was 0.80. It was hypothesized that shareholders would be more opposed to the presence of a union than would the non-shareholders, since a union would not be seen by the former as a likely instrument through which to improve their position.

The results of these various measures of personal satisfaction lend strong support to the hypothesis that ownership does make a difference. Those who owned stock manifested greater job satisfaction (a significant difference at $< .005$), were more committed to the organization ($p \leq .01$), and were more opposed to the presence of a union ($p \leq .005$).

EVOLVING PROBLEMS

The 1977 financial year replicated the good performance of the mill's first year of operation. Net profits registered a healthy $230,000 in what had been a disastrous period for the textile industry as a whole. The various indicators of productivity and employee attention remained consistently impressive. Moreover, the quitting rate was even lower than it had been the year before. Nonetheless, these objective data were masking some growing frustrations.

One of the problems of these companies flows from the very success of their formation. Their intense involvement in the campaign to save the company leads workers and/or union leaders to feel that in the future they will be treated more as the social equals of the management personnel and that their ideas will be valued. There is, undoubtedly, a legal foundation to these heightened expectations. There are avenues of influence for them as stockholders with voting power and as potential members on the board of directors. However, top management, used to acting without the constraint of normally distant shareholders, often has difficulty in perceiving the subtle change in role relationships. Despite the fact that the rank-and-file owners sometimes collectively possess more stock than the management members, management tends to see the prepurchase power distribution as the desirable state of affairs.

The critical point to be made about this type of employee-owned firm is that control is still based upon capital, not upon labor. Consequently, top management continues to view its function as representing the interests of the shareholders rather than the interests of all those who contribute their labor. One obvious repercussion is a disinclination to afford voting rights to those employees who did not partake in the initial investment gamble. But even within the ranks of the owners, there quickly develops an implicit realization of divided interests between the larger (mainly managerial) and smaller (mainly rank-and-file) shareholders. Only 12 months after the purchase, 86 percent of managerial shareholders believed that influence should be proportional to the amount of stock owned, while only 19 percent of rank-and-file shareholders were in agreement with this position. One clear conclusion that emanates from this case is that authority and legal ownership are additive. In other words, the long-term impact of employee ownership is a reinforcement of managerial status. This is because the functionaries of the absentee ownership have themselves become shareholders instead of being hired by the workers, as in the model producer cooperative.

Thus, the change of ownership from an absentee to a broad employee basis, when structured in the traditional stock form, merely enhances management's status. Such a development is facilitated by the absence of any environmental overload, that is, when it is felt that the top echelon itself can absorb all external pressures and achieve the company's goals. While the management team above first-level supervision was increasingly introduced into the central decision-making process, the internal briefings by the president on the state of the company, which were provided for all rank-and-file employees on an irregular basis, were no substitute. Apart from such attempts to open up the communications channels, there have been no structural changes within the mill. Once the survival of the

new firm had been ensured, the president began expressing a keen
interest in semiautonomous work groups as a mechanism for allowing
the mill's owners to attain control of their job environments. However, at the time of writing, no substantial developments can be reported in this area. This lack of action is unfortunate, for the internal structure of the organization was wide open for change during the
first few months of the experiment, as traditional roles were in a
state of flux, managers and supervisors being unsure of the form and
content of their relationships with subordinates. After this initial uncertainty, however, there was a refreezing of roles, which left authority relationships essentially the same.

It might be said that the rank and file could still make their influence felt at the annual shareholders' meetings. There seems little
doubt that many held that belief. The first survey had demonstrated
that the rank and file were, in many respects, as positive as the
managers in their attitudes. By the time of the second survey, this
was no longer the case. The only significant new experience for the
rank and file that occurred between the surveys was the first annual
shareholders' meeting. Since the overwhelming majority had not
owned stock before in any corporation, they were largely unprepared
for what was to eventuate. As one of the more detached management
observers of the process said: "A lot of them thought that it was going to be a fraternal sort of gathering, something like the American
Legion or the Elks." Of course, it was not. It was not a leisurely
meeting in which decisions would be taken on a one-man/one-vote
basis; neither was there a secret ballot. To have to publicly register
the amount of stock one owned in order to prove one's eligibility for
voting and to see proxies being voted by others were things that were
totally foreign to any past experience. The meeting was kept tightly
to the agenda, and little time was devoted to questions and answers.
In the words of one knitter, "Everyone was stunned." Another complained that "everything was set up even before you went to the meeting. I didn't want to have anything to do with the stock after that."
This sentiment is revealing because it was to be translated into concrete behavior. Only half of those who were at this gathering bothered
to attend the 1977 meeting.

Clearly, the existence of internal ownership can have an incre-
mental effect on morale in a negative as well as in a positive sense.
It is indicative of the change that had taken place that in the 1977 survey, there was now no significant difference between rank-and-file
owners and nonowners in two of the three attitudinal measures discussed above. Moreover, in response to another item, the rank and
file no longer felt a high sense of personal ownership in the firm and
were, in fact, indistinguishable from the nonowners in this respect.
It appears that they were beginning to adjust their aspirations to the

realities of the functioning of the new system. Rights, such as those inherent in ownership, take on psychological force only when they can be exercised.

Another relevant finding was the moderation of antiunion sentiment among the rank-and-file owners, which accords with several comments heard during a 1978 visit that there was talk of a union among some employees. Once it had become apparent that there was no meaningful influence flowing from ownership, many employees began to treat it as a financial investment only. A concentration on the material aspects of ownership, however, led to further dissatisfaction, First, there had been no dividends paid out (this was prohibited during the first three years of the company's existence by the terms of the bank loan); second, all employees (not just owners) took part in the annual profit sharing; third, the pay structure had not been equalized following the employee purchase, as many believed it would be, but was even more differentiated. In a real sense, the initial distinction constructed between the rank-and-file owners and nonowners was coming to be seen as increasingly artificial in the face of management's decision-making and material privileges.

The loss of commitment was reflected in the sale of stock by some employees. Between September 1977 and June 1978 alone, seven of the original investors had sold their shares. In light of this declining commitment, I was intrigued to know what the reaction of the shareholders would be to an attractive purchase offer from an outside buyer. The predominant reaction on the part of the individuals to whom I spoke recently was that the employees would or should sell. Most suggested that since the ordinary worker did not have much of a say anyhow, it did not matter all that much who was in charge. This is not a unique phenomenon. The stormy history of Vermont Asbestos Group, another spectacularly successful example of employee ownership in monetary terms, provides ample evidence on this point. Top management there made no provision for worker participation in decision making at the job level or for consultation with workers except through rank-and-file representation on the board. As the board attempted to circumvent majority stockholder opposition to two particular ventures, the rank and file began to argue that since they had no influence on the present board, there was no advantage in owning stock in the company. The old board was subsequently voted out, and a new board, representing an outsider who pledged himself to purchase stock at a set price from those wishing to sell, was voted in.

IMPLICATIONS

The reality of contemporary employee ownership has demonstrated some positive features: the maintenance of considerable em-

ployment within local communities, increased worker satisfaction
and higher productivity, more abundance for all, since there is no
longer a nonproductive labor factor to which an "adequate" return mus
be made, and a reorientation toward the managerial function of coordination and away from that of discipline. Such examples also seem
particularly congruent with a U.S. philosophy that is antigovernmen-
tal and prolocal initiative and self-reliance. Indeed, it could be argued that these worker and community actions reflect self-management (as opposed to a fatalistic acceptance of corporate decisions to
close a plant) regardless of the ultimate failure of some of these attempts as industrial democracies. The issue becomes, How can some
of the more negative consequences be avoided? There are, I believe,
several lessons to be extracted from these cases that are of value to
managers, union leaders, and workers who might be contemplating
similar action.

First, while it is understandable that there is a sense of exhaus-
tion and completion following the successful transfer of ownership,
problems will eventuate if the implementation and administration of
the new system are not immediately considered. The inevitable rise
in expectations among the rank and file needs to be matched by the appropriate learning experiences, both in how to handle and utilize the
new rights of ownership and in increased skills and technical training
to absorb the devolution of greater authority into a suddenly autonomo
enterprise.

Second, it needs to be recognized that the rights generated by
ownership can be comparatively small in the absence of a purposeful
attempt to extract their potential. We already know that where the
prescribed rights of ownership are abstract only, as in much of East-
ern Europe or in the nationalized industries of the West, the workers
do not appear to feel a meaningful degree of personal control as a result of the ownership itself. While workers have little power to effect
a change in these instances, in the case of employee ownership, there
is a legal title that can be disposed of when prescribed rights are not
actualized. The point is that workers will hold on to their freedoms
as long as they think they possess them. Once it becomes obvious tha
they have little influence in determining the direction of the new enterprise, it becomes susceptible to a takeover bid from an external party
One option that could be utilized to preempt the frustrations generated
by unmet expectations is to introduce a two-class system of common
stock. One class could be sold in any amounts to employees or to individuals outside the company, but would carry no voting rights. The
other class of stock would carry voting rights and no more than a single share would be sold to each member of the organization.

Third, the deliberate actions advocated thus far are all the less
likely to occur where there is no ideological basis underlying the em-

ployee ownership system. The cases described here are, after all, ad hoc responses to immediate problems generated by the threat of a plant shutdown. The workers have therefore missed out on the learning experiences that would have been created by a continuing struggle for control over a long period. Indeed, there is some evidence that ownership in the absence of a democratic ideology can come into conflict with participation. For example, a number of workers at the mill, who felt that what was produced was money in their own pockets, were resentful of the idea of regular consultative sessions, which took time away from productive activity. Managers for their part, unfamiliar with participation on a day-to-day basis, also might not possess much faith in the introduction of such innovations. Nor should we forget that managers are also shareholders—and tend to be the larger ones—and that they may react no differently in their relations with subordinates to the traditional owner-manager. If an ideology is to develop within this context, it is likely to be a renewal of faith in expertise. Those fundamentalist managers who assert that they are responsible only to the owners of the company, not to its employees, must feel uneasy when confronted with the prospect of an employee-owned company. If authority in these instances is not to be shared democratically, then a new ideology must be created to legitimate the lack of change in internal power relationships. The idea that influence should be in the hands of those with the expertise fills the void nicely.

Fourth, where no provision is made for nonmanagerial input, there will be a gradual drift back to the traditional adversary relationship. Without the balance provided by the experience of control, the benefits of ownership become much more subject to the presence or absence of satisfaction in the same sense as wages and other working conditions. Like them, particularly with a union in the equation, it will become a negotiable issue. There has been more than one example of the frustration of expectations in an employee-owned company leading to member support for a militant stance by the union at bargaining time. The union might also find a role for itself in protecting the independence of action and speech of worker representatives on the board of directors.

Finally, in order to ensure the long-term viability of employee ownership and control, the purchase or utilization of the stock probably needs to be collective. Forms of share ownership in which stock is individually held have historically proved to be unsuccessful.[10] It was Lauck's assessment that without a collective stimulus or desire for employee ownership and control, individual employees are inclined to dispose of their holdings for profit when prices advance or to secure needed funds in times of emergency. In either case, control inexorably slips away from the rank and file. When the opportunity does arise, collective purchase can take place through a union or a trust, which is directed how to vote by the employees. In the Temiscaming case in Quebec, in which the rank and file possess 30 percent of the stock, an arrangement has been made so that employee stock can be voted as a bloc where necessary.[11] The union established a holding company, which wields the workers' shares in the enterprise, and the workers each have a vote in electing the trustees of the holding company. Thus, the workers can maintain their influence collectively.

CONCLUSION

The thrust of this study has indicated that there are a number of intervening variables that can hinder the translation of employee ownership into employee control. This evidence thus provides support for those proponents of self-management who have been skeptical of the claim that stock ownership per se would bring about effective power sharing.[12] Employee ownership as practiced in North America presents us with an elitist form of self-management in which one sector of the working community has obvious predominance. As in other systems of self-management, however, there is a trial-and-error process of learning that is ongoing and that will provide invaluable lessons for practitioners and academics alike.

NOTES

1. P. Foner, History of the Labor Movement in the United States (New York: International, 1975), 1: 179.

2. C. A. Crosland, The Future of Socialism (London: Cape, 1956).

3. R. N. Stern and P. Comstock, Employee Stock Ownership Plans (ESOPs): Benefits for Whom? New York State School of Industrial and Labor Relations, Key Issue no. 23 (Ithaca, N.Y.: Cornell University Press, 1978).

4. See A. Bavelas, "Some Problems of Organizational Change," Journal of Social Issues, Summer 1948; E. Bennett, "Discussion, Decision, Commitment, and Consensus in 'Group Decision,'" Human Relations, 1955; G. Farris, "Organizational Factors and Individual Performance: A Longitudinal Study," Journal of Applied Psychology, April 1969; J. French, J. Israel, and D. As, "An Experiment in Participation in a Norwegian Factory," Human Relations, February 1960; N. Morse and E. Reimer, "The Experimental Manipulation of a Major Organizational Variable," Journal of Abnormal and Social Psychology, January 1956; and W. F. Whyte, Money and Motivation (New York: Harper, 1955).

5. Whyte, Money and Motivation, p. 247.

6. B. Garson, All the Livelong Day (New York: Doubleday, 1975), pp. 123-24.

7. E. W. Bakke, Unemployed Worker: A Study of the Task of Making a Living without a Job (Hamden, Conn.: Shoe String Press, 1971), pp. 29, 41.

8. R. Long, "The Effects of Employee Ownership on Job Attitudes and Organizational Performance: An Exploratory Study" (Ph.D. diss., Cornell University, 1977).

9. J. Nunnally, Psychometric Theory (New York: McGraw-Hill, 1967).

10. W. J. Lauck, Political and Industrial Democracy: 1776-1926 (New York: Funk & Wagnalls, 1926).

11. W. F. Whyte, "Worker Participation: Ownership and Control" (Paper presented at the Ninth World Congress of Sociology, Uppsala, Sweden, August 1978), p. 10.

12. P. Bernstein, Workplace Democratization: Its Internal Dynamics (Kent, Ohio: Kent State University Press, 1976); and J. Vanek, Self-Management: Economic Liberation of Man (Baltimore: Penguin, 1975).

# *Case 9*

## YUGOSLAV WORKER SELF-MANAGEMENT: SOME ADVANTAGES AND PROBLEMS

### Alan Whitehorn

This case study focuses on the Yugoslav system of worker self-management in an attempt to analyze the practical and sociological implications of workplace democratization. The author selects seven firms, four from Yugoslavia and three from Canada, for his study and evaluates the benefits and disadvantages of worker self-management in the Yugoslav and Canadian settings.

PURPOSE

One has seen a veritable explosion in recent years in the number of theoretical and academic writings on worker self-management. While most of the writings in the past reflect a polemical and an ideological tone, increasingly, empirically based studies are emerging. There is still a need, however, for more scientifically based yet popularly written works, which can be realistic guides to the practitioners in industrial relations.[1]

This case study focuses on the Yugoslav system of worker self-management in an attempt to analyze the practical sociological implications of workplace democratization. As such, some of the questions posed include the following: Have the actual experiences of workplace reorganization developed along the lines advocated by socialists and ad hoc industrial relations reformers? Have factory conditions improved? Is communications more effective in the democratic factory? What sort of enterprise policies are fostered by the establishment of worker councils? Are self-managed enterprise policies better than those achieved under traditional patterns of industrial relations? Is there a decline in job dissatisfaction with the advent of worker self-management, and if so, does this affect company productivity?

This study was conducted by Alan Whitehorn, Royal Military College, Kingston, Canada.

310

## RESEARCH METHODOLOGY

To attempt to answer these and other questions, we shall draw conclusions from a small case study of seven factories, four from the Yugoslav republic of Slovenia and three from central provinces in Canada. The study was conducted during the early 1970s.* In both countries, the sample case studies were selected from similar industries producing manufactured steel products and from comparable societies in terms of high literacy and living standards.

The data used in this study are based on anonymous survey questionnaires administered in each factory. Some data are also based on interviews with leading Yugoslav factory officials, such as the company director, the personnel director, a trade union official, the president of the worker council, and the Communist party secretary.

## BACKGROUND INFORMATION

### Enterprises

Since these case studies are drawn from factories producing manufactured steel products and all of the factories were in the highly industrialized republic of Slovenia, one should be careful to note that the statistical validity of this study is largely confined to a single industry within this republic and not to Yugoslavia as a whole.

### Formal Legal Participative Machinery at the Factory Level

The Yugoslav factories are noted for their organizational structure known as worker self-management. While other small-scale experiments at worker self-managed factories exist in the world, no other society has experimented as extensively with democratic factory parliaments.

Briefly stated, each factory (in 1972, when this study was undertaken) is organized so as to elect a representative worker council composed of members elected from among the factory work force. This legislature, in turn, is responsible for all long-term policies and selects a director to coordinate enterprise operations. The director thus becomes an elected "public" official, representing all factory employees (see Table 13).

---

*Since the study was conducted in the early 1970s, the latest attempts at decentralization of factory decision making are not discussed in this chapter.

TABLE 13

Selected Demographic Aspects of Yugoslav and Canadian Factories Studied

| | Yugoslav Factories | | | | Canadian Factories | | |
| --- | --- | --- | --- | --- | --- | --- | --- |
| | A | B | C | D | X | Y | Z[a] |
| Factory size | 1,352 | 780 | 566 | 1,096 | 361 | 177 | 2,085 |
| Location | Town | Town | Medium-sized city | Medium-sized city | Large city | Medium-sized city | Medium-sized city |
| Type of product | 1 | 2 | 3 | 4 | 1 | 2 | 3 |
| Profit per employee (dinars) | 5,178 | 7,179 | 9,604 | Loss | n.a.[b] | n.a. | n.a. |
| Percentage of unskilled employees | 48.7 | 43.5 | 24.2 | 62.5 | 83.1[b] | 14.0 | 84.3 |
| Percentage of male employees | 53.6 | 79.3 | 88.2 | 48.0 | n.a. | n.a. | n.a. |
| Percentage of employees who are Communists | 2.3 | 7.8 | 6.6 | 5.0 | n.a. | n.a. | n.a. |
| Other features to note | — | Two management boards; functional separation into (1) sales and finance and (2) personnel problems | — | No management board; only specialized committees, but collegium | Shop association; multilinguistic area | Union, new within year | Strong union; plant part of larger complex |

n.a. = not available

[a]Not presently used in this study.
[b]No differentiation available between skilled and unskilled blue-collar workers.

Source: Compiled by the author.

Since legislatures increasingly need an executive to propose and guide policy through the decision-making process, it is not surprising to discover that the Yugoslav factories have management boards that are chosen directly by the members of the worker council. The factory employees thus influence the choice of management board members only indirectly by their voting for the worker council assembly.

In the process of electoral accountability, formal authority is derived from the employees. The flow of power is upward from the employees as factory citizens. However, in terms of day-to-day decision making about work, authority flows from the director downward. Thus, communications flow is a complete and continuous cycle. Communication flows from employees as citizens to employees as workers and vice versa.* Management and legislative bodies act as the connecting links. The result is a communication system that promotes extensive and diverse input, responsible output, and informative feedback.

Labor Relations Climate in the Factories under Study

It is perhaps more difficult to evaluate the labor relations climate in Communist countries because of the relative newness of the regimes, the turbulent revolutionary experiences in the past, and the recentness of social science research.

Labor relations in the Slovenian factories is noted for a high degree of unionization, encompassing 89 percent of the labor force.[2] In the factories studied, union meetings are held once or twice monthly, and the factory union official devotes about one to two hours a day on union matters. The union's role largely involved education, recreation, and assisting in factory elections.

Since the introduction of worker councils with their policy-making powers, the role of unions has become more ambiguous. In theory, a fully participatory and representative worker council ought to diminish the significance of the union organization, and the survey showed that in fact within the factory, the union was ranked in influence below not only that of the worker council but also the director, the management board, the League of Communists, the technical staff, and the middle-level supervisors.

The presence of the worker councils structure seems to have gained widespread acceptance, since 80 percent of the factory respon-

---

*This is perhaps the practical political expression of the Marxist aspiration "From each according to his ability, to each according to his needs."

dents stated that they accepted worker self-management. More important, perhaps, 82 percent asserted that the system was successful in their own factory. Thus, the climate of industrial relations in the factories under study can be characterized as being perceived as both legitimate (that is, acceptable) and effective (that is, a success). These findings suggest stable social relations, and such attitudes should foster a sound, if not ideal, industrial relations climate.

Unique to Communist-led countries is the vanguard role of the Communist party. Membership in the League of Communists (the Yugoslav Communist party) as a percentage of all employees ranges in the factories studied from a low of 2.3 percent to a high of 7.8 percent. These variations in percentages of Communists active in each plant can significantly affect social relations and are worth noting here as having a general influence on the overall industrial relations climate. Obviously, a higher number of Communist party members will mean a greater degree of politicization in the factory; it thereby will have an effect upon employee attitudes about work, factory organization, and the factory's relations with the outside community.

To a considerable degree, underlying economic conditions can have an effect on factory labor relations in setting the general tone of optimism or pessimism. Three of the four Slovenian factories in the study earned a profit, and we can deduce from this that general economic conditions were not a serious hindrance to positive factory social relations.

Data on strikes in the factories were not collected, but strikes are a fairly recent and still relatively atypical development in Yugoslavia; where they do occur, they rarely last more than a day.[3]

One final aspect of general labor relations in the plants—ability to influence decisions—will be discussed next in the empirical findings section.


EMPIRICAL FINDINGS: BENEFITS AND PROBLEMS

In evaluating some of the benefits and disadvantages of introducing worker self-management, it is perhaps easiest to commence by outlining the successes. Sociological benefits can be characterized as three sorts: (1) effects on the factory decision-making process, (2) the impact on attitudes of the work force, and (3) company policies fostered by such a revised corporate structure.

The most impressive data about worker self-management are the high number of persons active in factory decision making by being elected to worker council bodies. The Yugoslav statistical yearbook estimates that in any one year, 180,000 persons are elected, and of these, over half are newly elected to the factory councils.[4] One consequence of greater rank-and-file participation in decision making is evident in this survey's finding that individual Slovene laborers indicate a greater sense of self-influence than Canadian laborers. Management replies to the same question provided similar results in that Slovene managers' perceptions were that they, too, had greater influence within the factories than their Canadian counterparts. An explanation for these seemingly contradictory phenomena of both Slovene laborers and managers feeling a greater sense of influence is that communication (that is, influence) patterns might be more effective in the Slovene system. The labor-management system, rather than being perceived as a conflict-oriented zero-sum game, in which one must lose for the other to gain, may be perceived as a cooperative plus-sum game. In such a social setting, all may feel that their sense of influence has increased. Such a hypothesis is also suggested by the empirical work of Likert, in which he found that among the more democratic U.S. factories, total influence by all groups was greater than among less democratic ones.[5] If factory social relations have in fact been transformed qualitatively from one dominated by a conflictual basis to one increasingly cooperative in nature, the decision-making model of worker self-management may offer a possible institutional means to greater industrial peace and, thereby in the long run, to higher productivity.

From the days of the early Hawthorne experiments in Chicago in the 1920s, we have seen that workplace attitudes can have a significant effect on an enterprise's operations.[6] In our study, we found that a majority of the Slovene respondents felt that worker self-management had improved their position within the factory. This finding was reinforced by the finding that job satisfaction for all groups of employees was found to be considerably higher in the Slovene factories than in the Canadian enterprises.[7] Work alienation levels were also lower in Slovenia than Canada.* While such results might be due less to the introduction of worker self-management and more to the tradi-

---

*In recent years, the concept of alienation has seen extensive usage. In this study, the term alienation will refer to the following three common aspects or dimensions: lack of ability to control one's own environment (powerlessness), sense of purposelessness (meaninglessness), and sense of separation from other individuals and groups (social isolation). In this study, work alienation will refer to social relations within the factory, while societal alienation will refer to the social relations outside the factory. See Dwight Dean, "Alienation: Its Meaning and Measurement," American Sociological Review 26 (1961): 753-58, for a more detailed explanation of the term alienation.

tional cultural attitudes about work in Yugoslavia, it seems unlikely that this is the case. Since the positive replies to the two work-related variables—job satisfaction and lack of work alienation—are also coupled with the suggestion that Yugoslav factory relations have improved over time, we can infer that such favorable evaluations of working conditions were not always the case in the past.

Confirming the idea that the introduction of worker self-management has had a positive effect on the attitudes of the work force is this survey's finding that participants in the factory worker councils were less likely to be alienated than those who did not participate. Participation then seems to have quite positive effects on employees' attitudes about the factory. This finding confirms the impression of many personnel managers that a more participatory managerial style is conducive to good management-staff relations.

Another way of judging the success of worker self-management in sociological terms is by analysis of factory policies, particularly as they relate to the distribution of economic benefits.

While some wage inequities are desirable, excessive extremes in earnings are probably conducive to industrial disharmony and class tensions. The Slovene factories' wage disparities were calculated as a ratio of average wage scales of the most highly paid enterprise individuals, such as the factory director, to that of the average wage rates for unskilled factory laborers. The ratios ranged from a high of 4.8:1 to 3.4:1. These differential ratios are certainly less than in contemporary capitalist countries, where ratios of 10:1 or higher are quite common. [8] This finding suggests that worker self-management may help to foster a more egalitarian distribution of wealth early on at the earning source—the workplace—and thereby reduces the need to redistribute wealth later and less effectively by taxation.

Perhaps less controversial to evaluate is the Slovene factory's propensity to foster positive involvement in the local community. Unlike the classic capitalist firm, in which profit maximization is the solitary motivating force, the Slovene self-managed enterprise performs important social roles. All of the sampled factories owned either apartment units or vacation lodges for their employees. In an age of spiraling housing costs in which young families struggle to afford decent accommodation, such services seem significant indeed. It seems likely that employee turnover might well decline when such services are provided. The Japanese factory, drawing upon benevolent paternalism, not democratic workplace decision making, provides similar housing benefits and has, perhaps as a result, an amazingly low level of labor turnover and high worker productivity. Creating a sense of work and factory commitment by offering some community services may be a key reason for the economic success of both Japan and Yugoslavia. Integrating the factory and the municipality more closely may be an effective way of combining an expanding and rich economy with a system of reasonably stable industrial relations.

Increasingly, newspaper headlines dwell on the crippling effects of large, lengthy, and seemingly self-destructive strikes. While strikes are legal and occur in both the Yugoslav and Canadian systems, strikes are far less numerous and are far shorter in duration in Yugoslavia than Canada. For example, in 1968 there were only 148 strikes, of which 34.6 percent lasted less than three hours in duration and 78.5 percent lasted not more than a day.[9] Indeed, another positive aspect was the decline in the number of strikes from the mid-1960s to the late 1960s. The above data suggest that there may be less need for production-stopping conflict and negative forms of communication in Yugoslavia. The Yugoslav model, based on a plus-sum game, provides strong incentives for strikes to occur sparingly, and only when the self-managing structure ceases to be representative in the eyes of the rank-and-file blue-collar workers do such strikes occur.[10] As long as a centralized and relatively remote worker council system prevails, some sociological manifestations of alienation, such as strikes, are likely to remain, but they certainly remain far less frequent than in Canada.[11]

It is rare for any social innovations to have no disadvantages whatsoever. The Slovene self-managed factories in this study are no exception. In the self-managed factory, there are a large number of monthly meetings by different organizations (for example, the management board, worker council, League of Communists, union), and thus, it seems to be an active social system. It is not known how closely the meetings cluster together, but certainly, the problems of overlapping membership and time limitations are likely. Indeed, one leading official (a member of the factory management board) suggested to me in an interview that "there are too many committees and meetings for a single individual to participate in." Time, then, is a scarce commodity, as Margaret Cole, a leading guild socialist and theorist on worker self-management, has noted, and worker self-management needs to resolve this problem more adequately, both in theory and in practice.

While there are very little data, in general, on the role of the specialized committees of the worker council (and, regrettably, my own study scarcely reduces this neglect), one thing is, however, clear. The analogy of the parliamentary system with its specialized committees composed entirely of legislative members breaks down in that very few worker council members are also on the council's committees.[12]

The large number of meetings suggests a reason for a low overlap of membership on the worker council and its specialized committees. While in some factories, council influence is still great because the chairperson of such committees must be either a member of the council or board, it would be unreasonable to estimate that since the key function of these committees is to draft proposals and since no Yugoslav data are available on committee composition, it is likely that the percentage of skilled and professional staff on these committees is high. Thus, the committees probably are performing a "civil service" function for the factory parliament and pose the same potential long-term danger of specialists and experts overwhelming the factory parliamentarians. Generalists, it seems, are on the decline.

More serious perhaps than the problems associated with added time demands for senior and key factory personnel is the lack of a supportive culture for worker self-management. While formal structures to enhance information access have been created, there is still a considerable lack of active utilization of such a format by a great many of the employees. Without sustained interest and detailed knowledge on the part of the employees, one must question how useful and reliable employee participation is and whether a democratic culture is being established.[13] Thus, while member attendance rates at the council meetings averaged a reasonable 69.0 percent at the sampled factories, nonmember attendance seemed remarkably low. Over 50.6 percent of the respondents replied that they never attend council meetings; 65.5 percent never attend management board meetings; and 49.8 percent never attend union meetings.[14] Indeed, these percentages are likely to be conservative indicators of nonattendance, since many unskilled persons, who in all likelihood did not attend board and union meetings, did not fill out this particular question, perhaps out of its seeming irrelevance or their embarrassment with their possible replies. Given the responses to the above questions, it is not surprising that the Slovene survey found that the overwhelming majority of persons did not know the answer to questions as to what were the enterprise's profits and income last year. A knowledgeable answer to such questions seems key to any effectively functioning worker self-management. Given the low attendance and information levels by non-council members, the likelihood that enterprise voting may be more erratic and concerned with short-term issues at the expense of long-term matters seems a plausible and potentially serious weakness in the system.

Contrary to expectation, one has found that alienation levels involving roles outside the factory are higher for the Slovene employees than the Canadians. This was the case both for laborers and management. While the rapid urbanization and societal change in Yugoslavia and the presence of a one-party system may account largely for these results, these findings do cast substantial doubt on the suggestion that altering the structure of work relations will necessarily alter nonwork attitudes and behavior.

While we have noted the significant and positive gains in increasing influence levels by all strata in the Slovene factories, it would be incorrect to infer that the Slovene factory is a fully egalitarian decision-making organization. There is still a marked dissimilarity between labor and management influence in the Slovene factories. In this sense, inequality persists, but simply on a different plateau. The base level of the least influential is higher than in non-self-managed factories, but is still below the levels of influence of those at the loftier places in the factory social pyramid. Inequality also is present in terms of both work alienation and societal alienation in that workers are more alienated than managerial personnel.* The worker self-managed factory then is also still an inegalitarian social system in terms of psychic rewards and personality development.

These variations in influence and alienation levels overlap and reinforce differences in knowledge levels, income, and attitudes. This has led one Yugoslav scholar pessimistically to suggest that what seems to have emerged is that while the "skilled and highly skilled workers . . . identify themselves with self-management and, thereby, participate actively in self-management bodies . . . the majority of semi-skilled and unskilled workers think and behave generally as wage labourers."[15] Certainly, the emergence of strikes in which 80 percent of the strikers are of blue-collar background suggests that the interests of a substantial number of persons are not altogether satisfied either in an objective or in a perceptual sense.[16] The above findings suggest that the gains of self-management may neither be as great nor as swift as some seem to hope. More important, it does suggest a curious persistence of classes and class conflict even in a socially owned and democratically managed factory. A panacea the worker self-management structure is not!

On this theme of conflict and fragmentation into differing strata, one Yugoslav sociologist noted another reason for such conditions when he stated that "decentralization did not bring about a democratic distribution of power but rather a fragmented one,"[17] since "top management and staff have power without responsibility, and the council has the responsibility without the power."[18] What this Yugoslav scholar seems to suggest is that a self-management pattern of social

---

*One important exception is that the three directors sampled scored higher on work alienation than the average score. In life alienation, however, they scored below the norm. What one must question, then, is whether greater work alienation may be an indication of leadership frustration in attempting to act in a less hierarchical factory system. See Ichak Adizes, Industrial Democracy: Yugoslav Style (Dordrecht: D. Reidel, 1970), p. 248, for a similar account.

relations, when overlaid upon a technological hierarchy, rather than increasing responsibility, may have lessened it in fact. A preoccupation with groups supervising other groups, "overgovernment" in the description by conservatives, might hamper the successful establishment of clear authority patterns and, thus, might undermine the positive goal of trying to establish greater social integration.

Recent reports by Yugoslav sociologists indicate that administrative and economic disputes have increased in recent years[19] and that the number of persons involved in strikes has increased even though the actual number of strikes has diminished.[20] In fairness, it should be noted that in both cases, the numbers of strikes and those involved are still quite small and may only now be reaching a typical level for an industrialized polity. Nevertheless, an increase in this area is a potentially serious warning signal that the self-managed factory is not always a highly efficient communications system and not always a completely acceptable system of rewards for some.

## CONCLUSION (SOME LESSONS FOR OTHER COUNTRIES)

While Yugoslavia is quite different from many other countries, the Slovene republic in which this case study took place is a highly industrialized, urbanized, and Westernized region. It is, therefore, possible to suggest that the findings of this case study may be of some significance to the North American and Western European settings.

The introduction of the formal machinery of an elected factory parliament has meant that there has been a very real alteration of power within the factory toward the direction of greater democracy. Contrary to the expectation of many managers, who might fear that the introduction of factory worker councils would mean a weakening of managerial powers, the data from this study suggest that managerial power has not diminished per se, but rather, the power of the workers has, instead, increased. Power has not been gained at the expense of the managerial group, but in conjunction with it. The Slovene factories studied suggest very powerful empirical evidence that a more cooperative and more effective factory system of communication is possible and that a new plateau of industrial relations can be reached. In an age concerned with the paralyzing effects of industrial conflict, this achievement seems significant indeed.

This case study suggests that the presence of worker self-management is associated with both positive and negative features regarding alienation. The more numerous positive features, some of which have been discussed at length in this case study, are the greater sense of improved work relations, sense of factory ownership, job satisfaction, lower work alienation, greater job security, and substantial housing, vacation, travel, and lunch meal benefits. On the negative side are higher societal alienation, a growing number of economic disputes, and high levels of industrial accidents, alcoholism, and suicides. In these findings, positive features outnumber the negative features, particularly within the factory. Thus, while muted by the observation of some societal alienation, one can conclude on a note of optimism regarding self-management's effect on improving factory relations and creating a sense of community within the enterprise. In an age of declining personal identity, community ties, and social stability, any mechanism that might recreate peaceful and equitable unity seems worthy of note, since it is difficult to imagine an economically productive society that is thrust into the midst of social turmoil.

Worker self-management is no panacea, and economic and social inequality will continue to persist, albeit at lower levels than in traditional capitalist factories. Whether these gaps in the quality of working life will be sufficiently great to foster anew class tensions is not certain. There are, however, significant indications that class disagreements will persist in the short run but that conflict will not take on the no-holds-barred class struggle that seems to be gripping much of contemporary Western industrial relations.

The final chapter on Yugoslav worker self-management is far from written, so it is difficult to offer any definitive final statements regarding the worker councils as a means to fostering greater industrial peace and productivity and, most important, socioeconomic justice. One statement is, however, possible. Anyone who suggests the imminent demise of worker self-management in Yugoslavia is very much mistaken. The structure is an established and accepted part of the Yugoslav culture. This fact was clearly confirmed in this survey. To offer this conclusion, however, is not to suggest that worker self-management will be unchanging. While the overwhelming majority of Slovenes accepted the system of self-management, almost half surveyed in the case study suggested some doubt that their own personal position had improved sufficiently. This may imply that changes have not occurred swiftly enough for a sizable number of persons and seems to substantiate the claim that certain aspirations for self-management may not yet be fully achieved.

Worker self-management paradoxically, then, is both a real and established fact in Yugoslavia and a dream of something not yet achieved. It is a vision of a more harmonious and productive factory operating within a more just society. As such, the appeal of a better society will be a continuing theme in industrial relations and politics and, as such, is worthy of further analysis and experimentation, both in Yugoslavia and elsewhere in the world.

NOTES

1. See, for example, Paul Blumberg, Industrial Democracy: The Sociology of Participation (London: Constable, 1968).
2. Statisticky godisnjak jugoslavije 1971 [Statistical yearbook of Yugoslavia] (Belgrade: Federal Institute for Statistics, 1971) (hereafter cited as SYY-1971).
3. Peter Jambrek, Development and Social Change in Yugoslavia (Lexington, Mass.: Lexington, 1975), p. 194.
4. SYY-1971.
5. Rensis Likert, New Patterns of Management (New York: McGraw-Hill, 1961), p. 98.
6. Elton Mayo, The Human Problems of an Industrial Society (New York: Viking Press, 1960).
7. For further details, see Alan Whitehorn, "Alienation and Industrial Society: A Case Study of Workers' Self-Management," in Canadian Review of Sociology and Anthropology, May 1979.
8. Michael Argyle, The Social Psychology of Work (Harmondsworth: Penguin, 1972).
9. Jambrek, Development and Social Change in Yugoslavia, pp. 193-94. Significantly, data on strikes are no longer available from the official Yugoslav statistical yearbooks. Interestingly, too, unemployment statistics by republic are also not available. Both sets of data are perceived by the regime, one suspects, as being too damaging to Yugoslavia's image to be published. The data are available, however, from the International Labour Office, Yearbook of Labour Statistics (Geneva: ILO, various years).
10. Ibid., p. 196. Jambrek notes that 80 percent of strikers are blue-collar workers.
11. R. Supek, "Discussion," in Yugoslav Workers' Self-Management: Proceedings, ed. M. J. Broekmeyer (Dordrecht: D. Reidel, 1970), p. 251.
12. Ichak Adizes, Industrial Democracy: Yugoslav Style (New York: Free Press, 1971), p. 36, confirms my findings.
13. Gabriel Almond and Sidney Verba, The Civic Culture (Boston: Little, Brown, 1963). On this point of the need for a democratic culture, one Yugoslav sociologist, Vlado Arzensek, has noted that merely introducing the formal machinery for democratic decision making is not sufficient to ensure democratic solving of conflicts. A democratic culture and democratic attitudes are also necessary. See International Sociological Association, "Industrial Conflict in Yugoslavia," Some Yugoslav Papers Presented to the Eighth Congress of the I.S.A. (Ljubljana: University of Ljubljana, 1974).
14. Note the similarity to Goldthorpe's finding in the United Kingdom that 60 percent never attend union meetings (p. 99) and that

52 percent never vote in union elections (p. 102). John Goldthorpe, The Affluent Worker, Industrial Attitudes and Behavior (Cambridge: At the University Press, 1968). In addition, I suspect very few citizens in the United Kingdom have ever attended a session of the House of Commons.

15. J. Goricar, "Workers' Self-Management: Ideal Type—Social Reality," in Participation and Self-Management (Zagreb, 1972), 1: 24.

16. Jambrek, Development and Social Change in Yugoslavia, p. 196.

17. Veljko Rus, "Limits of Organized Participation," in Participation and Self-Management, 2: 172.

18. Veljko Rus, "Influence Structure in Yugoslav Enterprises," Industrial Relations, vol. 9 (February 1970).

19. Z. Mlinar, "Social Values, Development, and Conflict," International Journal of Sociology, no. 4 (1972), pp. 384-418.

20. Jambrek, Development and Social Change in Yugoslavia, p. 193.

# Chapter Six

## INFORMATION, TRAINING, AND
## EFFECTIVE PARTICIPATION

Management decisions can be influenced through worker participation in different ways. These can be listed in a progressive scale: (1) disclosure of information, (2) advice and consultation, (3) codecision, and (4) self-management.[1]

These four approaches have been embodied in various participative schemes, which range from collective bargaining to codetermination and even full worker control of the total management process. One or more of these schemes have been established in many industrialized and developing countries, through legislation or by voluntary agreement between worker representatives and management.

Despite the fact that there exist in many countries ideological differences between labor and management representatives over the objectives of industrial democracy, the worker participation in most countries in various voluntary, contractual, or legal schemes presupposes that the minimum pragmatic objectives, that is, greater efficiency and labor productivity as a trade-off for improved worker job satisfaction and income, have been accepted by all concerned.

During the last decade, a great deal of research has been carried out on the institutional and legal aspects of worker participation in management. However, participation is more than the mere presence of the workers and/or their representatives in joint committees or supervisory boards; conditions must be fulfilled before worker participation in management becomes a meaningful effort. Some of these conditions are as follows:

1. The availability of accurate, opportune, systematic, and complete information;

2. Education and training of all those involved in participative schemes;

3. A strong and unified union movement (in unionized enterprises);

4. Management's recognition and acceptance of the concept of democratization of the workplace and work processes;

5. Direct involvement of employees in their immediate work environment in order to help them experience their personal values, provide outlets for their creativity, and give them a sense of responsibility; and

6. Finally, to be real, participation occurring at the appropriate levels in an enterprise, and various forms of participation (collective bargaining, shop floor democracy, works councils, board representation) integrated within the total system.

While all the above conditions are important, numbers 1 and 2 are the fundamental ones for the success of a participative scheme because information and knowledge are perceived potentially as powerful tools both by employers and worker representatives in increasing their influence over decision making in an enterprise.

## SCOPE AND PURPOSE

The scope of this chapter is limited to the study of condition numbers 1 and 2. To be more precise, this chapter surveys current provisions on disclosure of information (statutory and/or voluntary agreements) in Western industrialized countries; examines the problems that may arise owing to such disclosure and evaluates the Belgian, French, German, and British experience with regard to these problems; and stresses the importance of training and examines the types of training needed for all those involved in participative schemes.

## INFORMATION AND JOINT CONSULTATIVE BODIES

Essentially, joint consultative bodies (work councils, works committees, and so forth) are labor-management committees whose objective is to promote cooperation in the undertaking, to encourage greater productivity, and to give workers a say in matters that concern them. Joint consultative bodies are by far the most common form of machinery for worker participation in decision making within undertakings in both industrialized and developing countries. Though the size, composition, and competence of works councils and works committees vary among different countries, in all cases, employers are required to provide certain information about the enterprise.

The right of works council members to be informed in advance of important company decisions, such as major economic and financial development, is perceived by representatives of employees on works councils in many Western countries as a means of furthering their own interests. This can be seen by studying the functions of the works council, particularly, its watchdog function. The more complete the council's information on the employer's conduct in his or her day-to-day relationship with employees, the more valid is its assessment of whether the employer is meeting his or her legal obligations, as well as the obligations toward the employees under collective agreements.

Another function of the works council is that of barometer, that is, measuring the overall labor relations climate in a single plant and the larger company. The effectiveness of the works council in settling grievances and minimizing conflict depends heavily on the quantity and quality of the information it receives and on the rapport between labor and management representatives on the council.

### Provisions for Disclosure of Information

The information policies in each country are primarily determined by the industrial relations system and the institutions (works council, collective bargaining, or a mixture of the two) in operation in a particular country. We will notice that in a number of European countries, such as Belgium, France, Germany, and the Netherlands, the trend toward the extention of information is quite evident. The information to be given to the works council in these countries concerns the existing social and economic situation and the future prospects of the enterprise. The Belgian royal decree of November 27, 1973, concerning the detailed economic and financial information to be given to the works council is a clear example of this trend.

In Belgium the works council has the right to information on personnel matters, and sometimes on the competitive position of the enterprise, as well as on its plans for future investment and development. The Belgian royal decree not only outlines the substance of what economic and financial information should be disclosed to works council members but also lays down a procedure for providing such information. Every enterprise employing more than 150 people is required to have a works council. Each council member (management as well as employee representatives) must have all relevant documents 15 days in advance of a special meeting of the council, which is convened to discuss information. The employee representative could call an expert for advice, though management could object to a particular individual appearing as an expert. In cases of disagreement or complaints, the matter could be referred to the minister of Economic Affairs for arbitration. The royal decree makes it clear that the purpose of providing detailed information about production costs and about plans for future investments is to help the members of the works council to assess the relationship between the prevailing economic and financial conditions in the enterprise and their effect on the organization, employment, and personnel. The Belgian experience with the operation of the royal decree over a period of three years will be discussed later.

In France, at present, all firms with at least 50 employees are required to have a works council. Each council comprises management and labor representatives. According to the Ordinance of 1945, works council members have the right to be informed on economic and financial matters, as well as to have access to the annual report of the company's operations and its future prospects. Council members should also be provided with quarterly communications on the progress of production and employment. In limited-liability companies, they have the right to look at the balance sheet.

The French Parliament is expected to enact new legislation requiring every undertaking in France with more than 750 workers to draw up a "social balance sheet" on an annual basis for submission to its works council. The new bill states that this document "shall not be a substitute for any of the information already made available to workers' representatives." In particular "the weekly, quarterly and occasional consultative meetings already provided for under the Labour Code" should continue to take place.

According to the new bill, the annual social balance sheet should contain information on "employment, pay and related costs, conditions relating to health and safety, other working conditions, training, industrial relations as well as the living conditions of workers and their families so far as these depend on the undertaking." This information would not only cover the year in question but would provide a comparison with the development of social policy over the two preceding years.

The bill also states that after consultation with union and employer representatives, a ministerial decree will be introduced for each sector of French industry outlining the type of information that each social balance sheet compiled by undertakings in each of these sectors should contain. Provision is also made under the bill for each establishment in a multiplant undertaking to prepare a separate social balance sheet of its own (in addition to one at the level of the undertaking itself) as long as the individual establishment has more than 750 employees. Each works council member must be given the draft of the annual social balance sheet 15 days in advance of the next formal council meeting at which it is discussed. Union representatives and shareholders should also have access to this document.[2]

Under the Works Constitution Act of 1972, the works council in West Germany has far-reaching rights of information, consultation, and participation concerning social, staff, and economic matters. Stated briefly, the rights of the German works council under the terms of the 1972 act are the following:

1. There is the right to be informed and consulted on manpower planning, vacancies, training, termination of employment, construction, and alterations or extension of works and other premises belonging to the establishment.

2. There is the right to be informed about any proposed alteration that may affect the employees (for example, reduction of operations, closures, and so forth) or new work methods and production processes; where necessary, they may try to reach an agreement concerning social compensation.

3. Where specific matters are not subject to regulation or collective agreement, works councils have the right of codetermination in many social matters: these include hours of work, holidays, the introduction and use of technical devices to check on workers, safety and health regulations, the organization of social institutions within the company, internal wage fixing, and so forth.

4. There is the right to veto employers' decisions regarding dismissals.[3]

In Sweden the collective agreements specify that the employer should provide information on the production, economic, and personnel policy of the firm to the works council. To be more specific, the collective agreement of 1975 mentions three alternatives for the provision of economic information. It is up to the worker representatives on the works council to choose one or more of the alternatives suitable and convenient to it. The three choices are as follows:

1. The economy committee: The members of this committee are appointed by the works council; there should be a maximum of three representatives from the unions and three from the employers' side.

2. The internal workers' economic consultant: He or she should be appointed from among the employees of the firm.

3. The external workers' economic consultant: An outside expert should be appointed to serve as a consultant to the employee representatives on the works council on economic matters.

The most important task for the economy committee or the workers' economic consultant is to give advice and information on the economic situation and the development of the firm. Management is required to furnish research data and all documents concerning economic forecasts and analysis requested by the employee representatives on the works council.

The works council members in the Netherlands have a right to ask information on the progress of the enterprise and to discuss important decisions before they are made. The Dutch law also requires that unions be informed in advance and consulted concerning any measures constituting a transfer of control of an enterprise.[4] It should be noted that in all these countries, the right to information also includes the right of works council members to question and even to challenge the employer in the courts if he or she does not provide the necessary information. The influence of legislation concerning information in Belgium, France, Germany, and the Netherlands is quite apparent from the proposals for a European Works Council, prepared by the Commission on the European Communities.

The proposed Statute for European Companies requires the management board of a European company to give the following information to the European Works Council:

> First, the management board must meet regularly with the European works council, and in any event not less than four times a year. At least once a quarter, a report must be submitted on the general position of the company and its future development. The report must contain full and up-to-date information on general developments in the sectors of the economy in which the company and its subsidiaries operate; on the economic and financial position of the company and associated enterprises; on the development of the company's business; on the state of its production and marketing; on the employment situation of employees of the company and its subsidiaries and its future development; on the production and investment programme; on working methods, especially the introduction of new working methods; and on any other fact or project which may have an appreciable effect on the interests of the employees of the company.[5]

Outside Europe, such as in the United States, Canada, and Australia, while there are no legal systems of works council that compel employers to provide information, in actuality, there do exist voluntary consultative arrangements in many enterprises in these countries.

Relationship between the Provision of
Information to Works Councils and to
Other Participative Bodies

The quality and quantity of information provided to works councils can depend, in part, on the existence of other forms of employee participation in the decision-making bodies of the company. For example, in West Germany, the Biedenkopf report, in an evaluation of codetermination, noted that

there appeared to be a relationship between participation
of employees on the supervisory board, on the one hand,
and on the other hand the amount of cooperation between
the management and the works council. . . . Management's
willingness to impart information due to employees and
their representatives is likely to be reinforced if the managers know that their discharge of these obligations may be
scrutinized by a supervisory board some of the members
of which have been appointed by or subject to the approval
of the employees themselves.[6]

It is generally recognized that works councils receive more extensive information on social, financial, and economic matters than
do the unions in the United States, Canada, and the United Kingdom for
collective bargaining purposes. This fact was brought out in a survey
of 294 British companies:

There is a consistent pattern of preference for disclosure
to consultative bodies of information on company performance. On future plans, the "good news" item (expansion
plans) is also more usually released by joint consultation,
but by contrast the "bad news" item (closures) more often
falls within the province of the union. Joint consultative
bodies also receive more data about personnel employed
on a regular basis, though the incidence of preference for
joint consultation here is not as significant as with performance. However, as one would expect, trade unions are
more usually the recipients of information on incomes.
This reflects a tradition commonly occurring in organisa-
tions operating both bargaining and joint consultation:
namely, that the latter may not transgress on items properly the province of the former.[7]

## DISCLOSURE OF INFORMATION
## AND COLLECTIVE BARGAINING

Collective bargaining is probably one of the oldest indirect
forms of worker participation whereby employee representatives are
able to exercise countervailing power against managerial decisions
in an undertaking. In this century, collective bargaining has become
the main instrument for the negotiations of the terms and conditions
of employment in market economy countries. It is generally recognized that the key to effective collective bargaining is the presence
of a strong, well-informed union.

Importance of Disclosure

There seems to be a general agreement that the disclosure of company information is desirable. However, those who argue for disclosure often do so for different reasons. For example, proponents of disclosure from the employers' side tend to believe that it will lead to rational and objective bargaining. They claim that it will influence the behavior of members of unions and is likely to result in moderating some of their demands and attitudes. One the other hand, unions may support disclosure in the belief that it will redress power imbalance and will enable them to bargain as "equal" partners. Furthermore, it will assist them in mapping out their strategy, such as when management can least afford a strike, and will force management to justify their decisions. "Some observers believe that disclosure will promote acceptance of redundancy and the need for co-operation and change to avoid it; others view it in terms of advance warning and the need to prepare for factory occupations and other forms of resistance."[8]

Unions and organizations with leftist leanings, such as the CGT in France and the Institute of Workers' Control in England, perceive disclosure as a means of exposing antisocial practices of capitalism and of extending the scope of collective bargaining to such issues as company investment and other economic policies. Therefore, the subject matter and scope of collective bargaining, as well as the level at which bargaining is conducted, has a bearing on the subject of disclosure of information. The following examples from the United States, Canada, and Western Europe provide helpful guidelines about the requirements for the disclosure of information for collective bargaining purposes.

In certain countries in Western Europe, such as Belgium, France, the Netherlands, and West Germany, negotiations take place at the national and industrial levels and cover a large number of enterprises and employees. Collective bargaining in these countries is supplemented by works councils and/or by representation on the board of directors, as well as other forms of indirect representation. In other countries, such as the United States and Canada, collective bargaining is generally the sole method of worker participation in decision making at the enterprise level.

In the United States, in theory, there is no direct legal requirement for the disclosure of information, but in practice, various labor laws (the Taft-Hartley Act of 1947 and the Landum-Griffin Act of 1959) impose on both labor and management the obligation to "bargain in good faith." In the famous case of National Labor Relations Board v. Truit Manufacturing Company, the U.S. Supreme Court ruled that bargaining in good faith meant that both parties should make offers and counteroffers and if the employer claimed "inability to pay," it was important enough to require some sort of proof of its accuracy.[9] Furthermore, Section 204(a) (1) of the U.S. National Labor Relations Act emphasizes that both employers and employees "exert every reasonable effort to make and maintain agreements concerning rates of pay, bonus and working conditions." Consequently, an employer must furnish all information necessary and relevant to the performances of the union's collective bargaining responsibilities. This applies to the administration, as well as to the negotiation, of the labor agreement.[10]

In Canada, as in the United States, Section 148 of the Canada Labour Code (1973) requires both parties to "bargain in good faith." In the United Kingdom, there are three separate acts that have a bearing on the mandatory disclosure of information. Under the Employment Protection Act, the most important of the three, "The employer is required to disclose information 'on request' to the union, which places the onus on the unions to identify the areas where it needs information and then to establish a case for it."[11] One thing is clear from all these examples, namely, that unions are not entitled to information unless they ask for it and can prove that it is necessary for them to have information to perform their role effectively.

In Sweden the 1976 Act on Codetermination at Work enables workers and their representatives to exert greater influence over the organization of work and management of company affairs. However, the provisions of this act can be implemented only through appropriate collective agreements. The new act gives rights to unions in fields such as organization and allocation of work. They are entitled to negotiate on such issues as changes in working environment (restructuring of work organization, allocation of work, switching to new lines of business, and selling the firm), industrial health services, personnel policy, personnel transfer, the organization of work hours, and choice between alternative remunerative systems.

The underlying philosophy of the new act of 1976 is that workers must have the same right to comprehensive information about the enterprise's activities as the employer has for himself.[12]

In recent years, the scope of bargaining has been increasing substantially in other countries also. In some cases, it now includes such subjects as economic policy investments, new machinery, and plant layout. For example, in Italy, Fiat signed an agreement with the Metal Workers Federation in November 1974, which, among other things, states that "management and the union will jointly examine the continuing effects of the energy crisis on the transport sector with a view to reaching specific agreements on such points as investments in the South, hours and methods of work, volume of production and reallocation of work."[13] Agreements such as these are far more sophisticated than the average collective agreement. However, it is quite obvious from the above Italian agreement that employers must make all the necessary information about the enterprise available if they expect the union to make useful contributions toward its survival and growth.

## PROBLEMS OF DISCLOSURE

The problems concerning the provision of information on the operations of the enterprise fall under three main headings: behavioral; preparation, presentation, and administration of information; and confidentiality of information.

### Behavioral

When discussing disclosure, people often assume that it is a rational, almost scientific concept of industrial relations and that "facts" can bridge the gap between the goals and values of unions and those of management—two independent organizations with separate and partially incompatible goals. "Implicit in such a view is that information is accurate, objective and absolute. Not only can this be questioned, it is also unlikely that information however accurate will always be accepted or given its due weight."[14] Because collective bargaining involves gamemanship, unions are not likely to be constrained by the disclosure of facts, while discussing their demands, if they do not wish to be so. They would like to retain their freedom to maneuver and may accept or reject the "facts" as the situation warrants.

### Preparation, Presentation, and Administration of Information

The information demanded by worker representatives in the indirect forms of participation (works council, collective bargaining, and supervisory boards) is generally of an economic and financial nature. Unions demand not only more information but also insist that new and simpler methods be found for giving correct information in comprehensible terms. This problem is even more acute in large companies (multiplant and multinational), where the accounting systems are highly complex.

There is, for instance, no such thing as the profit. "Profit" is the result of a comparison of costs and revenues and one's

perception of "cost" and "revenue" can vary with the period
of time, the unit of report and whether or not one sees a
transaction as a marginal activity. To take an example, an
integrated oil company might consist of a number of sequential divisions—exploration, production, refining and distribution. One division "sells" to another down the chain at
a transfer price. Each division might also supply outside
companies who will subsequently be competitors of the integrated company's downstream division. It might be to the
latter's advantage that pricing is so arranged that artifi-
cially high transfer prices are charged both to inside and
outside customers, to the outsider's disadvantage. By the
end of the chain, the distortion is ironed out in the integrated company but the artificiality of the transfer pricing
system distorts costs and revenues as between divisions so
as to make individual measures of profitability meaningless.
. . .

There may be compelling reasons from a top management
standpoint to adopt such a pricing policy, but it will be difficult to say what the true cash flow or return earned by different divisions are.[15]

In such a situation, if the union wants to know the comparative
cost and profit situation within each division and among various divisions, it cannot receive the relevant information because management
has not prepared such a breakdown. Preparation of such information,
according to management, requires much time and is very costly.

On a more general level, there is need for a change in the way
the financial accounts are prepared. Fogarty suggests the following
steps:

a) the reform of financial accounting to provide for social
   accounting, alongside other developments such as inflation accounting or stronger general provision for disclosure; for example by focussing attention on enterprises'
   gross margin or net value added, and the use made of
   it for the benefit of all parties to an enterprise, rather
   than on net earnings which are primarily of interest to
   shareholders;
b) social auditing; the development of specific, largely
   non-financial, formulas for reporting on performance
   in relation to each of the interests involved in an enterprise;
c) the development of codes of practice as a basis for auditing, reporting, and with necessary sanctions by professional bodies, trade organizations, or the State.[16]

Not only the type of information disclosed but also the timing of disclosure is critical. In many instances, information is given to workers when the decision has already been finalized. Worker participation in decision making under those circumstances is an exercise in futility. In matters involving changes and innovations affecting the majority of the work force in the enterprise, provision of information in the formative stage of decision making can be helpful to employees and their representatives. In the early stages, attitudes and opinions on both sides can be accommodating, and proposals can be easily altered. Decisions arrived at in this manner can be implemented more easily.

In many enterprises, the first-line supervisors and other junior management staff members frequently receive information about the enterprise not from senior management officials but through the grapevine, from members of the works council who have access to vital information much earlier than the others. This can create serious morale problems for management.

## Confidentiality of Information

In some countries, members of works councils and joint decision-making bodies are obliged to keep the information confidential until the senior management is in a position to release it to all interested parties simultaneously. However, this policy does not always work in practice. In Belgium, the Netherlands, West Germany, and other countries, there are legal provisions whereby employers are authorized to withhold certain information. The question as to what is confidential or where to draw the line is necessarily one that has to be answered and justified by management. Policy on confidentiality may vary from company to company, but is likely to include details of projected company mergers and takeovers, as well as other information to which the stock market might react sensitively. Marketing information, which might affect the company's competitive position, is also usually considered to be confidential. [17]

While management may decide as to what is private or confidential, the criteria on which such a decision is based has to be negotiated with the unions and agreed upon by both parties. The obligation of worker representatives on joint decision-making bodies to keep the information secret creates a dilemma for the unions, that is, "How can the rank and file employees participate in a meaningful way if the information given to a minority of them must be kept secret?"[18] The disclosure also creates a dilemma for management. Confidential information supplied by management could be used by unions to enhance their influence and power and even to achieve their political ends. For example, the CGT, the largest French union, takes the position that works committees constitute "a weapon in the class struggle and should not be considered as an instrument for cooperation between employers and workers."[19] Unions could also undermine the position of management in collective bargaining. In many countries, the information given to the members of the works councils often finds its way to the collective bargaining sessions. This is equally true for the employees who sit on the supervisory boards and are also members of the unions.

In the absence of clearly defined legal obligations on disclosure of information, interested parties in joint decision-making bodies have a tendency to interpret disclosure of information obligations to suit their own purposes. It is a safe generalization that employers tend to interpret the disclosure obligation rather restrictively, while worker representatives tend to interpret them broadly. The Belgian experience is relevant here.

Belgian Experience

The Belgian royal decree on disclosure of information became operative in 1974. The Belgian unions and employers have conducted independent studies of the actual operations of the royal decree over a period of three years. The Social Christian Trade Union (CSC) surveyed the situation experienced by its members in nearly 300 undertakings in Flanders and metropolitan Brussels. About one-half of these firms provided the necessary information. Two-thirds of the remainder were deficient on technical grounds: inadequate documentation, late information, or no special meetings. The rest did not put into practice the royal decree at all.

The employers' federation, in a survey of 200 of their member firms, found that in the French-speaking Wallonia region, the progress was much slower because the "employers in Wallonia seem more prepared to defend their traditional managerial prerogative."[20] The findings of these surveys indicate the following obstacles to the free flow of information, as outlined in the royal decree:

1. Little or no information on price calculation, on the details of management budgets, on the salaries of higher management.
2. In the union survey it is claimed that many firms treat even basic information as confidential. They do not allow the members of the works council, who already have access to the information, to release it to all employees.
3. The ambivalence of unions as to their role vis-à-vis the works council. The Socialist union (F.G.T.B.) is pri-

marily interested in extending workers' control through bargaining rather than in the effectiveness of the works councils.

4. The Christian union (C.S.C.) estimates that five per cent of its members are true activists, who play a leading part in both the works council and the union delegation. These are the ones who really benefit from disclosure of information and serve as catalysts to make the Royal Decree operational.

5. The use of outside experts has caused major problems. The employers resent the manner in which the expert tends to become the leader or chief spokesman for the employees. They fear that the presence of an outside expert in the works council detracts from its consultative nature and increases the possibility of bargaining.[21]

Findings on France, Germany,
and the United Kingdom

The findings of a pilot study on the experience of employee representatives and management in France, West Germany, and the United Kingdom on the disclosure of information indicate that generally speaking, they felt that practices concerning the provision of information were satisfactory.[22] However, the study identified problems in the following areas: the timely provision of information, confidential information, and the level and extent of information.

The main conclusions and recommendations of this study on the above areas are summarized below:

1. The timeliness of information requires definition in terms of the particular situation for which the various types of employee representatives need such information. An approach involving specific timing of information disclosure, such as is found in the EEC councils' directive on mass redundancy (as well as reflected in certain national legislation such as the U.K. Employment Protection Act of 1975) could be useful.

2. Problems regarding the confidential nature of information arise out of a situation where the business requirements of the enterprise are in conflict with the information requirements of employee representatives. It would seem that the business interest should nevertheless give way to a greater extent than at present where the essential interest of employees are at stake and in particular on matters of employment security.

Problems of this nature are obviously much less felt where there is employee representation on the boards, irrespective of the secrecy they are supposed to observe.

Disclosure of company information will not of itself be of much use unless the workers and their representatives have the ability to understand, evaluate, and use it. Therefore, any consideration for the improvement of the preparation, presentation, and administration of information has implications for training and education for all those involved in participative schemes.

## EDUCATION AND TRAINING

At the ILO symposium on worker participation, it was generally agreed that management, workers, and their representatives needed training for the effective implementation of participative decision-making systems.[23] Broadly speaking, the main objectives of education and training for all those involved in participative systems appear to be (1) the acquisition of systematic knowledge and experience in participation, (2) the development of positive attitudes toward the democratization of the workplace and work processes, and (3) the recognition and handling of power relationships.

Tanic, a researcher at the Institute for Social Science in Belgrade, in a study of works councils over a period of ten years in Yugoslavia found that "there is a positive correlation between the level of education [of workers] and participation in management activities. . . . But the level of education is only one variable. . . . Knowledge increases with experience in self-management.[24]

### Importance of Economic Education

The workers and/or their representatives who are called upon to spend much of their time on problems of an economic nature in their formal or informal capacity, such as shop stewards, members of works councils, union representatives on boards, or members of work groups on the shop floor, need training and education in economic matters. It has been suggested that the rank and file's lack of knowledge and understanding of basic economic concepts might be a factor "retarding the more complete organization of workers into trade unions."[25] The lack of economic education among the organized workers sometimes could lead to decisions being made on emotional grounds, such as the refusal by the rank and file to ratify collective agreements reached by their union leaders after a careful analysis of the economic position of the company and the industry.

Furthermore, in order to fulfill the workers' aspirations for economic democracy and greater participation at all levels, it is necessary to design educational programs of basic applied economics suited to the basic needs and functions of the workers and their representatives at various levels. As far as the aims of economic education are concerned, a report of the ILO Seminar on the Economic Education of Trade Unionists states that "no single or exhaustive definition of the aims of economic education can be made. It is the national, economic and social structure, as well as the position of the trade unions, that will determine the specific educational needs of different target groups, each having its own profile and its specific goals."[26]

Training for Participative Bodies

The focus of education and training for worker representatives at the level of the enterprise varies among various countries because of the differences in their legislative and institutional arrangements. For example, in the Netherlands and West Germany, where union representation at the plant and enterprise level is indirect, the main educational effort is directed at the members of the works council. However, in the United Kingdom, where unions are directly involved with worker representation at various levels of the enterprise, the educational effort is almost entirely concentrated on the shop stewards. "The role and rights of work place representatives in the one case (Britain) derive primarily from collective bargaining and associated procedure agreements, whether formal or informal; in the other case (Holland and West Germany), the main basis is legislative."[27] However, in certain countries, where there is a dual system of works council and shop stewards at the plant and enterprise levels, the distinction between the role and functions of the shop stewards and the members of the works councils becomes blurred. This creates problems for unions in terms of their own priorities and the training needs of their representatives at the plant or enterprise level.

> The conclusions of the debate now in progress concerning the implications of workers' participation will depend to a great extent on the role of trade union leadership on the distribution of decision-making powers, whether at the shop floor level or at a higher level. In all circumstances, trade unionists should become more conversant with the various types of workers' participation to enable them to express their policy preferences.[28]

Education for Works Councils

As far as unions in West Germany are concerned, the principal objective of their educational efforts "is to familiarize the workers' representatives on bi-partite bodies with their duties and to teach them how to translate political demands into social realities."[29] For example, the DGB and other unions run residential schools, which restrict their courses to works council members and other officials. In these schools, the major emphasis is placed on such subjects as analyzing the functions of works councils, the priorities in union educational objectives, economics, law, and social science. In the Netherlands, education for workers and their representatives has been focused on three main areas: (1) information on the legal framework within which the works councils operate, (2) information on the Dutch socioeconomic system and its functioning, and (3) information on the internal relationships within the firm—industrial management, economics, industrial sociology, and so forth.

Training in the Handling of Power

However, the imparting of factual knowledge in the above areas will be of little value to the workers and their representatives on the works councils unless they have the ability to understand and use it. Mulder stresses the need for training the members of the works council in the handling of power. In his research on the power distance theory and its implications, Mulder argued that there are differences in the degree of power exercised by the various members of works councils. For example, managers and top specialists have more expertise and information about problems pertaining to the organization than ordinary workers simply because they spend more time on such items as financial resources and on relationships between technology and production and between the organization and outside influences. These are crucial to the survival of the system. Managers and specialists have more experience in communications and human relations. "These built-in socio-psychological handicaps lead to the paradox that introducing participation systems for the less powerful (rank and file workers and staff delegates) will increase rather than decrease the actual power distance."[30] This is evident from data on the Yugoslavian worker self-management experience and on the operation of works councils in the Netherlands. However, Mulder maintains that it is possible to train people in recognizing and handling power relationships.

In Sweden unions employ outside experts and consultants to assist the worker representatives on such bodies in "bridging the power distance," because it is difficult, if not impossible, for workers and their representatives to match the resources for information and expertise that management has at its disposal.

Education for Collective Bargaining

In recent years, the question of access to information, as well as the training for the interpretation and use of such information, has assumed a great deal of importance not only for works council members but also for shop stewards and other union officials who are involved in collective bargaining. For example, in the United Kingdom and Italy, the subject matter of collective bargaining has extended from the traditional concerns with wages and working conditions to the role of workers and their representatives at the workplace and to other areas. In recent years, British unions, in view of their opposition to plant closures, have asked the employer not only for financial information but also for a social cost-benefit analysis in the handling of such situations.

Unions are realizing that in order to cope with such complex situations, workers and their representatives need multidisciplinary education. An outstanding recent example has been the British Broadcasting Corporation (BBC) series on "Productivity Bargaining," a form of collective bargaining in which pay increases are related to changes in the use of resources and labor practices designed to increase productivity. At the suggestion of the Trade Union Congress, the series was directed at the shop stewards and the role they play in handling productivity bargaining sessions. Groups of local union representatives were organized in many factories during working hours to watch the programs and then to discuss them. Group leaders were provided with a booklet produced by the BBC to accompany the television program. A major organizational effort was made to provide for effective group work and to monitor the results.[31]

OBSTACLES TO TRAINING

At the Organization for Economic Cooperation and Development Seminar on Education in Economics for Workers and Their Representatives, the participants identified the following problems:

1. Sheer number of people to be trained: The participants recognized that the sheer number of worker representatives to be trained was too big a task for unions alone to handle; for example, there are over 140,000 works council members in West Germany, nearly

200,000 shop stewards in the United Kingdom, and 40,000 worker delegates in Belgium. Furthermore, there are financial constraints that limit the union's capacity to meet these educational demands.

2. Release from work for training purposes: Access to paid educational leave could greatly facilitate the training and education of the work force representatives who participate in various decision-making bodies in an undertaking.

In addition to acquiring economic and technical knowledge, the representative capacity of these people requires them to develop effective communication skills (1) in relation to the group that elected them, (2) in dealing on their behalf with management, (3) in relation to their union, and (4) with representatives of other work groups.


CONCLUSION

Despite these problems, the education and training of workers and management are important contributory factors to successful participation. Educational and training programs not only provide workers and managers with the required knowledge and skills for effective participation in consultative and decision-making bodies but also help to develop the necessary cooperative attitudes. Experience has shown that legislated or negotiated participative schemes cannot be made to work effectively without prior appropriate changes or improvements in the attitudes of all interested parties.

According to Jecchinis, a fruitful approach to labor affairs education in Canada would involve the cooperation and participation of the federal and provincial governments, labor and management organization, and a selected group of colleges and universities, which could provide the required teaching facilities and some of the teaching staff. He proposes short study courses for practitioners in the field of industrial relations and manpower planning who are interested in working together for the solution of problems of mutual concern. He argues that such an educational approach would lead to objective analysis and better understanding of the pressing problems confronting all interested parties and that it would contribute to the reduction of conflict, the improvement of labor-management relations, and the eventual increased productivity through the establishment of appropriate institutional arrangements, which could reduce conflict by preventive rather than corrective action. In a way, it would be education "for" labor as well as "about" labor.[32]

NOTES

1. Roger Blanpain, "Provision of Information" (Paper presented at the Organization for Economic Cooperation and Development Seminar on Workers' Participation, Paris, March 1975), p. 3.

2. See European Industrial Relations Review, no. 40 (April 1977).

3. European Economic Community, Commission of the European Communities, Employee Participation and Company Structures in the European Community, Bulletin of the EEC, supp. 8/75 (Brussels, 1975), pp. 59-60.

4. Ibid., p. 89.

5. Ibid., p. 107.

6. Ibid., p. 26.

7. Robin Smith, "Keeping Employees Informed: Current U.K. Practice on Disclosure," Management Survey Report (London), no. 31 (1975), p. 11.

8. Arthur Marsh and Roger Rosewell, "A Question of Disclosure," Industrial Relation Journal 7 (Summer 1976): 8.

9. Robin Smith, "Management Experts' Meeting on Information and Communication in the Firm" (Organization for Economic Cooperation and Development Background Paper), mimeographed (Paris: OECD, July 1974), p. 11.

10. Blanpain, "Provision of Information," p. 4.

11. Smith, "Keeping Employees Informed," p. 22.

12. Sweden, Ministry of Labor, "Act on Co-Determination at Work" (Svenska Arbetsgivareföreningen, doc. no. 1532), mimeographed (1976).

13. European Economic Community, Commission of the European Communities, Employee Participation and Company Structures, p. 22.

14. Marsh and Rosewell, "Question of Disclosure," p. 10.

15. Robin Smith et al., "Company Information and the Development of Collective Bargaining," reprint from Three Banks Review, September 1973, p. 15, as quoted in Blanpain, "Provision of Information, p. 8.

16. M. P. Fogarty, "The Social Responsibility of the Business Enterprise as a Work Organization" (Paper delivered at the Fourth World Industrial Relations Congress, Geneva, September 1976), p. 14.

17. Smith, "Management Experts' Meeting," p. 24.

18. Blanpain, "Provision of Information," p. 17.

19. Ibid., p. 13.

20. Robin Smith, "Company Information to Trade Unions: Can Britain Learn from Belgium?" unpublished (1977).

21. Ibid.

22. International Institute for Labour Studies, "Pilot Study on Relations between Management of Transnational Enterprises and Employee Representatives in E.E.C. Countries," mimeographed (Geneva: IILS, May 1977), p. 64.

23. International Labour Organisation, Workers Participation in Decisions within Undertakings, Oslo Symposium, Labour Management Series, no. 48 (Geneva: ILO, 1975).

24. David Jenkins, Job Power: Blue and White Collar Democracy (London: Heinemann, 1974), p. 106.

25. Organization for Economic Cooperation and Development, Education in Economics for Workers and Their Representatives, Final report of an OECD seminar held in Düsseldorf, November 1971 (Paris: OECD, 1971), p. 5.

26. International Labour Organisation, "Symposium on Economic Education for Trade Unionists" (Discussion Paper), mimeographed (Geneva: ILO, 1974), p. 7.

27. Organization for Economic Cooperation and Development, Education in Economics for Workers, p. 14.

28. International Labour Organisation, "Symposium on Economic Education," p. 14.

29. Organization for Economic Cooperation and Development, Education in Economics for Workers and Their Representatives, Final Report of an OECD seminar held in Düsseldorf, November 1971, supp. (Paris: OECD, 1972), p. 54.

30. Mauk Mulder, "Power Equalization through Participation," Administrative Science Quarterly, March 1971, pp. 31-38.

31. Organization for Economic Cooperation and Development, Education in Economics for Workers, Final Report, supp., p. 118.

32. Chris Jecchinis, "A Tripartite Approach to Labour Affairs Education under Consideration in Canada," Lakehead University, Staff Discussion Paper, no. 79-01 (Port Arthur, Ont., 1979).

# Chapter Seven

## LESSONS FROM THE EUROPEAN EXPERIENCE

The great "participation debate" continues unabated in North America. In the last three years, the Labour Gazette, an organ of the Canadian Department of Labour, has published more than 20 articles on the European model of worker participation in management. These articles have been written by executives, journalists, academics, trade unionists, and politicians. Their views range from enthusiastic support to outright rejection. In the United States, a number of articles on participation have appeared in such prestigious journals as the Academy of Management Review, the Harvard Business Review, the Journal of Applied Behavioral Sciences, and Fortune magazine. The entire May 1977 issue of the Annals of the American Academy of Political and Social Sciences was devoted to industrial democracy, not to mention a number of books published on this topic during the last decade.

The fascination with the European style of industrial democracy stems from a number of factors. The slackening productivity, growing industrial unrest, and persistent inflation in the last decade have forced managers to take notice of the relative industrial peace and increased labor productivity enjoyed by their competitors in many European countries. Consequently, they have become keenly interested in European employee relations and institutions that might promote industrial peace and productivity.

Conversely, because of the high rate of unemployment, inflation, and job uncertainty, labor leaders in North America are under great pressure from the rank and file to promote measures that will create more jobs and protect the present ones. Unemployment levels in North America, as a percentage of the labor force, have been for some years about one-third higher than those in some European countries, such as West Germany, Austria, France, and the Netherlands. In many European countries, union participation in social and economic planning at the national level gives union leaders leverage to influence governmental policy and measures such as job creation, job security, and wage indexation. Naturally, labor leaders in North America are interested in such developments.

There are major differences between the European and North American industrial relations systems. Even within Western Europe, there are variations among the industrial relations systems. Each country is evolving a distinctive form of worker participation, distinctive in its major components, as well as in nuances. Therefore, it is futile to transplant or transfer directly the basic institutional arrangements or forms of participation from one country to another. However, the differences between North America and Western Europe should not preclude the adaptation of some of the more successful European techniques and experiments in worker participation to the North American scene. The relevance of the European experiments in worker participation to the North American environment and the lessons one can learn from the European experience will be discussed below under two main headings: (1) the need to reform the traditional collective bargaining system at both the structural and attitudinal levels and (2) the need to democratize the decision-making process within the enterprise.

## REFORMING COLLECTIVE BARGAINING

Experience has shown that the conventional collective bargaining system has fallen short of the expectations of those who consider it as a sort of panacea for all labor-management ills. It is a fair generalization that collective bargaining, on both sides of the Atlantic, has not developed as the complete answer to the question of worker participation in management, that is, how workers can and should influence the decision-making process of enterprise. If collective bargaining is to remain the main road to worker participation in management in North America, then it is necessary to introduce reforms in the existing bargaining system and to supplement it with other permanent institutional arrangements.

### Structural Reforms (Enterprise Level)

One feature of the North American system of collective bargaining is that once a contract is signed, management, under the residual rights theory, feels free to initiate short-term and long-term changes, within the contract's parameters. These changes may have a significant impact on the work force. Management is not obliged to inform or consult employee representatives or involve workers directly in the process by which short-term and long-term plans are formulated.

This characteristic of the North American collective bargaining system is in direct contrast with the European system of works councils, whereby employee representatives are involved in problem-solving and decision-making processes throughout the course of the contract.

In Canada, as well as in the United States, legislation requires both parties to bargain in good faith, which essentially means that employers are obliged to furnish information necessary and relevant to the performance of the union's collective bargaining responsibilities. But employers are not obliged to furnish information to unions about their future plans. It is generally recognized that works councils in Europe receive more extensive information on social, financial, and economic matters than do the unions in North America for collective bargaining purposes. Recognizing the comparative paucity of information that unions have to work with as bargaining agents, the Canadian Labour Congress (CLC) in a recent manifesto demanded that present labor relations, as well as securities legislation, be amended and that the following basic financial and nonfinancial information be made available to unions as bargaining agents: (1) the firm's status, (2) its competitiveness in the market, (3) its production and productivity, (4) the firm's financial structure, (5) budget and cost accounting, (6) staff costs, (7) the firm's program and outlook for the future, (8) scientific research, (9) all forms of public support received, and (10) the firm's organizational chart.[1] The following statement helps put this long list of demands in perspective:

> Broadened information rights tend, in and for themselves, to foster a widened scope of bargaining. This link is likely to follow just as logically in North America as in Western Europe. Past North American notions about confidentiality of information and exclusivity of employer residual rights are bound to prove increasingly passé in any and all areas where vital employee interests pertaining to their income, security and working conditions are involved.[2]

Throughout its history, the North American system of collective bargaining has tended to play more of a conflictual role than a consensual role. The central issue in the North American context is, Can collective bargaining with its adversary character be modified in such a way that it can accommodate both integrative and distributive issues? Experience so far indicates that in North America, union-management cooperation and quality-of-working-life programs have had a short life. Except in certain well-publicized cases, the common attitude of union leaders toward such programs is one of suspicion and distrust. If cooperative issues cannot be meaningfully dealt with on a permanent basis within the framework of the existing collective bargaining system, would it not be advisable to supplement it with other institutional arrangements? It is in this context that a modified version of the concept of European works councils could become relevant to the North American scene.

It should be emphasized that the European system of works councils can be combined with provisions that ensure that where workers are organized, the unions will play their proper role in the system. An interesting example of plant-level representation is the Danish system of "cooperation committees" (works councils); in this system, the employee representatives on cooperation committees consist both of members elected by all the employees in secret ballot elections and of the shop stewards representing the unionized workers in the plant, who are automatically members of this committee. In order to involve as many employees as possible in joint activities, the cooperation committee sets up permanent subcommittees in the different departments of the enterprise. It also encourages the formation of subcommittees (either permanent or temporary) to deal with specific issues having short-term or long-term implications. The primary objectives of the cooperation committees are to promote cooperation in the enterprise, to encourage greater productivity, and to give employees a say in matters that concern them.

The unions benefit from works councils in that they enjoy greater access to information. The more complete the council's information on the employer's conduct of his or her day-to-day relationship with employees, the more valid is its assessment of whether the employer is meeting its legal obligations, as well as the obligations toward the employees under collective agreements. The works council serves as a barometer, measuring the overall labor relations climate in a plant, as well as in the enterprise as a whole, and can respond to problems quickly as they arise. They could also provide a legitimizing context for joint cooperative programs, such as improving the quality of life at the workplace, which might otherwise be perceived by the unions as unilateral and manipulative management schemes. Furthermore, European experience tells us that despite the differences in size, composition, and competence of works councils or works committees among different European countries, they have demonstrated, over a period of time, a capacity to find solutions to major problems in the enterprise before they evolve into hardened issues.

In nonunionized enterprises, there is a real need for a permanent formal representative machinery. Regardless of the form of the representative mechanism (joint labor-management committee or works councils), such an institution or institutions are necessary, both for employees and management, if decisions that affect employees in their immediate environment are to be properly considered and implemented. Such machinery has a vital role to play in communicating local concerns and ideas to management and vice versa. It is the principle of employee representation at the workplace that is far more important than the form of representative machinery.

There is no denying the fact that unions in North America are opposed to the concept of works councils or employee representation plans outside the unions. They are afraid that such bodies would be dominated by employers. Many union leaders perceive such bodies as rival organizations and believe they would eventually undermine the role and strength of the unions. These fears seem to be exaggerated. The European experience indicates that works councils have provided a foothold for unions in unorganized enterprises. The existence of a works council in a nonunionized company presents an opportunity for union organizers to present the case for unionization to a group of employees who have, by their membership in the works council, already shown an interest in employee affairs. The British Trade Union Council acknowledges that "the tendency in the U.K. has been for long established works councils to become part of the trade union machinery."[3]

## National Level

Because of the highly decentralized and fragmented nature of bargaining structures in North America, a settlement reached at the plant level may take into account factors important to a particular firm in a particular industry, but it may overlook larger national interests. John Crispo, a specialist in public policy, elaborates on this point:

> The idea of a free collective bargaining system functioning almost oblivious to national economic and social development and priorities is becoming increasingly untenable. Yet neither employers nor unions in North America are really prepared for anything else. Instead they engage in a largely uncoordinated and unrestrained dog-eat-dog free-for-all over the spoils of different plants, companies and industries as well as the overall income distribution of the two nations involved. . . .
> A more enduring and intelligent way must obviously be found to bring some degree of compatibility between labour and management wage and price setting procedures and government fiscal, monetary and related policies. The two sets of mechanisms involved cannot continue on their own often distinct and separate courses without setting the stage for some frequent serious collision between them.[4]

The European system of tripartite consultative mechanisms at the national level deserves consideration. It allows labor and management representatives to have meaningful input into the overall socio-economic-political decision-making process. Roger Blanpain, of the University of Louvain, at a conference held in Toronto, stressed the growing interdependence of the political, business, and labor communities in Western Europe. "Their interlocking interests are such that they cannot but be affected by one another's actions and their consequences, making it absolutely necessary for the parties involved to meet, to consult and to develop common strategies and goals."[5]
These consultative mechanisms help labor, management, and government to reach a consensus on specific subject areas, such as wage developments, job security, training, and working time. The consensus arrived at the national level on specific subjects is then used as a trade-off at the microlevel of collective bargaining to enable the government to gain acceptance for certain of its policies, such as price and wage restraints.

In North America, the obstacles to meaningful tripartite consultation and cooperation at the national level are formidable indeed. The national labor federations and employer associations periodically exert influence as political lobbies, but they do not participate in the formulation of socioeconomic policies. The main criteria for the success of a workable tripartite system is that the participants must be able to commit their constituents to policies and objectives agreed at the national level by all the interested parties. But the national labor federations in North America do not have such authority over their affiliates. To illustrate this point, the CLC at its 1976 annual convention demanded a say in the formulation of national social and economic policy and asked for the establishment of a tripartite consultative body. The government was somewhat responsive to the CLC's demands, but by the fall of 1977, the probability of a permanent tripartite structure being established had greatly diminished. This was partly due to the opposition within CLC ranks, particularly from powerful unions, such as the Canadian Union of Public Employees. They feared that such a mechanism would result in labor's co-optation and would weaken the labor movement's links with the New Democratic party.

The business and industrial community in Canada has its own structural problems. At present, there are four different organizations that speak for business, and there is no single central body that has authority or extensive powers over its affiliates. Furthermore, Canada's federal system of government makes it difficult for the federal government to commit itself to a concerted action because it must share or defer jurisdiction to the provinces in several key areas, such as natural resources, industrial relations, education, urban affairs, health, and welfare. Provincial governments sometimes adopt different and conflicting approaches to social and economic issues, and the federal government is powerless to resolve such conflicts. In spite of all these difficulties, the prime minister and the premiers of the ten provinces agreed in February 1978 to set up 23 task forces involving businessmen, labor leaders, and academics to look at 23 sectors of the Canadian economy and make recommendations for their improvement. Upon the completion of these studies, an umbrella committee, called the Second Tier Committee, consisting of five prominent members from the ranks of labor and five prominent business figures, was established to analyze the sector reports. The degree of accord between labor and management over the recommendations to be made to the federal and provincial governments was surprising even to the committee members themselves. A mere handful of the issues on which they agreed include the following:

1. Encouragement should be given to the formation of consortia to take advantage of export opportunities.

2. Industry and labor should meet regularly to forecast needs and recommend training and educational programs in manpower areas where training and planning are inadequate.

3. An autonomous body jointly supported by provincial and federal governments and by business and labor should integrate manpower inventories and needs and advise on manpower policy, training, and educational requirements.

Obviously, there were some differences of opinion between labor and management, but there were more areas of agreement than disagreement. Both parties agreed to pursue cooperation rather than confrontation in the future. They agreed to establish a labor–business committee that would report to the prime minister and to all the provincial premiers. Its task is to examine labor–business relations on such basic matters as standardization of labor codes, union certification, labor relations boards, the resolution of impasses in negotiations, union security, picketing codes, the rights of parties during strikes, and the right to strike in essential services. This committee has started an era of consultation and working together. Whether it will evolve into something more permanent remains to be seen. Recently, the CLC accused the federal government of exploiting the above recommendations of the Second Tier Committee for political purposes. Other developments, particularly in the Province of Quebec, seem to indicate that unions are moving away from pragmatism to radicalism and that some of them reject collaboration or cooperation with either management or government.

In the United States, the Joint Economic Committee of Congress serves as a forum for an annual debate and discussion based on the

report of the president's Council of Economic Advisors. Much more
could be done by this committee to encourage frequent and regular
labor-management consultation. North American governments should
establish mechanisms for regular consultation between governments
(provincial and federal in the case of Canada), unions, and employers
on national, social, and economic policies. Governments should consult labor and management before proposing legislation in these fields.
Such a machinery could conceivably help the government in formulating a set of policies better directed toward the attainment of such objectives as a lower rate of inflation and a higher level of employment.

Attitudinal Reforms

The involvement of union and management in collaborative and
cooperative endeavors requires a change in the attitudes and value
systems on the part of both parties. The introduction of any new participative schemes through legislation will not be successful unless
accompanied by such changes. It would be unwise to impose statutory
works councils or other legislated mechanisms until unions and employers have had a chance either to see for themselves how these
schemes work out in practice or to learn from the experience of
others.

The most difficult aspect of introducing any new participative
mechanism is knowing where to start and the procedure to follow. It
is in this context that the case studies of successful experiments of
collaborative mechanisms in North America and Western Europe (described in this book) can be most helpful in providing useful insights
to the pragmatic industrial relations professionals in North America.

In a recent study of 67 cases of change-efforts in the United
States, Dunn and Swierczek found that the following contributed to
successful change-efforts: (1) a collaborative strategy, in which both
employees and management participate in setting goals and where
each party enjoys an equal opportunity to change those goals; and (2)
a participative orientation, which implies the use of such techniques
as group problem solving, in order to tap the knowledge and creative
potential of participating employees. They also pointed out that organizational development and participative management were the two
strategies of organizational change that were explicitly oriented toward the participative processes and that had resulted in effective
change outcomes.[6]

The best participative structure for an individual company,
whether unionized or nonunionized, is the one that is worked out voluntarily and agreed upon jointly by its management and work force.
Large and medium-sized companies in North America could conduct

viability studies to decide what is the best form of participation for
the firm. These studies could be conducted by a team of management
and employee representatives with the assistance of outside experts
and/or independent governmental agencies. The task of the proposed
joint study teams would be to examine both the needs and constraints
of (1) company technology—its objectives and operation problems;
(2) management policies and practices, including systems of controls
and styles of managing; (3) employee attitudes and expectations; (4)
industrial relations processes and procedures; (5) external pressures
of the markets, fiscal policies, and other legislative measures, as
well as social and political values; and (6) educational and training requirements of employees for participation. [7]

Independent governmental agencies could play an important role
as educators and facilitators. They could work out guidelines for developing voluntary participative schemes and publish a code of good
industrial relations practices, including employees' rights to information, consultation, education, and training. They could carry out a
program of demonstration projects and educational activities and provide financial and expert advice to those companies that need such
help. In the United States, the Federal Mediation and Conciliation
services have consistently encouraged the establishment of labor-
management committees, particularly as a form of preventive mediation. Mediators have acted as neutral chairpersons of joint union-
management committees and have helped them to identify problems
of mutual interest, concentrating on work issues that are not usually
matters of negotiation or grievances. In Canada an independent agency
having somewhat similar functions and powers is needed. The Federal Mediation and Conciliation services could assist the parties in
implementing the participative schemes and could monitor their progress.

The history of industrial democracy in North America, the legacy of individualism, and distrust for governmental control dictate
that any reforms or legislative proposals be implemented only after
a period of educational process conducive to the gradual introduction
and acceptance of participative schemes.

WORKER PARTICIPATION IN DECISION
MAKING WITHIN THE ENTERPRISE—
CURRENT STATUS AND FUTURE
TRENDS IN NORTH AMERICA

Within an enterprise, decision making usually takes place at
three broad levels: corporate, plant and department, and shop floor.
The participative processes whereby employees may be involved in

TABLE 14

Decision Making at Three Levels: Participative Processes
Involving Employees

| Organizational Hierarchy | Nature of Decisions Undertaken | Participative Processes |
|---|---|---|
| Corporate level (long-range) | Strategic policy decisions | Employee directors on corporate boards |
| Plant and departmental level (short-term) | Administrative decisions | Works councils, joint labor-management consultative committes |
| Shop floor (day-to-day) | Operating decisions | Work organization and restructuring |

Source: Compiled by the author.

decision making at each of the above levels are briefly summarized, as shown in Table 14.

Worker participation in management is most successful when it is a part of an overall strategy involving efforts to increase worker influence at appropriate organizational levels through various forms (direct and indirect) simultaneously. One can safely generalize that in this respect, Europeans are well ahead of North Americans. However, institutions developed in a foreign setting cannot be transplanted easily regardless of their potential advantages. For example, there is little likelihood of employee representation on ecompany boards in North America in the near future. Except in a few isolated cases, North American employers and unions have shown no interest in this concept in spite of the fact that in the adversary atmosphere of labor-management relations, the voluntary appointment of union leaders on the board of directors would facilitate openness and mutual trust by enhancing the status of the rival group. The major obstacles to the appointment of worker-directors are the conflict of interest for union officials, certain aspects of confidentiality of information, and above all, lack of interest on the part of union officials in becoming involved with the management of the enterprise.

While the trend in Western Europe is toward greater participation by labor representatives in company management, the basic shift in the United States is toward a more active and independent board of directors. The trend seems to be in the direction of an active role for shareholders in the selection of outside directors. There is a need for the representation of public interest on major company boards. Even if such representatives are not given the right to vote, they could perform a useful watchdog role. According to Crispo, "In such a capacity they could be charged with the responsibility of issuing an annual report of existing laws of the land, advertisement claims and warranties, and applicable codes of ethics."[8] The attitude of North American union leaders toward employee representation on company boards is not likely to change in the near future because they do not wish to be saddled with the responsibility for joint decisions, which in the end might result in a negative outcome for the workers.

As far as employee representation at the plant level is concerned, it was pointed out earlier that most union leaders in North America are opposed to the concept of works councils. However, it is interesting to note that rank-and-file members do not necessarily share their leaders' views. In a study on U.S. auto workers, Garson found "majority support for [the] works council."[9]

In North America, collective bargaining is the dominant form of employee participation in managerial decision making at the plant level. However, as pointed out earlier, traditional collective bargaining does not provide a framework for the recognition of the mutuality of interests or joint responsibility for the success of the organization. Many organizations in the United States and Canada have recognized the limitations of collective bargaining and have voluntarily established special joint labor-management committees on the model of the European works councils. In an article in the Harvard Business Review, Fenn and Yankelovich argue that "many people want to reach more deeply into corporate decisions than they have before; they want a larger, more formal and more institutionalized role in the issues that affect their lives."[10] They cite the existence of two forms of information and consultation committees in a number of firms (both union and nonunion). The purpose of these committees is to satisfy the growing desire on the part of many employees to have the organization justify and explain its decisions.

## Special Manager-Employee Councils

Special manager-employee councils meet from two to six times a year to discuss their problems; they have a formal agenda submitted by both management and workers. The agenda is published in advance, and the subsequent disposition of each item is publicly listed. These councils are often accompanied by attendant subcouncils organized around work groups that air ideas and criticisms.

## "Cracker-Barrel" Meetings between
## Supervisors and Employees

Most of the critics of such manager-employee councils argue that these committees do not have a built-in capacity to achieve desirable results, since there are no formal requirements for them to do so. In view of the fact that many of these committees have succeeded in solving the problems they were faced with, the critics' failure to examine objectively and dispassionately many such innovations at the plant level in North America is unfortunate.

Finally, to be successful, worker participation must extend to the shop floor level. Workers in both unionized and nonunionized firms want information about what is happening and why. They want to have a bigger say in decisions that affect their jobs and immediate work environment. A number of organizations in both the United States and Canada have experimented with new ways of organizing work and with quality-of-working-life projects. These experiments are aimed at increasing productivity, as well as at reducing job alienation and improving the labor-management climate.

It appears that most of the quality-of-working-life programs and other cooperative projects in North America have been stimulated by the existence of some problem. Several major industries, such as steel, automobiles, railroads, and retail foods, which undertook cooperative projects, were faced with serious competitive pressures or industrial relations problems, and both unions and management felt that the traditional collective bargaining process was incapable of solving these problems. The question arises, What are the long-term prospects of labor-management cooperation and quality-of-working-life programs in North America? The impression gained from the few well-publicized and successful cases and from the attempts made by centers for productivity and quality of life both in the United States and in Canada to disseminate information, organize educational activities, and so forth, is that there is a genuine movement in this direction. However, upon reflection, this movement appears to be the result of initiatives taken largely by management. In a number of cases, these programs have had a short life. Changes in work reorganization involve a reshuffling of the existing power structure, which affects particularly the traditional authority of supervisors and technical specialists. While individual work reorganization experiments have had a fairly good success rate, the diffusion of these new work experiments has been extremely poor. With a few exceptions, most union leaders believe that these experiments are manipulative management schemes to increase output without regard to the interest of the employees. Furthermore, quality-of-working-life issues at this time of high unemployment and inflation are not priority issues for many union leaders. Given the traditional adversary model of labor-management relations in North America, it appears that joint union-management projects in the area of work reorganization and humanization movement will not make much headway in major industries unless unions are really willing to cooperate with employers.

Undoubtedly, collective bargaining will continue to dominate the industrial relations scene in North America, but worker participation is much more than collective bargaining. It involves the democratization of enterprises that have been in the past largely hierarchical or authoritarian in nature. At present, admittedly many collective agreements provide advance notice and other safeguards against changes in policies and procedures that may adversely affect the workers' interest at the workplace, and there are many joint union-management committees that monitor the implementation of such agreements. However, unions in North America do not perceive their role as working with employers within the framework of consensual or cooperative sharing of decision making, which, in my opinion, is the essence of "participation."

The socioeconomic challenges confronting both the United States and Canada are grave enough to warrant a concerted action on the part of government, unions, and management to achieve increased productivity, to regain competitiveness in the international markets, to solve the problems of unemployment and inflation, and to bring about a prolonged period of industrial peace. Before present economic and social problems reach a state of crisis and the government is forced to solve them, it is in the enlightened self-interest of both labor and management to find ways and means to interact more regularly at various levels of the organization and to experiment with new participative approaches that are based on cooperation rather than confrontation.

NOTES

1. "Corporate Disclosure," Canadian Labour, June 1978, p. 42.

2. John Crispo, Industrial Democracy in Western Europe: A North American Perspective (Toronto: McGraw-Hill-Ryerson, 1978), p. 152.

3. Trade Union Council, Industrial Democracy, Report by the TUC General Council to the 1974 Trade Unions Congress (London: HMSO, 1974), p. 40.

4. Crispo, Industrial Democracy in Western Europe, p. 153.

5. Ed Finn, "Tripartite Consultation at the National Level," Labour Gazette 78 (February-March 1978): 66.

6. William Dunn and Fredric W. Swierczek, "Planned Organizational Change," Journal of Applied Behavioral Science 13 (1977): 135-57.

7.  Chris A. Jecchnis, "Employees' Participation in Management: International Experiences and the Prospects for Canada," Lakehead University, Department of Economics, Staff Discussion Paper, no. 77-04, mimeographed (Port Arthur, Ont.), p. 33.

8.  Crispo, Industrial Democracy in Western Europe, p. 159.

9.  G. David Garson, "Paradoxes of Worker Participation," in Worker Self-Management in Industry: The Western European Experiment, ed. G. D. Garson (New York: Praeger, 1977), p. 224.

10.  Dan H. Fenn and Daniel Yankelovich, "Responding to the Employee Voice," Harvard Business Review, May-June 1972, p. 86.

# BIOGRAPHICAL NOTES

HEM C. JAIN is Professor of Management at the University of New Brunswick (Canada). From 1973 to 1976, he was the Chairman of the Division of Social Science and Business Administration. He was a visiting professor at the European Institute for Advanced Studies in Management, the University of Leuven (Belgium); Boston University in Brussels; and the University of Ottawa. Until 1971 Dr. Jain was a professor at Sir George Williams University.

In 1976 Professor Jain served as an external collaborator with the International Labour Office (ILO) in Geneva on a research project on worker participation. He is the author of two books on Canadian Labour and Industrial Relations and has published more than 20 articles in professional journals in the United States, Canada, Belgium, and the United Kingdom. In 1975 he served as President of the Canadian Industrial Relations Association and is at present a member of its executive board. He was the Canadian representative to the Council of International Industrial Relations Associations in Geneva in 1976 and in Paris in 1979.

Professor Jain has served as the Chairman of Conciliation and Arbitration Boards in Canada. Dr. Jain holds an M.S. and a Ph.D. from the University of Illinois. Over 50 organizations have used Professor Jain as a consultant on staff training, organization development, and industrial relations.

GENEVIEVE LALOUX JAIN is an honorary research associate at the School of Graduate Studies of the University of New Brunswick and a freelance writer and editor. From 1965 to 1972 she was a professor at St. Joseph Teachers' College and at McGill University, Montreal, Canada.

Dr. G. Jain's field of interest is comparative cultural studies, in particular the relationship between nationalism and education in various countries. Her Ph. D. thesis on Canadian nationalism and the teaching of history was published by Université Laval Presses, Quebec. She was co-author of one of the studies commissioned by the Royal Commission on Bilingualism and Biculturalism.

Geneviève Jain holds a Licence from the University of Lille, France, an M.A. from the University of Illinois, and a Ph. D. from McGill University.